WELCOME no.5 TOMO TAKEUCHI

TO THE BALLROOM

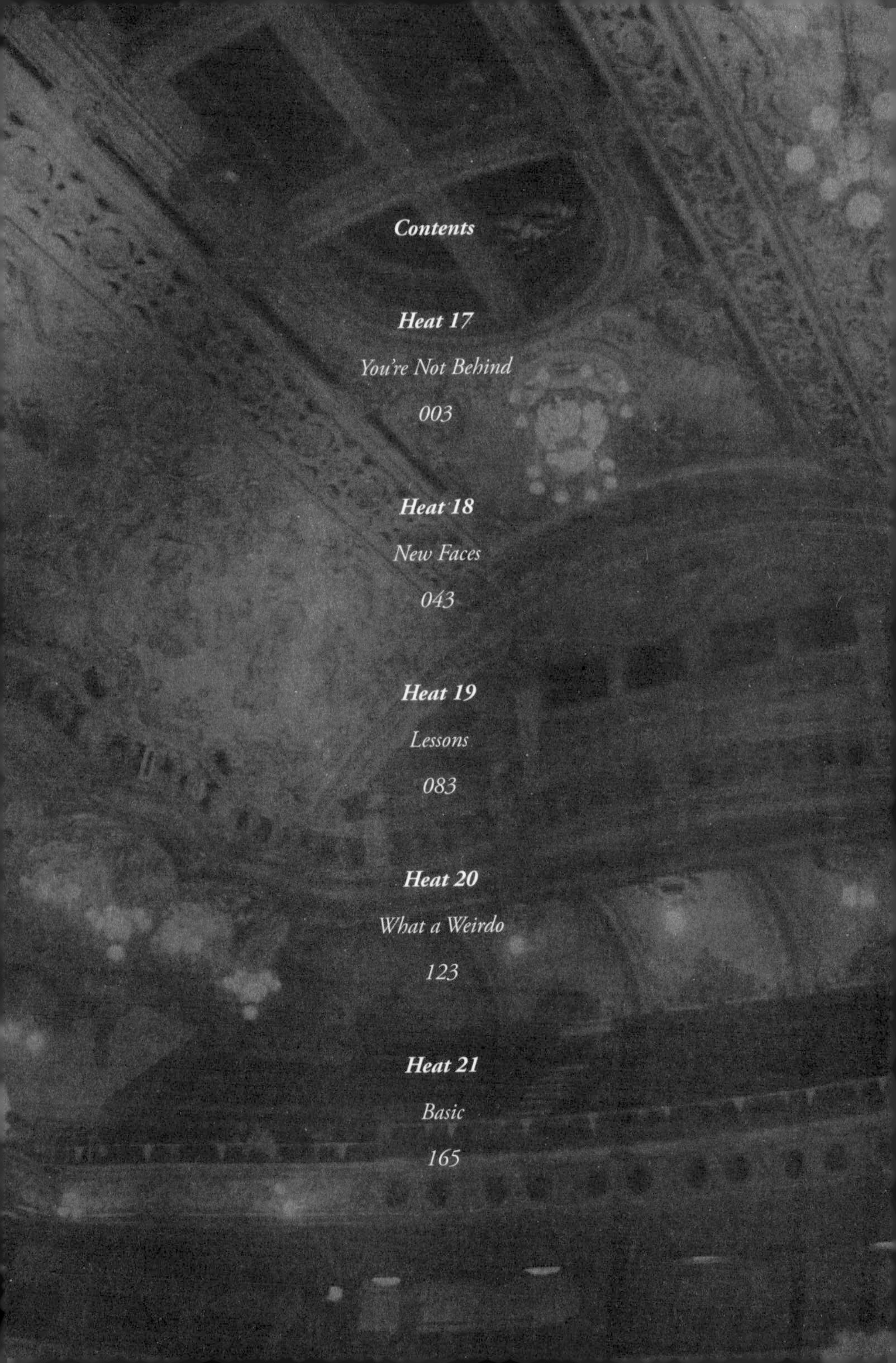

Contents

Heat 17

You're Not Behind

003

Heat 18

New Faces

043

Heat 19

Lessons

083

Heat 20

What a Weirdo

123

Heat 21

Basic

165

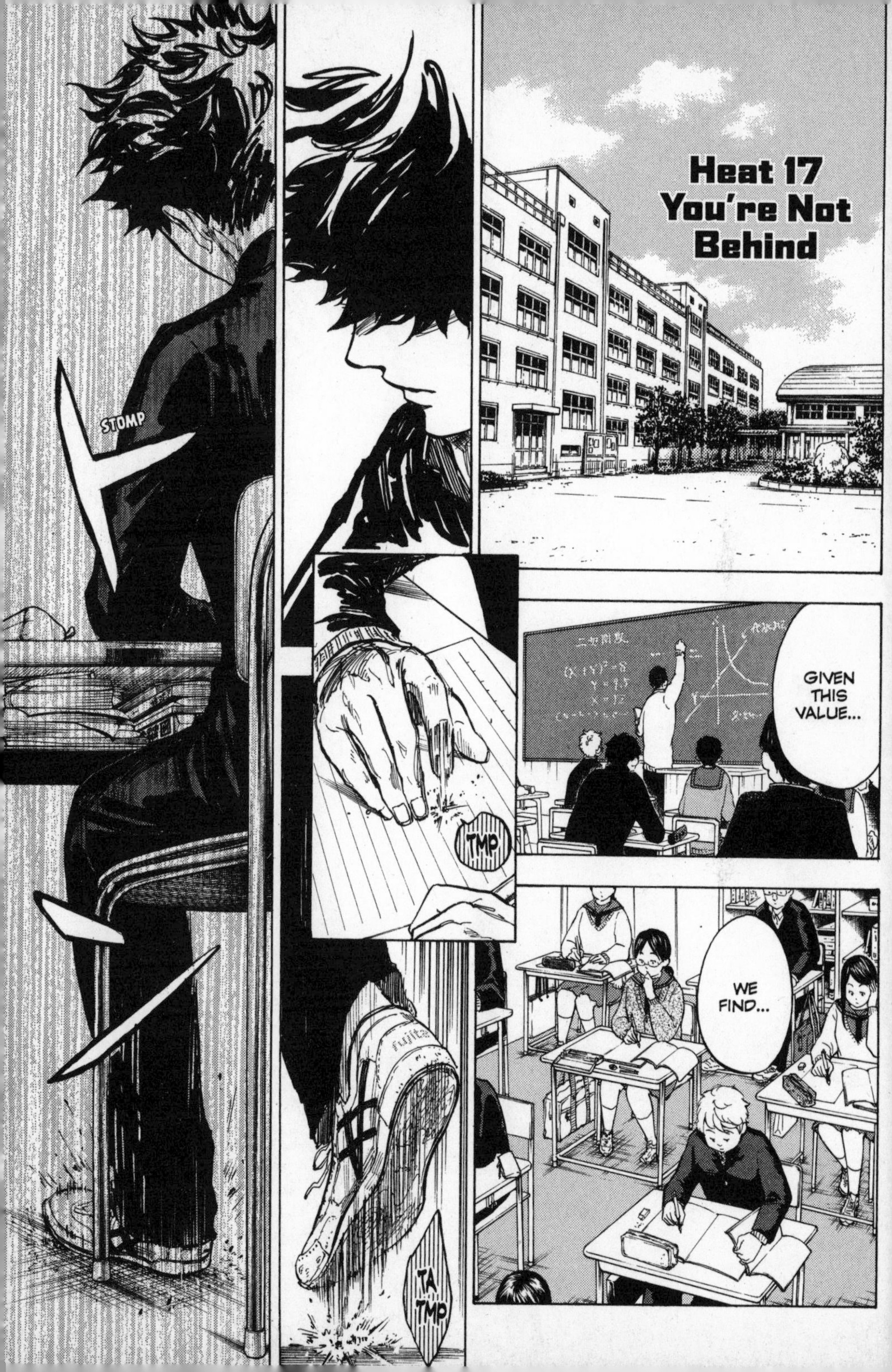
Heat 17
You're Not
Behind
GIVEN THIS VALUE...
WE FIND...
TMP
TA TMP
STOMP

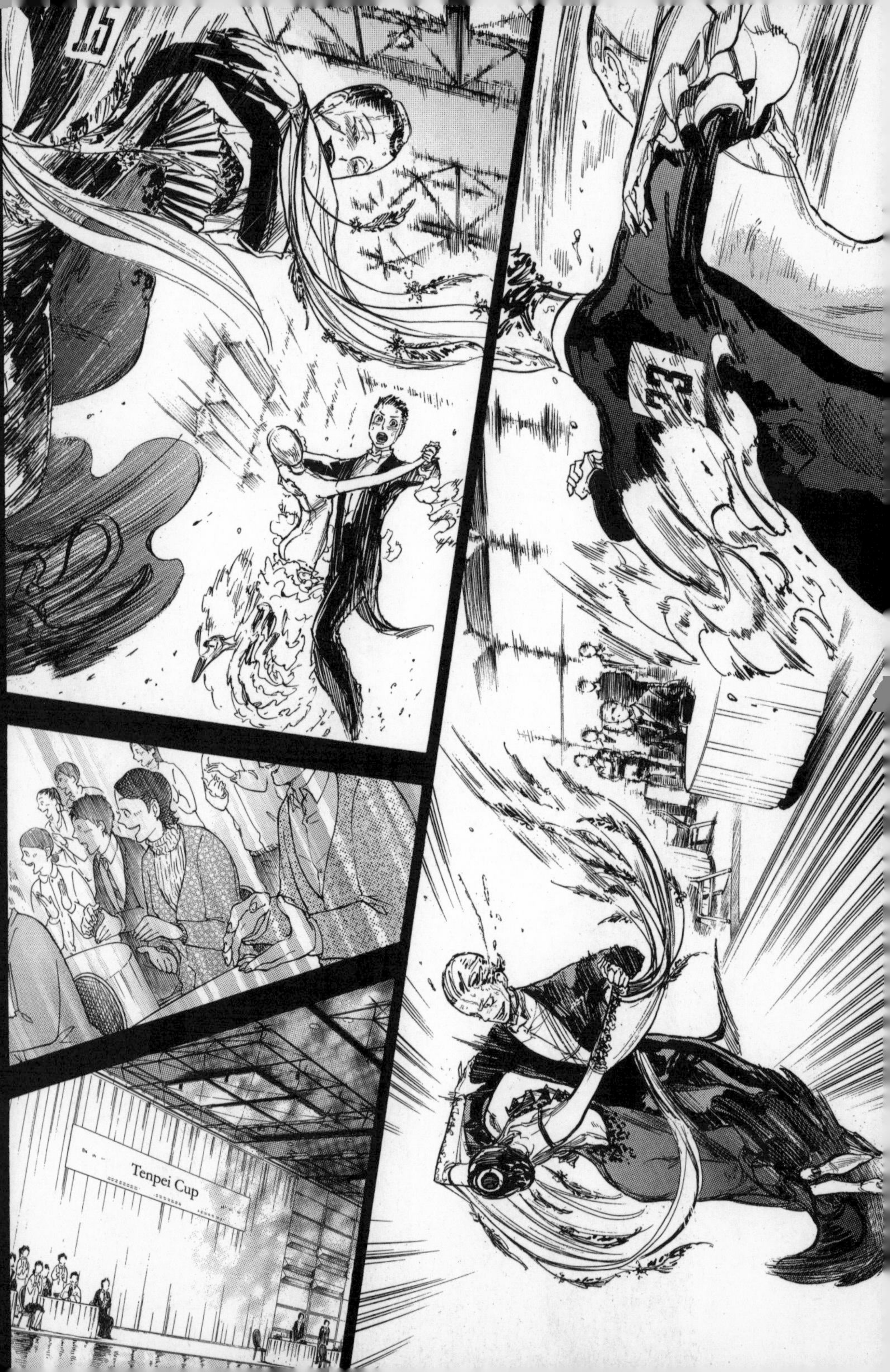
Tenpei Cup

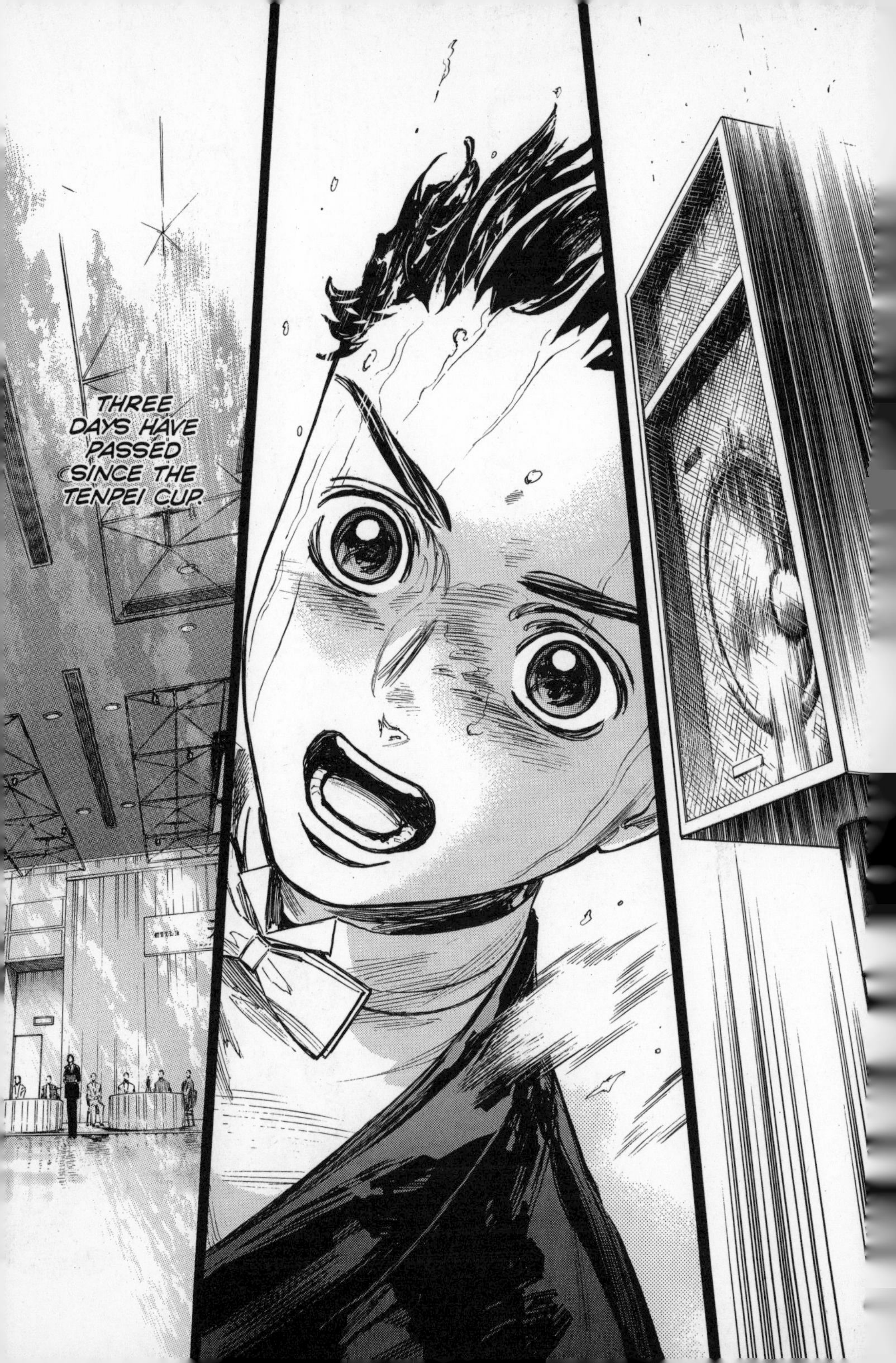
THREE DAYS HAVE PASSED SINCE THE TENPEI CUP.

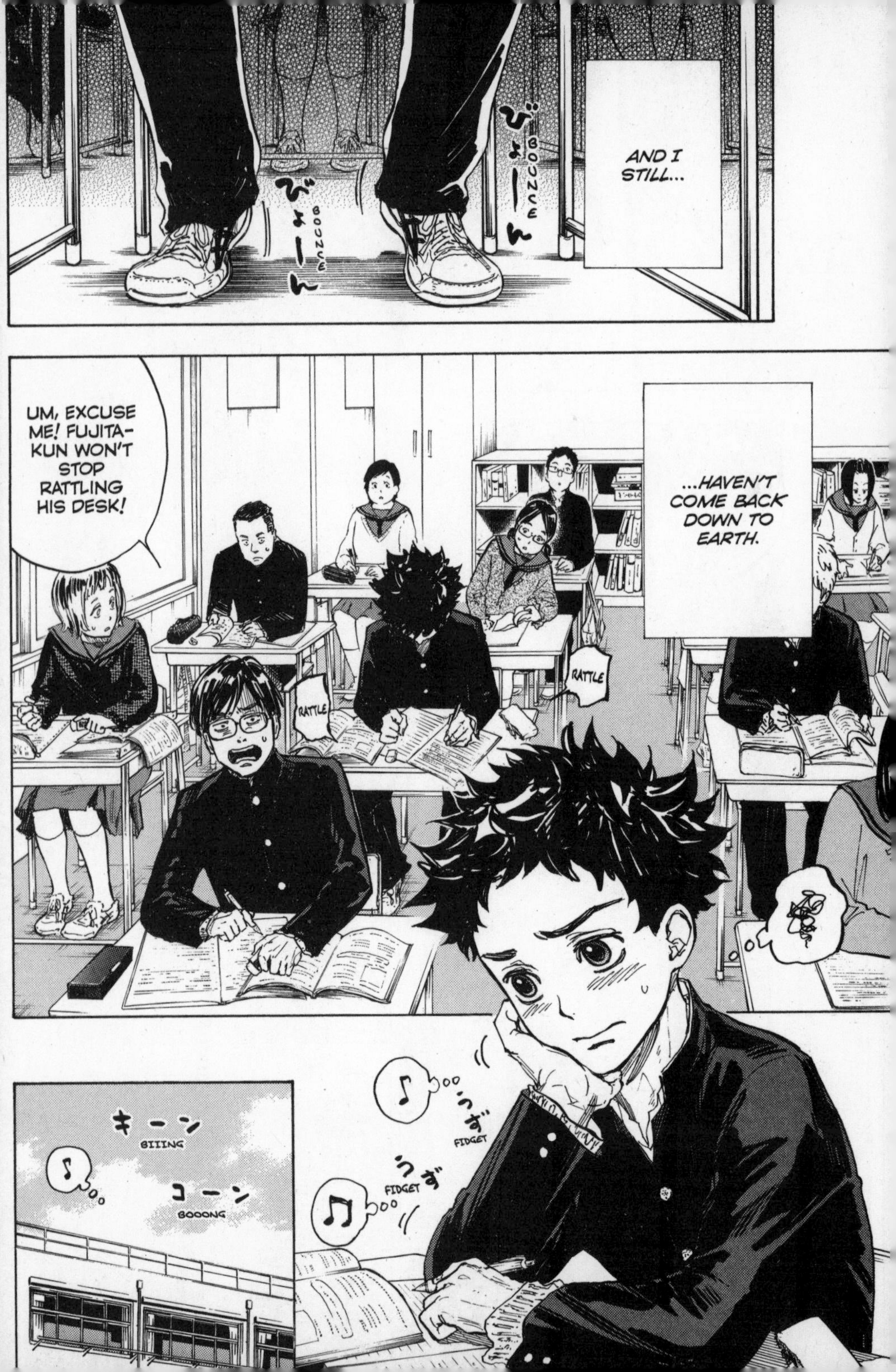
AND I STILL...
びょーん
BOUNCE
びょーん
BOUNCE
...HAVEN'T COME BACK DOWN TO EARTH.
UM, EXCUSE ME! FUJITA-KUN WON'T STOP RATTLING HIS DESK!
RATTLE
RATTLE
うず
FIDGET
うず
FIDGET
キーン
BIIING
コーン
BOOONG

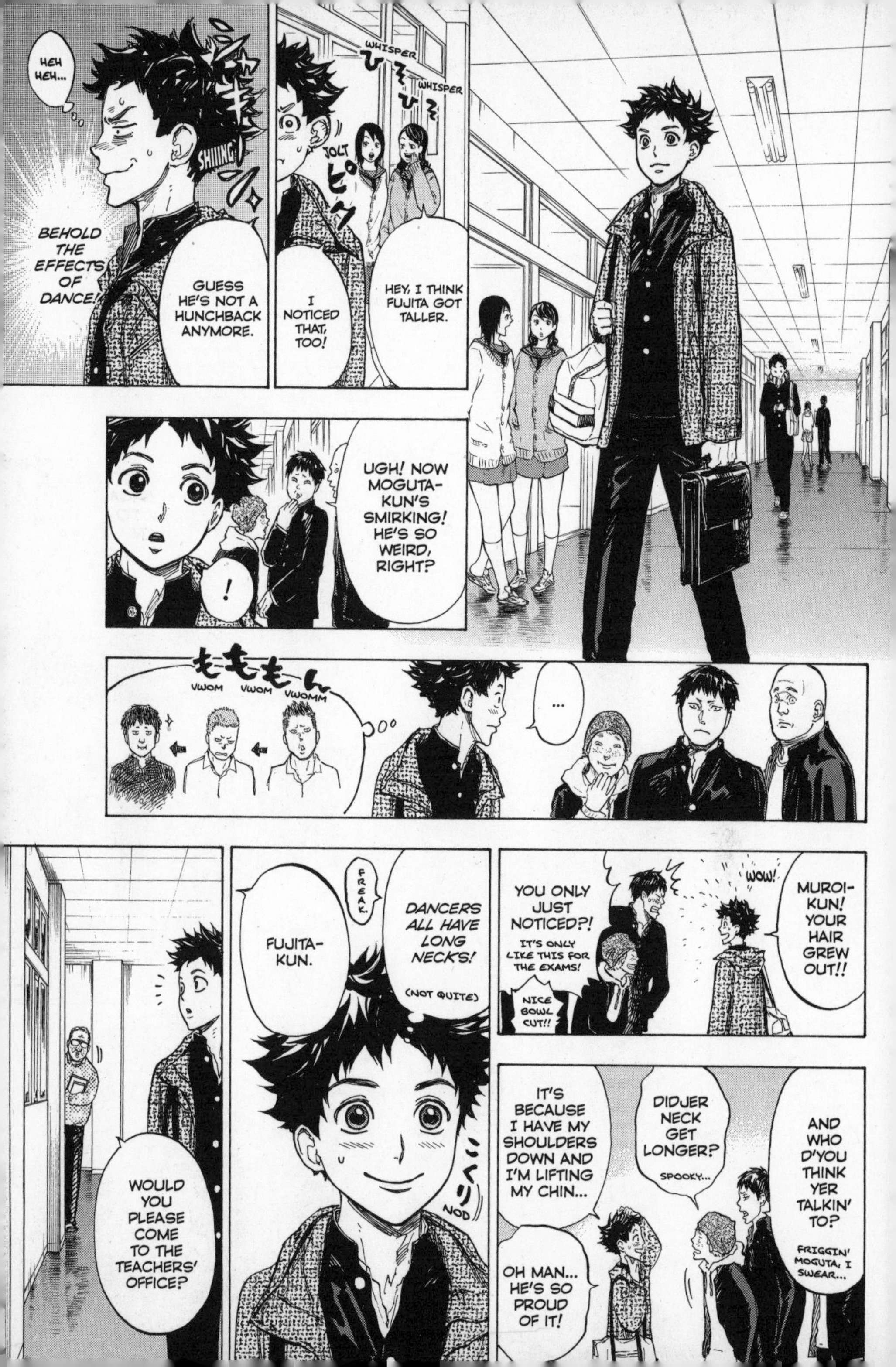
WHISPER
WHISPER
JOLT
HEY, I THINK FUJITA GOT TALLER.
I NOTICED THAT, TOO!
GUESS HE'S NOT A HUNCHBACK ANYMORE.
SHIIING
HEH HEH...
BEHOLD THE EFFECTS OF DANCE!!
UGH! NOW MOGUTA-KUN'S SMIRKING! HE'S SO WEIRD, RIGHT?
!
...
VWOM VWOM VWOMM
MUROI-KUN! YOUR HAIR GREW OUT!!
WOW!
YOU ONLY JUST NOTICED?!
IT'S ONLY LIKE THIS FOR THE EXAMS!
NICE BOWL CUT!!
AND WHO D'YOU THINK YER TALKIN' TO?
FRIGGIN' MOGUTA, I SWEAR...
DIDJER NECK GET LONGER?
SPOOKY...
IT'S BECAUSE I HAVE MY SHOULDERS DOWN AND I'M LIFTING MY CHIN...
OH MAN... HE'S SO PROUD OF IT!
DANCERS ALL HAVE LONG NECKS!
(NOT QUITE)
FREAK.
FUJITA-KUN.
NOD
WOULD YOU PLEASE COME TO THE TEACHERS' OFFICE?

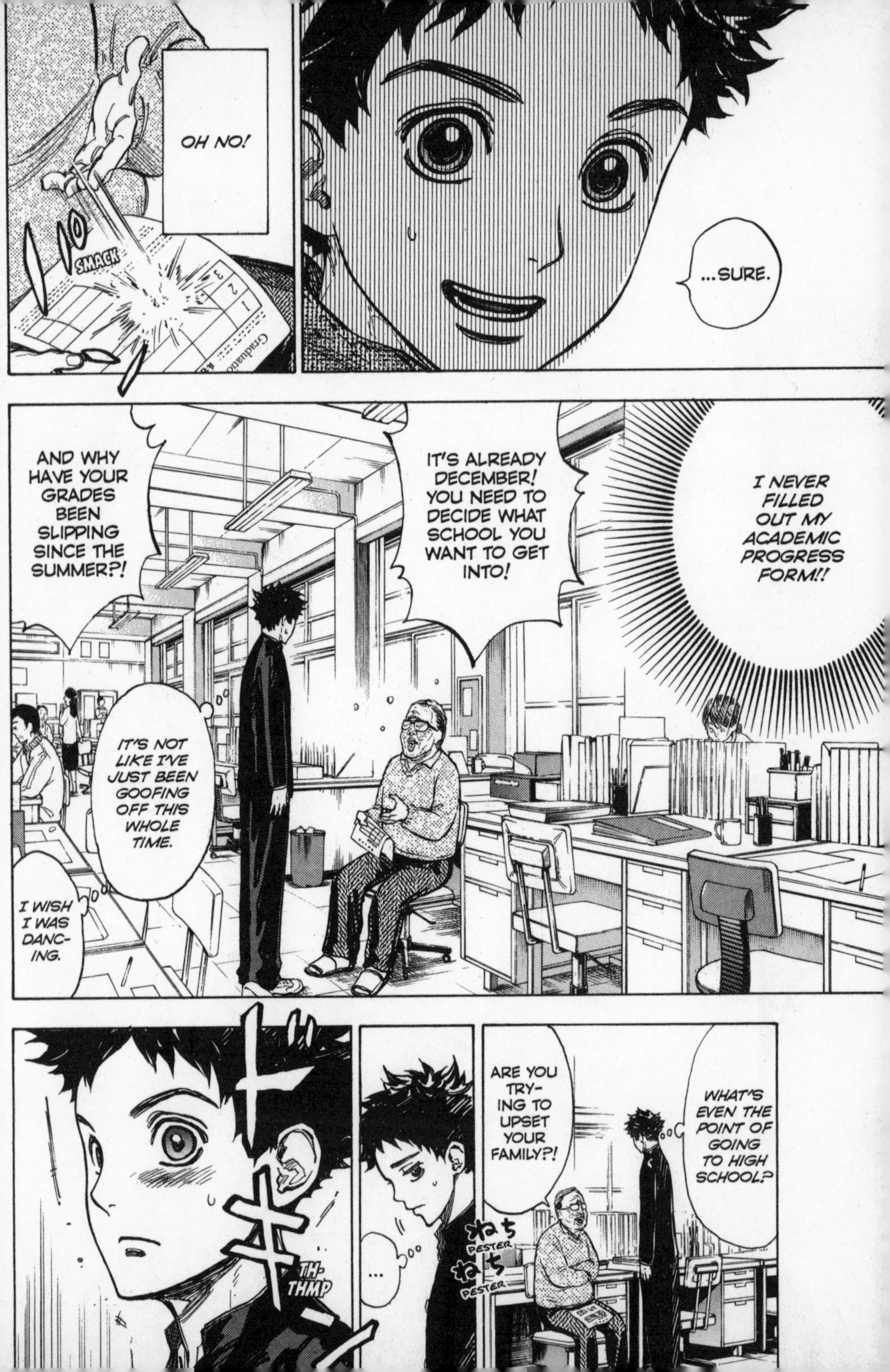
...SURE.
OH NO!
SMACK
I NEVER FILLED OUT MY ACADEMIC PROGRESS FORM!!
IT'S ALREADY DECEMBER! YOU NEED TO DECIDE WHAT SCHOOL YOU WANT TO GET INTO!
AND WHY HAVE YOUR GRADES BEEN SLIPPING SINCE THE SUMMER?!
IT'S NOT LIKE I'VE JUST BEEN GOOFING OFF THIS WHOLE TIME.
I WISH I WAS DANCING.
WHAT'S EVEN THE POINT OF GOING TO HIGH SCHOOL?
ARE YOU TRYING TO UPSET YOUR FAMILY?!
ねち PESTER
ねち PESTER
...
TH-THMP

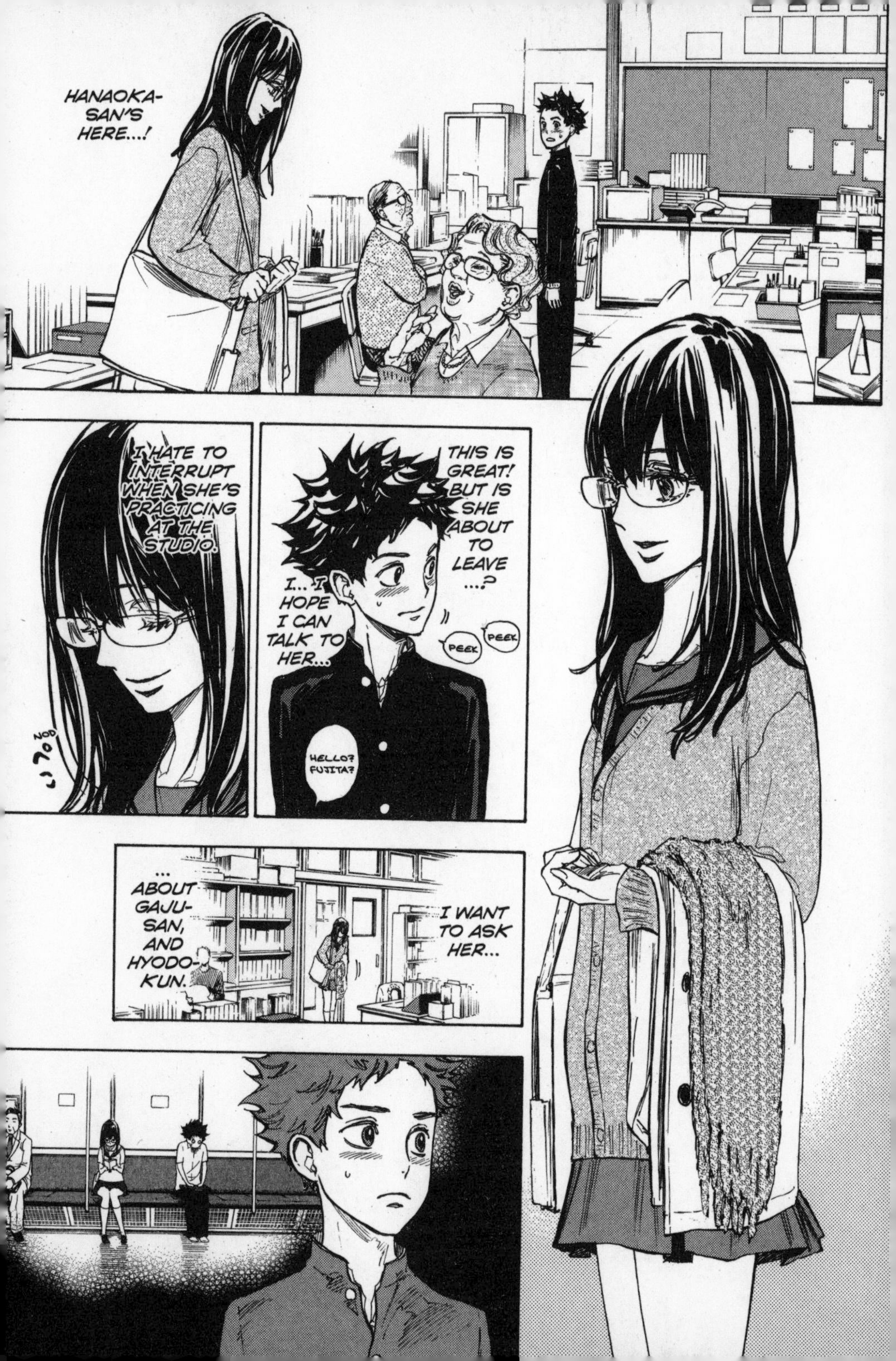
HANAOKA-SAN'S HERE...!
THIS IS GREAT! BUT IS SHE ABOUT TO LEAVE ...?
I... I HOPE I CAN TALK TO HER...
PEEK
PEEK
HELLO? FUJITA?
I HATE TO INTERRUPT WHEN SHE'S PRACTICING AT THE STUDIO.
NOD
I WANT TO ASK HER...
... ABOUT GAJU-SAN, AND HYODO-KUN.

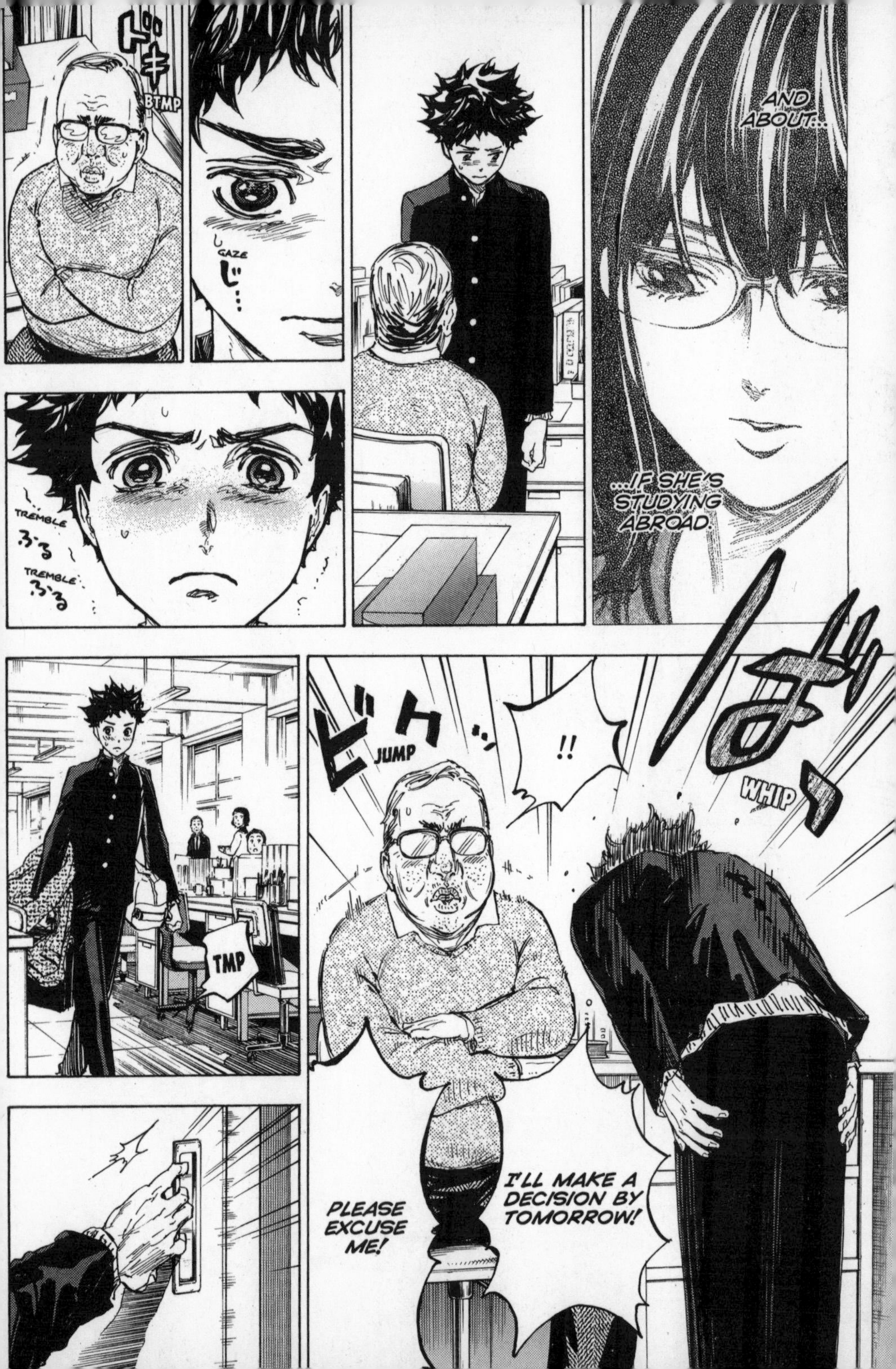
AND ABOUT...
...IF SHE'S STUDYING ABROAD.
じ…
GAZE
ドキ
BTMP
TREMBLE
ぶる
TREMBLE
ぶる
ばっ
WHIP
ビクッ
JUMP
!!
I'LL MAKE A DECISION BY TOMORROW!
PLEASE EXCUSE ME!
TMP

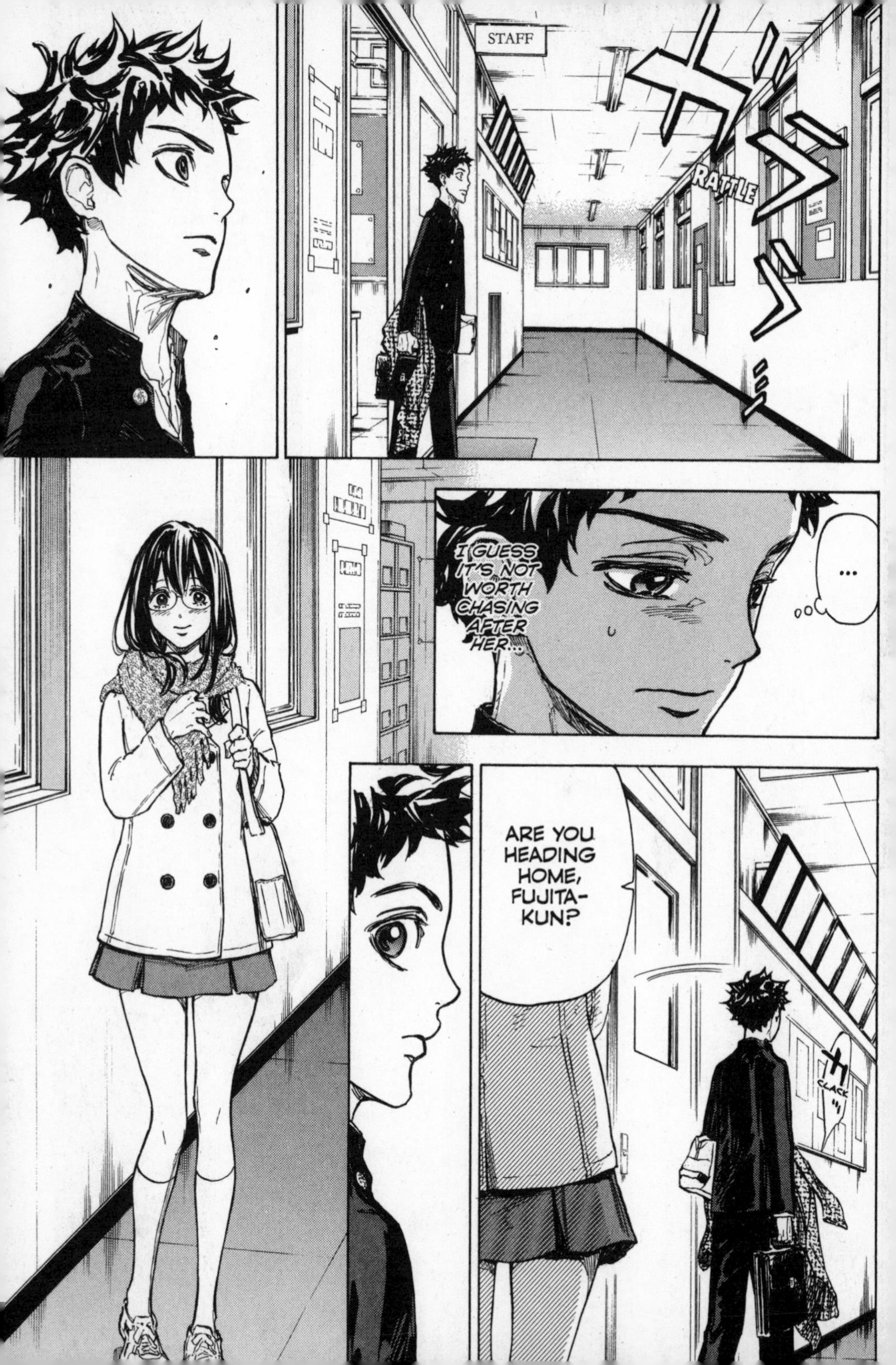
STAFF
RATTLE
...
I GUESS IT'S NOT WORTH CHASING AFTER HER...
ARE YOU HEADING HOME, FUJITA-KUN?
CLACK

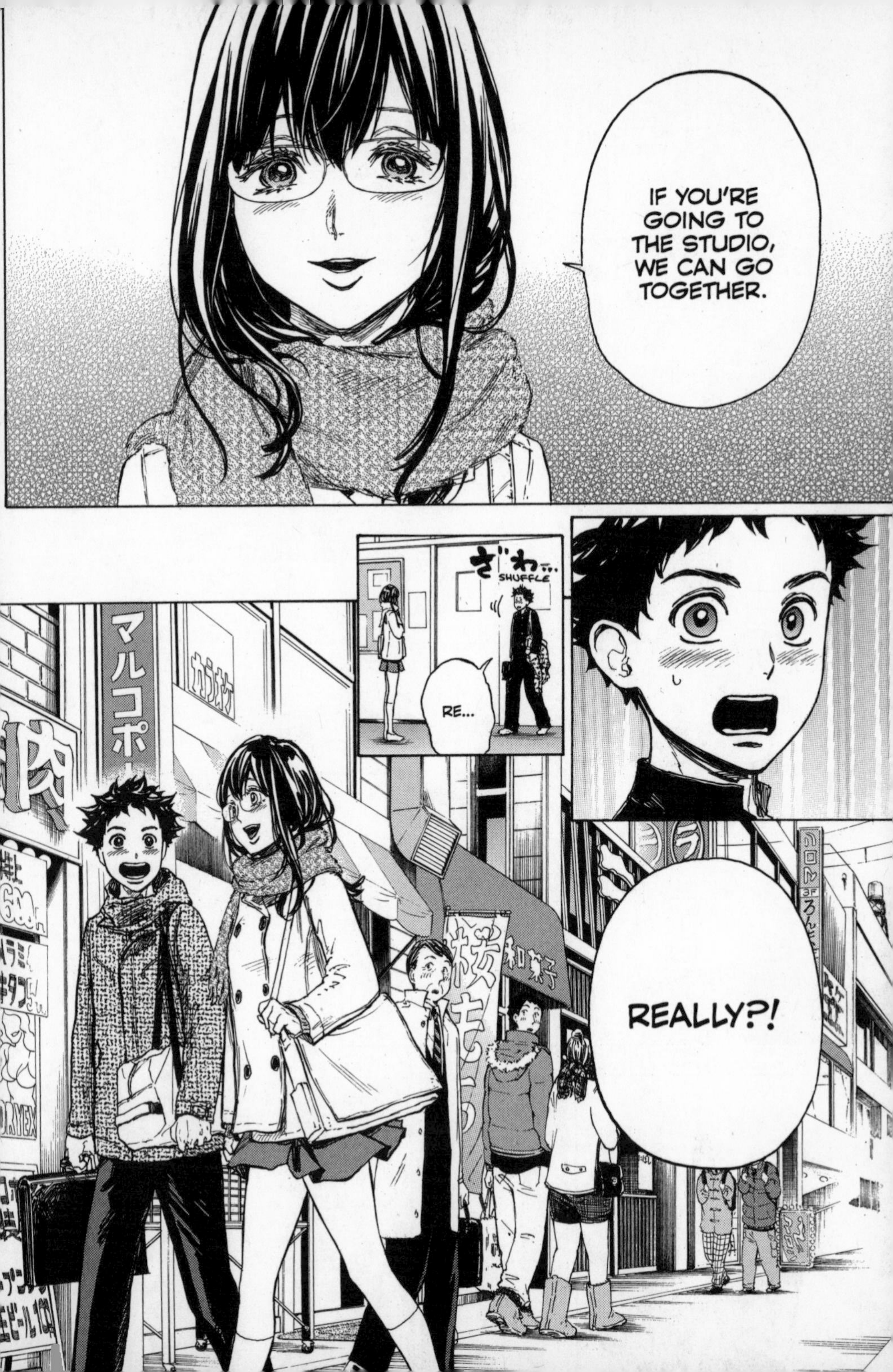
IF YOU'RE GOING TO THE STUDIO, WE CAN GO TOGETHER.
ざわ…
SHUFFLE
RE...
マルコポ
肉
和菓子
REALLY?!

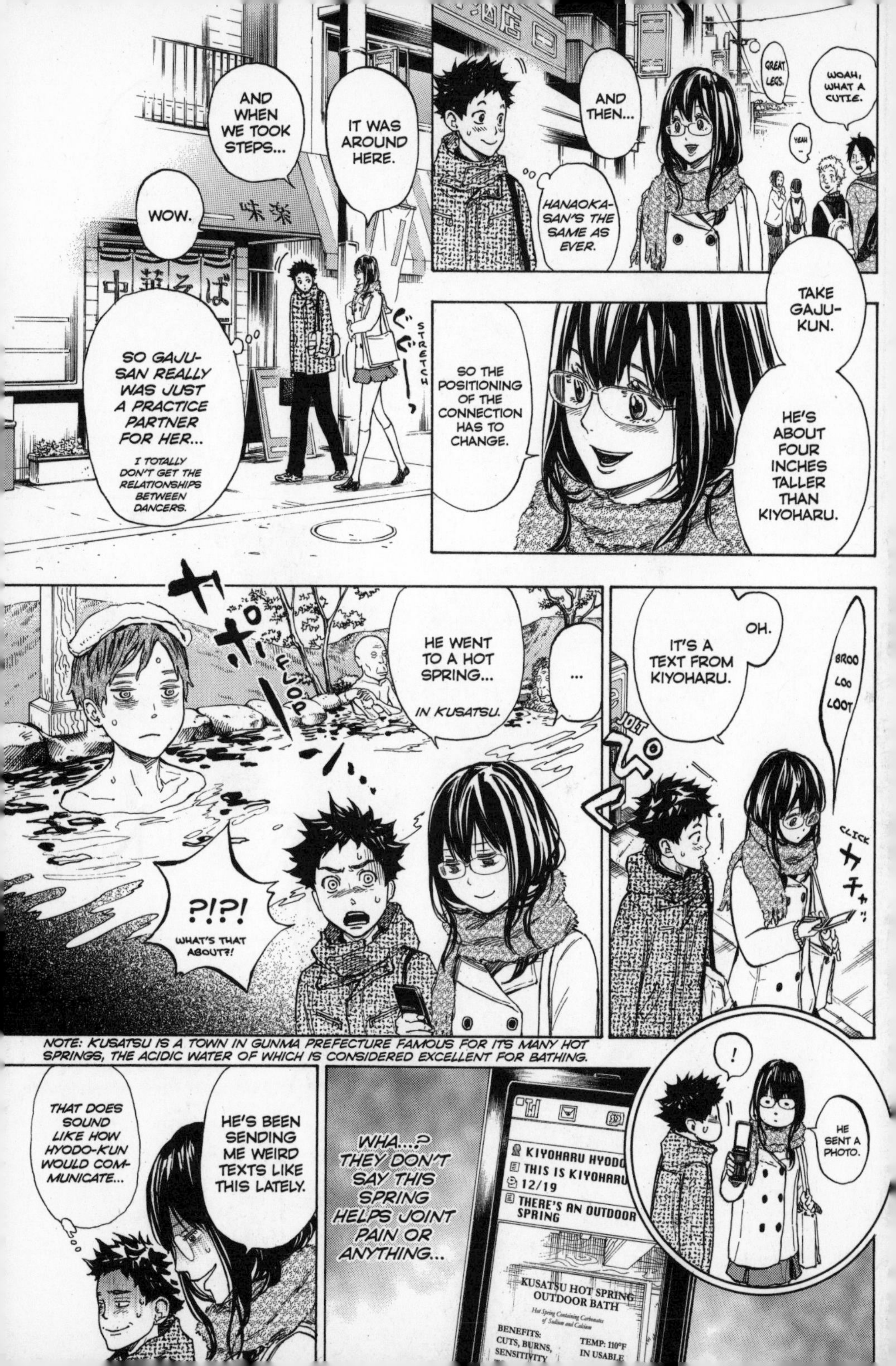
WOAH, WHAT A CUTIE.
YEAH ...
GREAT LEGS.
AND THEN...
HANAOKA-SAN'S THE SAME AS EVER.
TAKE GAJU-KUN.
HE'S ABOUT FOUR INCHES TALLER THAN KIYOHARU.
SO THE POSITIONING OF THE CONNECTION HAS TO CHANGE.
IT WAS AROUND HERE.
AND WHEN WE TOOK STEPS...
WOW.
STRETCH
SO GAJU-SAN REALLY WAS JUST A PRACTICE PARTNER FOR HER...
I TOTALLY DON'T GET THE RELATIONSHIPS BETWEEN DANCERS.
OH.
IT'S A TEXT FROM KIYOHARU.
BROO LOO LOOT
JOLT
CLICK
HE WENT TO A HOT SPRING...
IN KUSATSU.
...
FLOP
?!?!
WHAT'S THAT ABOUT?!
NOTE: KUSATSU IS A TOWN IN GUNMA PREFECTURE FAMOUS FOR ITS MANY HOT SPRINGS, THE ACIDIC WATER OF WHICH IS CONSIDERED EXCELLENT FOR BATHING.
!
HE SENT A PHOTO.
KIYOHARU HYODO
THIS IS KIYOHARU
12/19
THERE'S AN OUTDOOR SPRING
KUSATSU HOT SPRING OUTDOOR BATH
Hot Spring Containing Carbonates of Sodium and Calcium
BENEFITS: CUTS, BURNS, SENSITIVITY
TEMP: 110°F IN USABLE
WHA...? THEY DON'T SAY THIS SPRING HELPS JOINT PAIN OR ANYTHING...
HE'S BEEN SENDING ME WEIRD TEXTS LIKE THIS LATELY.
THAT DOES SOUND LIKE HOW HYODO-KUN WOULD COMMUNICATE...

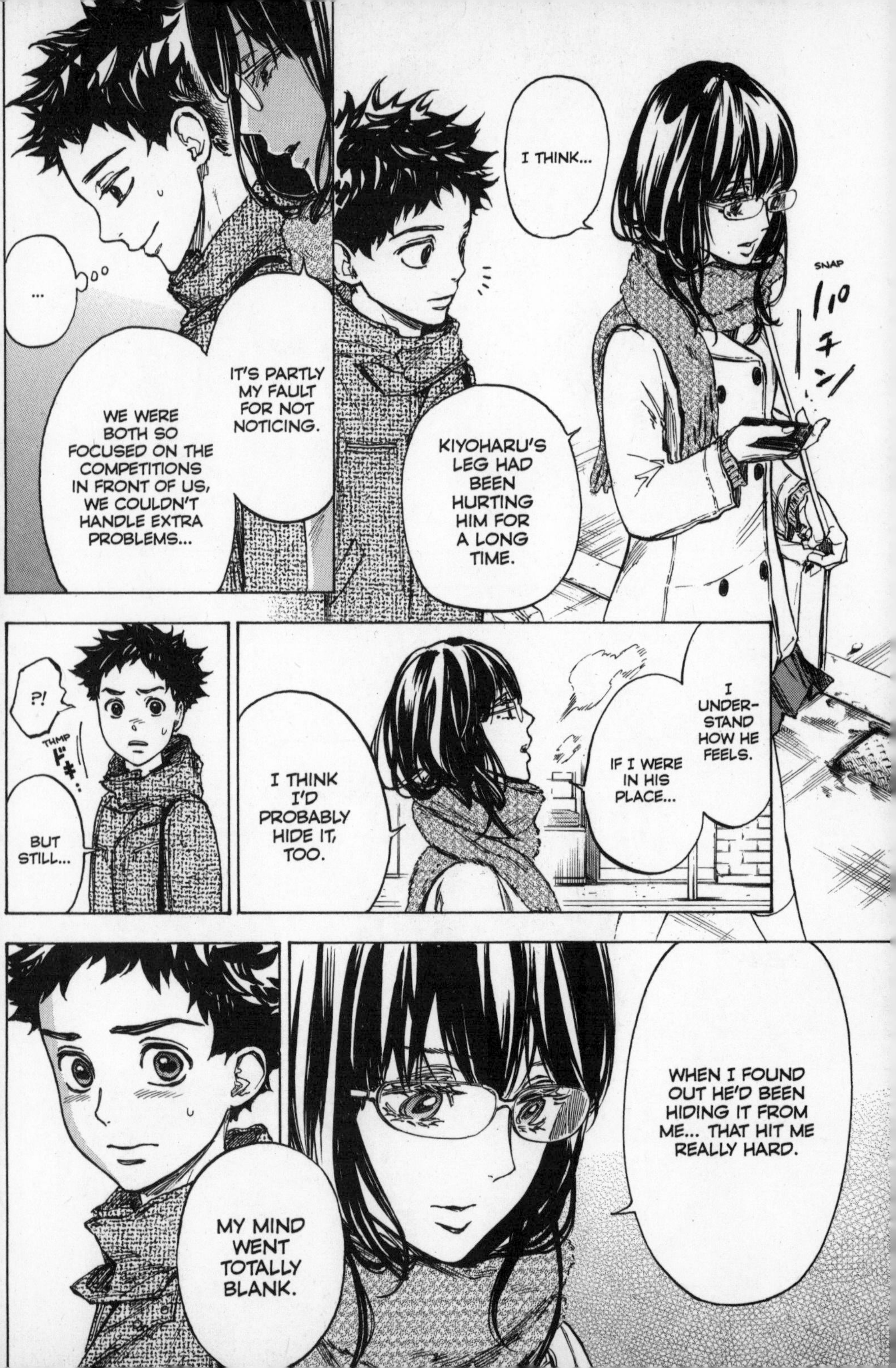

SNAP
パチン
I THINK...
KIYOHARU'S LEG HAD BEEN HURTING HIM FOR A LONG TIME.
...
IT'S PARTLY MY FAULT FOR NOT NOTICING.
WE WERE BOTH SO FOCUSED ON THE COMPETITIONS IN FRONT OF US, WE COULDN'T HANDLE EXTRA PROBLEMS...
I UNDERSTAND HOW HE FEELS.
IF I WERE IN HIS PLACE...
I THINK I'D PROBABLY HIDE IT, TOO.
?!
THMP
ドキ
BUT STILL...
WHEN I FOUND OUT HE'D BEEN HIDING IT FROM ME... THAT HIT ME REALLY HARD.
MY MIND WENT TOTALLY BLANK.

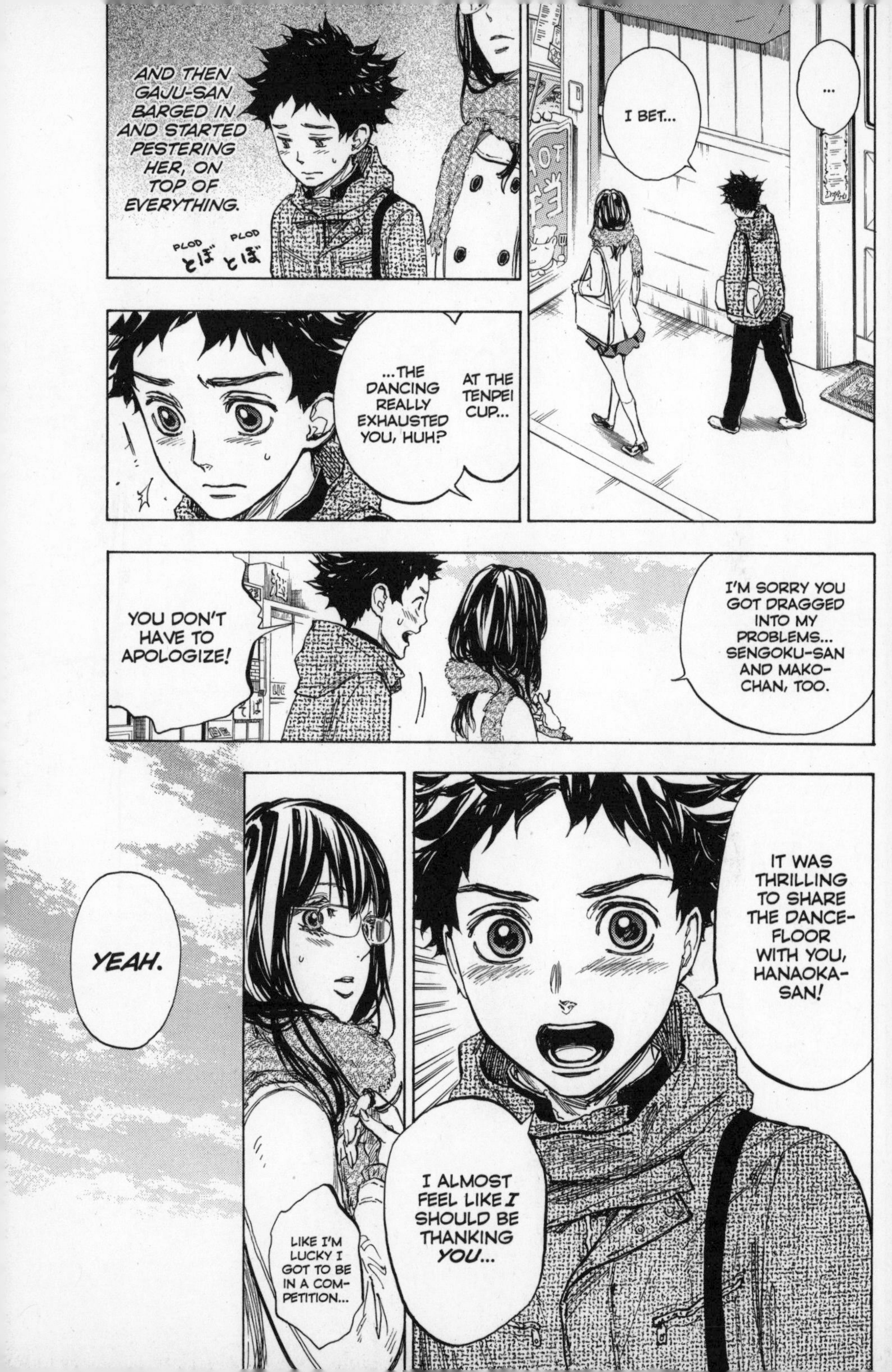
...
I BET...
AND THEN GAJU-SAN BARGED IN AND STARTED PESTERING HER, ON TOP OF EVERYTHING.
PLOD PLOD
とぼ とぼ
AT THE TENPEI CUP...
...THE DANCING REALLY EXHAUSTED YOU, HUH?
I'M SORRY YOU GOT DRAGGED INTO MY PROBLEMS... SENGOKU-SAN AND MAKO-CHAN, TOO.
YOU DON'T HAVE TO APOLOGIZE!
IT WAS THRILLING TO SHARE THE DANCE-FLOOR WITH YOU, HANAOKA-SAN!
I ALMOST FEEL LIKE *I* SHOULD BE THANKING *YOU*...
LIKE I'M LUCKY I GOT TO BE IN A COMPETITION...
YEAH.

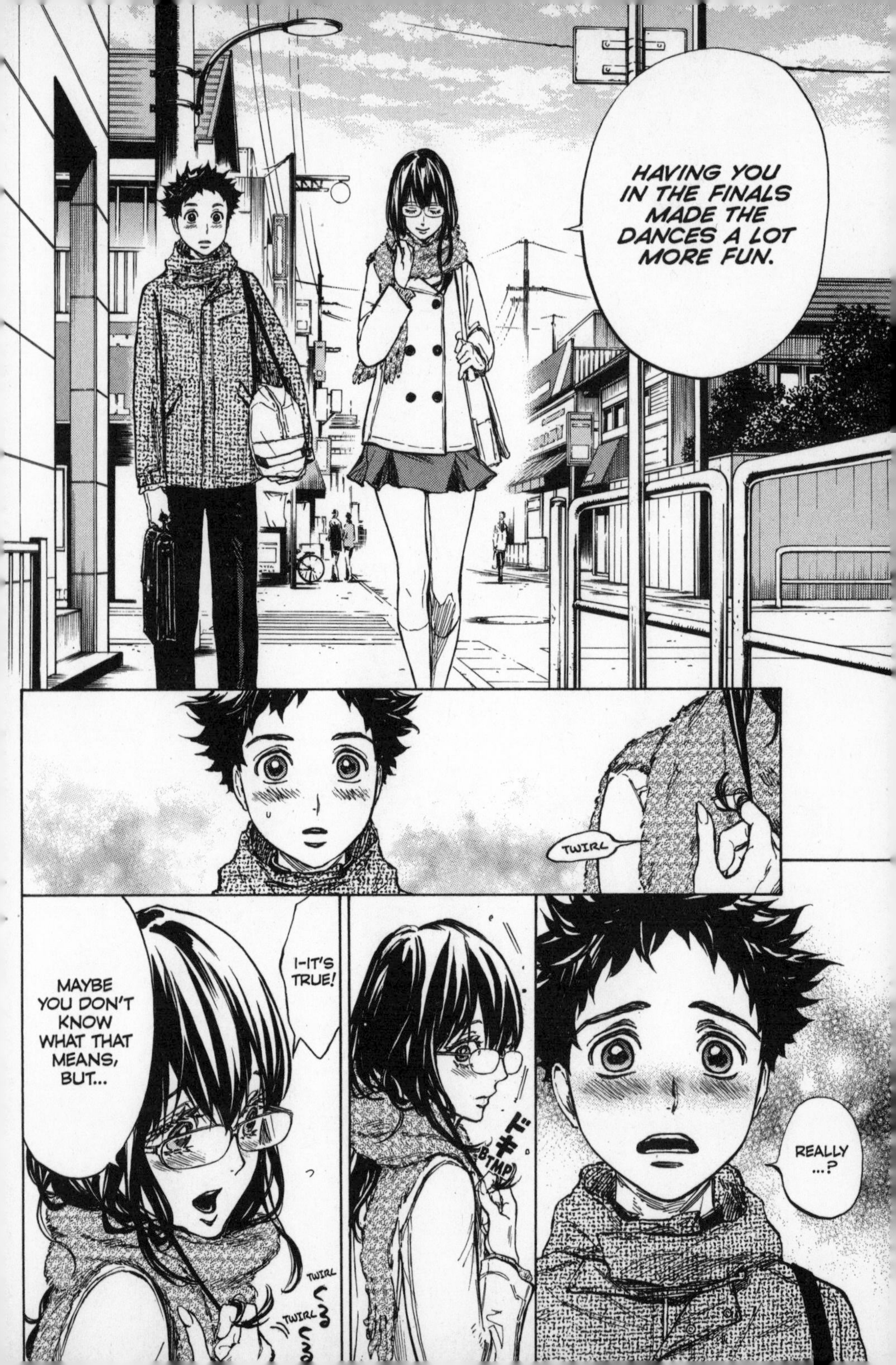
HAVING YOU IN THE FINALS MADE THE DANCES A LOT MORE FUN.
TWIRL
REALLY ...?
ドキ
BTMP
I-IT'S TRUE!
MAYBE YOU DON'T KNOW WHAT THAT MEANS, BUT...
TWIRL
TWIRL

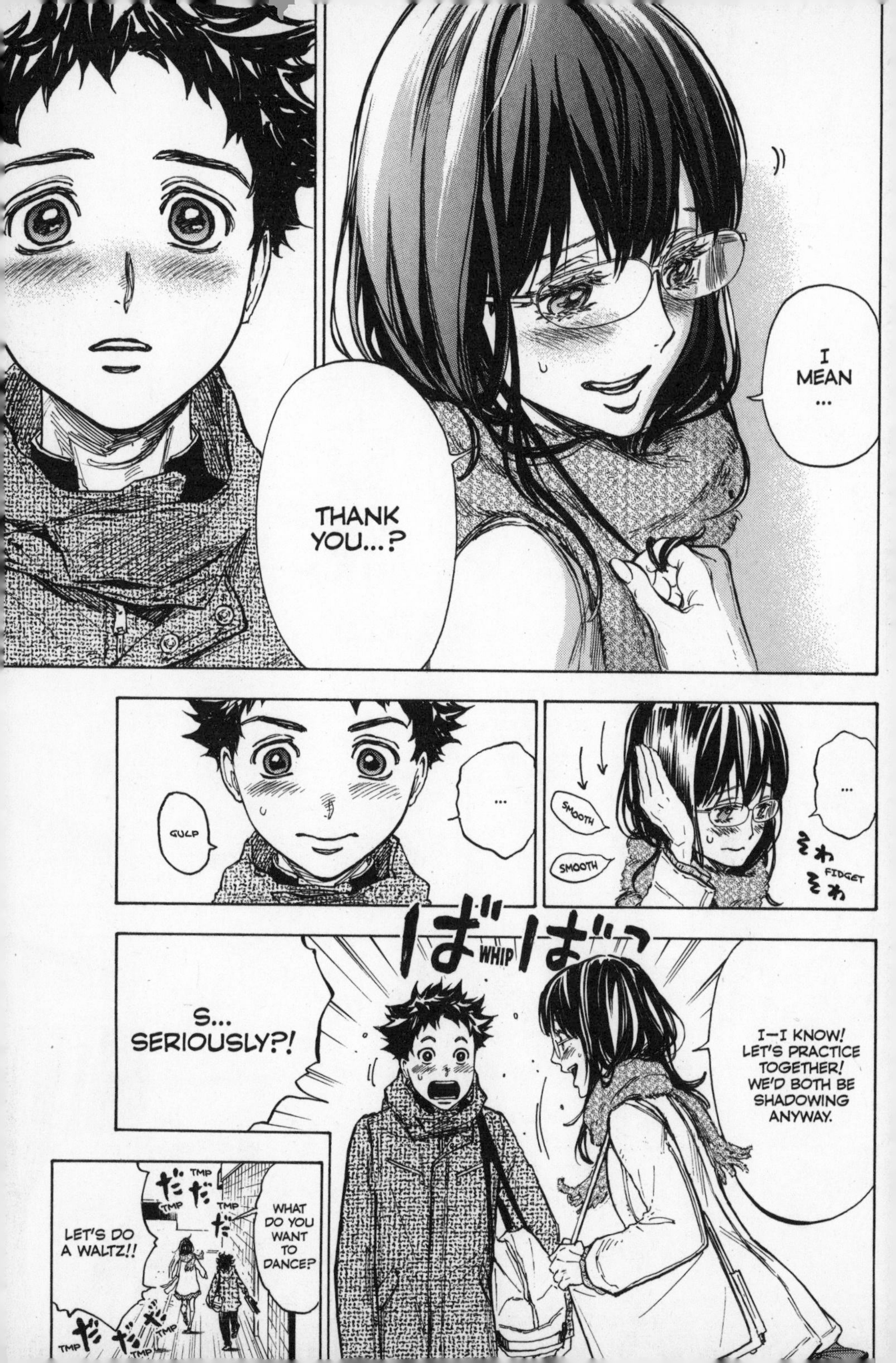
I MEAN ...
THANK YOU...?
...
SMOOTH
SMOOTH
そわ そわ FIDGET
...
GULP
ばばっ WHIP
I—I KNOW! LET'S PRACTICE TOGETHER! WE'D BOTH BE SHADOWING ANYWAY.
S... SERIOUSLY?!
WHAT DO YOU WANT TO DANCE?
LET'S DO A WALTZ!!
だだだ TMP TMP TMP
だだだ TMP TMP TMP

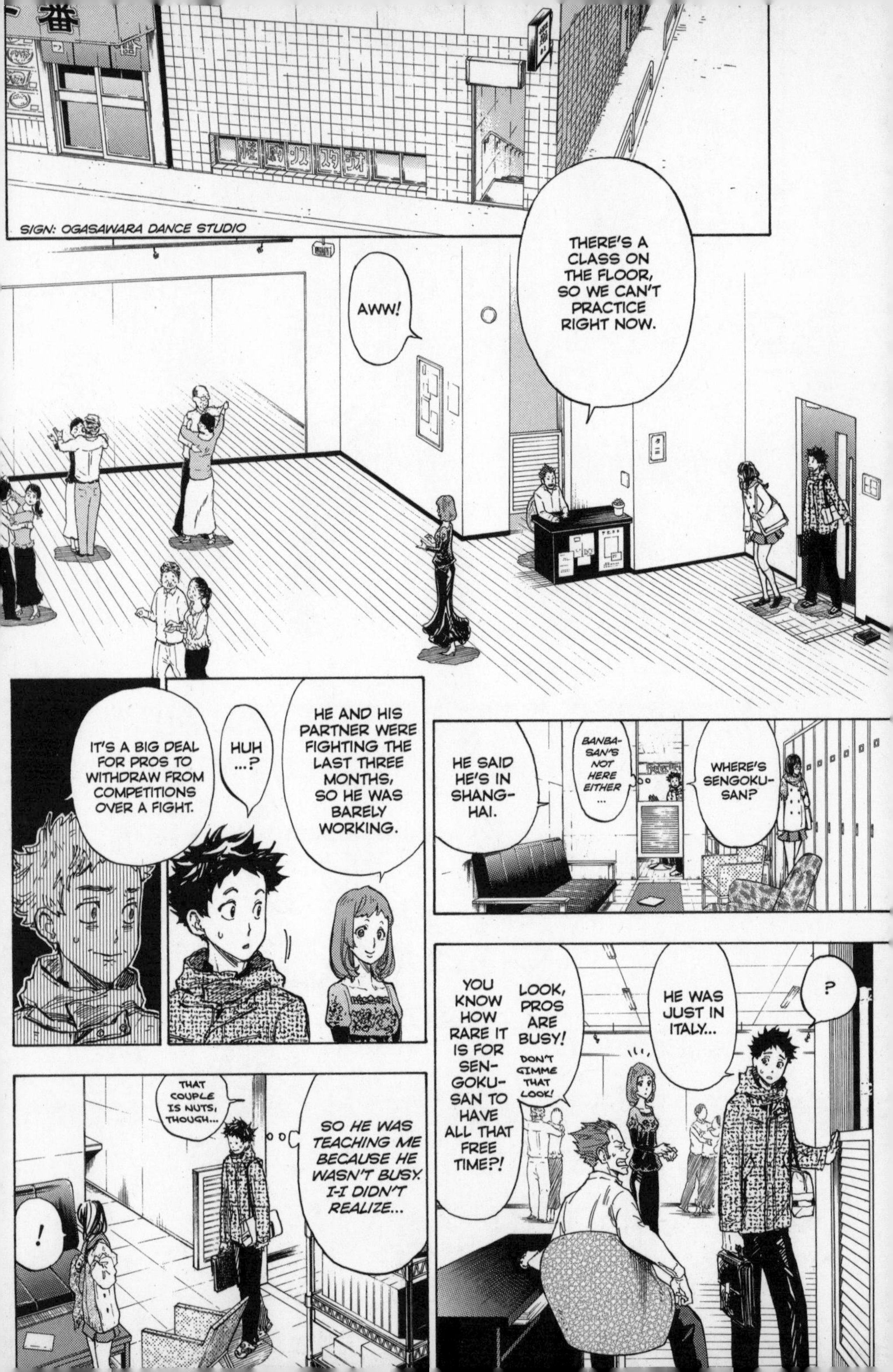
SIGN: OGASAWARA DANCE STUDIO
THERE'S A CLASS ON THE FLOOR, SO WE CAN'T PRACTICE RIGHT NOW.
AWW!
WHERE'S SENGOKU-SAN?
BANBA-SAN'S NOT HERE EITHER...
HE SAID HE'S IN SHANG-HAI.
HE AND HIS PARTNER WERE FIGHTING THE LAST THREE MONTHS, SO HE WAS BARELY WORKING.
HUH ...?
IT'S A BIG DEAL FOR PROS TO WITHDRAW FROM COMPETITIONS OVER A FIGHT.
?
HE WAS JUST IN ITALY...
LOOK, PROS ARE BUSY!
DON'T GIMME THAT LOOK!
YOU KNOW HOW RARE IT IS FOR SEN-GOKU-SAN TO HAVE ALL THAT FREE TIME?!
SO HE WAS TEACHING ME BECAUSE HE WASN'T BUSY. I-I DIDN'T REALIZE...
THAT COUPLE IS NUTS, THOUGH...
!

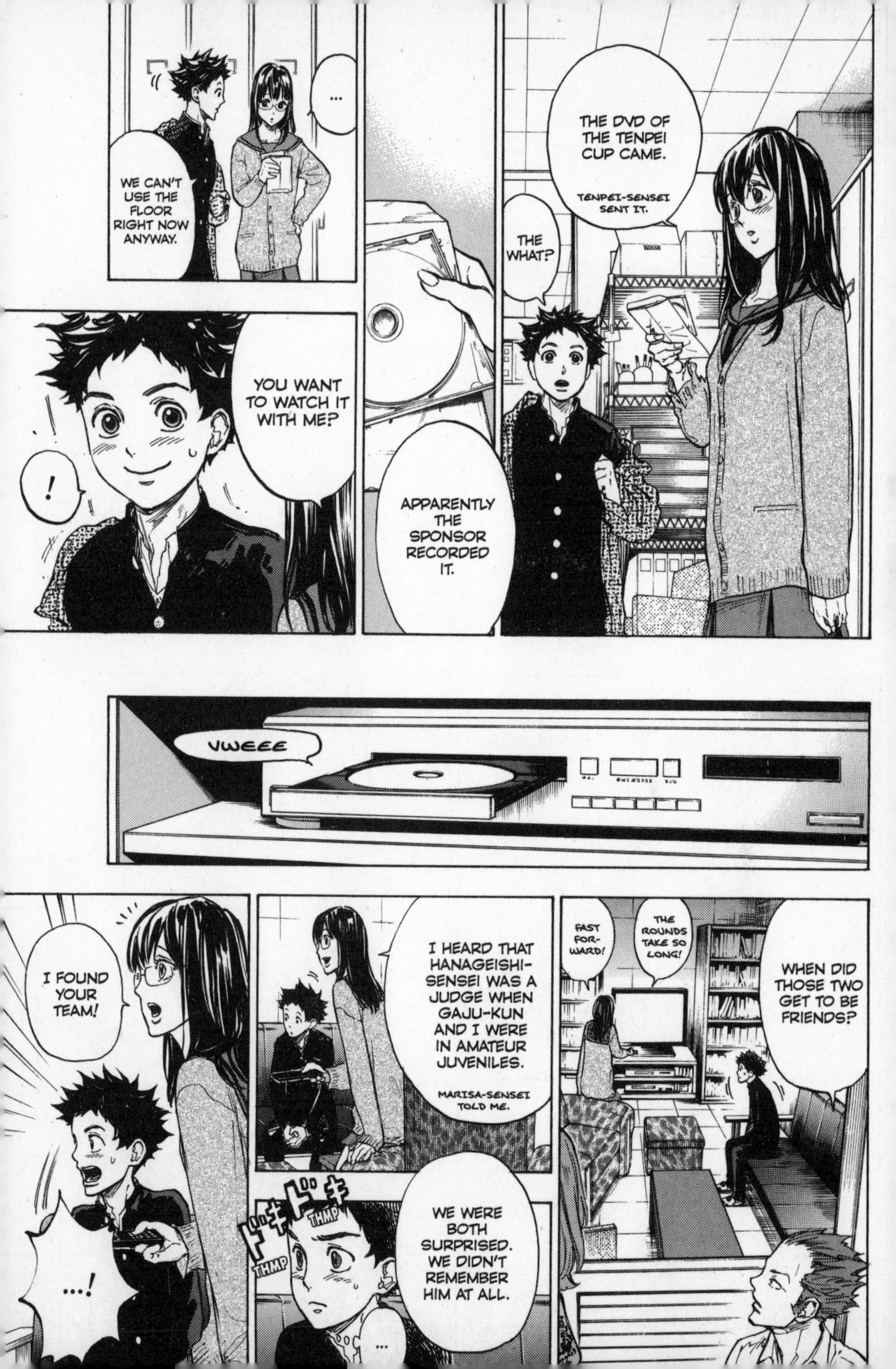
THE DVD OF THE TENPEI CUP CAME.
TENPEI-SENSEI SENT IT.
THE WHAT?
APPARENTLY THE SPONSOR RECORDED IT.
...
WE CAN'T USE THE FLOOR RIGHT NOW ANYWAY.
YOU WANT TO WATCH IT WITH ME?
!
VWEEE
WHEN DID THOSE TWO GET TO BE FRIENDS?
THE ROUNDS TAKE SO LONG!
FAST FOR-WARD!
I HEARD THAT HANAGEISHI-SENSEI WAS A JUDGE WHEN GAJU-KUN AND I WERE IN AMATEUR JUVENILES.
MARISA-SENSEI TOLD ME.
WE WERE BOTH SURPRISED. WE DIDN'T REMEMBER HIM AT ALL.
THMP
THMP
...
I FOUND YOUR TEAM!
...!

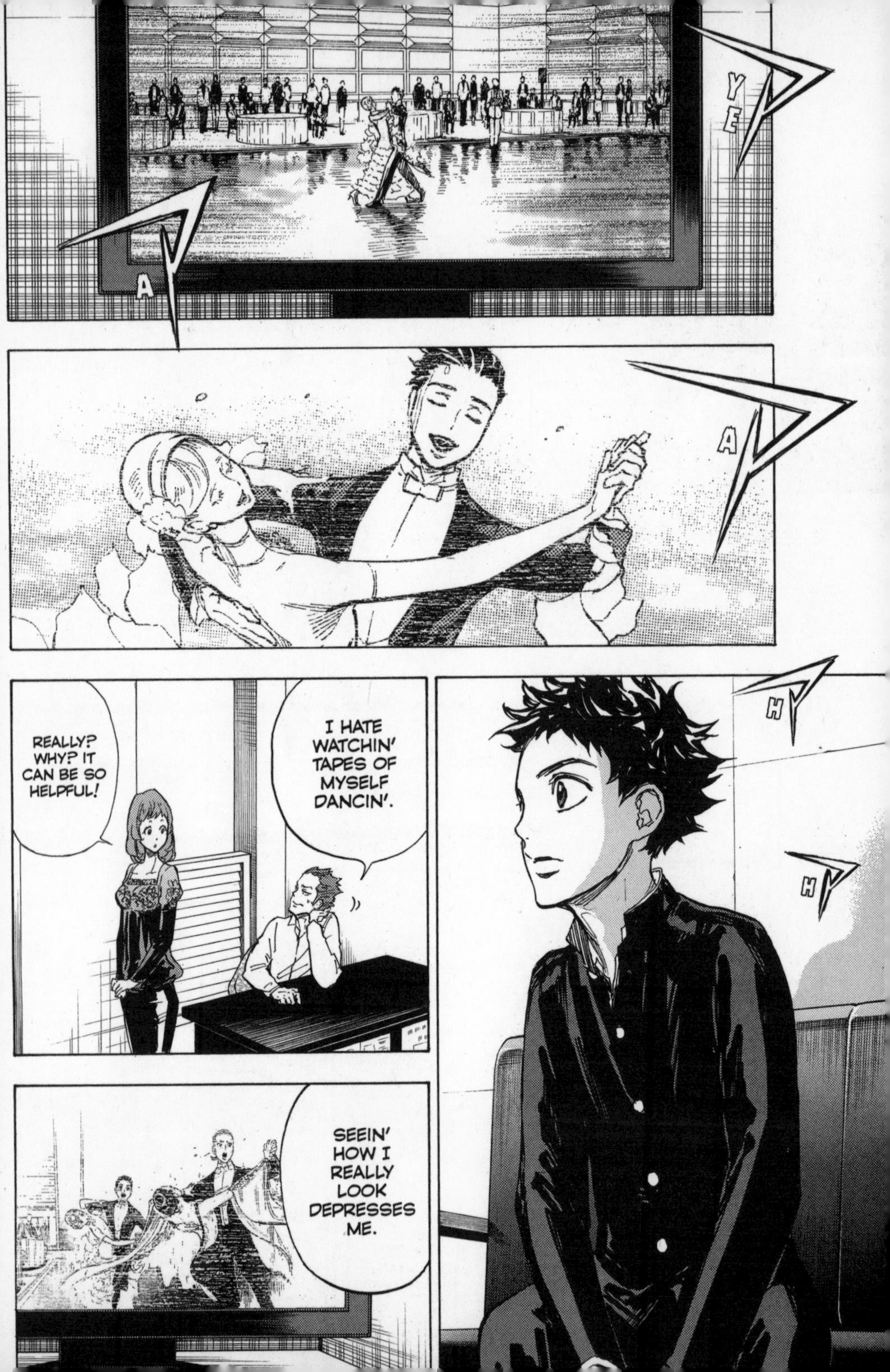
YE
A
A
H
H
I HATE WATCHIN' TAPES OF MYSELF DANCIN'.
REALLY? WHY? IT CAN BE SO HELPFUL!
SEEIN' HOW I REALLY LOOK DEPRESSES ME.

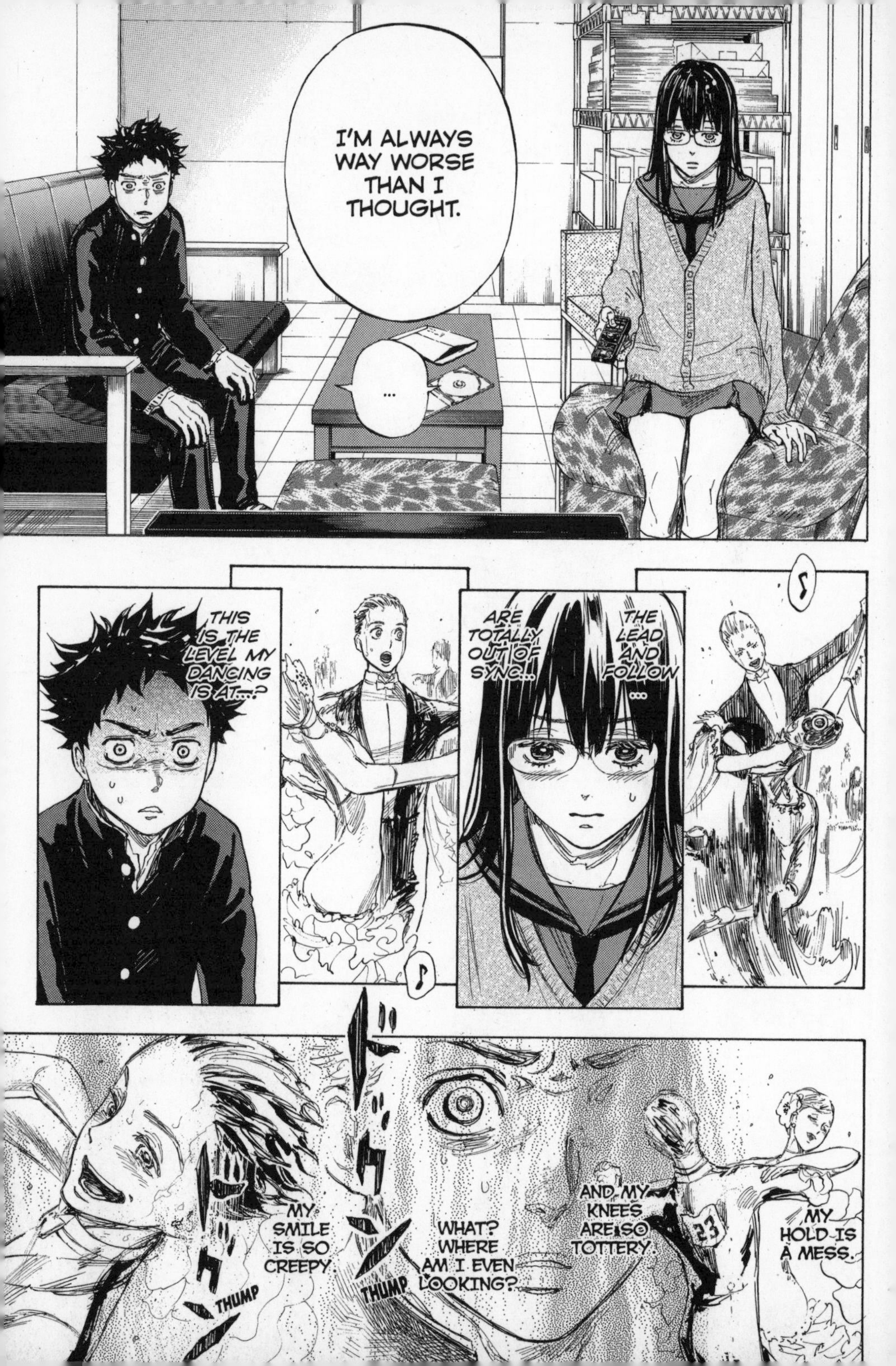
I'M ALWAYS WAY WORSE THAN I THOUGHT.
...
♪
THE LEAD AND FOLLOW ...
ARE TOTALLY OUT OF SYNC...
♪
THIS IS THE LEVEL MY DANCING IS AT...?
MY HOLD IS A MESS.
23
AND MY KNEES ARE SO TOTTERY.
WHAT? WHERE AM I EVEN LOOKING?
THUMP
MY SMILE IS SO CREEPY.
THUMP

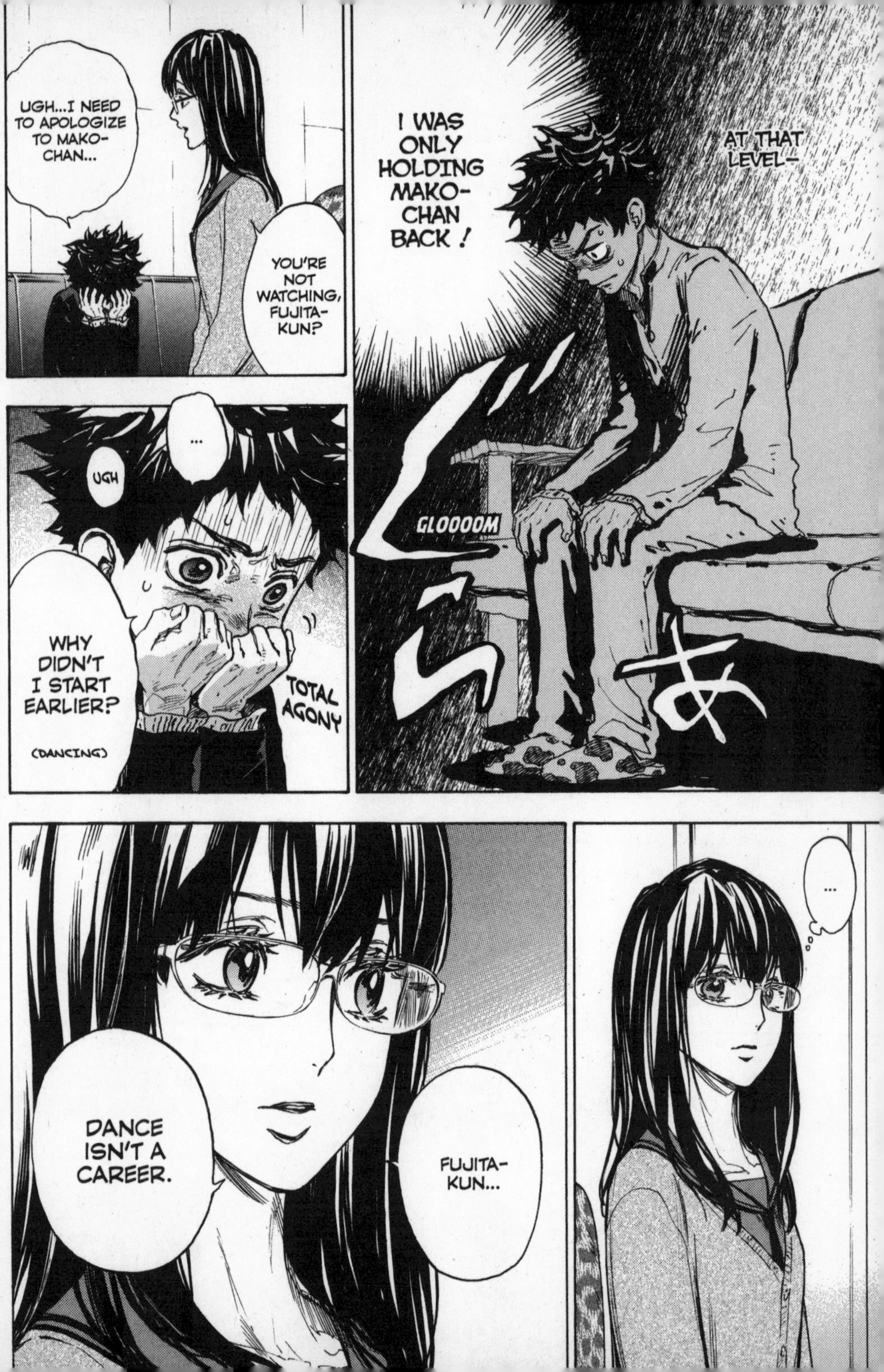
I WAS ONLY HOLDING MAKO-CHAN BACK!
AT THAT LEVEL–
GLOOOOM
YOU'RE NOT WATCHING, FUJITA-KUN?
UGH...I NEED TO APOLOGIZE TO MAKO-CHAN...
...
UGH
TOTAL AGONY
WHY DIDN'T I START EARLIER?
(DANCING)
...
FUJITA-KUN...
DANCE ISN'T A CAREER.

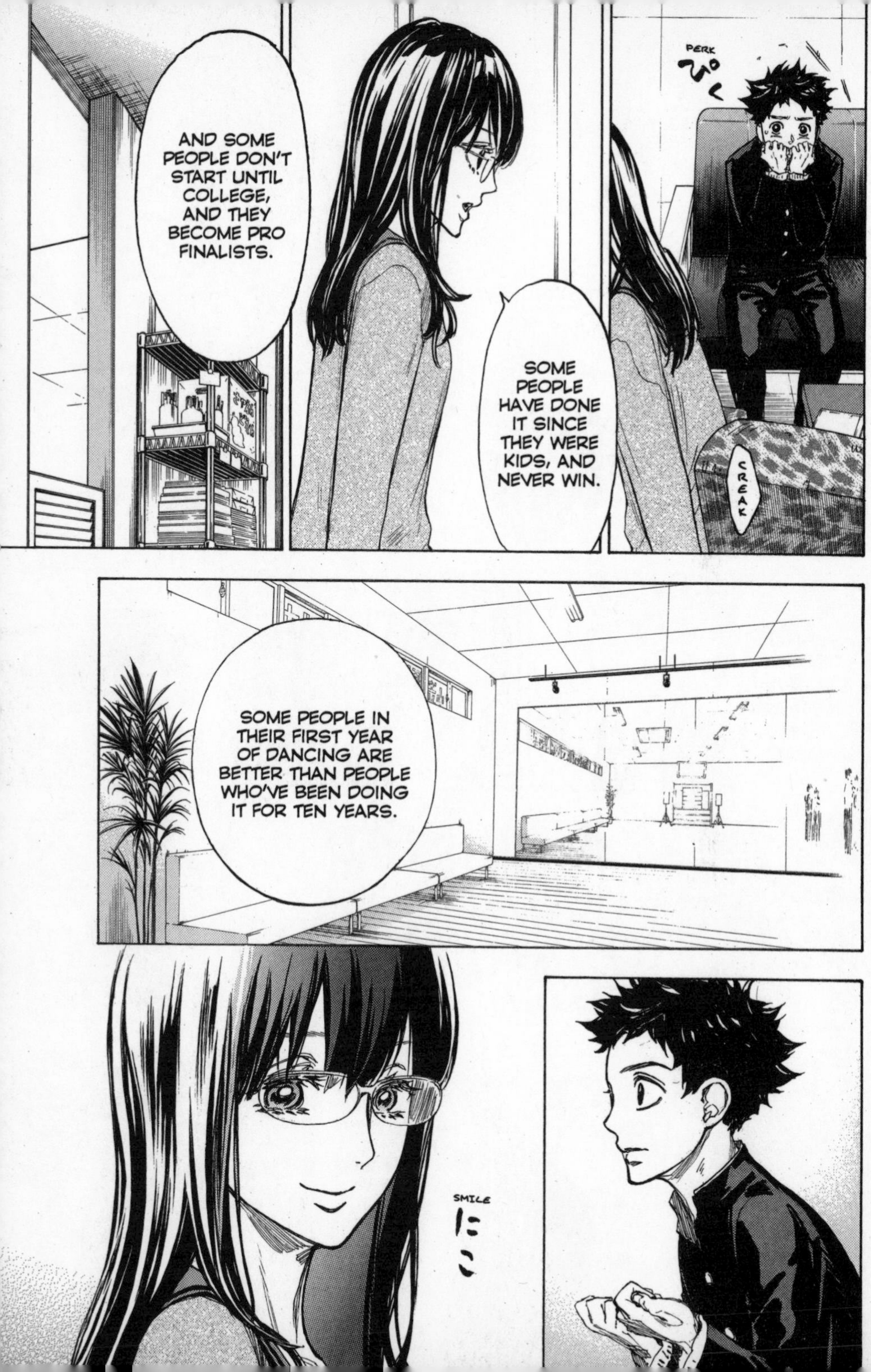
PERK
ぴく
CREAK
SOME PEOPLE HAVE DONE IT SINCE THEY WERE KIDS, AND NEVER WIN.
AND SOME PEOPLE DON'T START UNTIL COLLEGE, AND THEY BECOME PRO FINALISTS.
SOME PEOPLE IN THEIR FIRST YEAR OF DANCING ARE BETTER THAN PEOPLE WHO'VE BEEN DOING IT FOR TEN YEARS.
SMILE
にこ

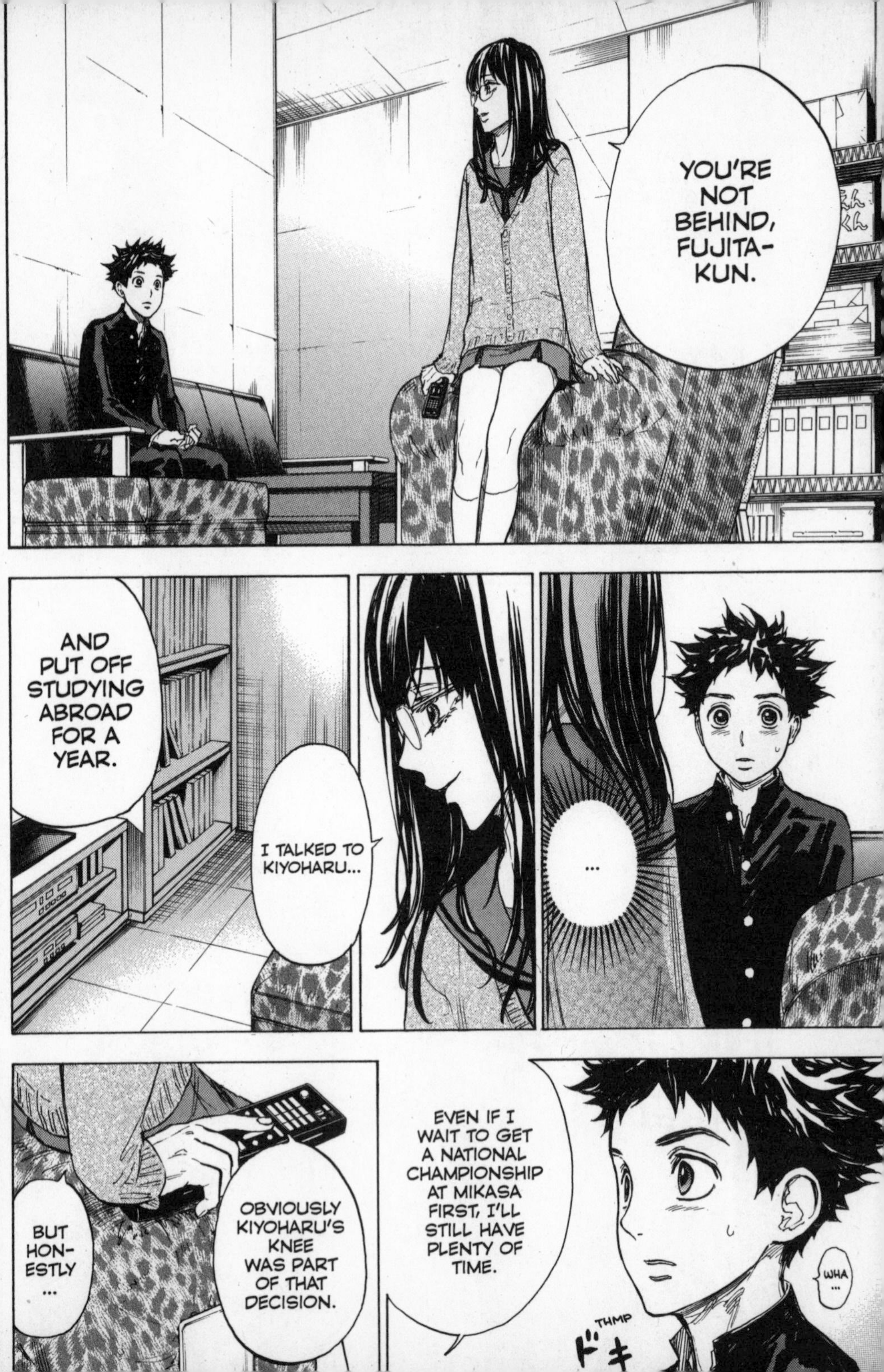
YOU'RE NOT BEHIND, FUJITA-KUN.
...
I TALKED TO KIYOHARU...
AND PUT OFF STUDYING ABROAD FOR A YEAR.
WHA...
THUMP ドキ
EVEN IF I WAIT TO GET A NATIONAL CHAMPIONSHIP AT MIKASA FIRST, I'LL STILL HAVE PLENTY OF TIME.
OBVIOUSLY KIYOHARU'S KNEE WAS PART OF THAT DECISION.
BUT HON-ESTLY...

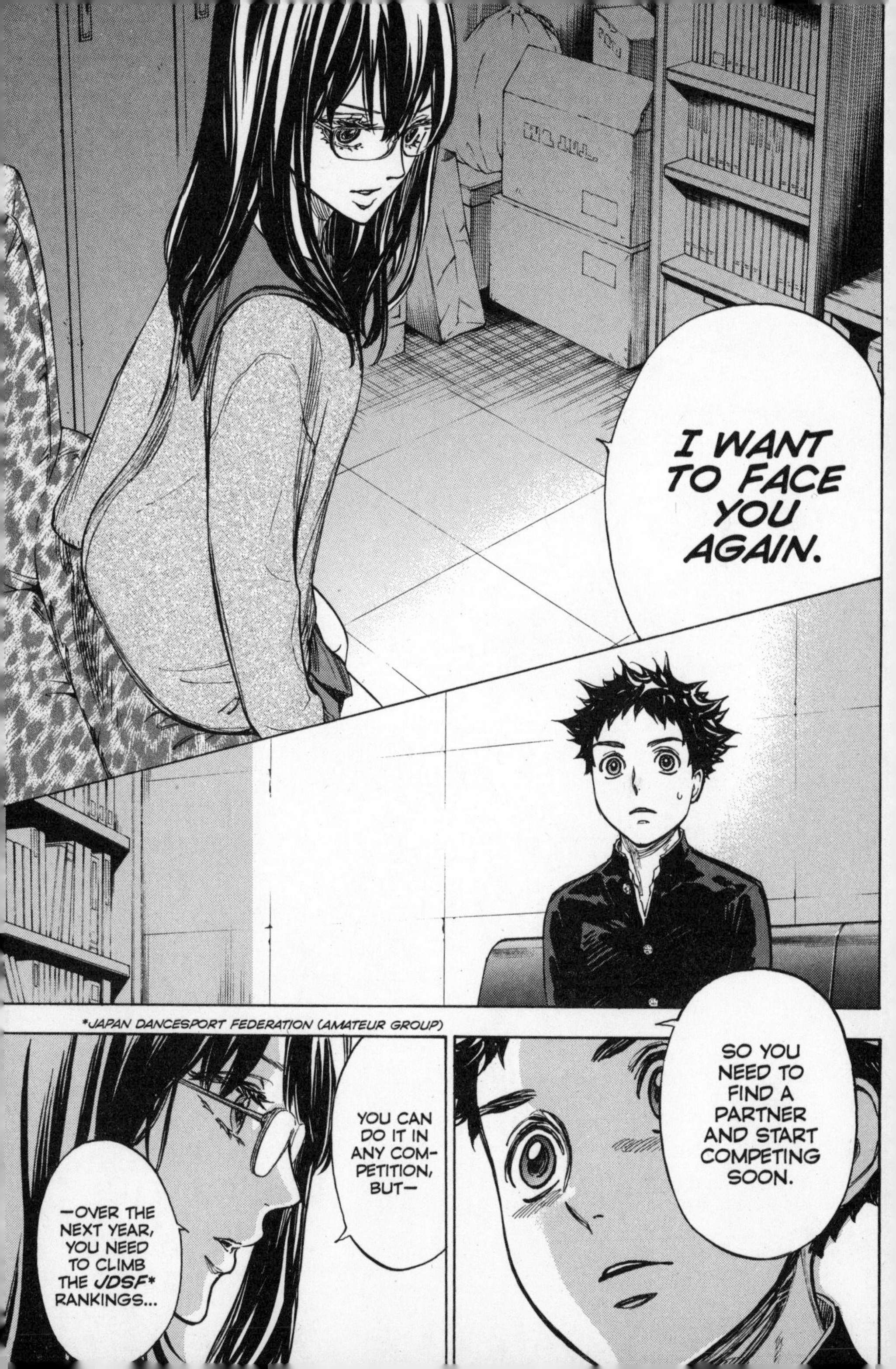
I WANT TO FACE YOU AGAIN.
*JAPAN DANCESPORT FEDERATION (AMATEUR GROUP)
SO YOU NEED TO FIND A PARTNER AND START COMPETING SOON.
YOU CAN DO IT IN ANY COMPETITION, BUT—
—OVER THE NEXT YEAR, YOU NEED TO CLIMB THE *JDSF** RANKINGS...

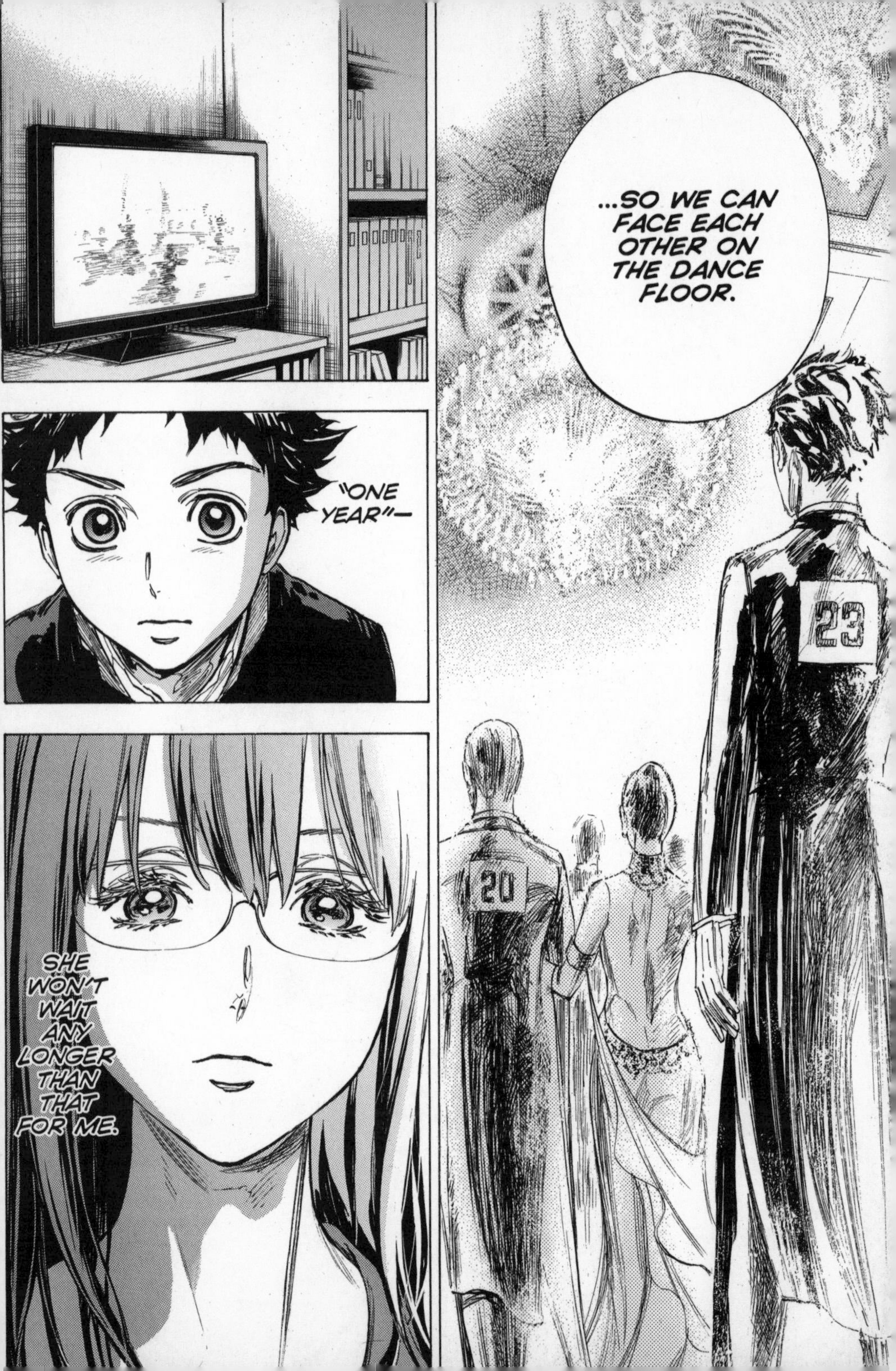
...SO WE CAN FACE EACH OTHER ON THE DANCE FLOOR.
23
20
"ONE YEAR"—
SHE WON'T WAIT ANY LONGER THAN THAT FOR ME.

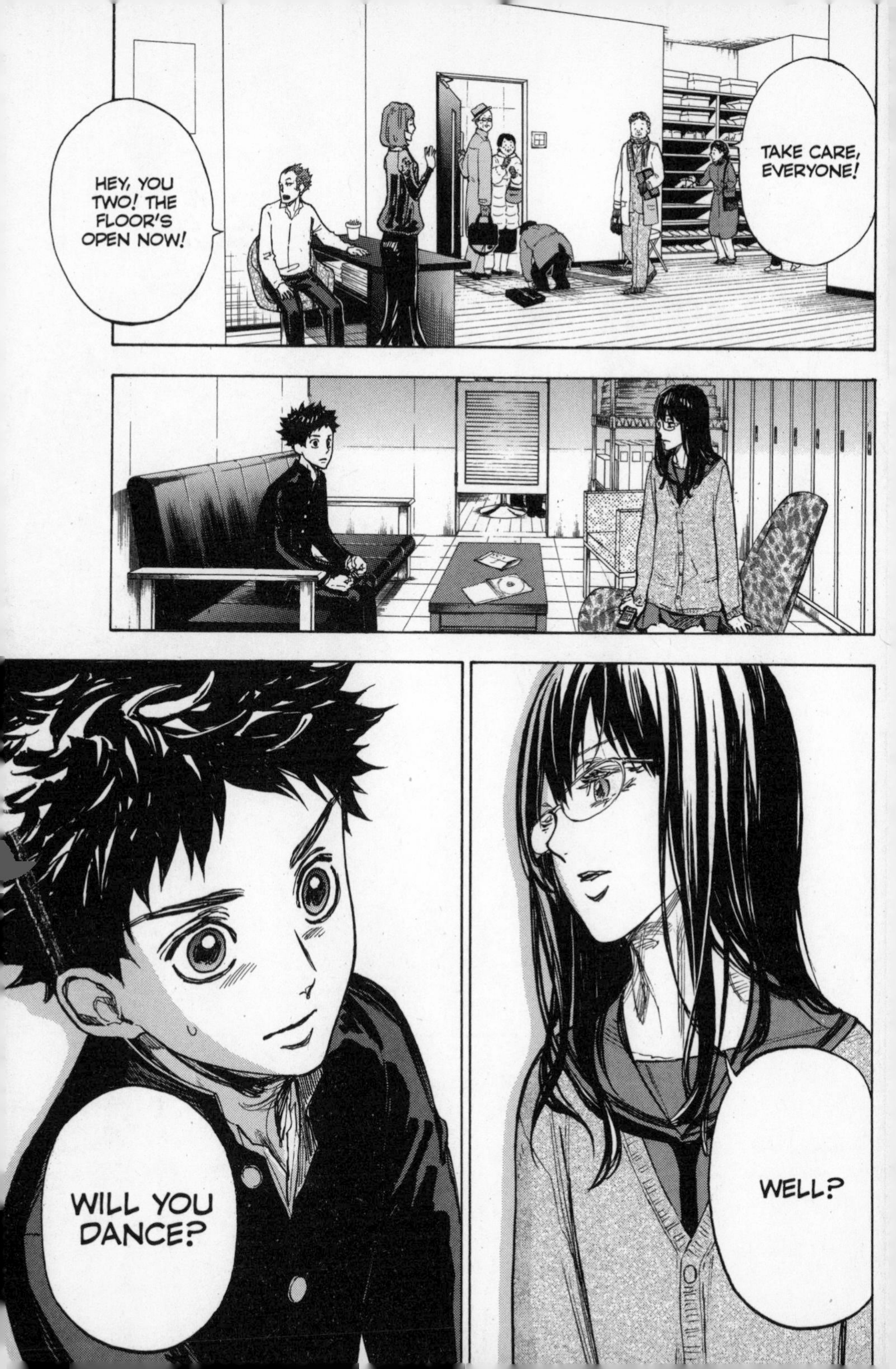
TAKE CARE, EVERYONE!
HEY, YOU TWO! THE FLOOR'S OPEN NOW!
WELL?
WILL YOU DANCE?

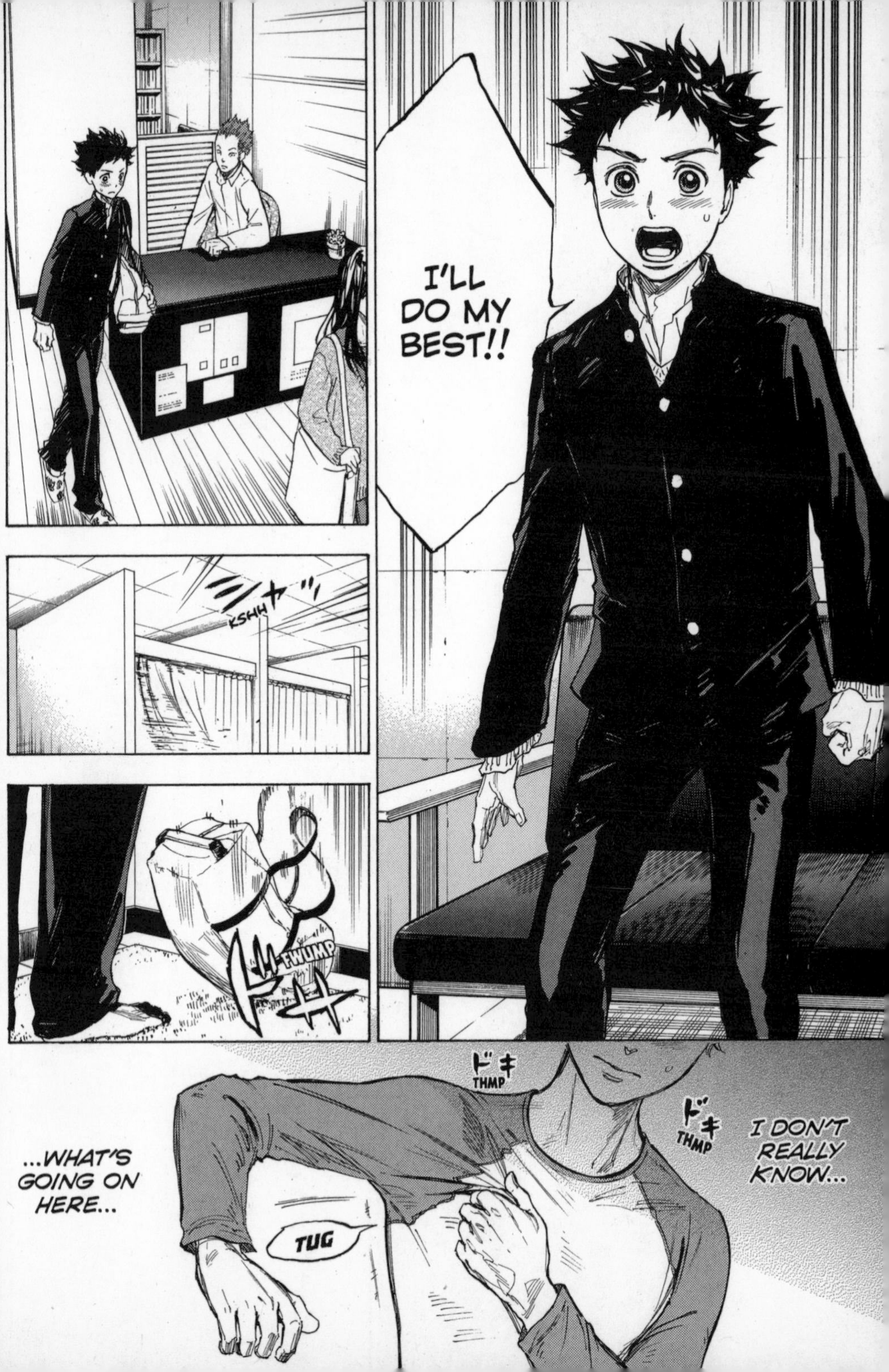
I'LL DO MY BEST!!
KSHH
FWUMP
ドキ
THMP
ドキ
THMP
I DON'T REALLY KNOW...
TUG
...WHAT'S GOING ON HERE...

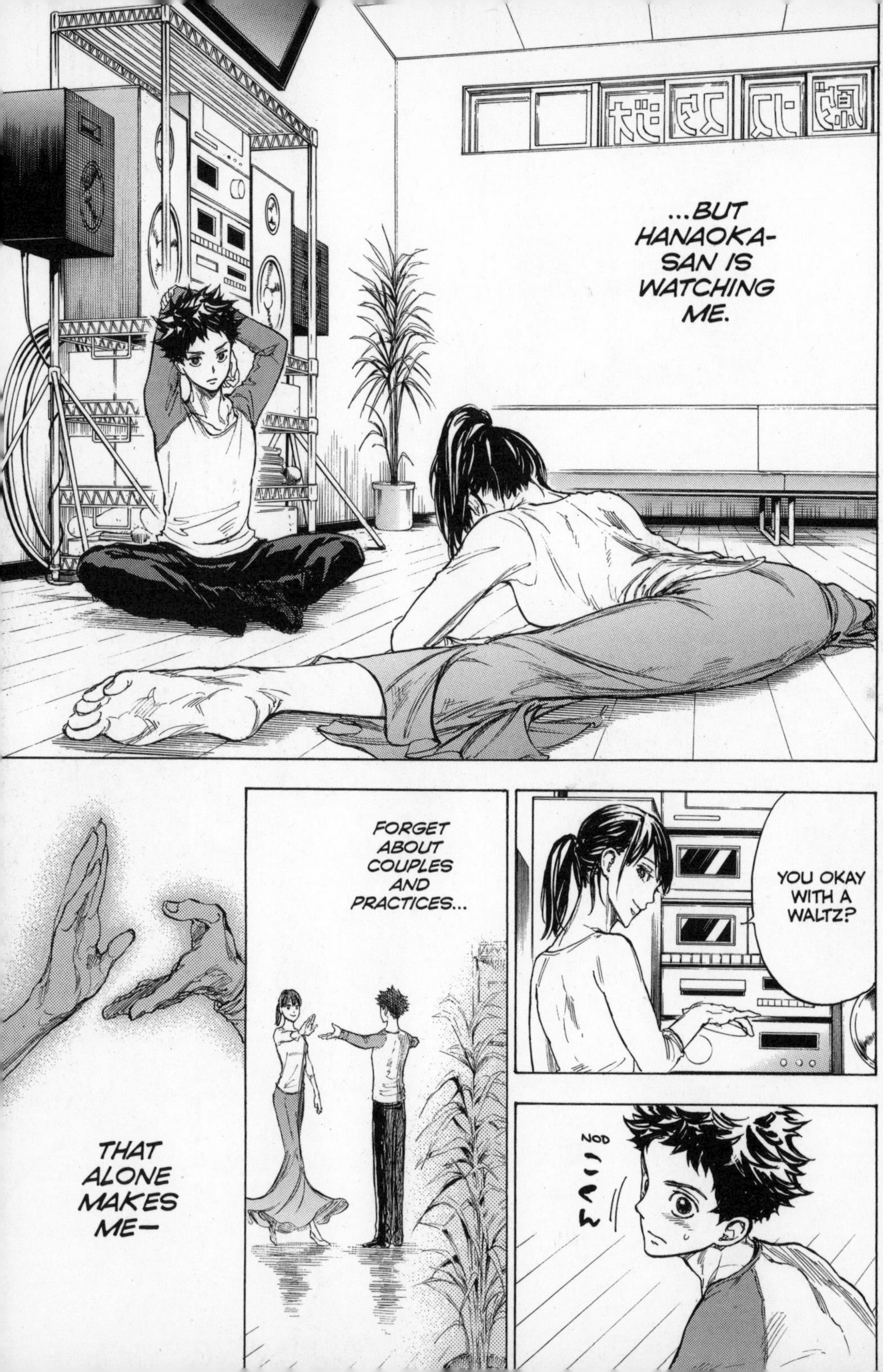
...BUT HANAOKA-SAN IS WATCHING ME.
YOU OKAY WITH A WALTZ?
NOD
FORGET ABOUT COUPLES AND PRACTICES...
THAT ALONE MAKES ME—

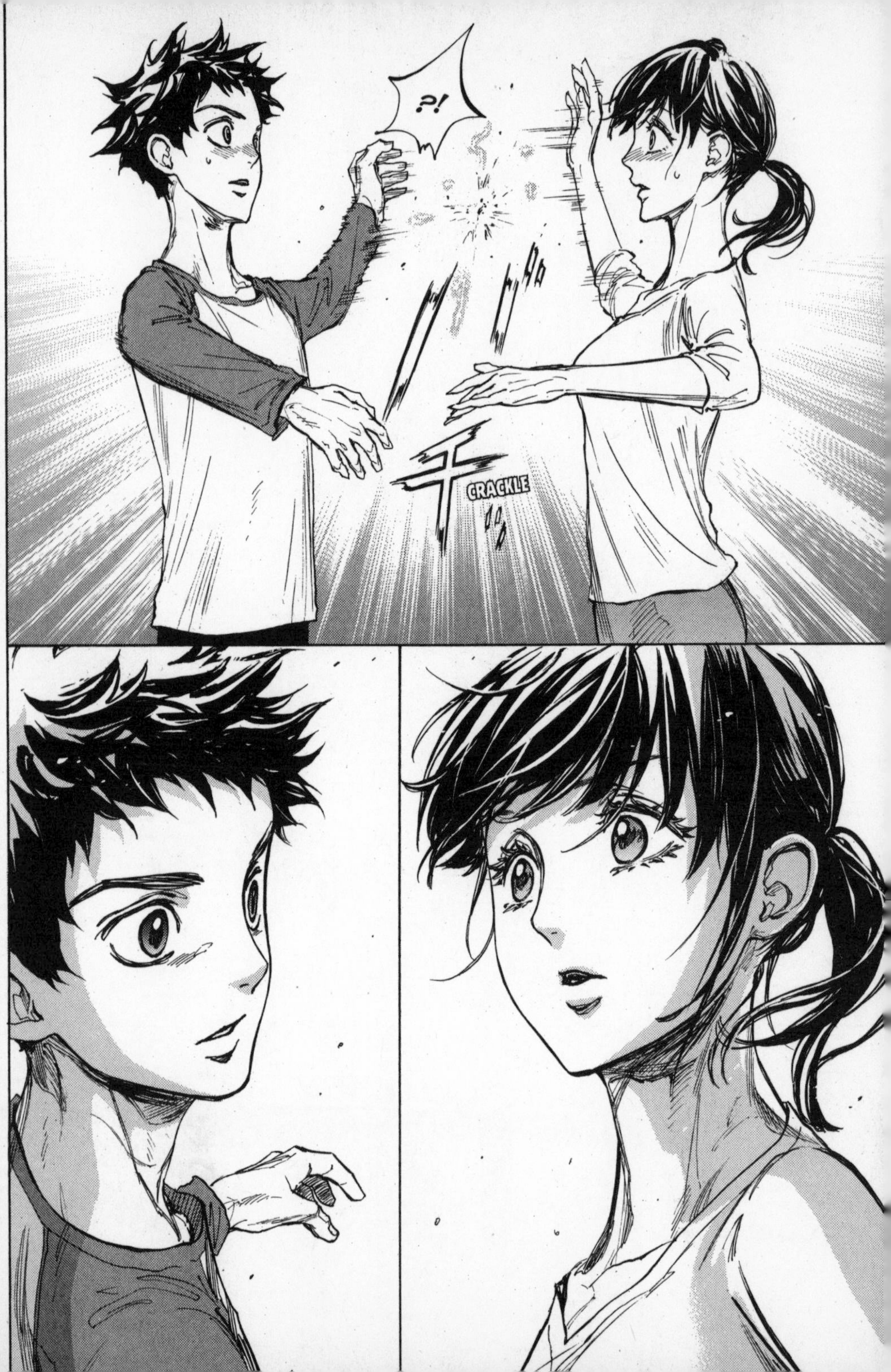
?!
CRACKLE

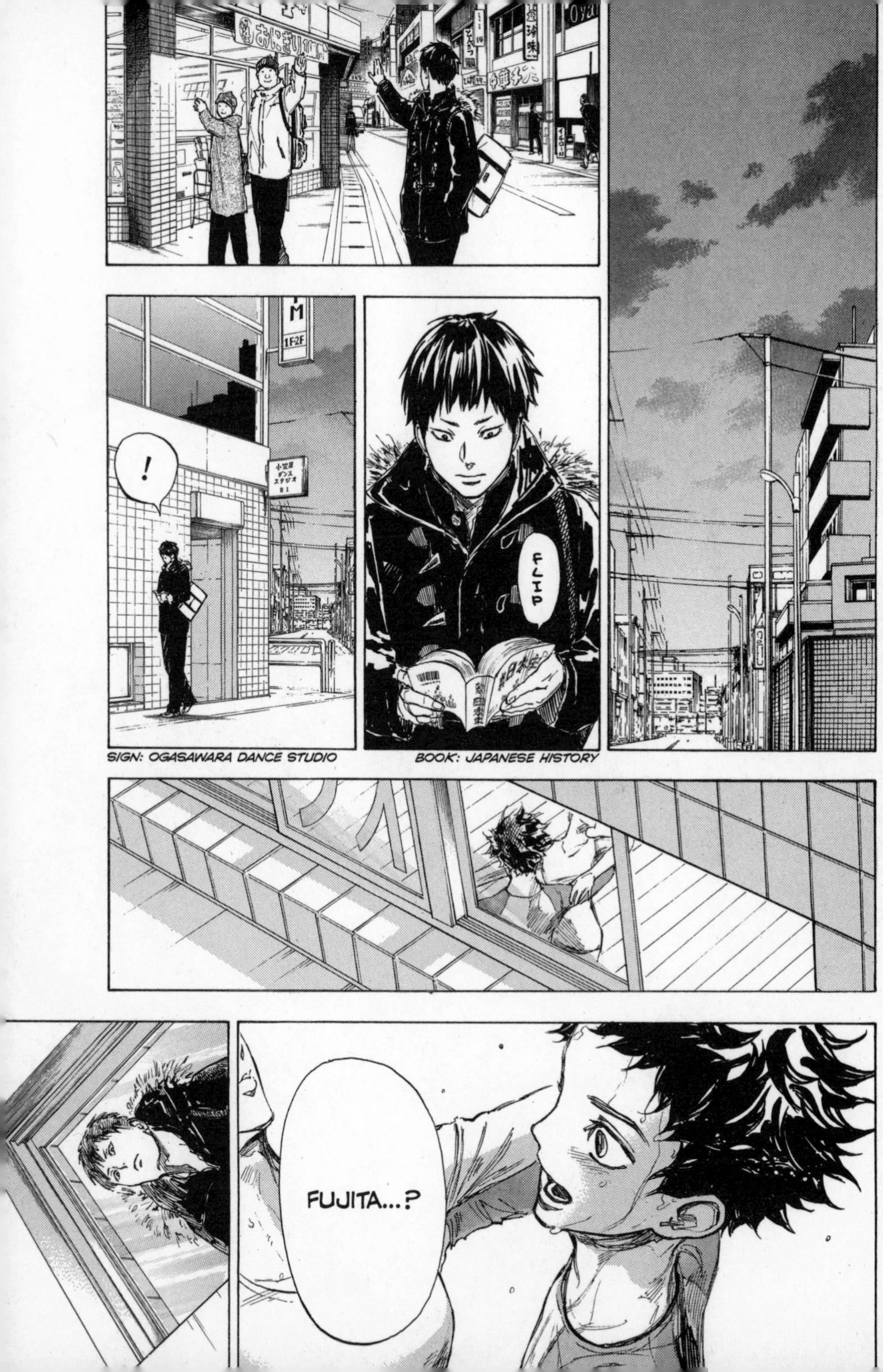
FLIP
BOOK: JAPANESE HISTORY
!
SIGN: OGASAWARA DANCE STUDIO
FUJITA...?

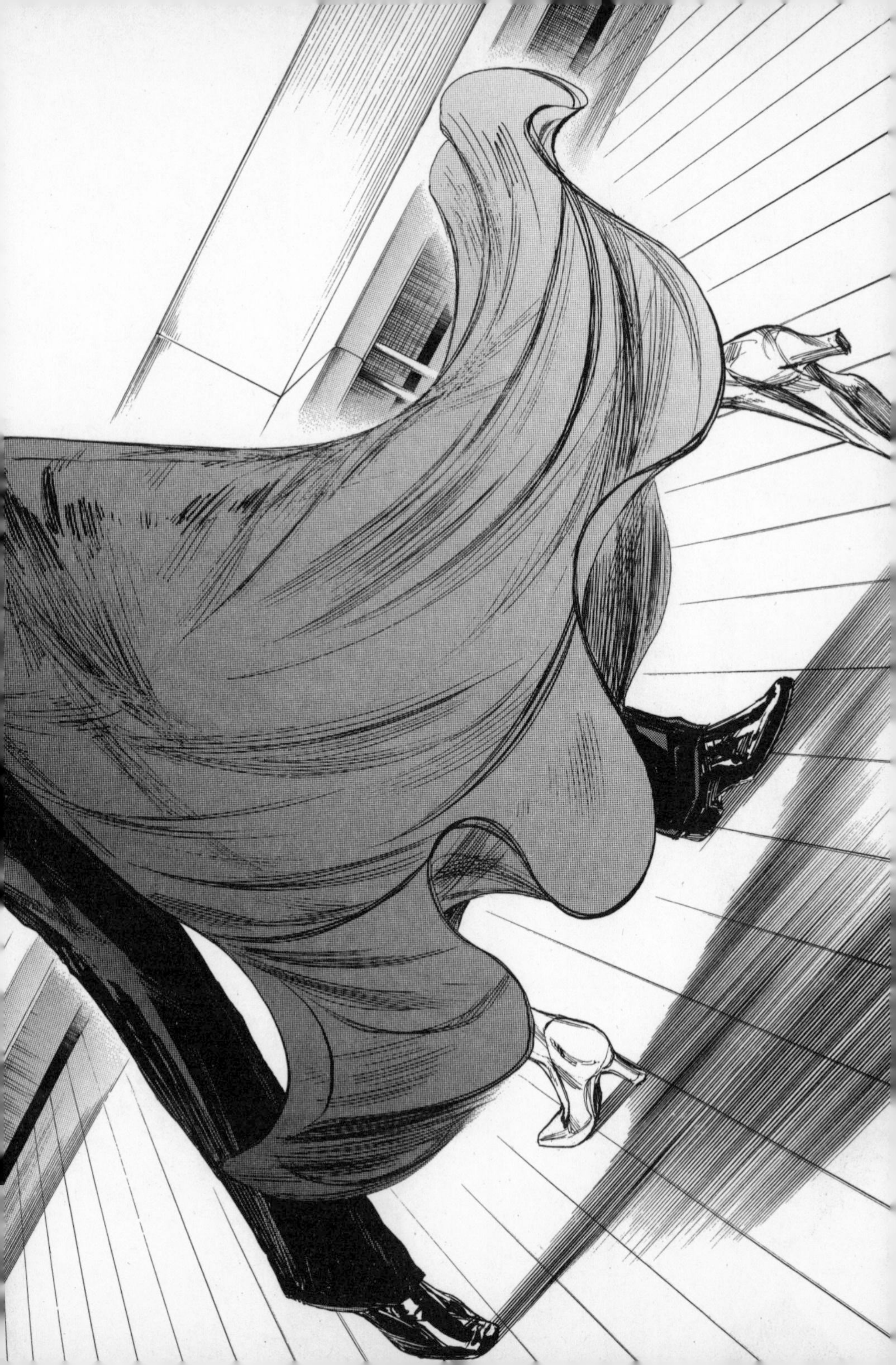

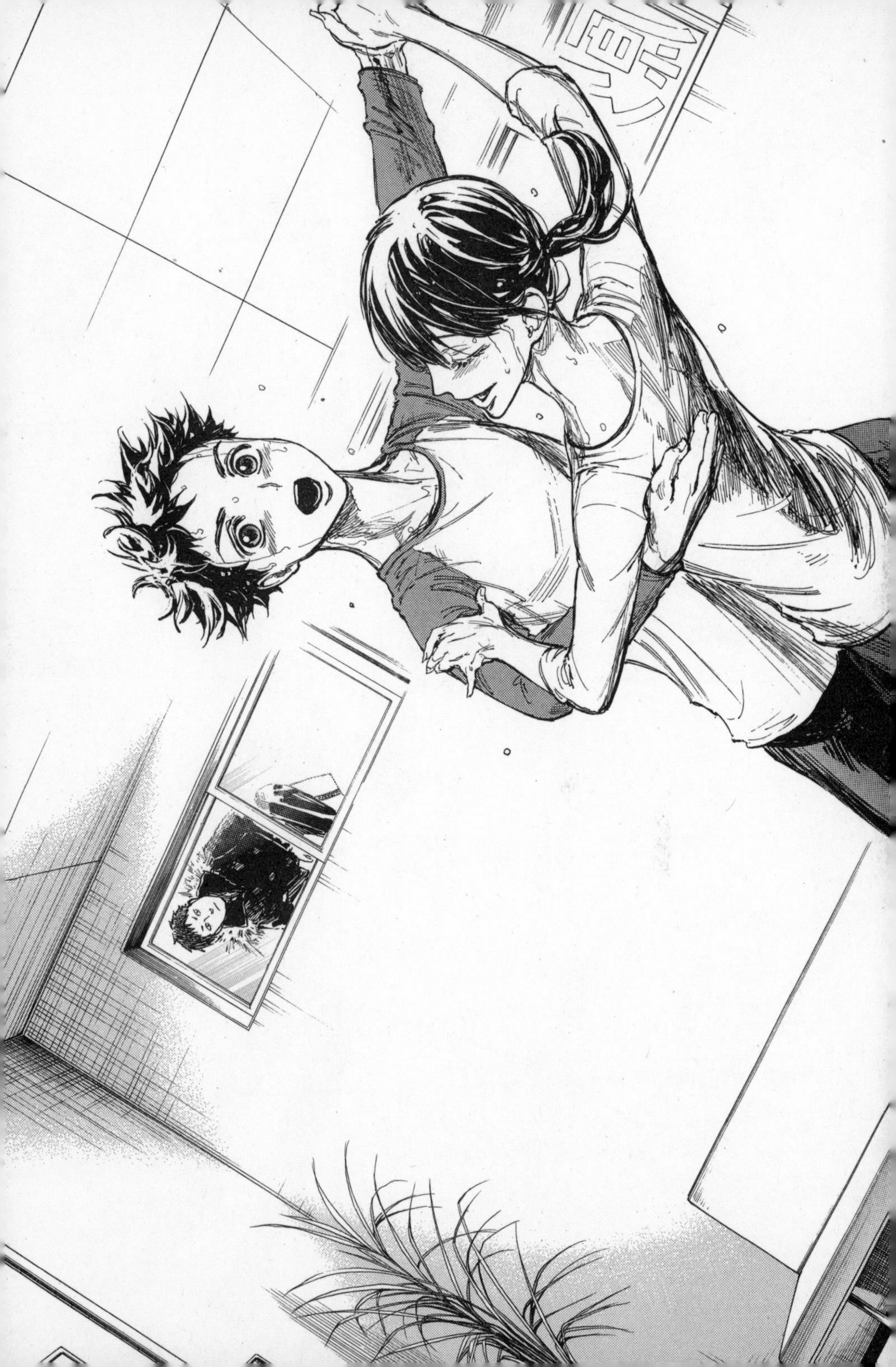

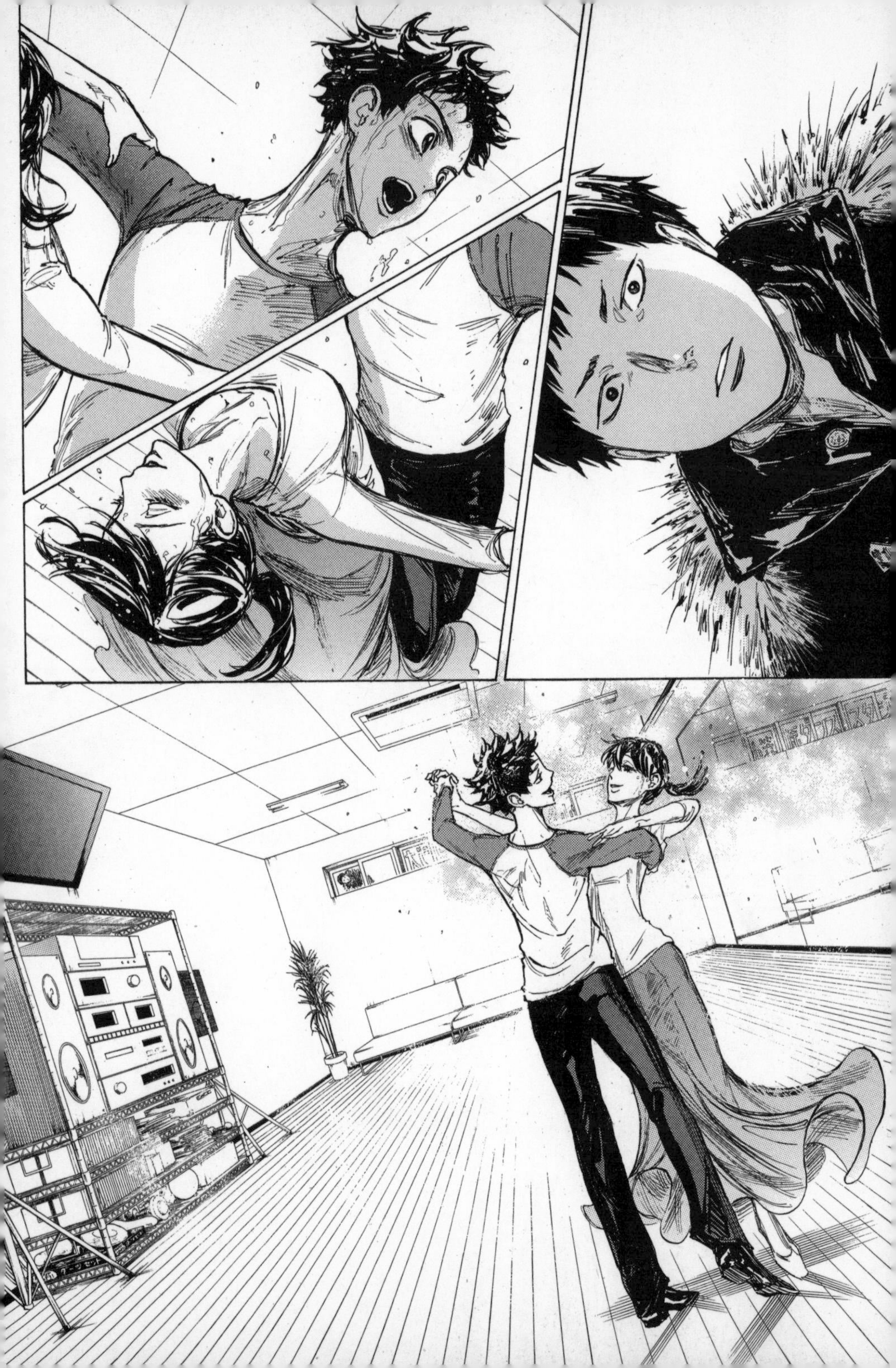

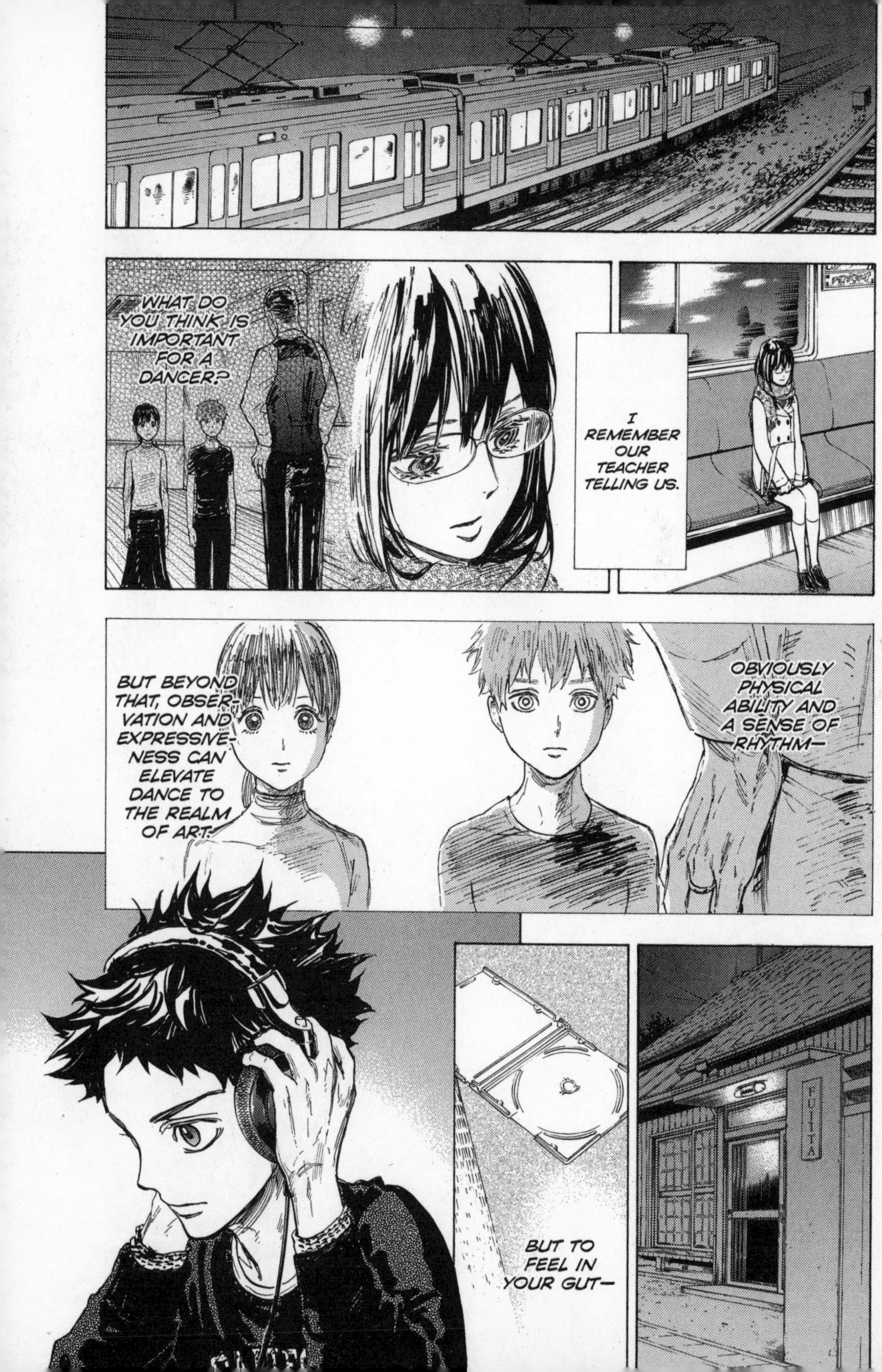
I REMEMBER OUR TEACHER TELLING US.
WHAT DO YOU THINK IS IMPORTANT FOR A DANCER?
OBVIOUSLY PHYSICAL ABILITY AND A SENSE OF RHYTHM—
BUT BEYOND THAT, OBSERVATION AND EXPRESSIVENESS CAN ELEVATE DANCE TO THE REALM OF ART.
BUT TO FEEL IN YOUR GUT—

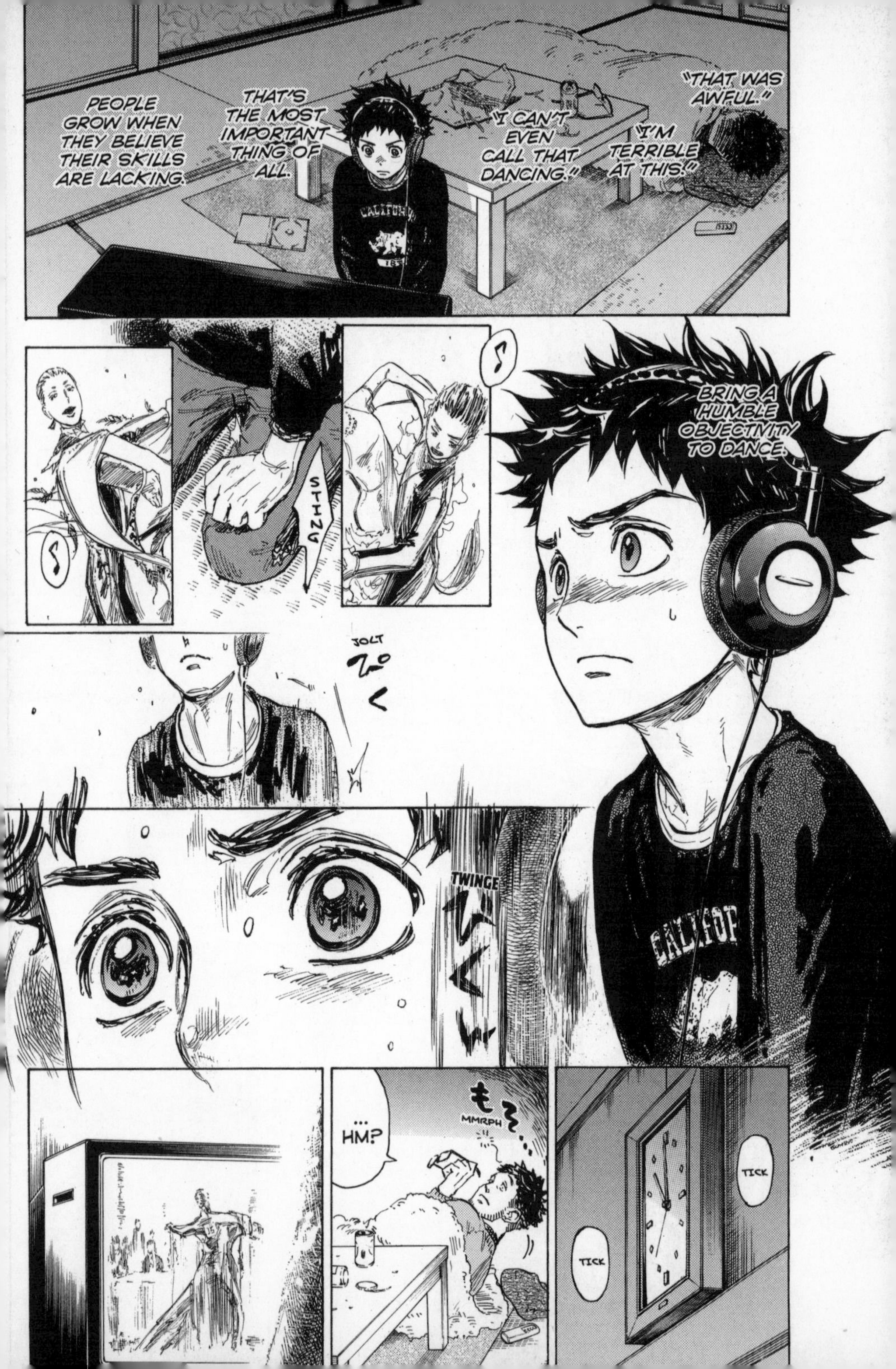

"THAT WAS AWFUL."
"I'M TERRIBLE AT THIS."
"I CAN'T EVEN CALL THAT DANCING."
THAT'S THE MOST IMPORTANT THING OF ALL.
PEOPLE GROW WHEN THEY BELIEVE THEIR SKILLS ARE LACKING.
BRING A HUMBLE OBJECTIVITY TO DANCE.
STING
JOLT
TWINGE
TICK
TICK
MMRPH
... HM?

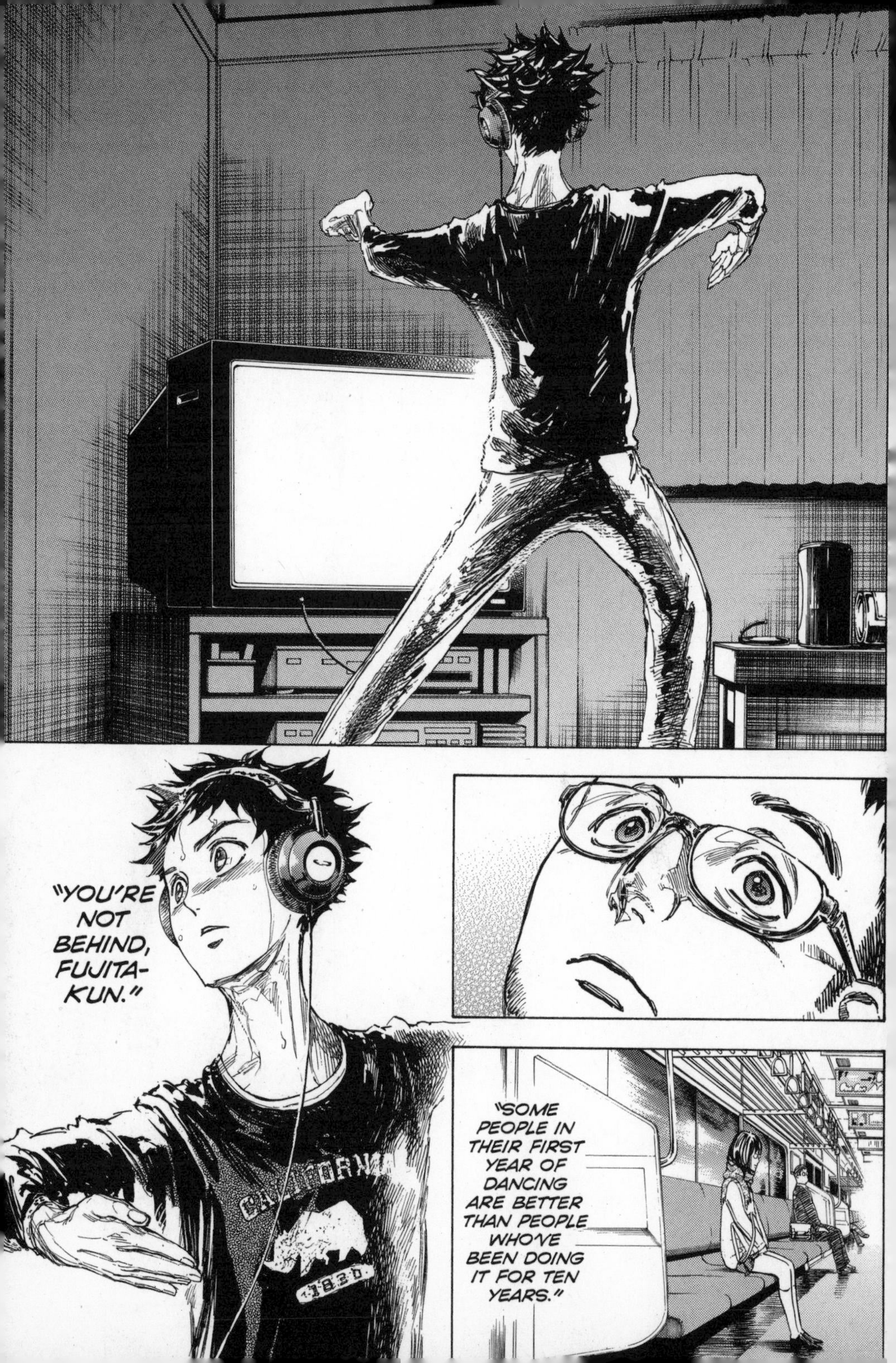
"SOME PEOPLE IN THEIR FIRST YEAR OF DANCING ARE BETTER THAN PEOPLE WHO'VE BEEN DOING IT FOR TEN YEARS."
"YOU'RE NOT BEHIND, FUJITA-KUN."

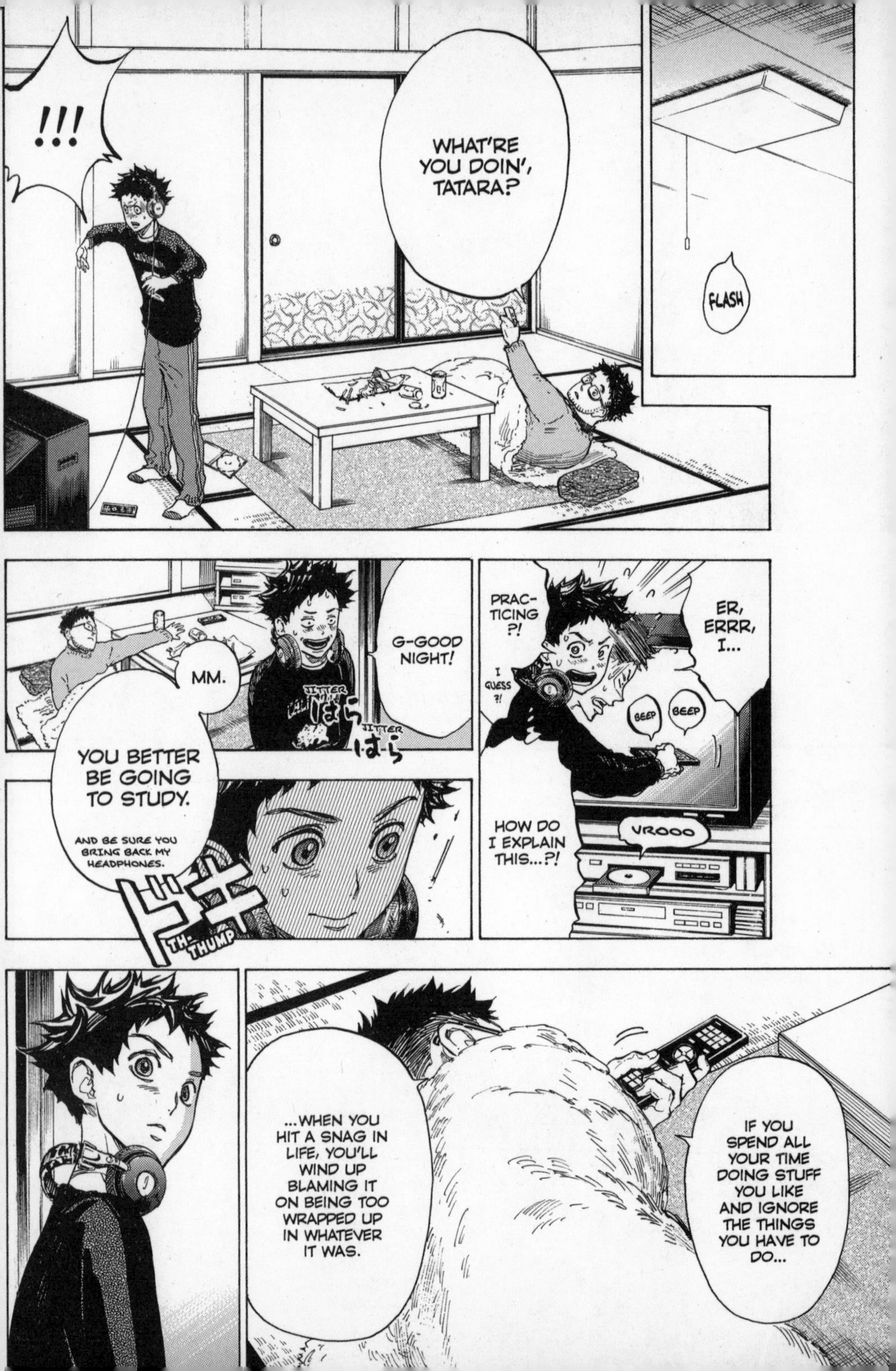
FLASH
WHAT'RE YOU DOIN', TATARA?
!!!
ER, ERRR, I...
PRACTICING?!
I GUESS?!
BEEP
BEEP
HOW DO I EXPLAIN THIS...?!
VROOO
G-GOOD NIGHT!
JITTER はら
JITTER はら
MM.
YOU BETTER BE GOING TO STUDY.
AND BE SURE YOU BRING BACK MY HEADPHONES.
ドキ TH-THUMP
IF YOU SPEND ALL YOUR TIME DOING STUFF YOU LIKE AND IGNORE THE THINGS YOU HAVE TO DO...
...WHEN YOU HIT A SNAG IN LIFE, YOU'LL WIND UP BLAMING IT ON BEING TOO WRAPPED UP IN WHATEVER IT WAS.

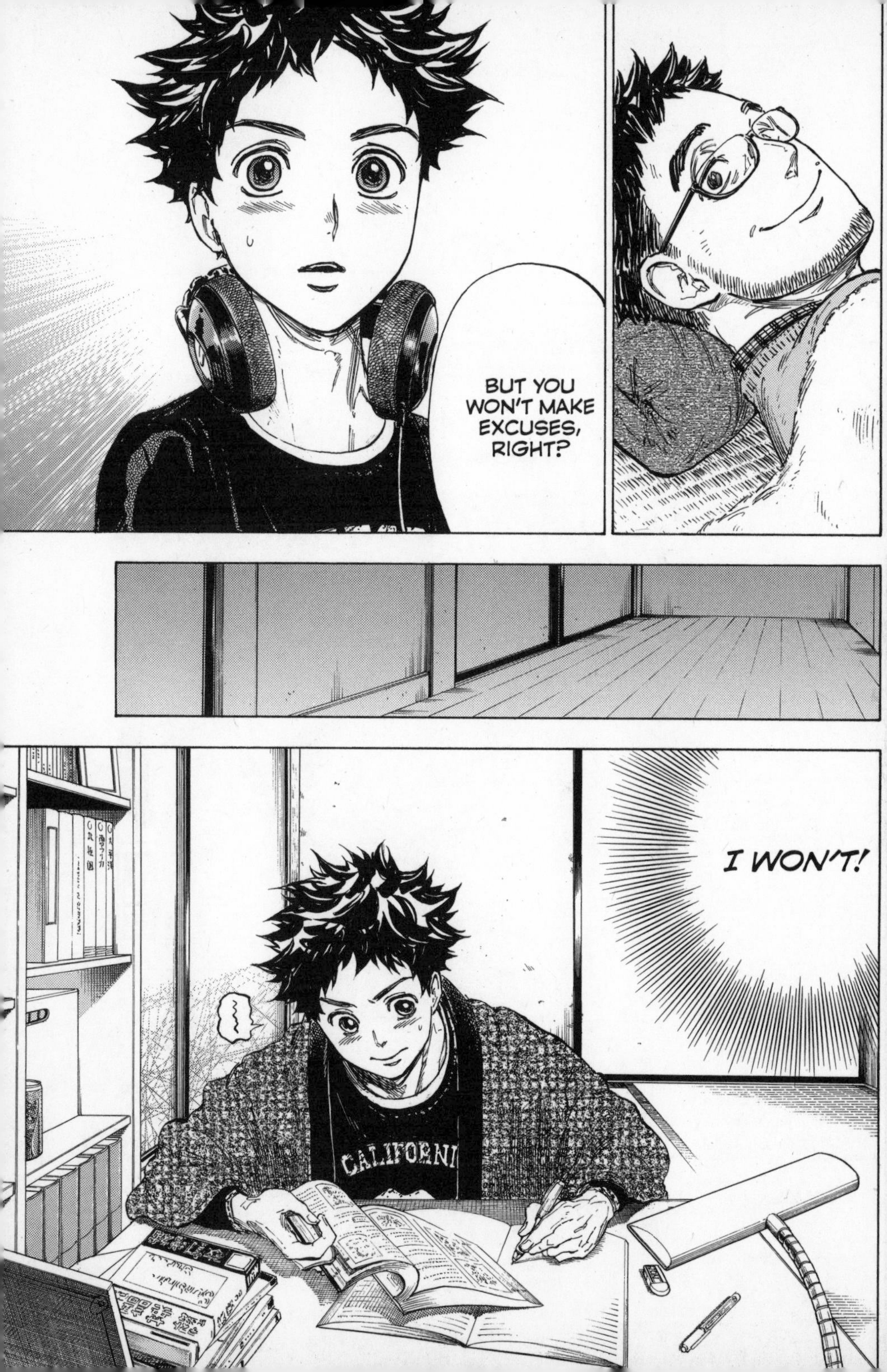
BUT YOU WON'T MAKE EXCUSES, RIGHT?
I WON'T!

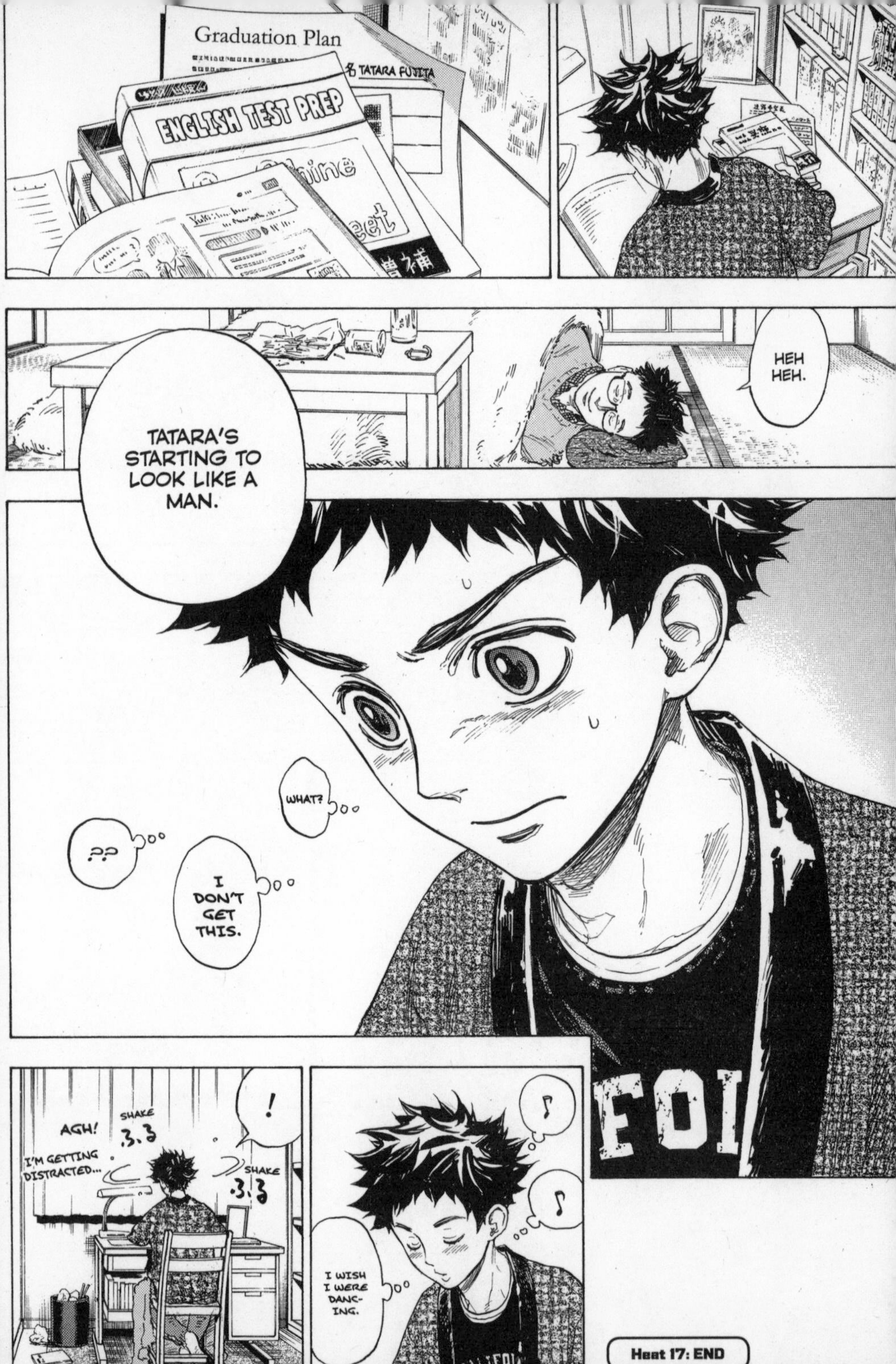

Graduation Plan
TATARA FUJITA
ENGLISH TEST PREP
HEH HEH.
TATARA'S STARTING TO LOOK LIKE A MAN.
WHAT?
I DON'T GET THIS.
??
♪
♪
I WISH I WERE DANC-ING.
!
AGH!
SHAKE
I'M GETTING DISTRACTED...
SHAKE
Heat 17: END

WELCOME TO THE BALLROOM

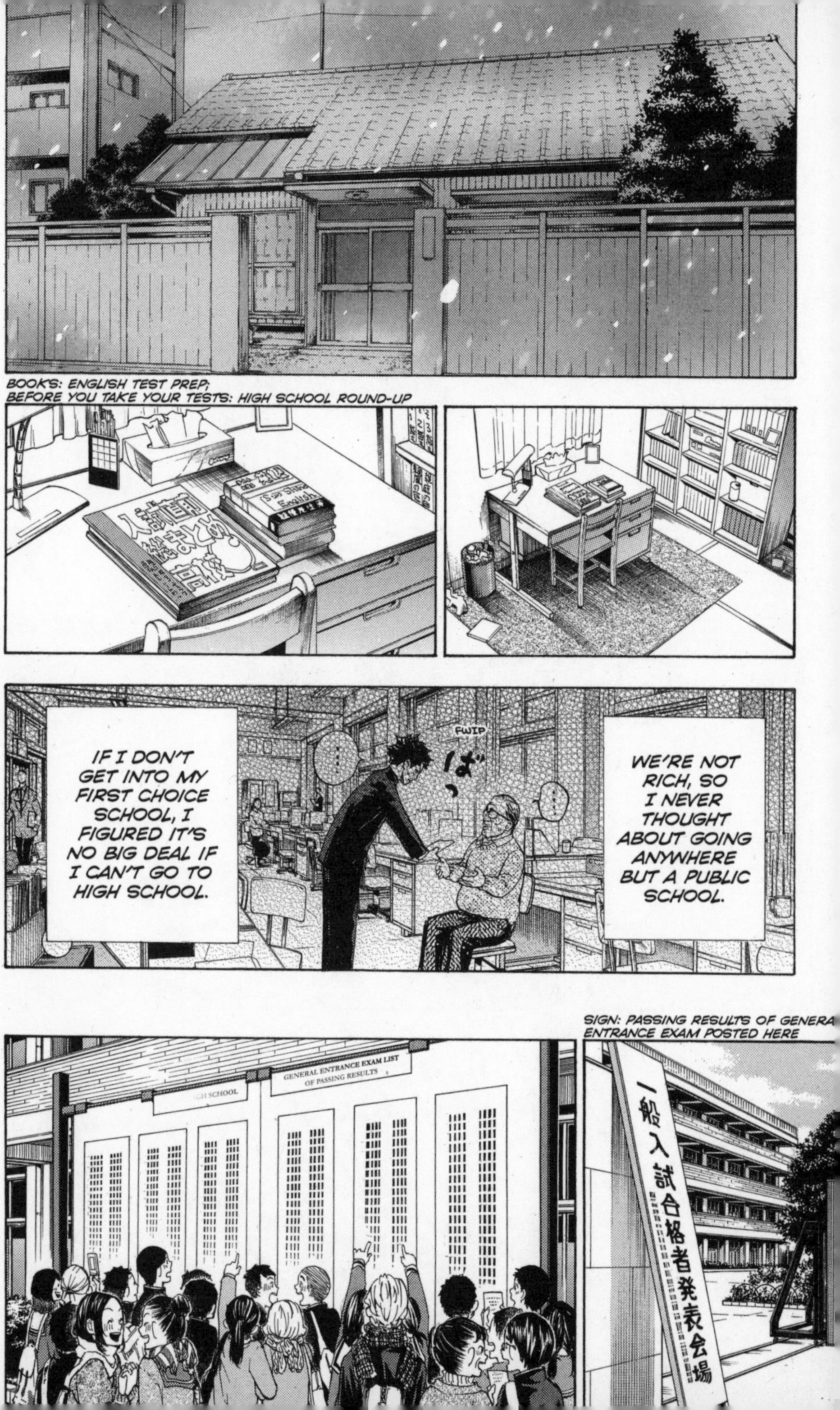
BOOKS: ENGLISH TEST PREP;
BEFORE YOU TAKE YOUR TESTS: HIGH SCHOOL ROUND-UP
WE'RE NOT RICH, SO I NEVER THOUGHT ABOUT GOING ANYWHERE BUT A PUBLIC SCHOOL.
FWIP
ばっ
IF I DON'T GET INTO MY FIRST CHOICE SCHOOL, I FIGURED IT'S NO BIG DEAL IF I CAN'T GO TO HIGH SCHOOL.
SIGN: PASSING RESULTS OF GENERA
ENTRANCE EXAM POSTED HERE
一般入試合格者発表会場
GENERAL ENTRANCE EXAM LIST OF PASSING RESULTS
IGH SCHOOL

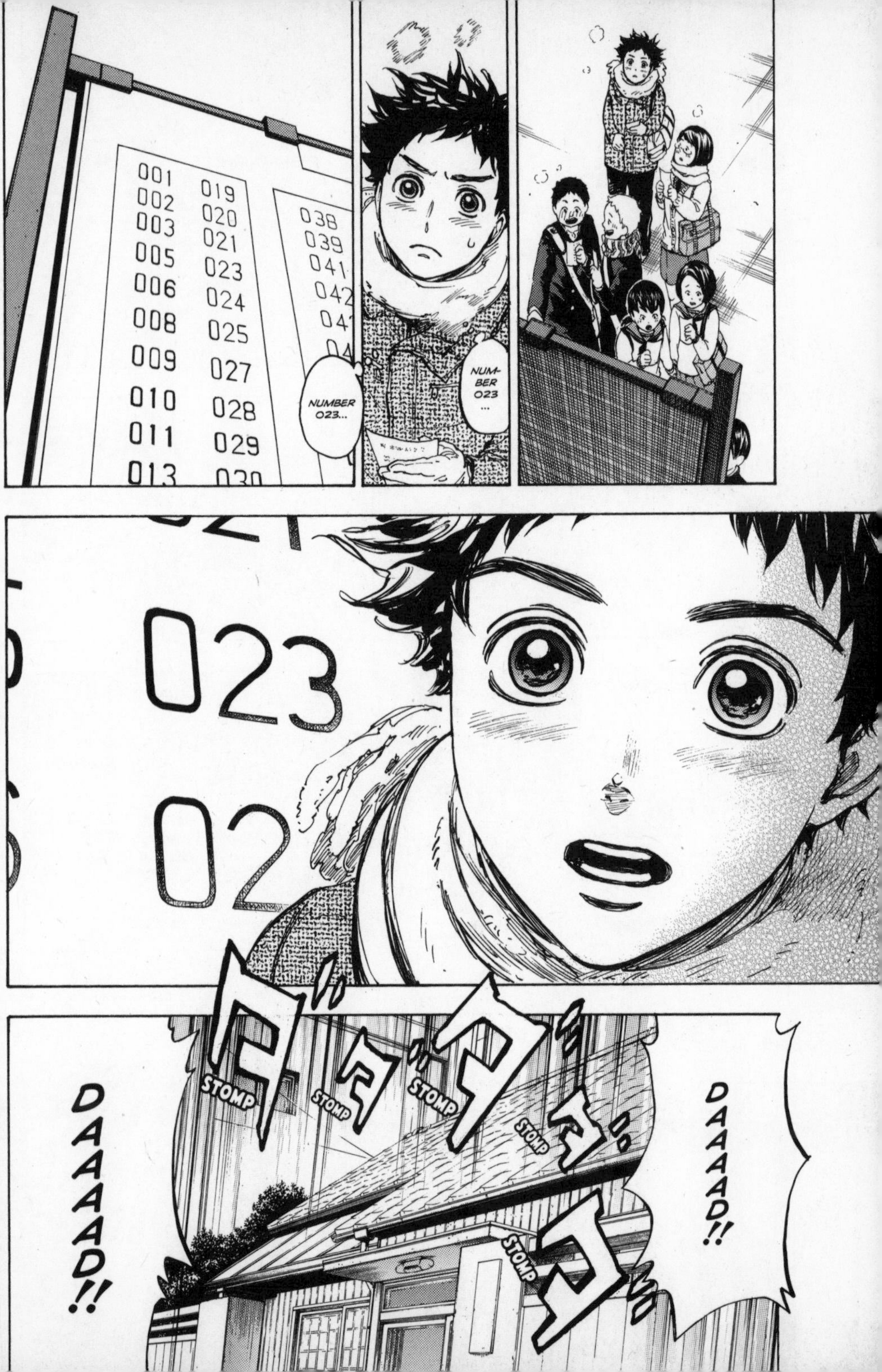
NUMBER 023...
NUMBER 023...
001
002
003
005
006
008
009
010
011
013
019
020
021
023
024
025
027
028
029
030
038
039
023
DAAAAAD!!
STOMP
STOMP
STOMP
STOMP
STOMP
DAAAAAD!!

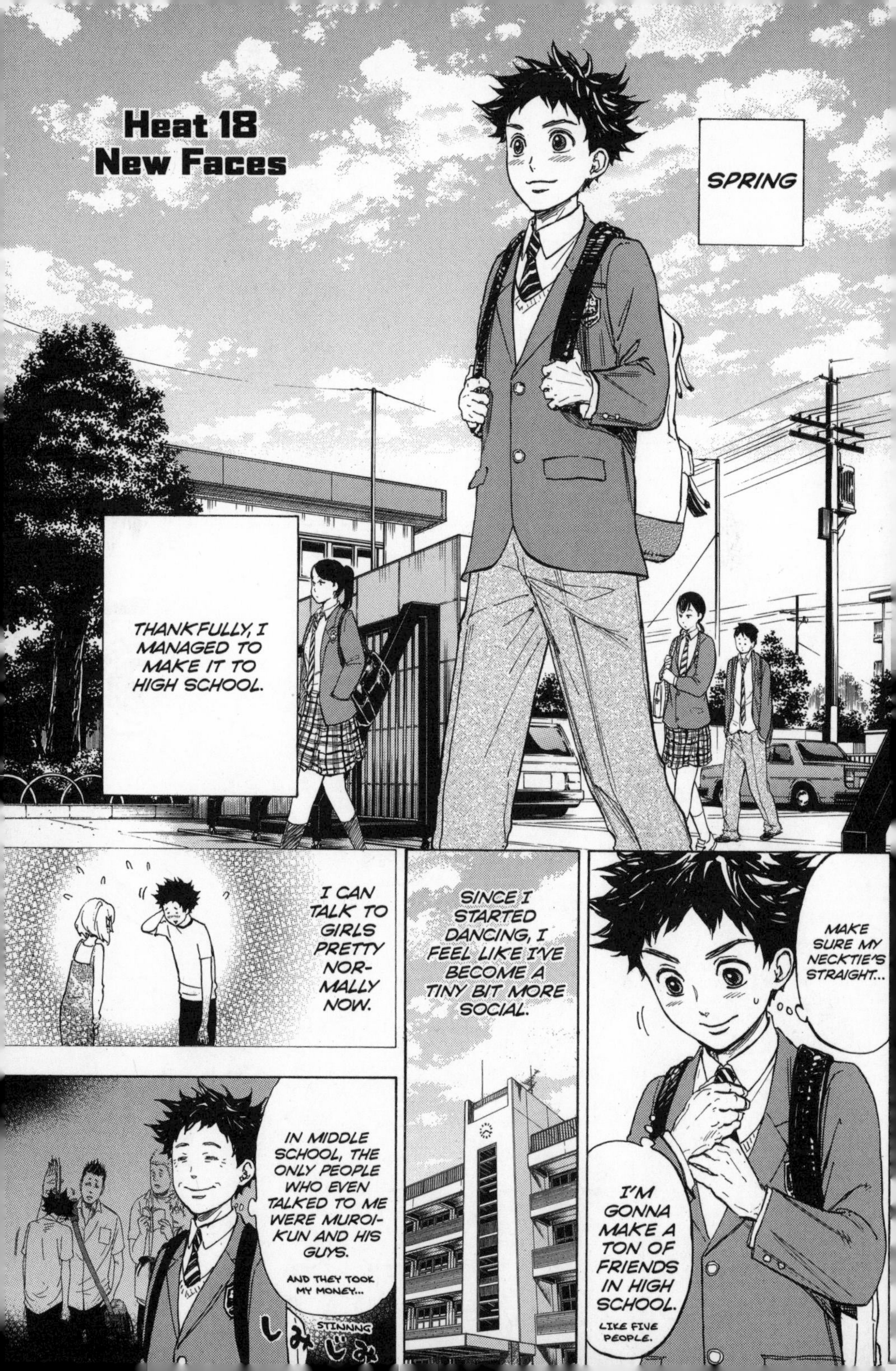
Heat 18
New Faces
SPRING
THANKFULLY, I MANAGED TO MAKE IT TO HIGH SCHOOL.
MAKE SURE MY NECKTIE'S STRAIGHT...
I'M GONNA MAKE A TON OF FRIENDS IN HIGH SCHOOL.
LIKE FIVE PEOPLE.
SINCE I STARTED DANCING, I FEEL LIKE I'VE BECOME A TINY BIT MORE SOCIAL.
I CAN TALK TO GIRLS PRETTY NOR-MALLY NOW.
IN MIDDLE SCHOOL, THE ONLY PEOPLE WHO EVEN TALKED TO ME WERE MUROI-KUN AND HIS GUYS.
AND THEY TOOK MY MONEY...
STINNNG

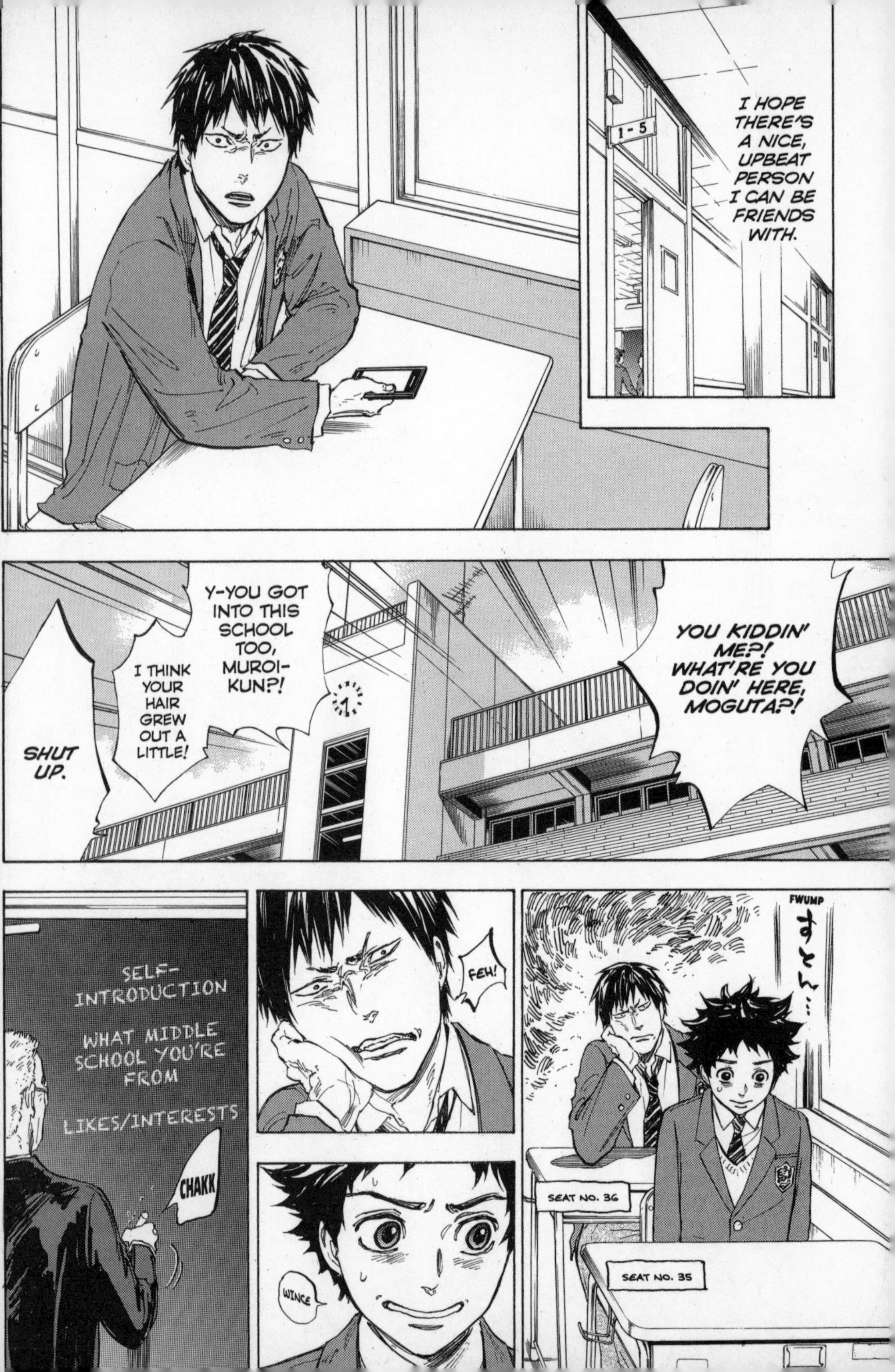
I HOPE THERE'S A NICE, UPBEAT PERSON I CAN BE FRIENDS WITH.
1-5
YOU KIDDIN' ME?! WHAT'RE YOU DOIN' HERE, MOGUTA?!
Y-YOU GOT INTO THIS SCHOOL TOO, MUROI-KUN?!
I THINK YOUR HAIR GREW OUT A LITTLE!
SHUT UP.
FWUMP
すとん…
SEAT NO. 36
SEAT NO. 35
FEH!
WINCE
SELF-INTRODUCTION
WHAT MIDDLE SCHOOL YOU'RE FROM
LIKES/INTERESTS
CHAKK

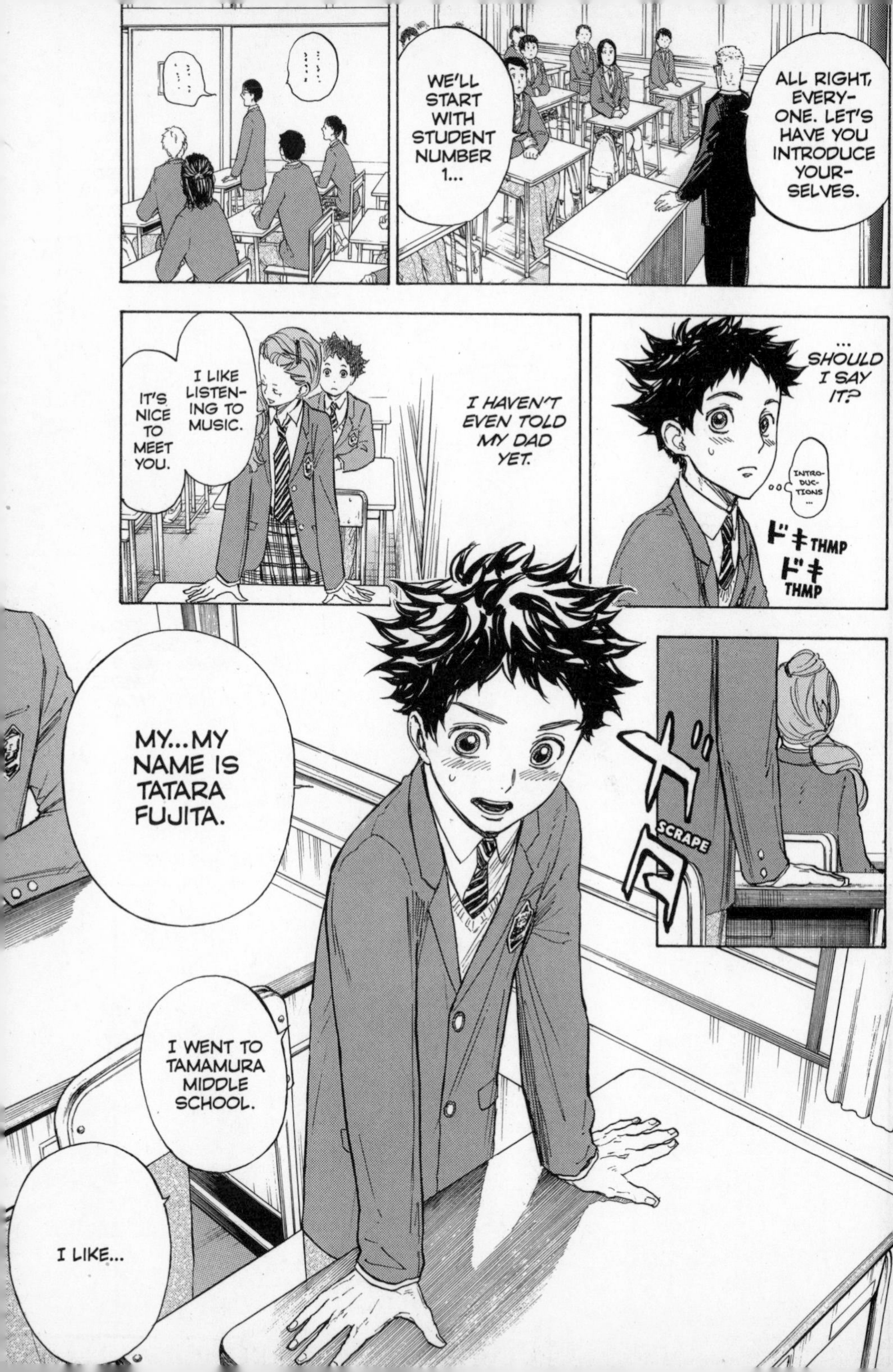
ALL RIGHT, EVERYONE. LET'S HAVE YOU INTRODUCE YOURSELVES.
WE'LL START WITH STUDENT NUMBER 1...
... SHOULD I SAY IT?
INTRODUCTIONS...
ドキ THMP
ドキ THMP
I HAVEN'T EVEN TOLD MY DAD YET.
I LIKE LISTENING TO MUSIC.
IT'S NICE TO MEET YOU.
SCRAPE
MY...MY NAME IS TATARA FUJITA.
I WENT TO TAMAMURA MIDDLE SCHOOL.
I LIKE...

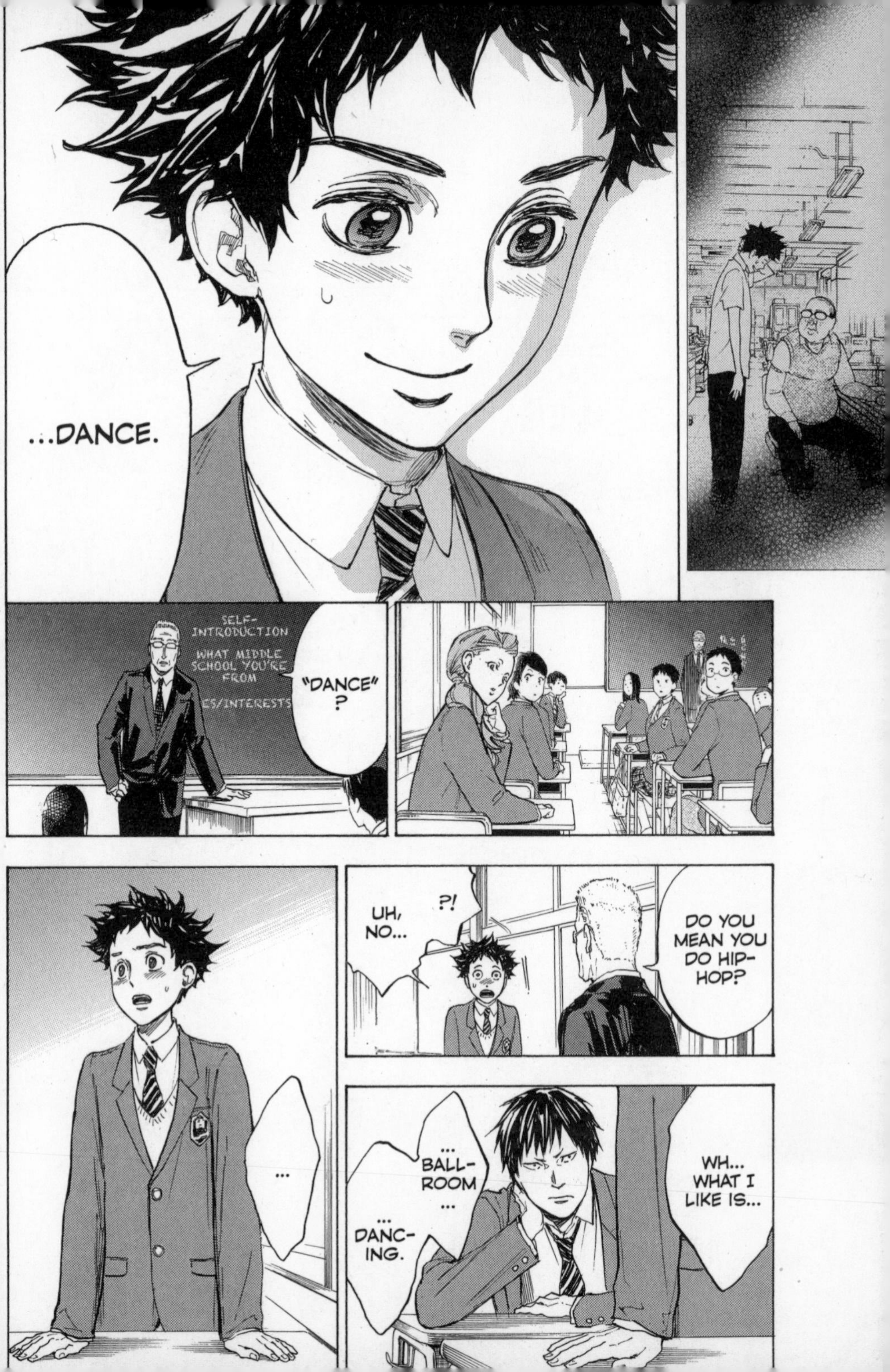
...DANCE.
SELF-INTRODUCTION
WHAT MIDDLE SCHOOL YOU'RE FROM
ES/INTERESTS
"DANCE"?
DO YOU MEAN YOU DO HIP-HOP?
?!
UH, NO...
WH... WHAT I LIKE IS...
...BALLROOM...
...DANCING.
...

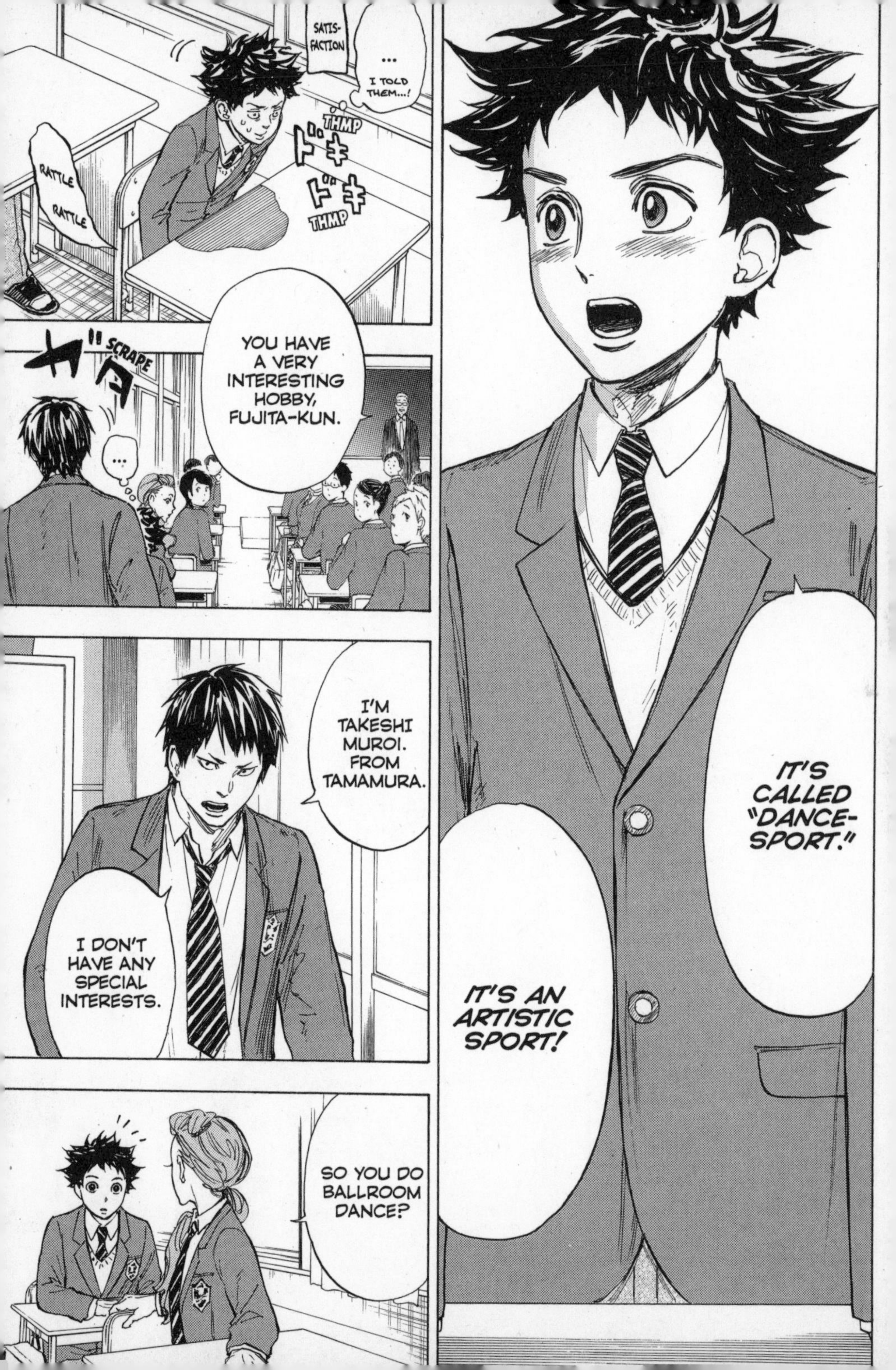
IT'S CALLED "DANCE-SPORT."
IT'S AN ARTISTIC SPORT!
SATIS-FACTION
... I TOLD THEM...!
THMP
ドキ
ドキ
THMP
RATTLE RATTLE
YOU HAVE A VERY INTERESTING HOBBY, FUJITA-KUN.
SCRAPE
...
I'M TAKESHI MUROI. FROM TAMAMURA.
I DON'T HAVE ANY SPECIAL INTERESTS.
SO YOU DO BALLROOM DANCE?

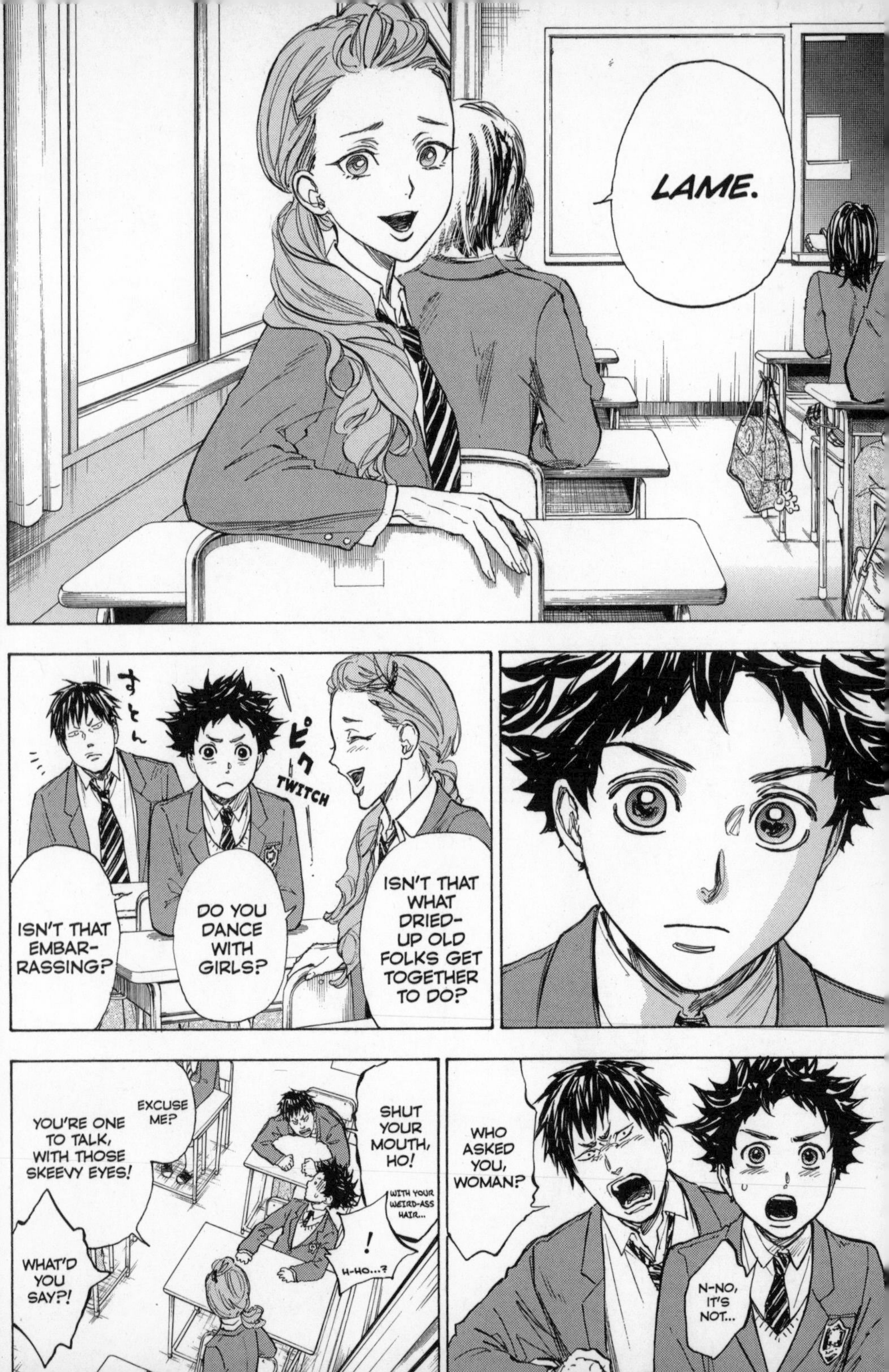
LAME.
ISN'T THAT WHAT DRIED-UP OLD FOLKS GET TOGETHER TO DO?
ピク
TWITCH
すとん
DO YOU DANCE WITH GIRLS?
ISN'T THAT EMBARRASSING?
WHO ASKED YOU, WOMAN?
N-NO, IT'S NOT...
SHUT YOUR MOUTH, HO!
EXCUSE ME?
WITH YOUR WEIRD-ASS HAIR...
YOU'RE ONE TO TALK, WITH THOSE SKEEVY EYES!
!
H-HO...?
WHAT'D YOU SAY?!

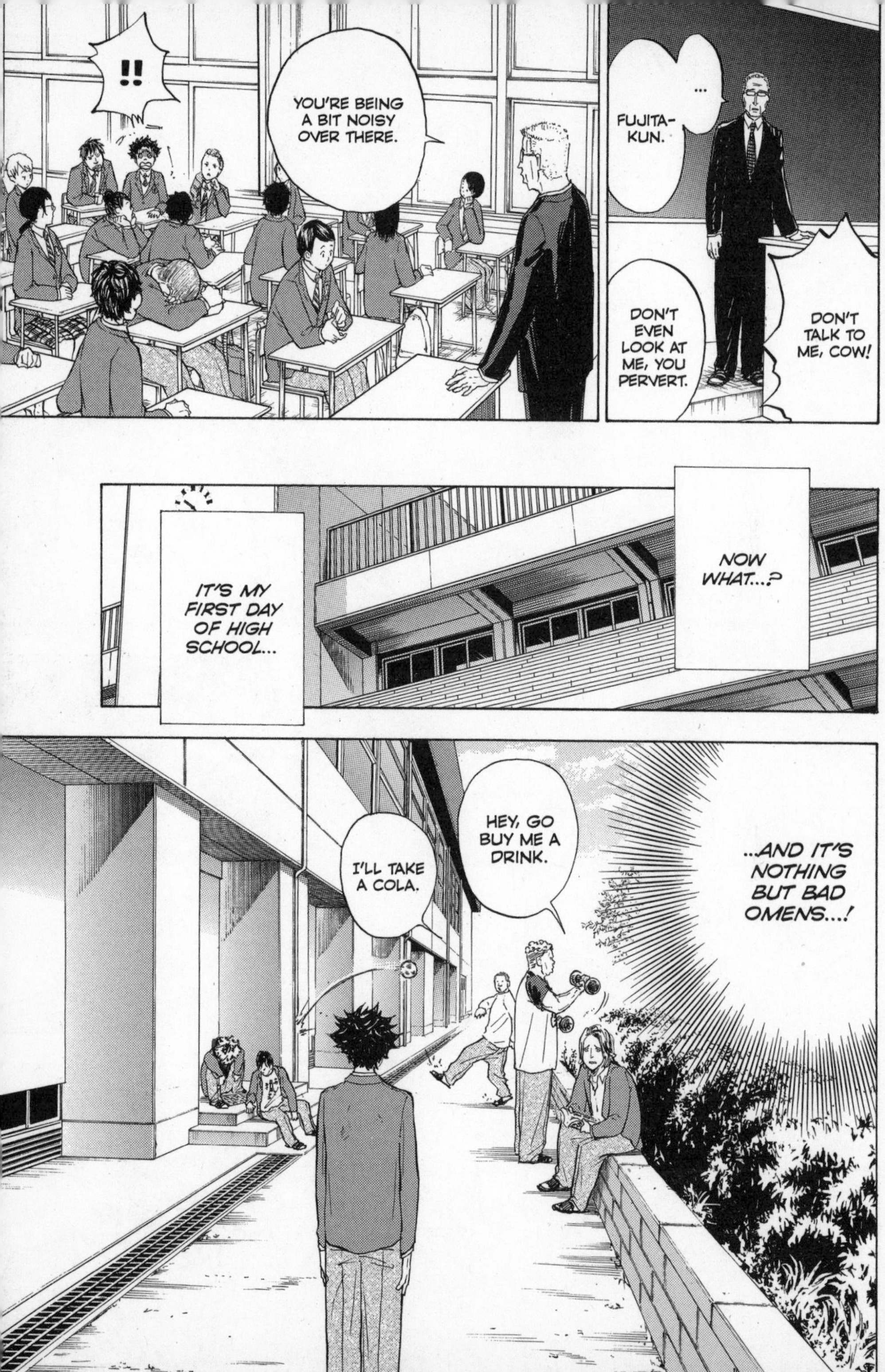
...
FUJITA-KUN.
DON'T TALK TO ME, COW!
DON'T EVEN LOOK AT ME, YOU PERVERT.
YOU'RE BEING A BIT NOISY OVER THERE.
!!
NOW WHAT...?
IT'S MY FIRST DAY OF HIGH SCHOOL...
...AND IT'S NOTHING BUT BAD OMENS...!
HEY, GO BUY ME A DRINK.
I'LL TAKE A COLA.

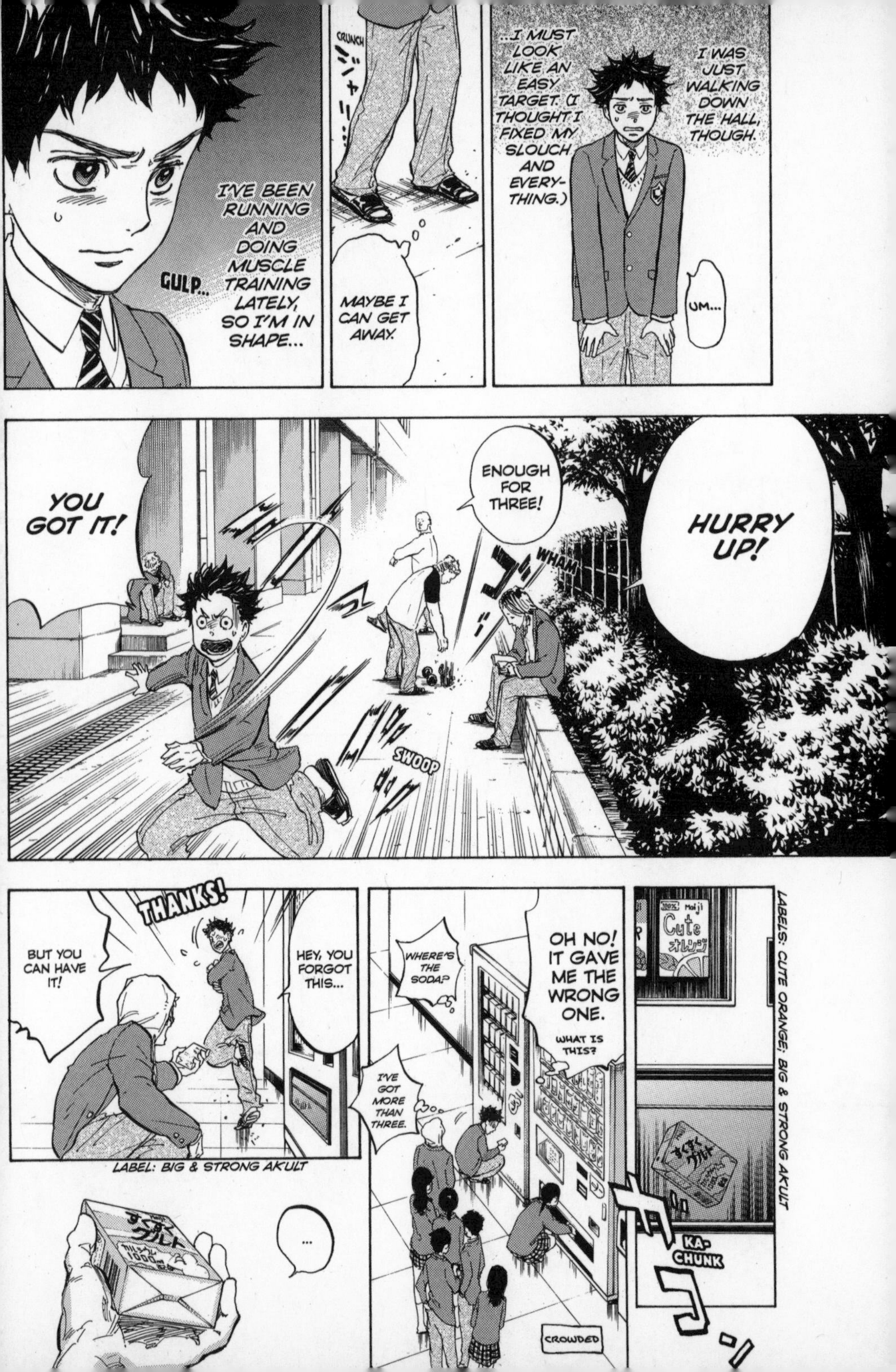
I WAS JUST WALKING DOWN THE HALL, THOUGH.
...I MUST LOOK LIKE AN EASY TARGET. (I THOUGHT I FIXED MY SLOUCH AND EVERYTHING.)
UM...
CRUNCH
MAYBE I CAN GET AWAY.
I'VE BEEN RUNNING AND DOING MUSCLE TRAINING LATELY, SO I'M IN SHAPE...
GULP...
HURRY UP!
ENOUGH FOR THREE!
WHAM
SWOOP
YOU GOT IT!
LABELS: CUTE ORANGE; BIG & STRONG AKULT
KA-CHUNK
OH NO! IT GAVE ME THE WRONG ONE.
WHAT IS THIS?
WHERE'S THE SODA?
I'VE GOT MORE THAN THREE.
CROWDED
HEY, YOU FORGOT THIS...
THANKS!
BUT YOU CAN HAVE IT!
LABEL: BIG & STRONG AKULT
...

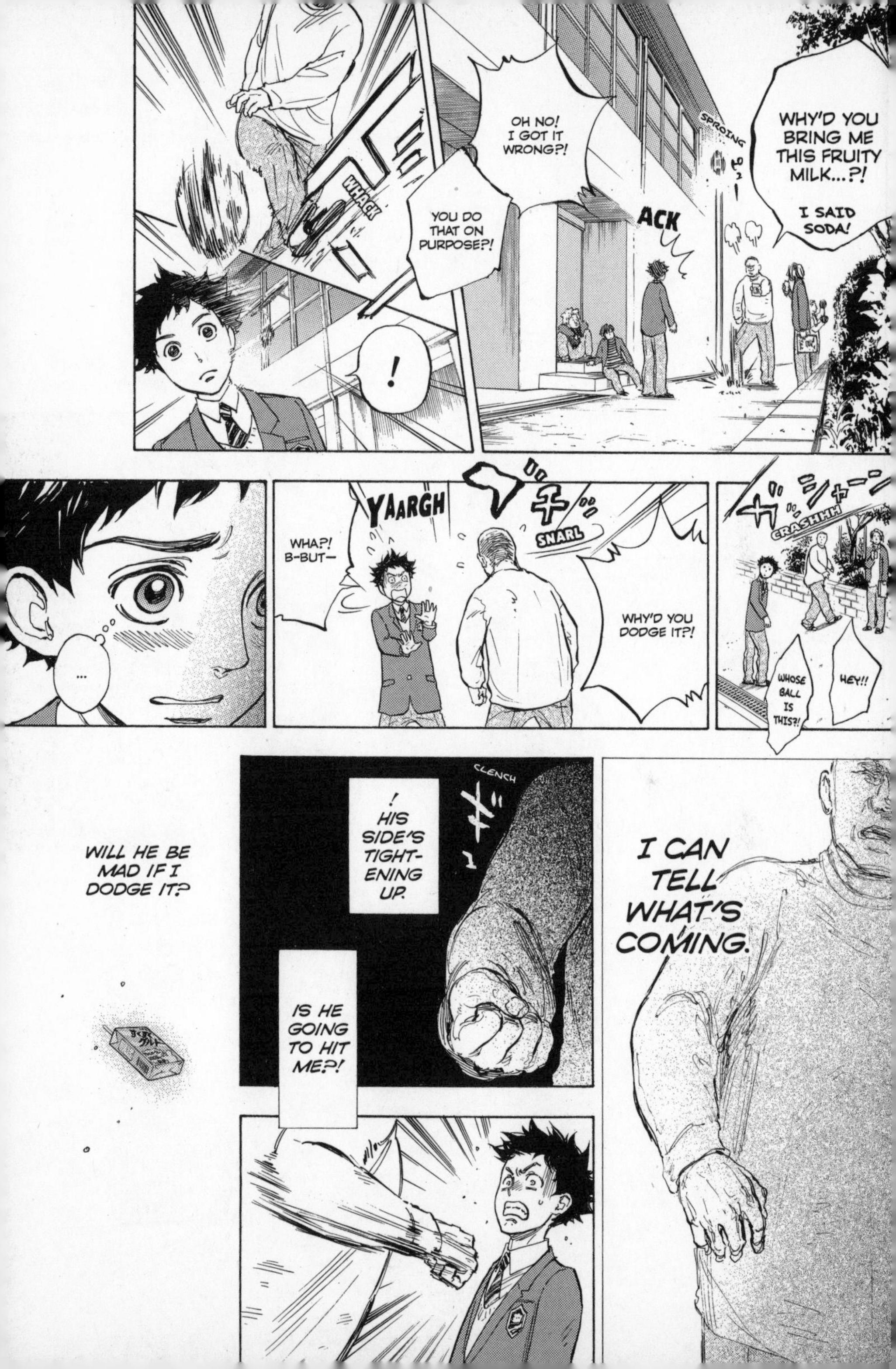
WHY'D YOU BRING ME THIS FRUITY MILK...?!
I SAID SODA!
SPROING
ACK
OH NO! I GOT IT WRONG?!
WHACK
YOU DO THAT ON PURPOSE?!
!
CRASHHH
HEY!!
WHOSE BALL IS THIS?!
SNARL
WHY'D YOU DODGE IT?!
YAARGH
WHA?! B-BUT—
...
I CAN TELL WHAT'S COMING.
CLENCH
! HIS SIDE'S TIGHT-ENING UP.
IS HE GOING TO HIT ME?!
WILL HE BE MAD IF I DODGE IT?

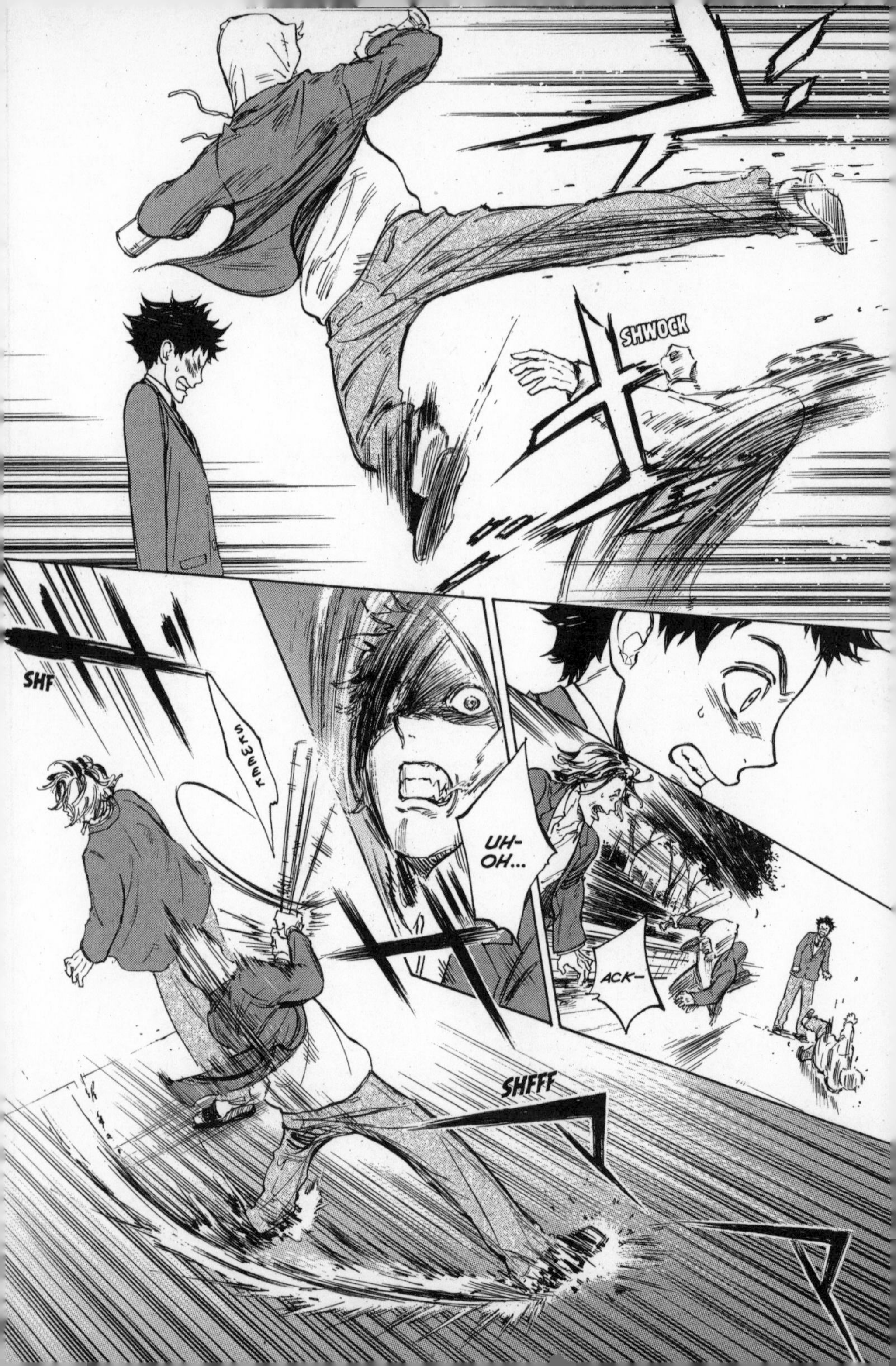
SHWOCK
ACK-
UH-OH...
SHF
SKWEEK
SHFFF

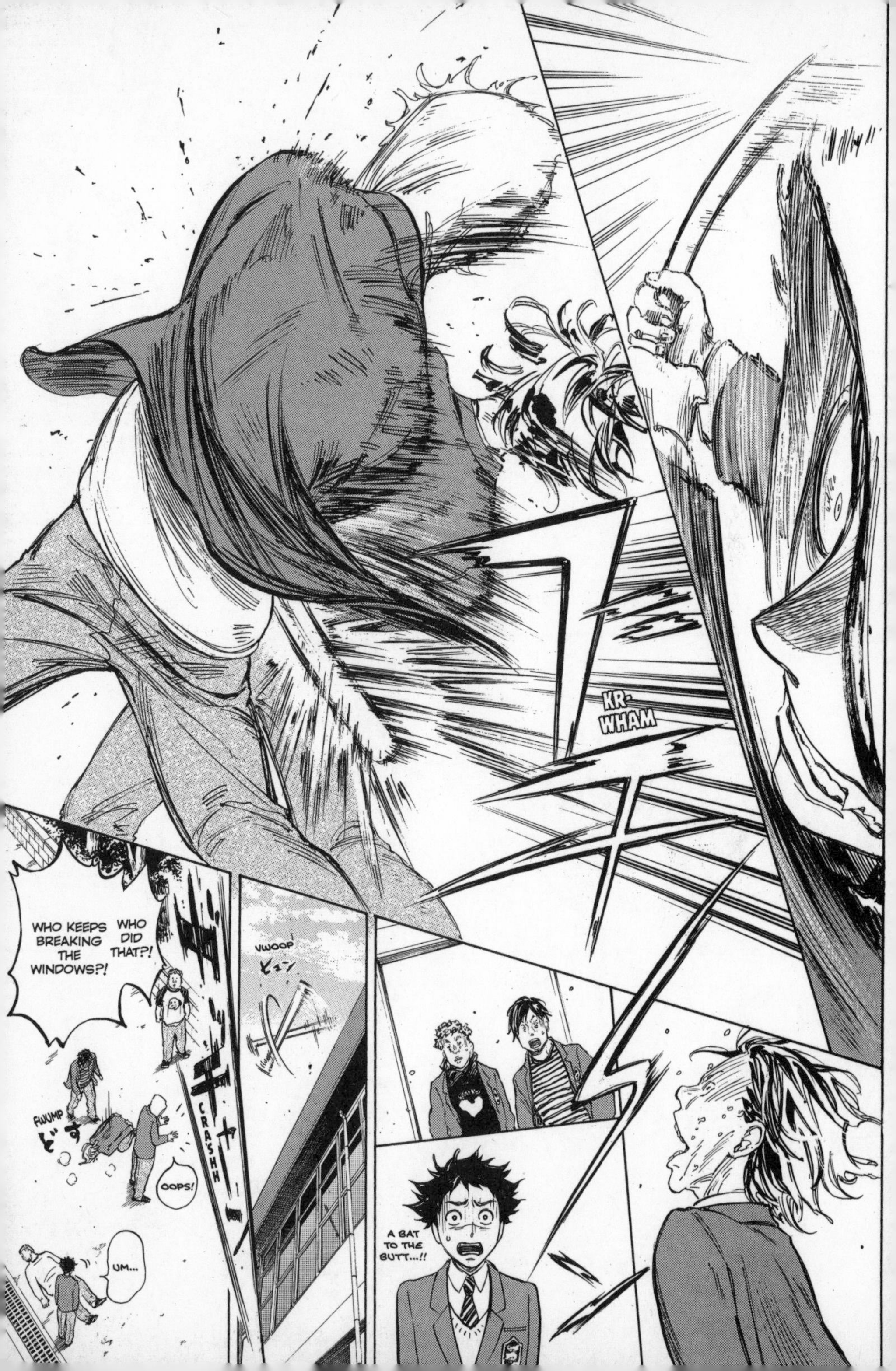
KR-WHAM
A BAT TO THE BUTT...!!
VWOOP
CRASHH
WHO DID THAT?!
WHO KEEPS BREAKING THE WINDOWS?!
FWUMP
どす
OOPS!
UM...

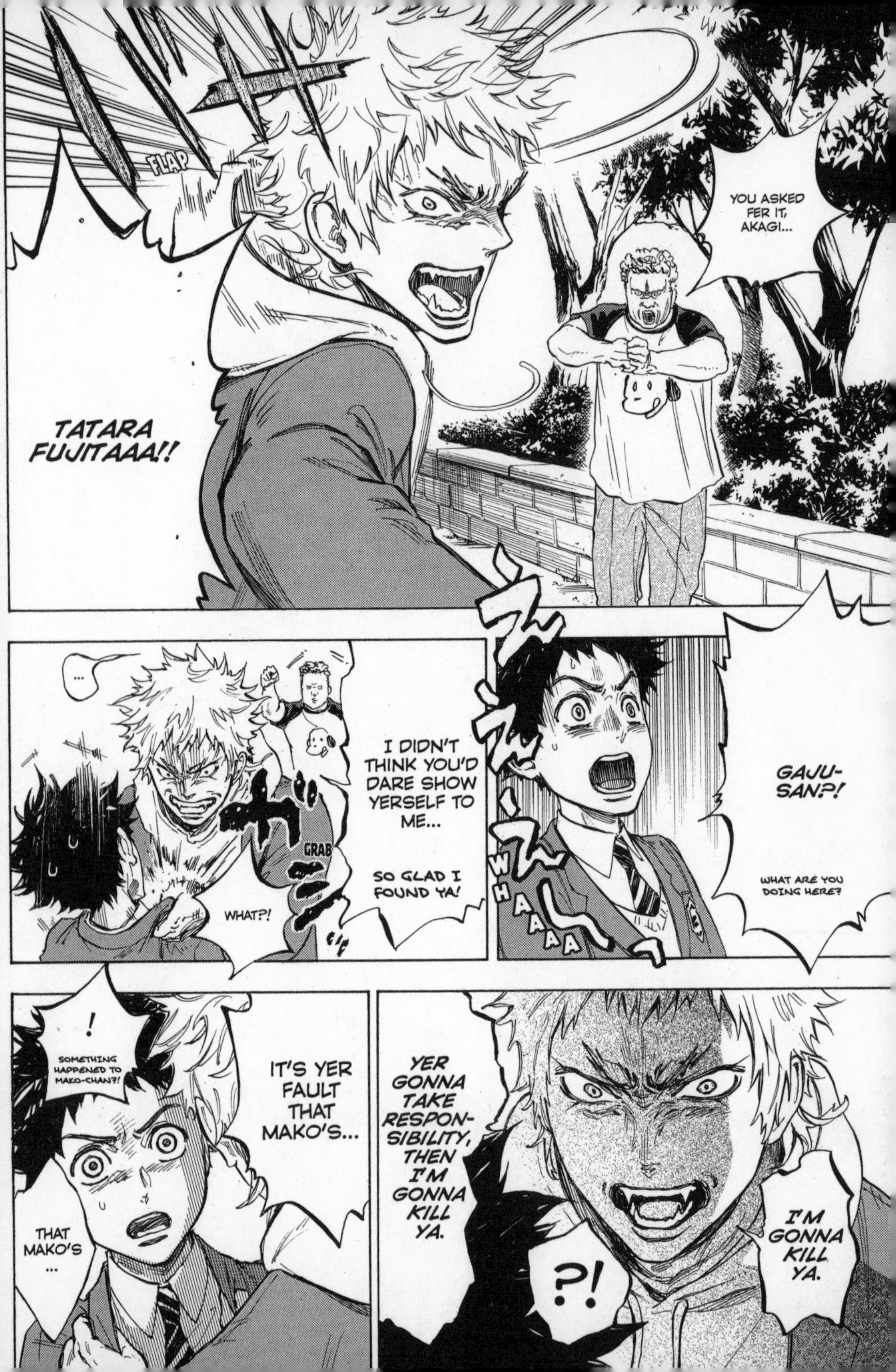
YOU ASKED FER IT, AKAGI...
FLAP
TATARA FUJITAAA!!
GAJU-SAN?!
WHAT ARE YOU DOING HERE?
WHAAAA
I DIDN'T THINK YOU'D DARE SHOW YERSELF TO ME...
SO GLAD I FOUND YA!
GRAB
WHAT?!
...
I'M GONNA KILL YA.
YER GONNA TAKE RESPONSIBILITY, THEN I'M GONNA KILL YA.
?!
IT'S YER FAULT THAT MAKO'S...
!
SOMETHING HAPPENED TO MAKO-CHAN?!
THAT MAKO'S ...

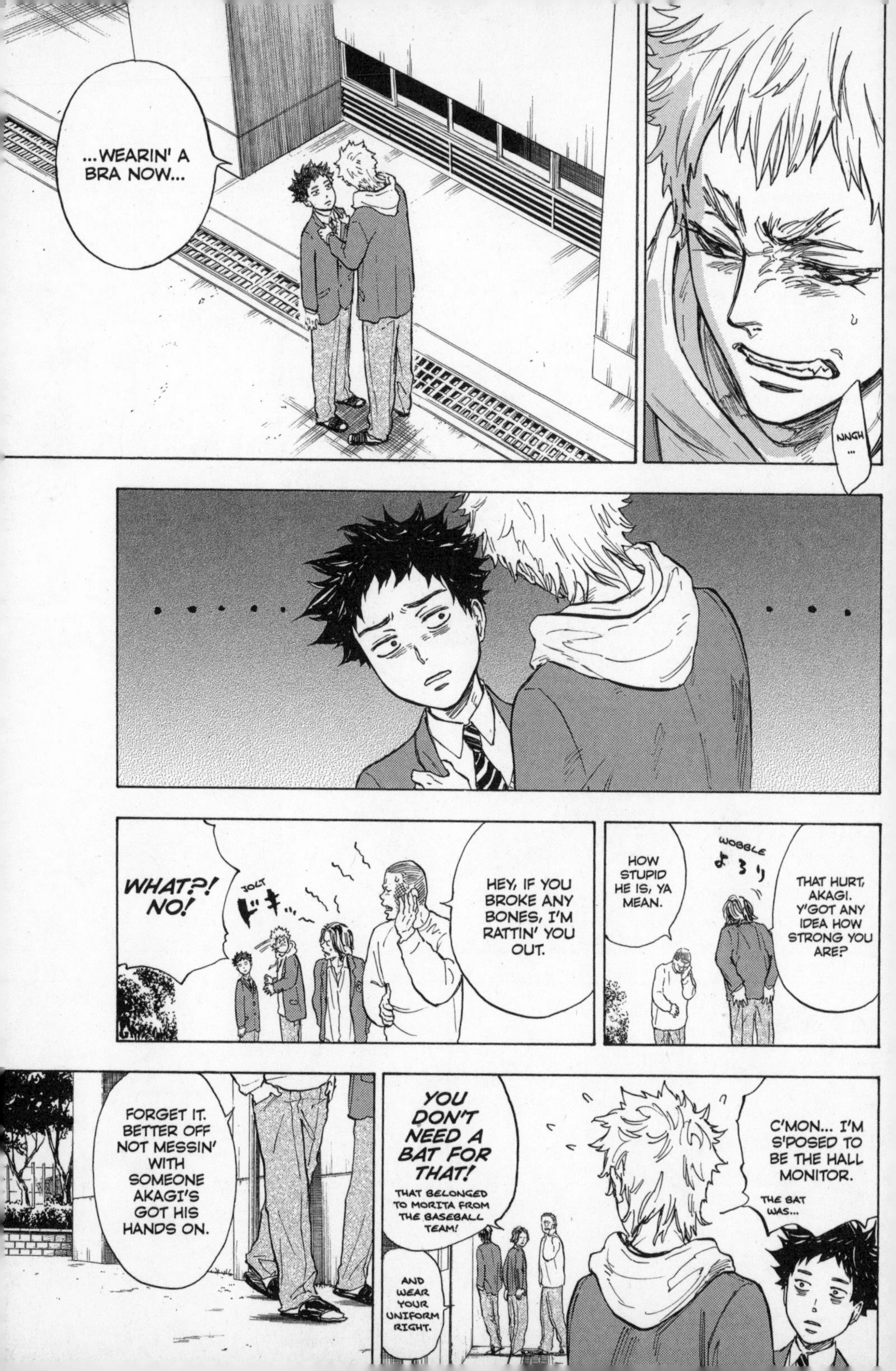
NNGH ...
...WEARIN' A BRA NOW...
THAT HURT, AKAGI. Y'GOT ANY IDEA HOW STRONG YOU ARE?
WOBBLE
よろり
HOW STUPID HE IS, YA MEAN.
HEY, IF YOU BROKE ANY BONES, I'M RATTIN' YOU OUT.
JOLT
ドキッ
WHAT?! NO!
C'MON... I'M S'POSED TO BE THE HALL MONITOR.
THE BAT WAS...
YOU DON'T NEED A BAT FOR THAT!
THAT BELONGED TO MORITA FROM THE BASEBALL TEAM!
AND WEAR YOUR UNIFORM RIGHT.
FORGET IT. BETTER OFF NOT MESSIN' WITH SOMEONE AKAGI'S GOT HIS HANDS ON.

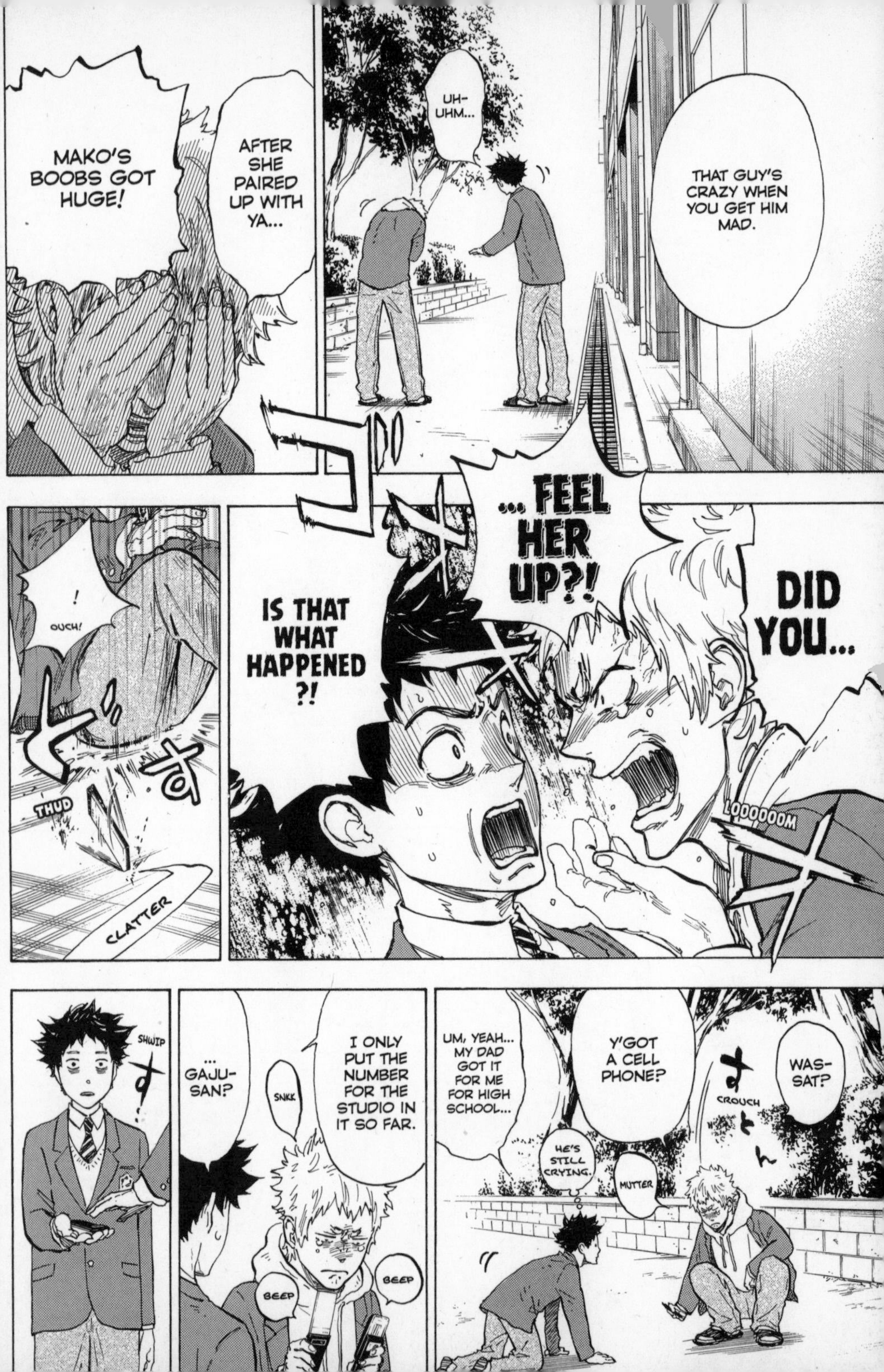
THAT GUY'S CRAZY WHEN YOU GET HIM MAD.
UH-UHM...
AFTER SHE PAIRED UP WITH YA...
MAKO'S BOOBS GOT HUGE!
DID YOU...
...FEEL HER UP?!
IS THAT WHAT HAPPENED ?!
LOOOOOOM
!
OUCH!
THUD
CLATTER
WAS-SAT?
CROUCH
Y'GOT A CELL PHONE?
MUTTER
HE'S STILL CRYING.
UM, YEAH... MY DAD GOT IT FOR ME FOR HIGH SCHOOL...
I ONLY PUT THE NUMBER FOR THE STUDIO IN IT SO FAR.
SNKK
BEEP
BEEP
... GAJU-SAN?
SHWIP

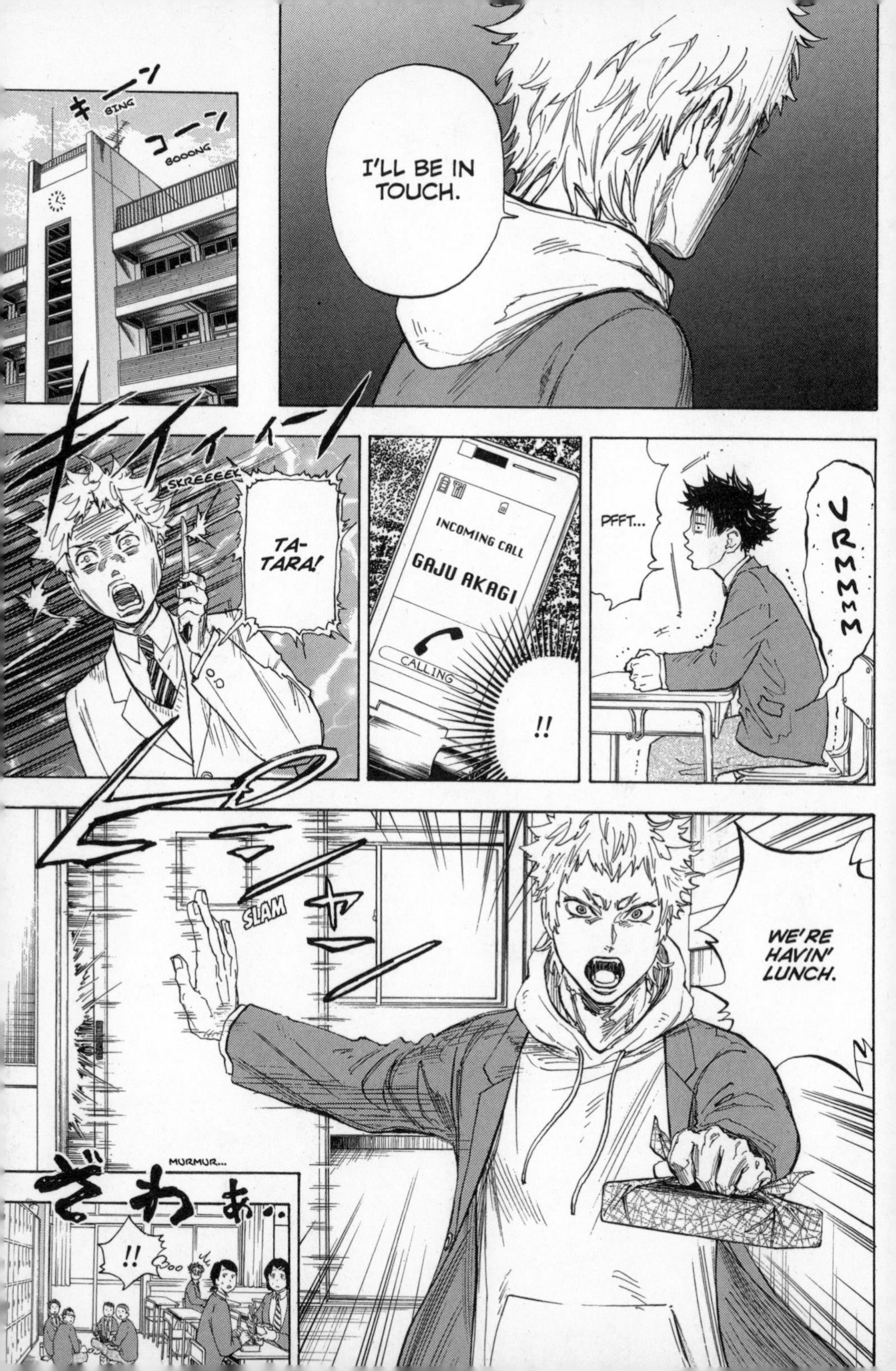
I'LL BE IN TOUCH.
BING
BOOONG
PFFT...
URMMMM
INCOMING CALL
GAJU AKAGI
CALLING
!!
SKREEEEK
TA-TARA!
WE'RE HAVIN' LUNCH.
SLAM
MURMUR...
!!

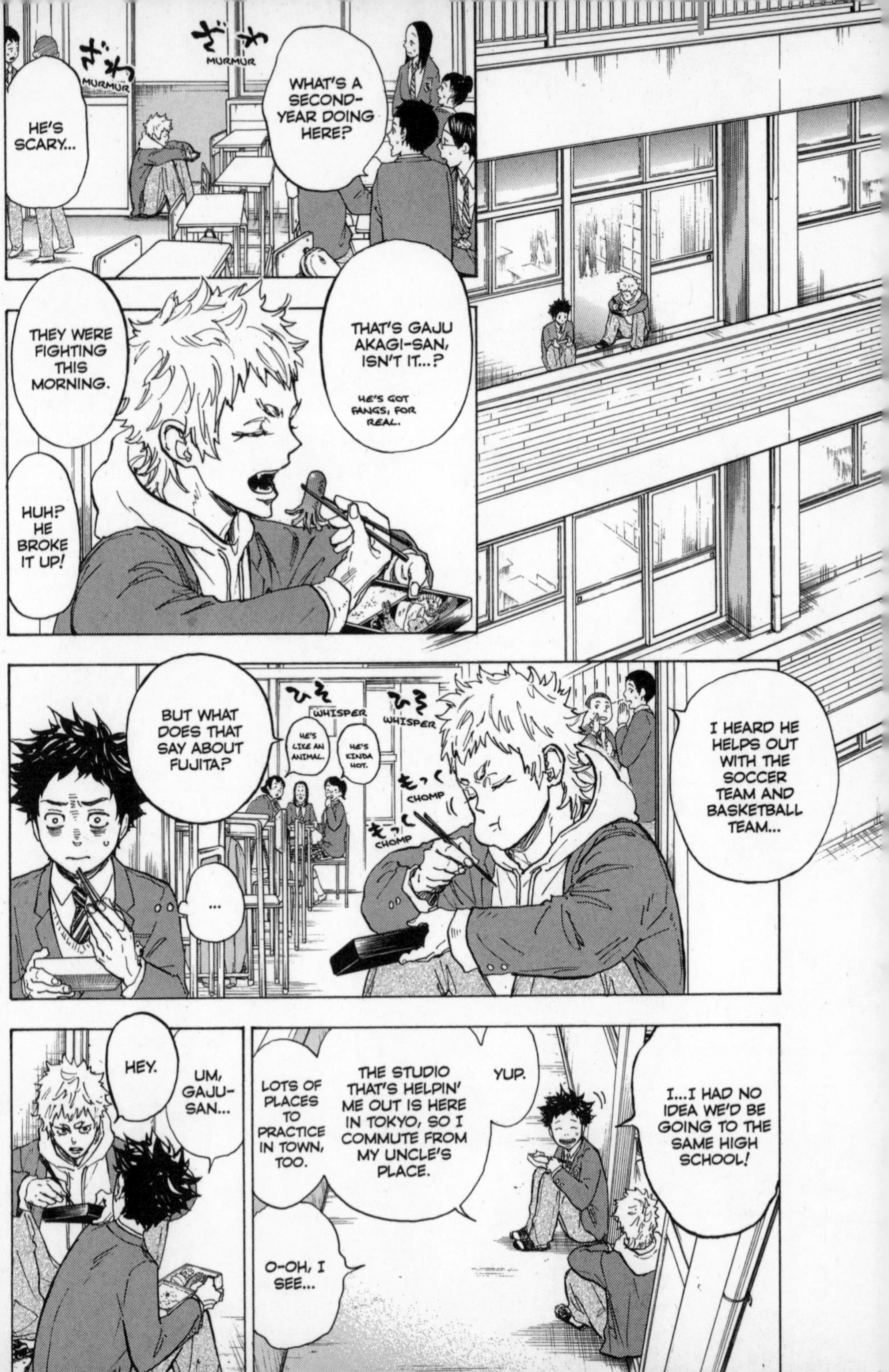
ざわ
MURMUR
ざわ
MURMUR
WHAT'S A SECOND-YEAR DOING HERE?
HE'S SCARY...
THAT'S GAJU AKAGI-SAN, ISN'T IT...?
HE'S GOT FANGS, FOR REAL.
THEY WERE FIGHTING THIS MORNING.
HUH? HE BROKE IT UP!
I HEARD HE HELPS OUT WITH THE SOCCER TEAM AND BASKETBALL TEAM...
ひそ
WHISPER
ひそ
WHISPER
HE'S KINDA HOT.
HE'S LIKE AN ANIMAL.
もっく
CHOMP
もっく
CHOMP
BUT WHAT DOES THAT SAY ABOUT FUJITA?
...
I...I HAD NO IDEA WE'D BE GOING TO THE SAME HIGH SCHOOL!
YUP.
THE STUDIO THAT'S HELPIN' ME OUT IS HERE IN TOKYO, SO I COMMUTE FROM MY UNCLE'S PLACE.
LOTS OF PLACES TO PRACTICE IN TOWN, TOO.
O-OH, I SEE...
UM, GAJU-SAN...
HEY.

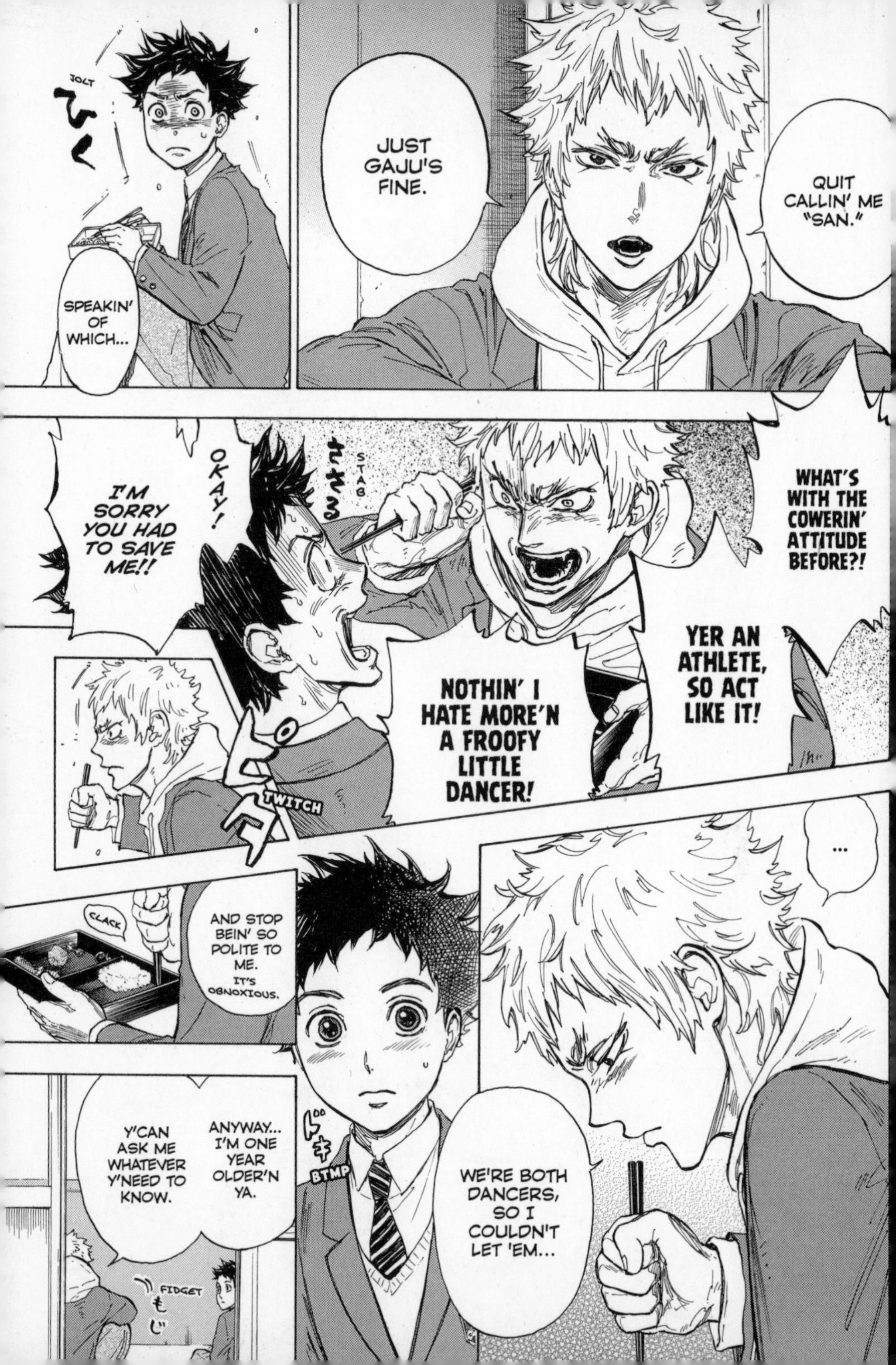

QUIT CALLIN' ME "SAN."
JUST GAJU'S FINE.
JOLT
ひく
SPEAKIN' OF WHICH...
WHAT'S WITH THE COWERIN' ATTITUDE BEFORE?!
YER AN ATHLETE, SO ACT LIKE IT!
NOTHIN' I HATE MORE'N A FROOFY LITTLE DANCER!
ささる
STAB
OKAY!
I'M SORRY YOU HAD TO SAVE ME!!
TWITCH
...
WE'RE BOTH DANCERS, SO I COULDN'T LET 'EM...
ドキ
BTMP
CLACK
AND STOP BEIN' SO POLITE TO ME.
IT'S OBNOXIOUS.
ANYWAY... I'M ONE YEAR OLDER'N YA.
Y'CAN ASK ME WHATEVER Y'NEED TO KNOW.
FIDGET
もじ

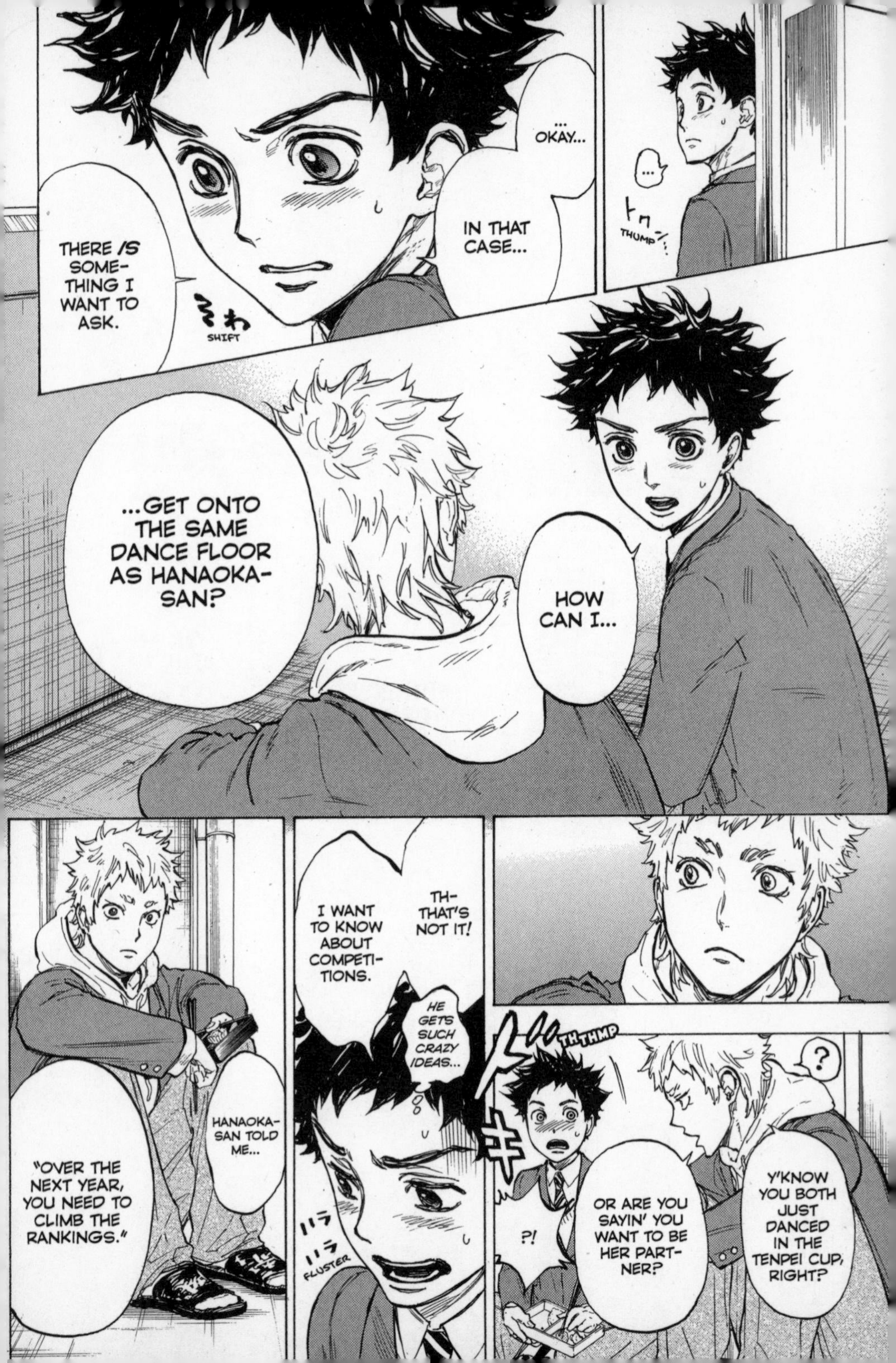
...
トン THUMP
... OKAY...
IN THAT CASE...
THERE IS SOMETHING I WANT TO ASK.
そわ SHIFT
HOW CAN I...
...GET ONTO THE SAME DANCE FLOOR AS HANAOKA-SAN?
?
Y'KNOW YOU BOTH JUST DANCED IN THE TENPEI CUP, RIGHT?
OR ARE YOU SAYIN' YOU WANT TO BE HER PARTNER?
?!
TH THMP
TH-THAT'S NOT IT!
I WANT TO KNOW ABOUT COMPETITIONS.
HE GETS SUCH CRAZY IDEAS...
ハラハラ FLUSTER
HANAOKA-SAN TOLD ME...
"OVER THE NEXT YEAR, YOU NEED TO CLIMB THE RANKINGS."

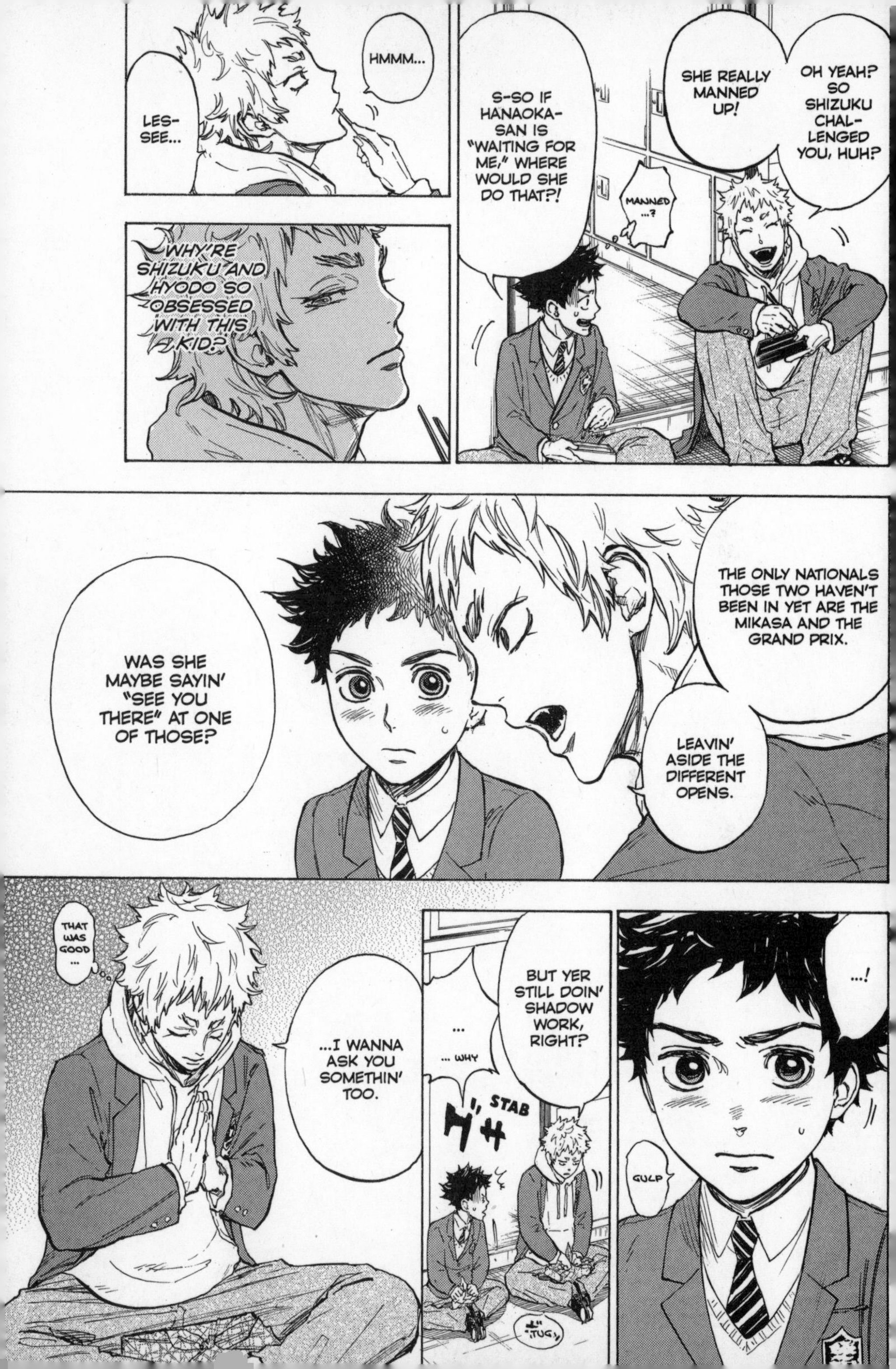
OH YEAH? SO SHIZUKU CHAL-LENGED YOU, HUH?
SHE REALLY MANNED UP!
MANNED ...?
S-SO IF HANAOKA-SAN IS "WAITING FOR ME," WHERE WOULD SHE DO THAT?!
HMMM...
LES-SEE...
WHY'RE SHIZUKU AND HYODO SO OBSESSED WITH THIS KID?
THE ONLY NATIONALS THOSE TWO HAVEN'T BEEN IN YET ARE THE MIKASA AND THE GRAND PRIX.
LEAVIN' ASIDE THE DIFFERENT OPENS.
WAS SHE MAYBE SAYIN' "SEE YOU THERE" AT ONE OF THOSE?
...!
GULP
BUT YER STILL DOIN' SHADOW WORK, RIGHT?
...
... WHY
STAB
TUG
...I WANNA ASK YOU SOMETHIN' TOO.
THAT WAS GOOD ...

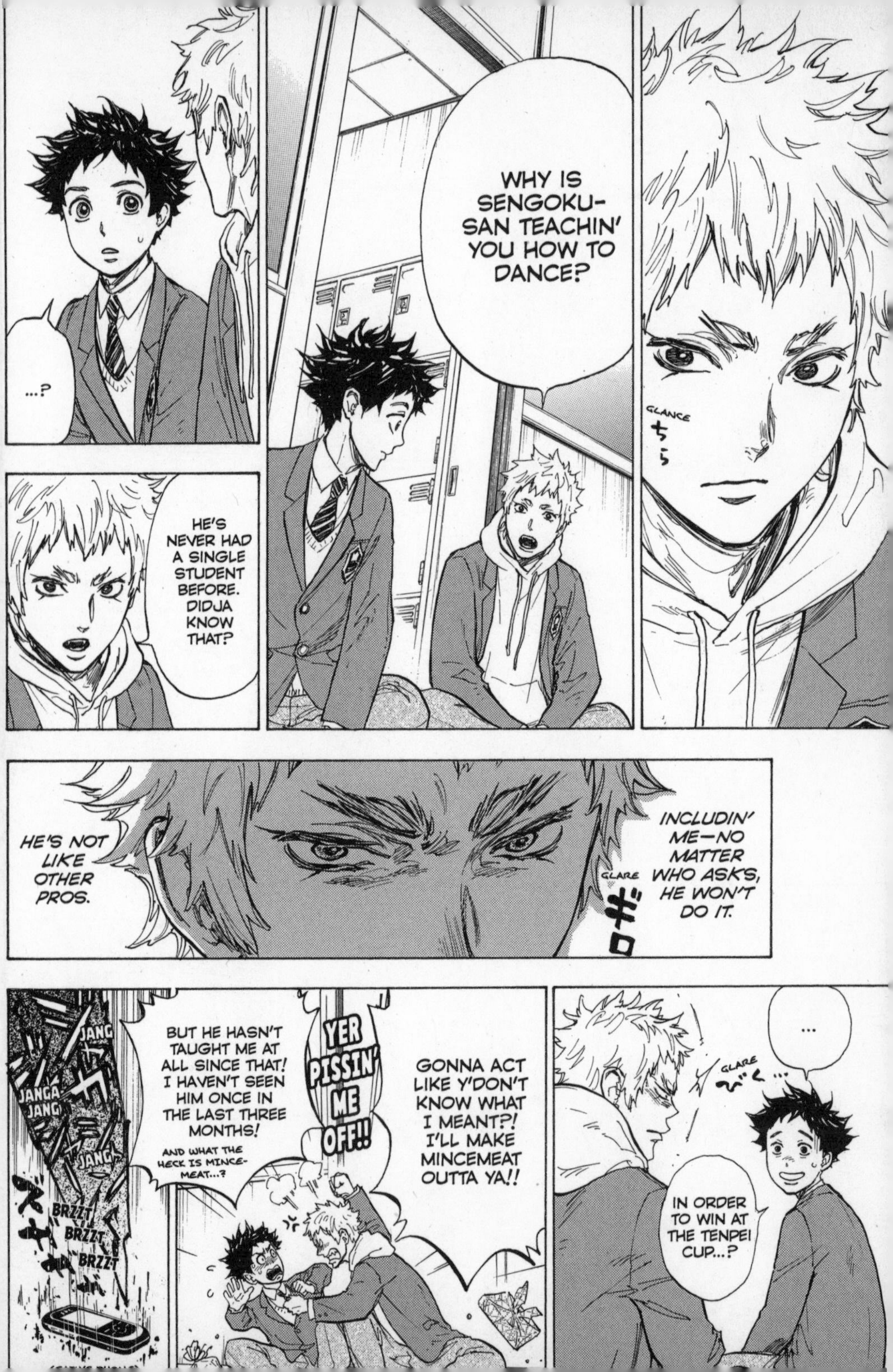
GLANCE
ちら
WHY IS SENGOKU-SAN TEACHIN' YOU HOW TO DANCE?
...?
HE'S NEVER HAD A SINGLE STUDENT BEFORE. DIDJA KNOW THAT?
INCLUDIN' ME—NO MATTER WHO ASKS, HE WON'T DO IT.
GLARE
ギロ
HE'S NOT LIKE OTHER PROS.
...
GLARE
...
IN ORDER TO WIN AT THE TENPEI CUP...?
GONNA ACT LIKE Y'DON'T KNOW WHAT I MEANT?! I'LL MAKE MINCEMEAT OUTTA YA!!
YER PISSIN' ME OFF!!
BUT HE HASN'T TAUGHT ME AT ALL SINCE THAT! I HAVEN'T SEEN HIM ONCE IN THE LAST THREE MONTHS!
AND WHAT THE HECK IS MINCE-MEAT...?
JANG
JANGA JANG
JANG
BRZZT
BRZZT
BRZZT

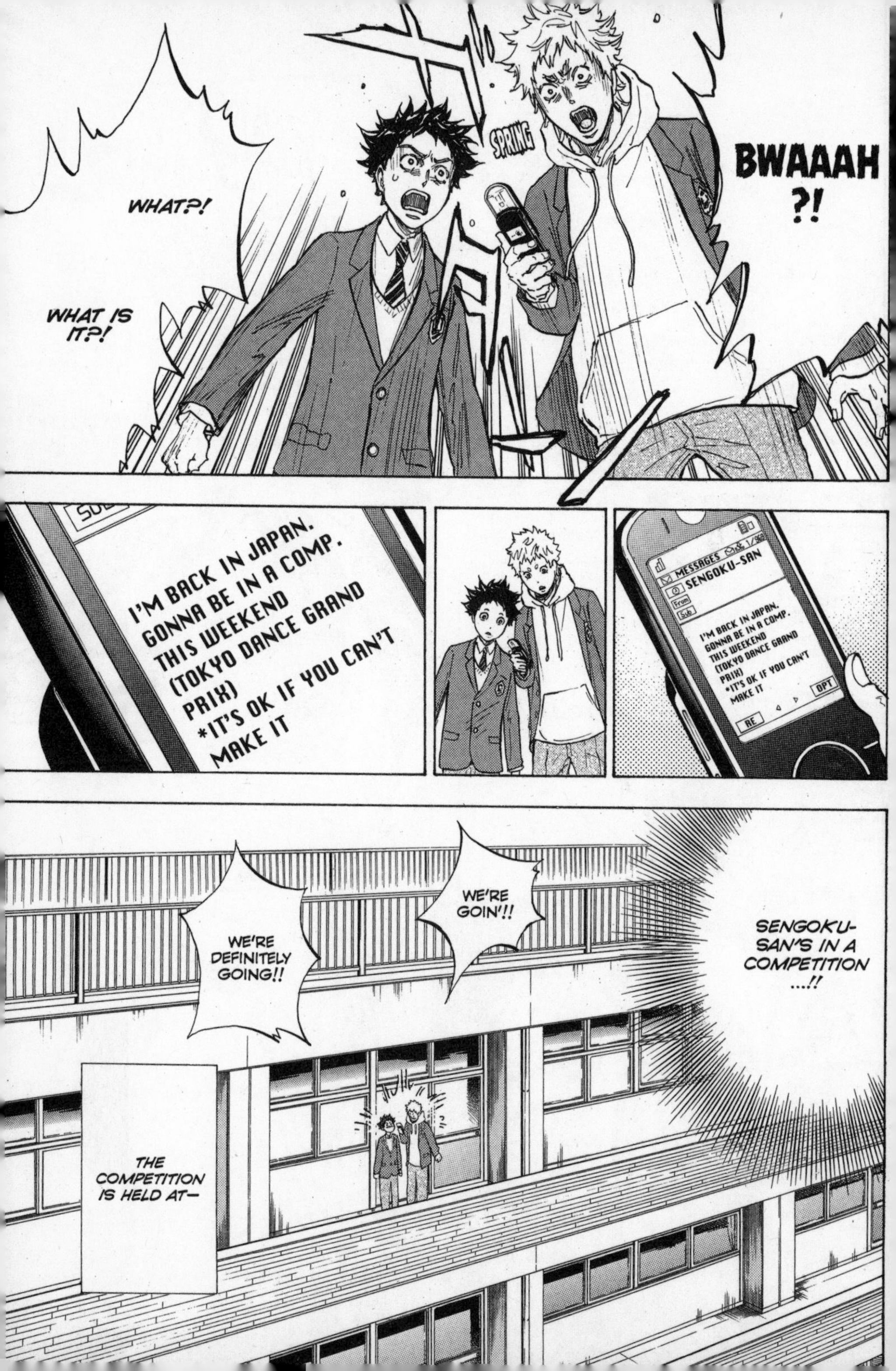
BWAAAH ?!
SPRING
WHAT?!
WHAT IS IT?!
MESSAGES
SENGOKU-SAN
From
Sub
I'M BACK IN JAPAN. GONNA BE IN A COMP. THIS WEEKEND (TOKYO DANCE GRAND PRIX) *IT'S OK IF YOU CAN'T MAKE IT
RE
OPT
I'M BACK IN JAPAN. GONNA BE IN A COMP. THIS WEEKEND (TOKYO DANCE GRAND PRIX) *IT'S OK IF YOU CAN'T MAKE IT
SENGOKU-SAN'S IN A COMPETITION ...!!
WE'RE GOIN'!!
WE'RE DEFINITELY GOING!!
THE COMPETITION IS HELD AT—

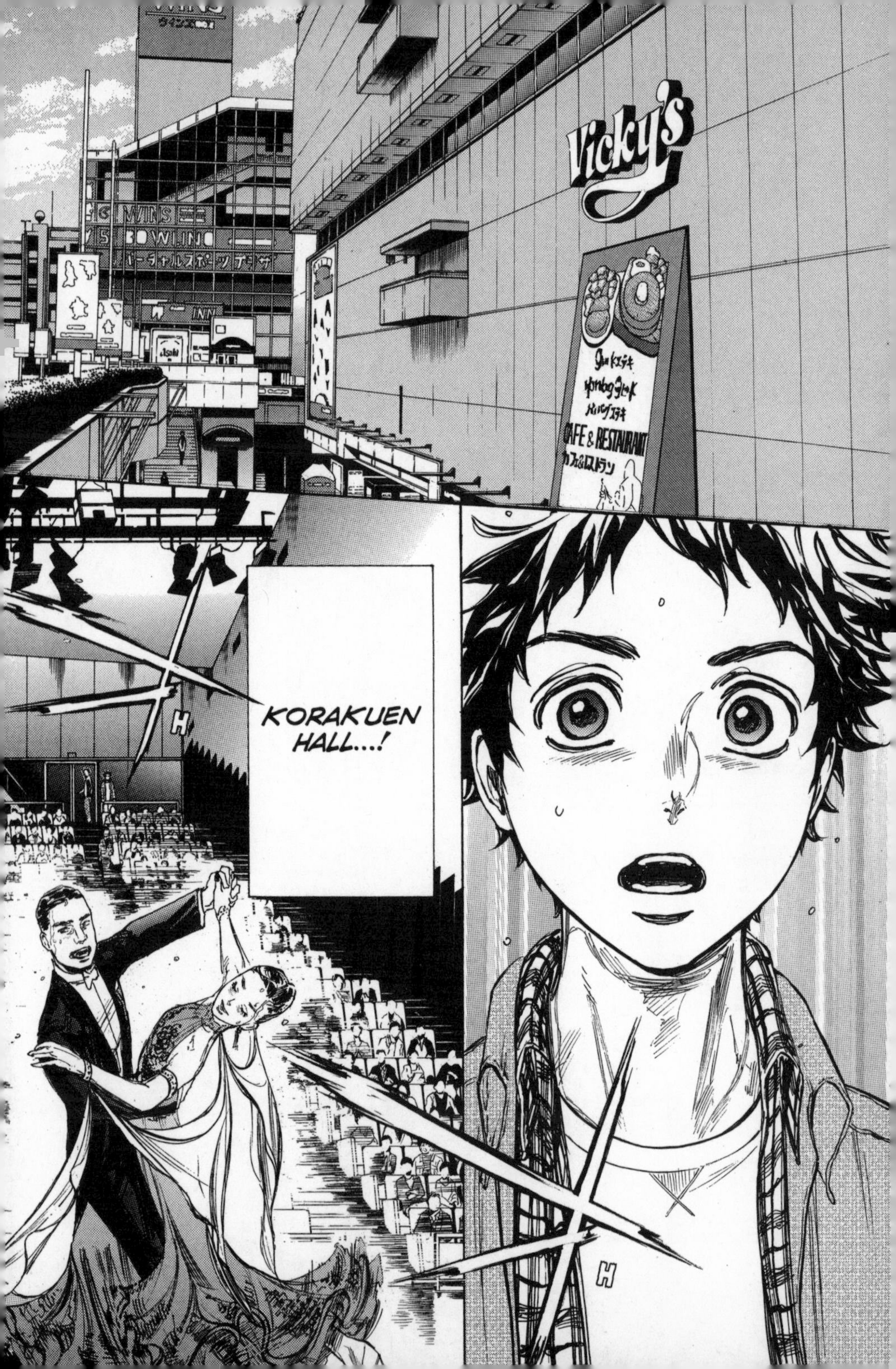
Vicky's
CAFE & RESTAURANT
KORAKUEN HALL...!

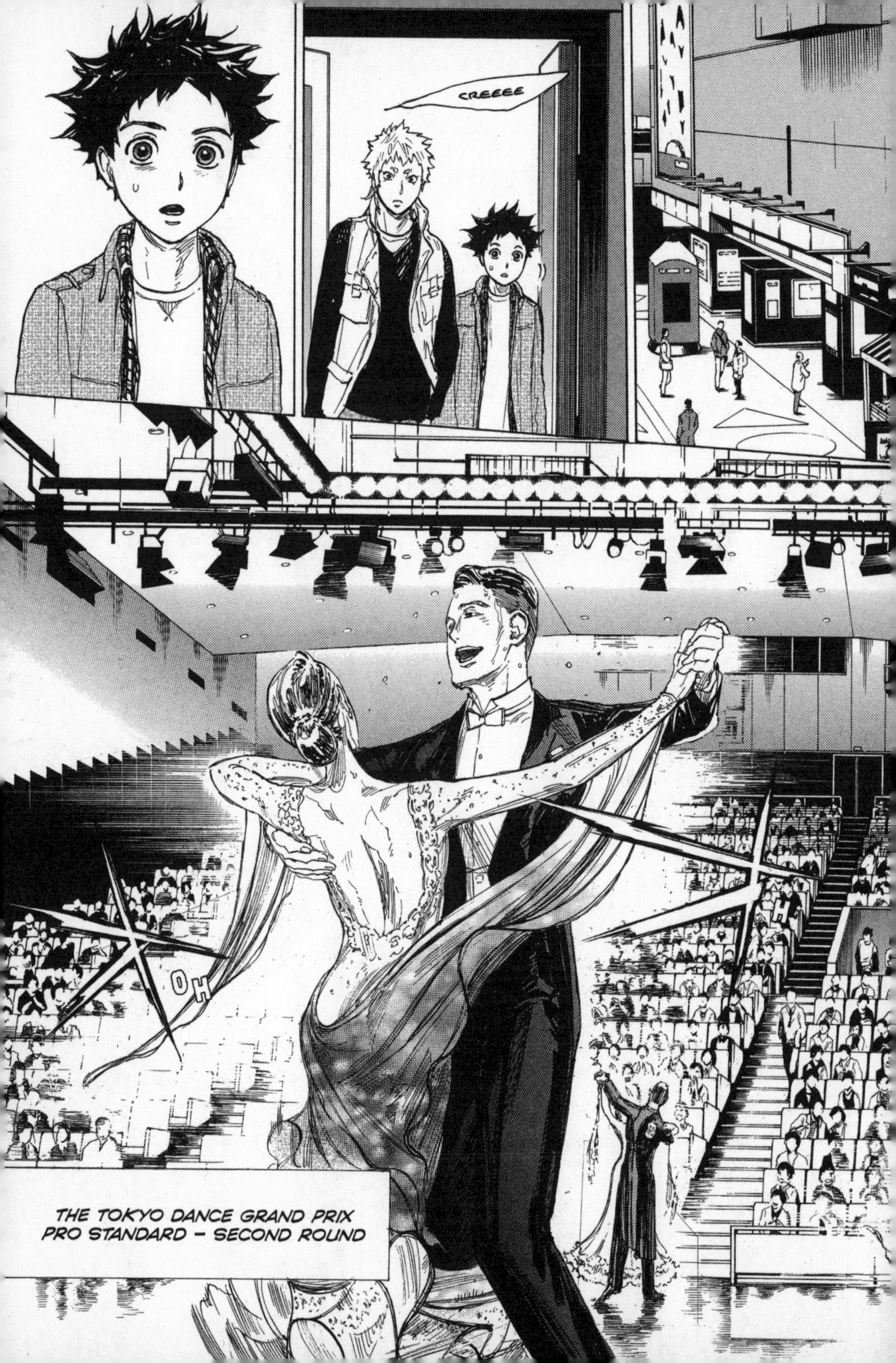
CREEEE
OH
THE TOKYO DANCE GRAND PRIX
PRO STANDARD – SECOND ROUND

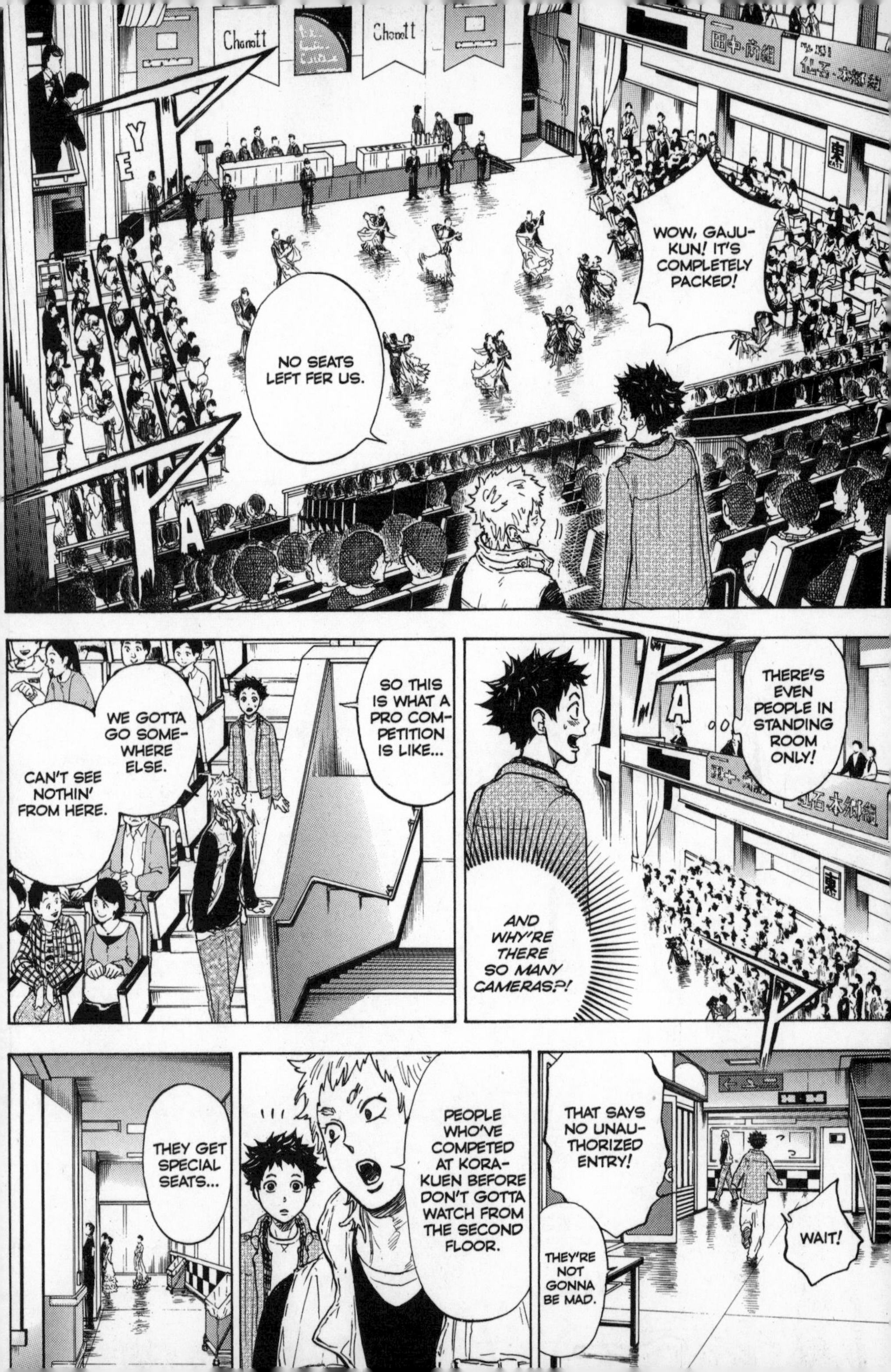
WOW, GAJU-KUN! IT'S COMPLETELY PACKED!
NO SEATS LEFT FER US.
THERE'S EVEN PEOPLE IN STANDING ROOM ONLY!
AND WHY'RE THERE SO MANY CAMERAS?!
SO THIS IS WHAT A PRO COMPETITION IS LIKE...
WE GOTTA GO SOMEWHERE ELSE.
CAN'T SEE NOTHIN' FROM HERE.
THAT SAYS NO UNAUTHORIZED ENTRY!
WAIT!
THEY'RE NOT GONNA BE MAD.
PEOPLE WHO'VE COMPETED AT KORAKUEN BEFORE DON'T GOTTA WATCH FROM THE SECOND FLOOR.
THEY GET SPECIAL SEATS...

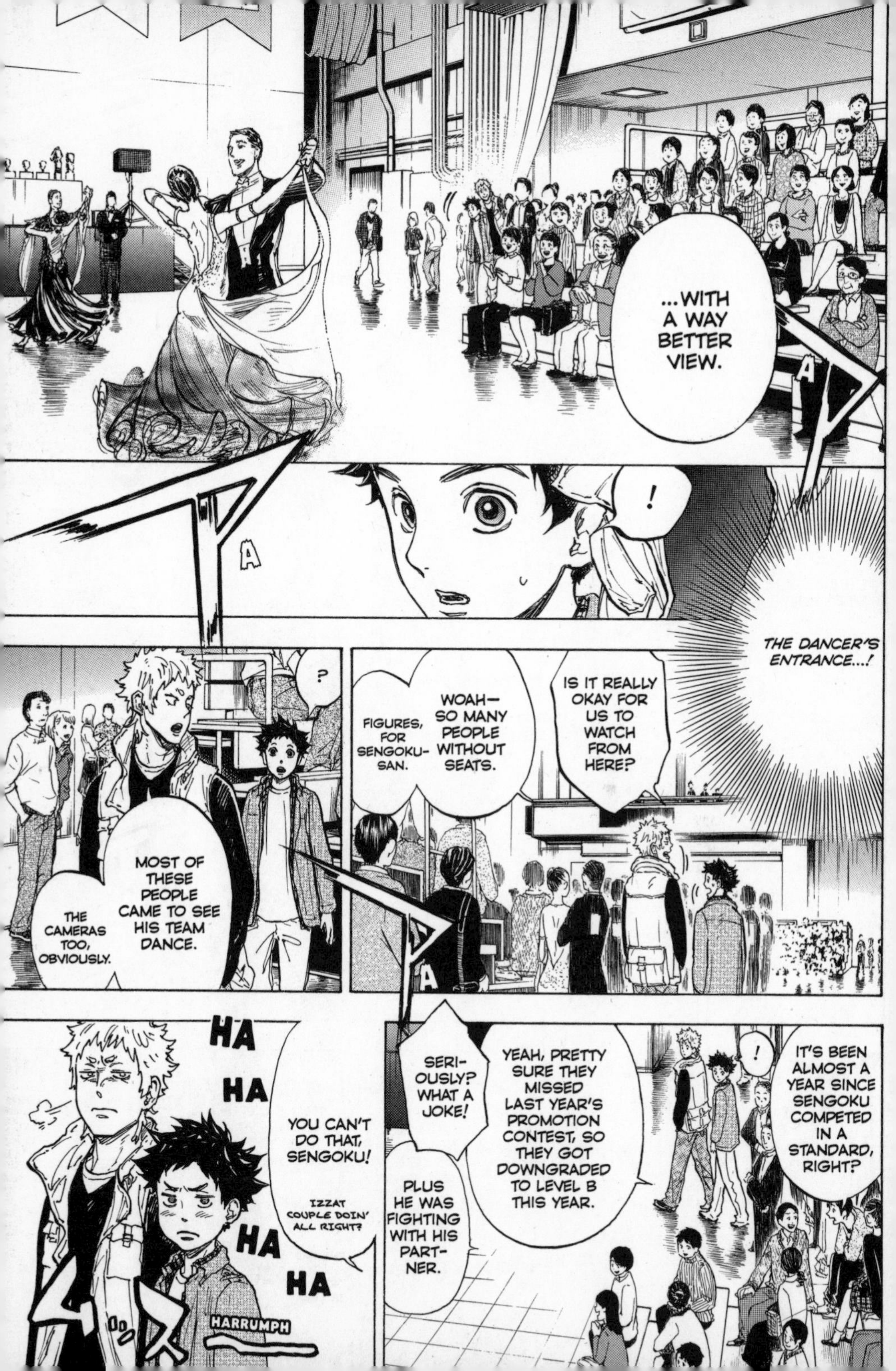
...WITH A WAY BETTER VIEW.
A
!
A
THE DANCER'S ENTRANCE...!
IS IT REALLY OKAY FOR US TO WATCH FROM HERE?
WOAH— SO MANY PEOPLE WITHOUT SEATS.
FIGURES, FOR SENGOKU-SAN.
A
?
MOST OF THESE PEOPLE CAME TO SEE HIS TEAM DANCE.
THE CAMERAS TOO, OBVIOUSLY.
!
IT'S BEEN ALMOST A YEAR SINCE SENGOKU COMPETED IN A STANDARD, RIGHT?
YEAH, PRETTY SURE THEY MISSED LAST YEAR'S PROMOTION CONTEST, SO THEY GOT DOWNGRADED TO LEVEL B THIS YEAR.
SERI-OUSLY? WHAT A JOKE!
PLUS HE WAS FIGHTING WITH HIS PART-NER.
YOU CAN'T DO THAT, SENGOKU!
IZZAT COUPLE DOIN' ALL RIGHT?
HA HA HA HA
HARRUMPH

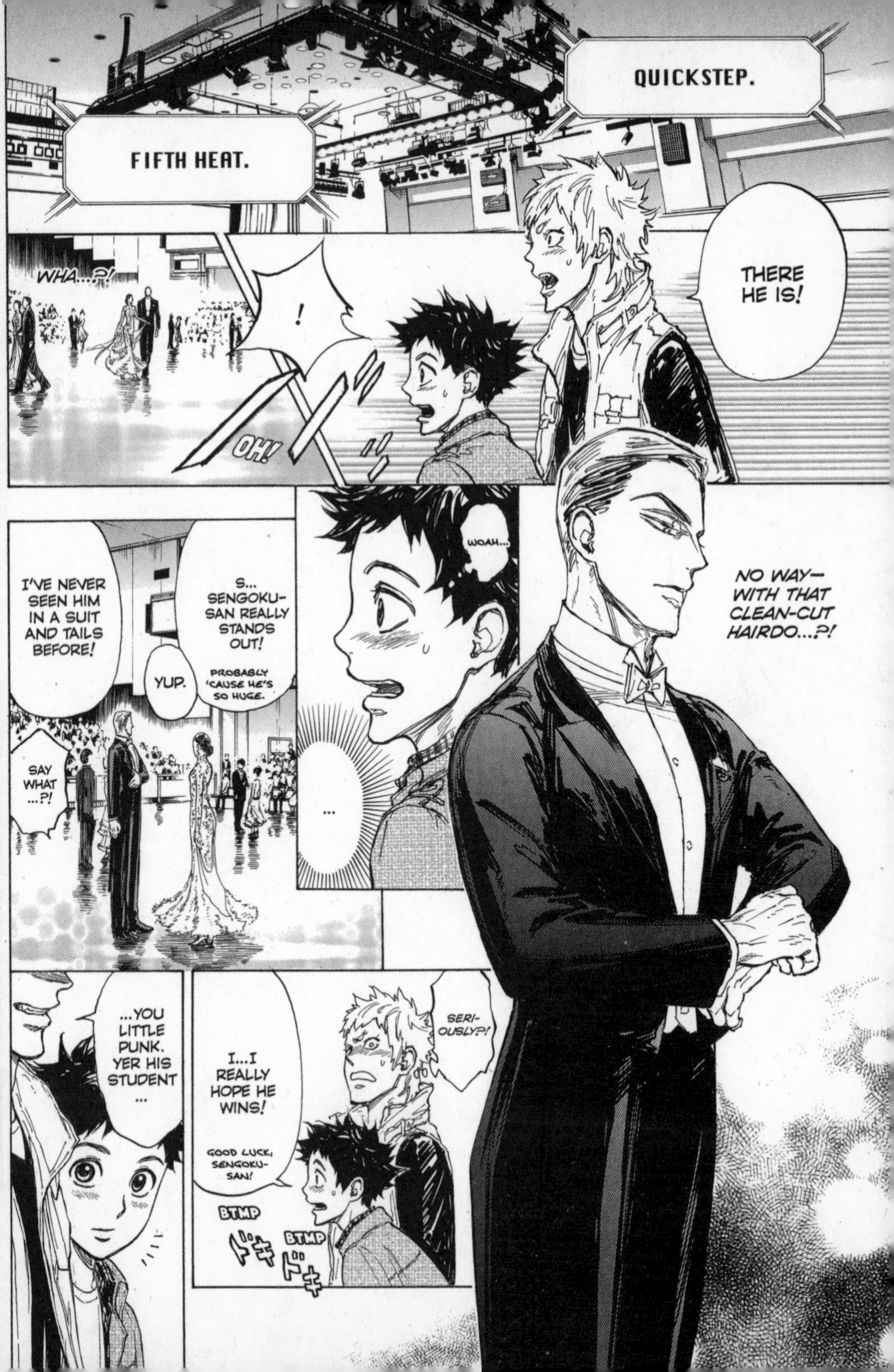
QUICKSTEP.
FIFTH HEAT.
THERE HE IS!
!
OH!
WHA...?!
NO WAY— WITH THAT CLEAN-CUT HAIRDO...?!
WOAH...
...
S... SENGOKU-SAN REALLY STANDS OUT!
I'VE NEVER SEEN HIM IN A SUIT AND TAILS BEFORE!
YUP.
PROBABLY 'CAUSE HE'S SO HUGE.
SAY WHAT ...?!
SERI-OUSLY?!
I...I REALLY HOPE HE WINS!
GOOD LUCK, SENGOKU-SAN!
BTMP
BTMP
...YOU LITTLE PUNK. YER HIS STUDENT ...

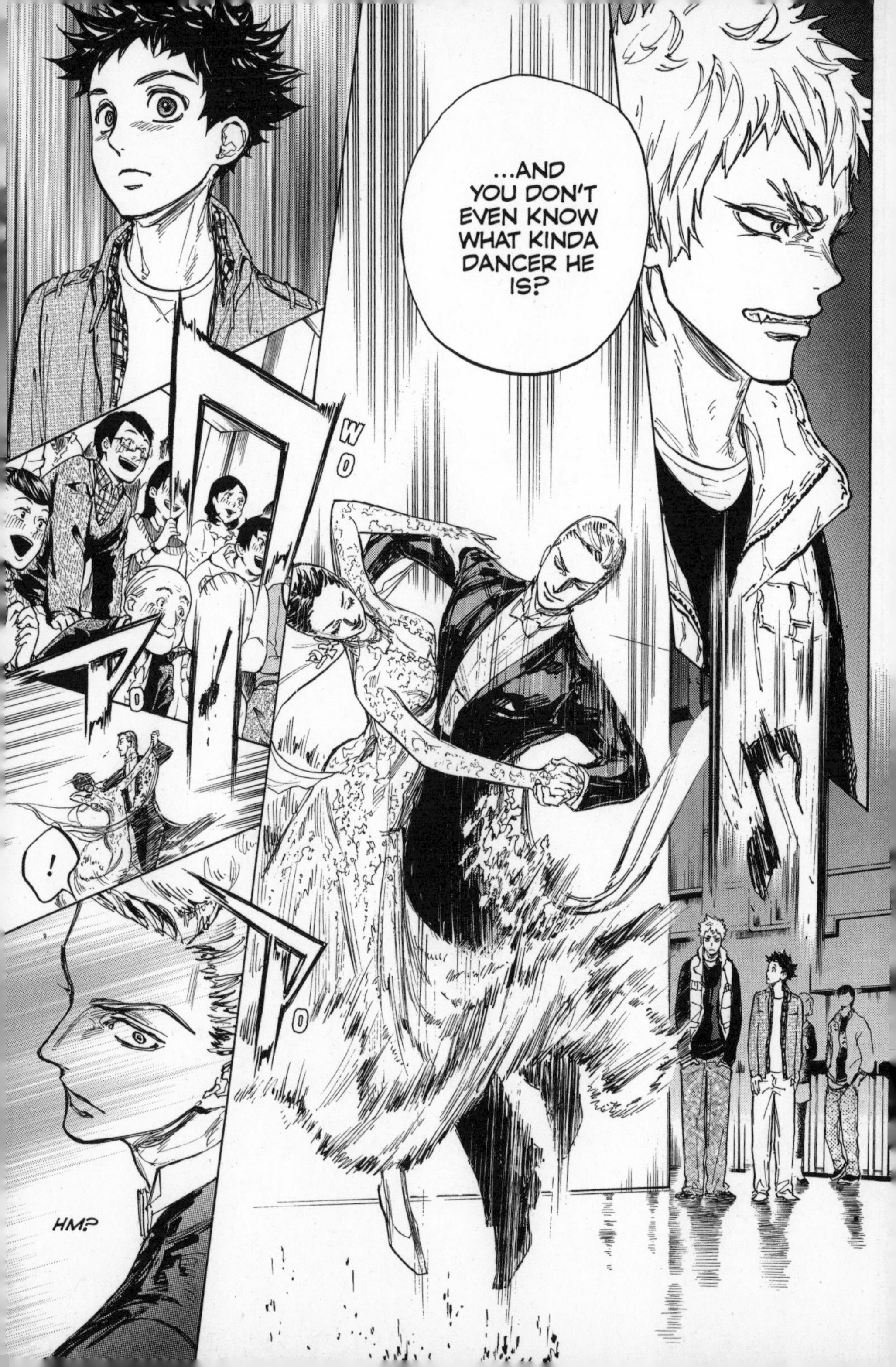
...AND YOU DON'T EVEN KNOW WHAT KINDA DANCER HE IS?
WOOOO
!
HM?

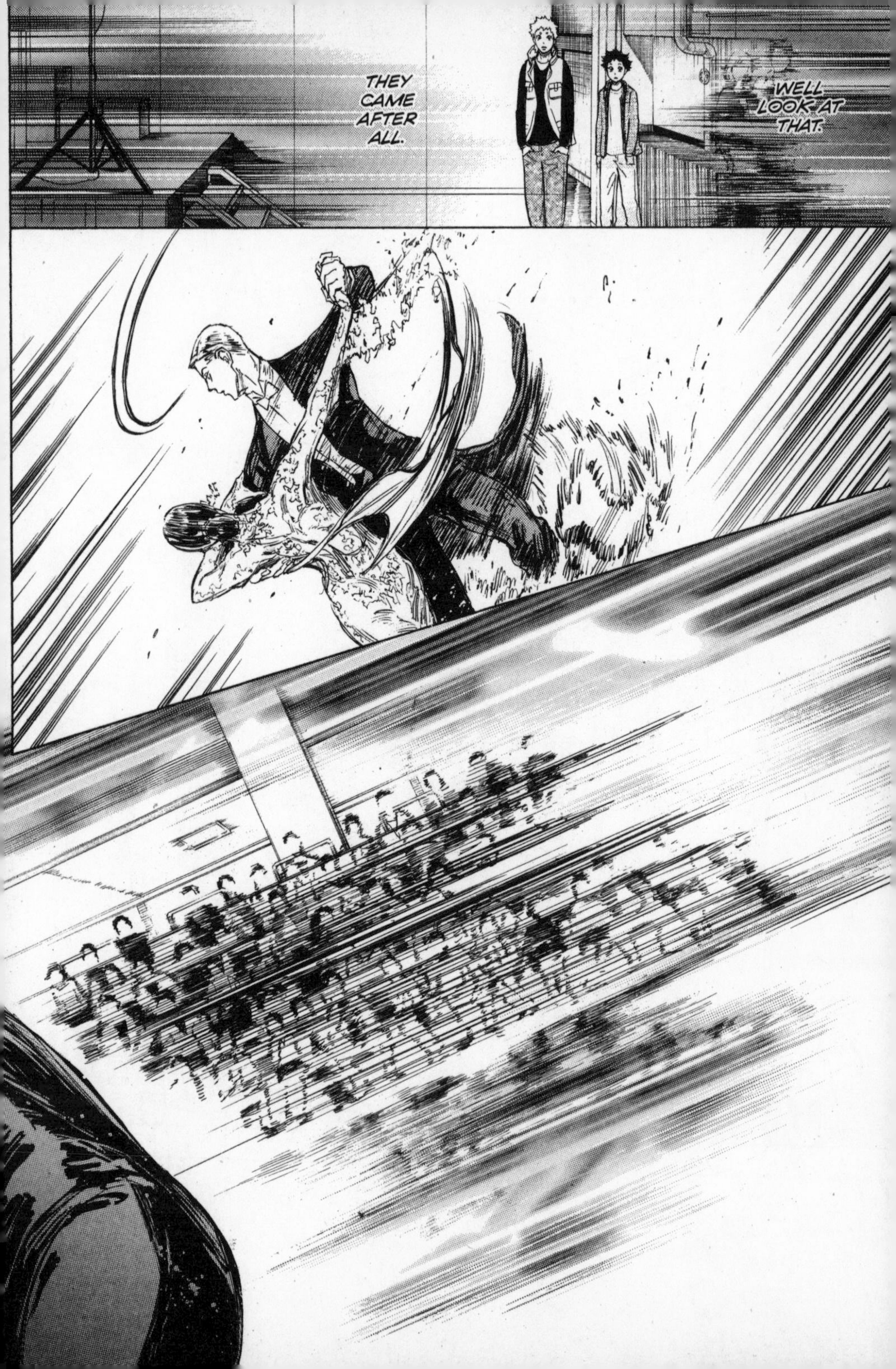
WELL LOOK AT THAT.
THEY CAME AFTER ALL.

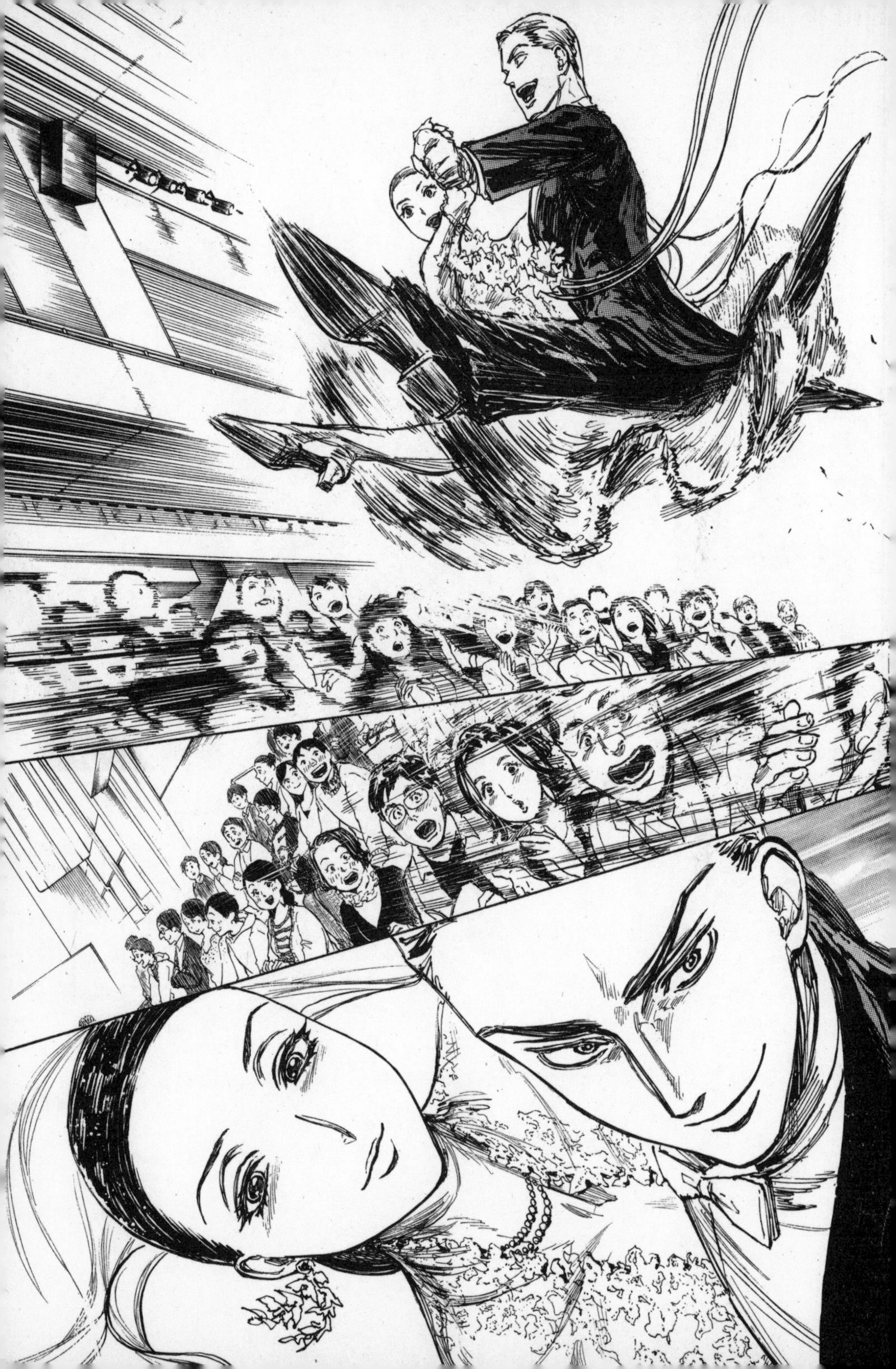

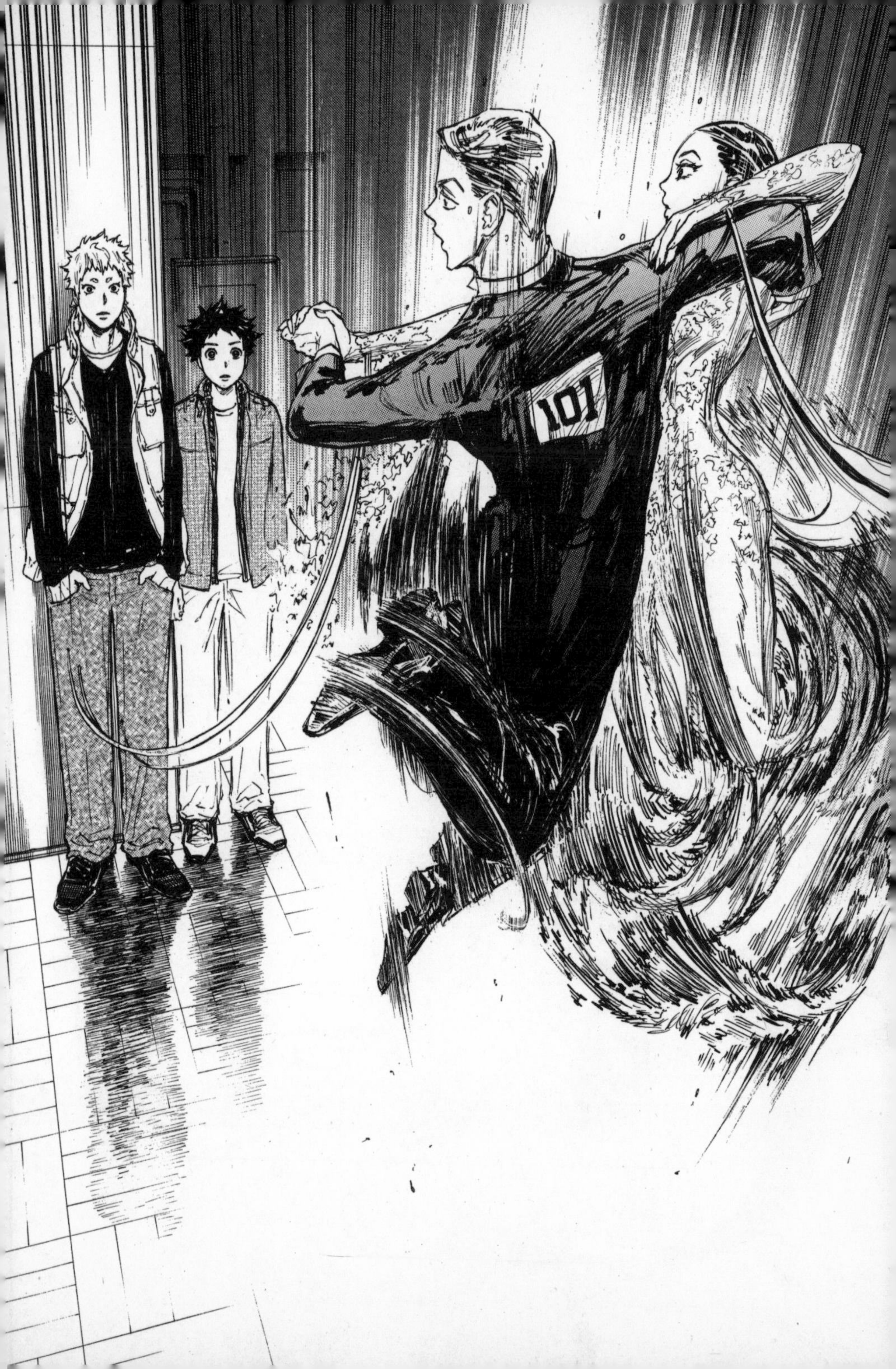
101

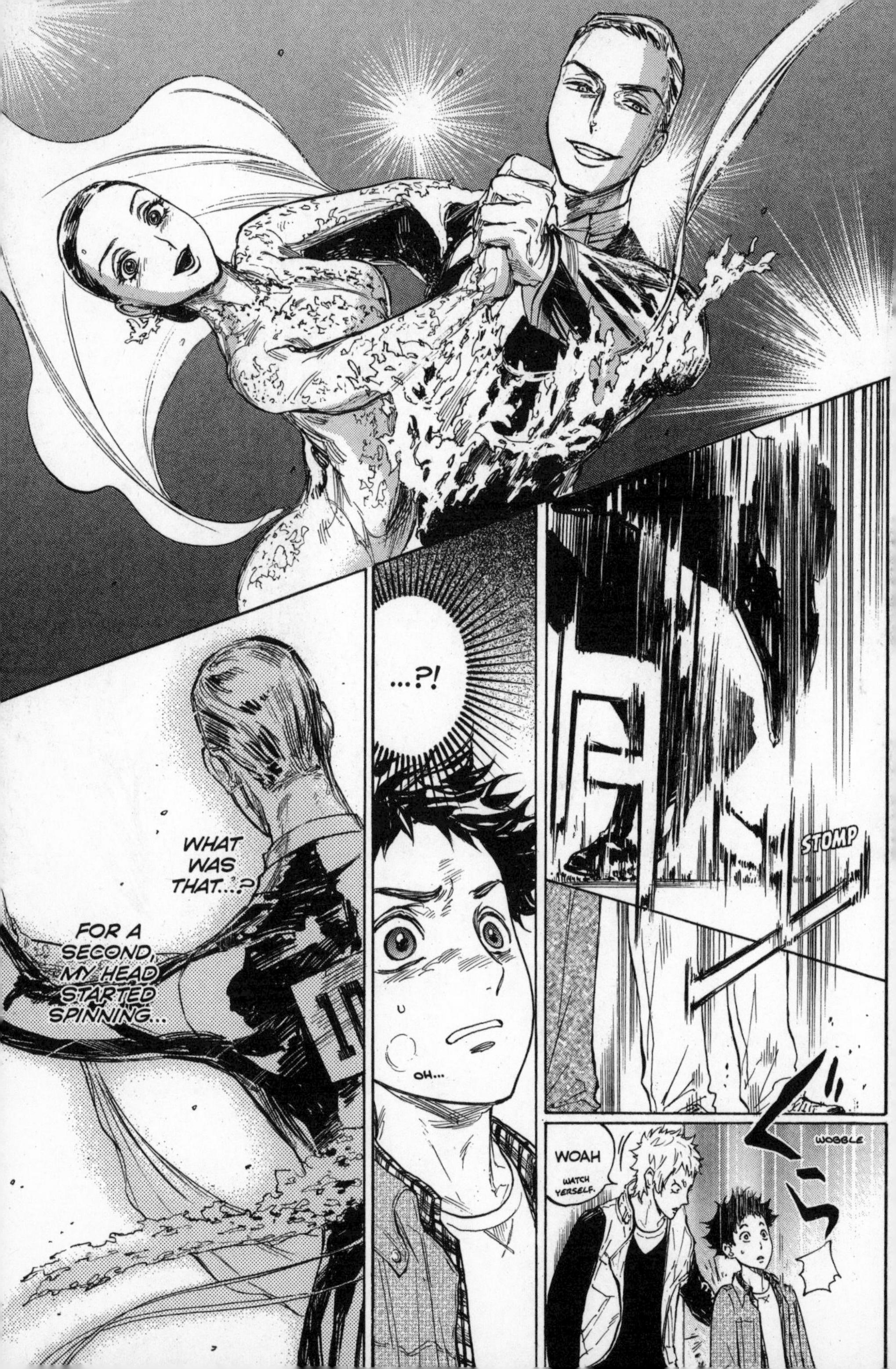
STOMP
WOAH
WATCH YOURSELF.
WOBBLE
...?!
OH...
WHAT WAS THAT...?
FOR A SECOND, MY HEAD STARTED SPINNING...

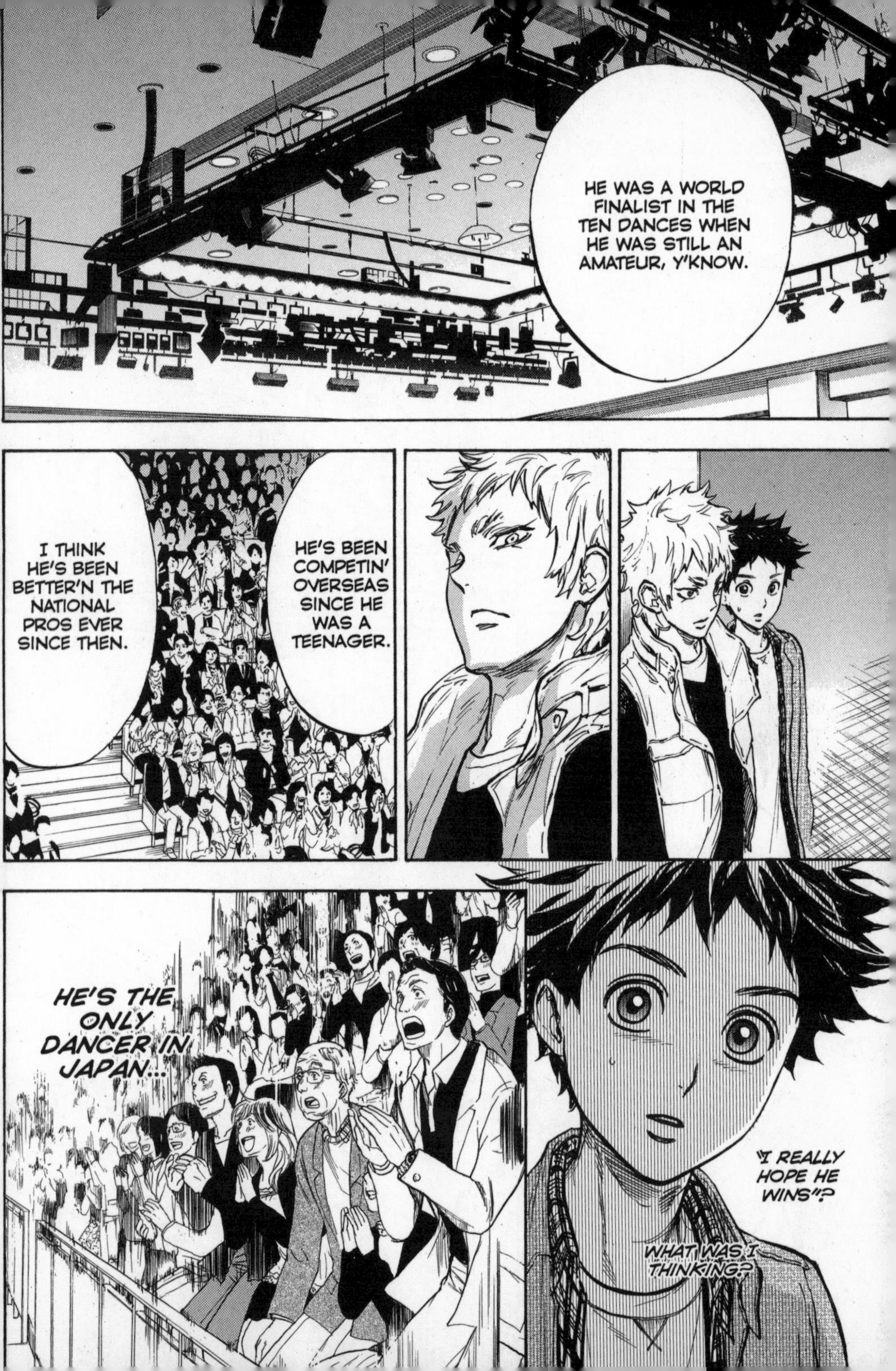
HE WAS A WORLD FINALIST IN THE TEN DANCES WHEN HE WAS STILL AN AMATEUR, Y'KNOW.
HE'S BEEN COMPETIN' OVERSEAS SINCE HE WAS A TEENAGER.
I THINK HE'S BEEN BETTER'N THE NATIONAL PROS EVER SINCE THEN.
"I REALLY HOPE HE WINS"?
WHAT WAS I THINKING?
HE'S THE ONLY DANCER IN JAPAN...

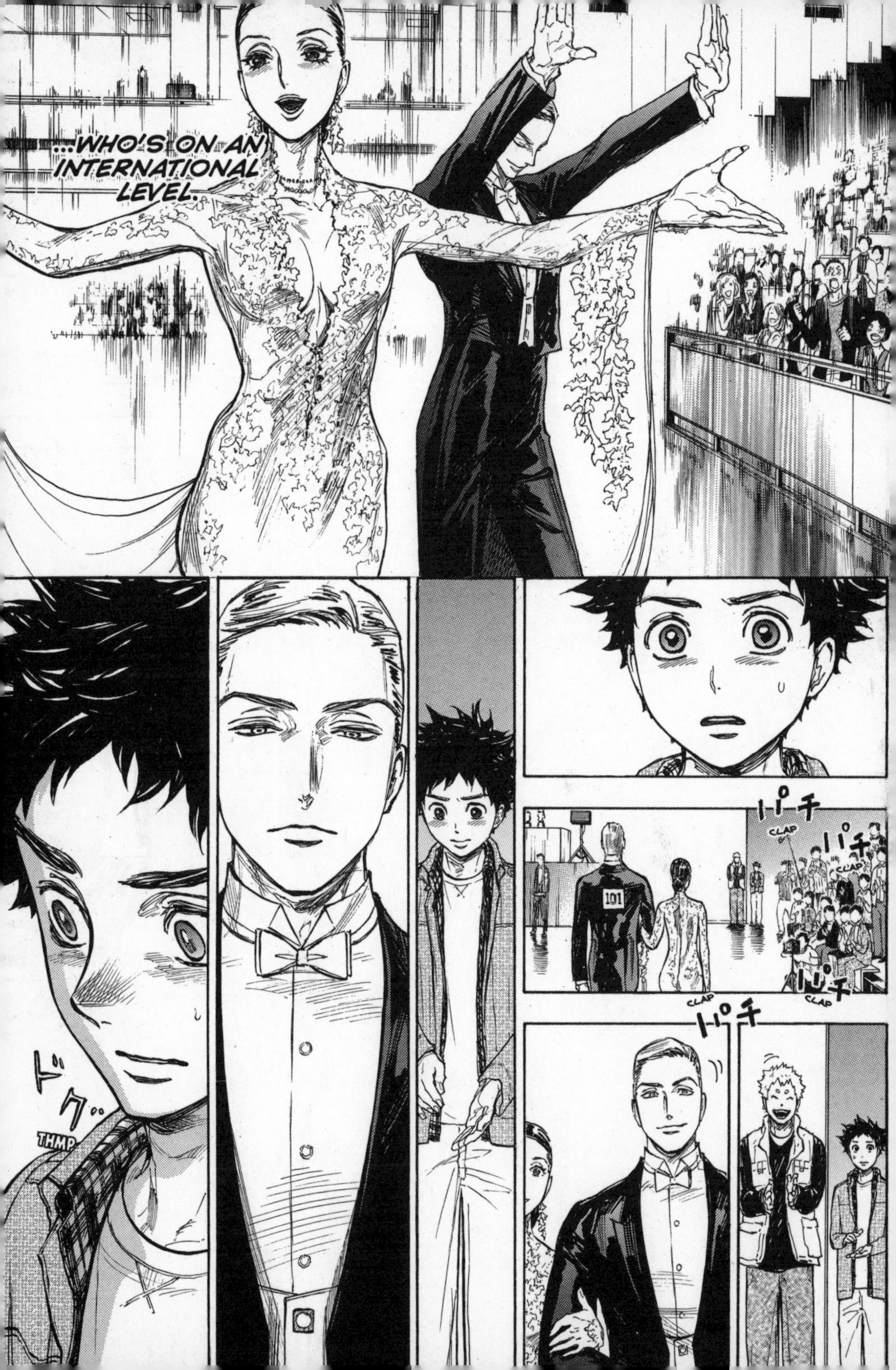

...WHO'S ON AN INTERNATIONAL LEVEL.
パチ
CLAP
パチ
CLAP
パチ
CLAP
パチ
CLAP
ドク
THMP

GET A GOOD LOOK.

MR. SENGOKU, COULD WE GET A QUICK COMMENT FROM YOU?

CAN I GET A PICTURE?

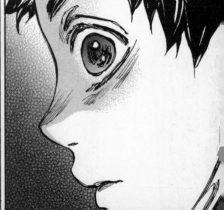

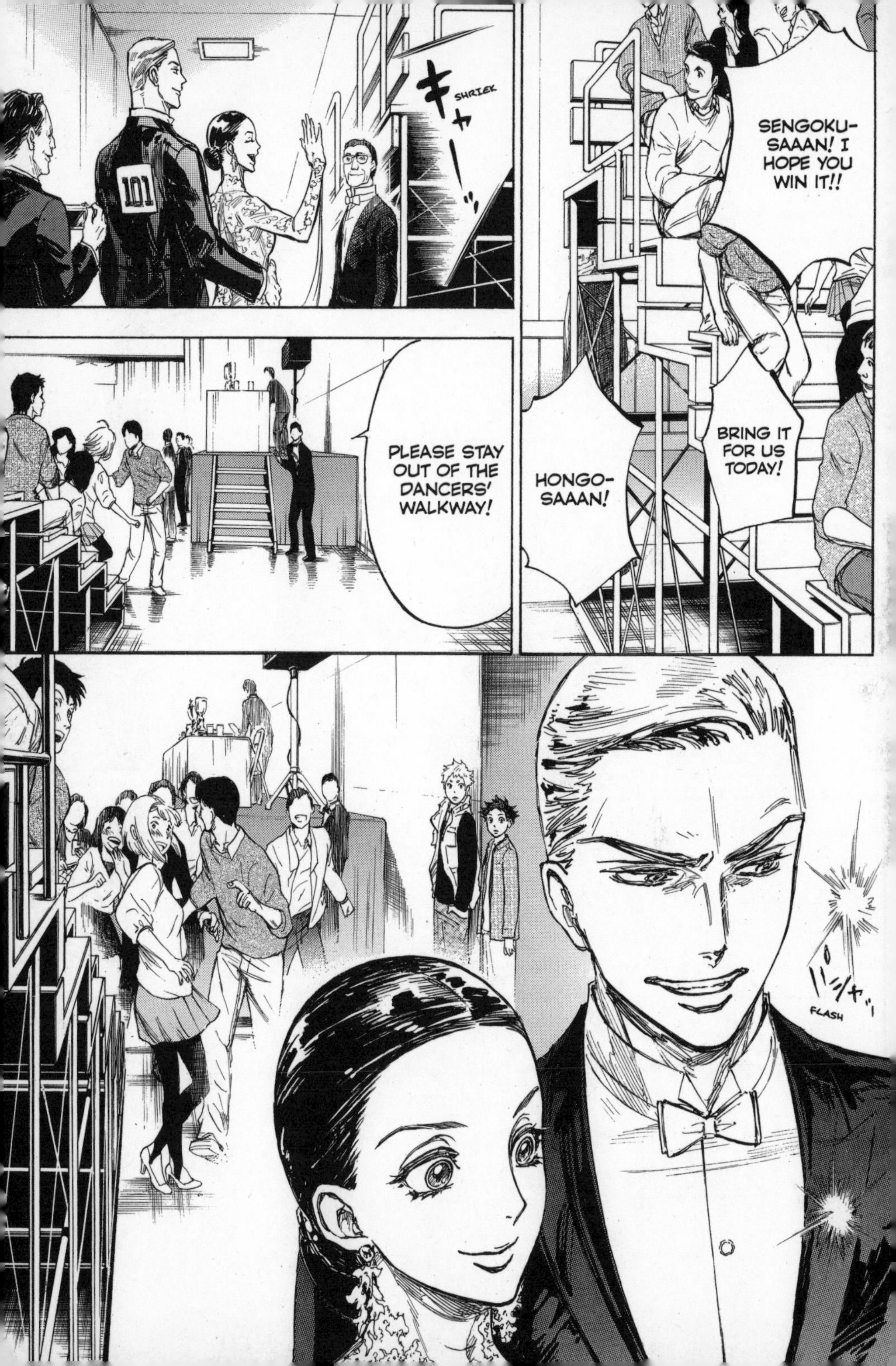
SENGOKU-SAAAN! I HOPE YOU WIN IT!!
BRING IT FOR US TODAY!
HONGO-SAAAN!
SHRIEK
PLEASE STAY OUT OF THE DANCERS' WALKWAY!
FLASH

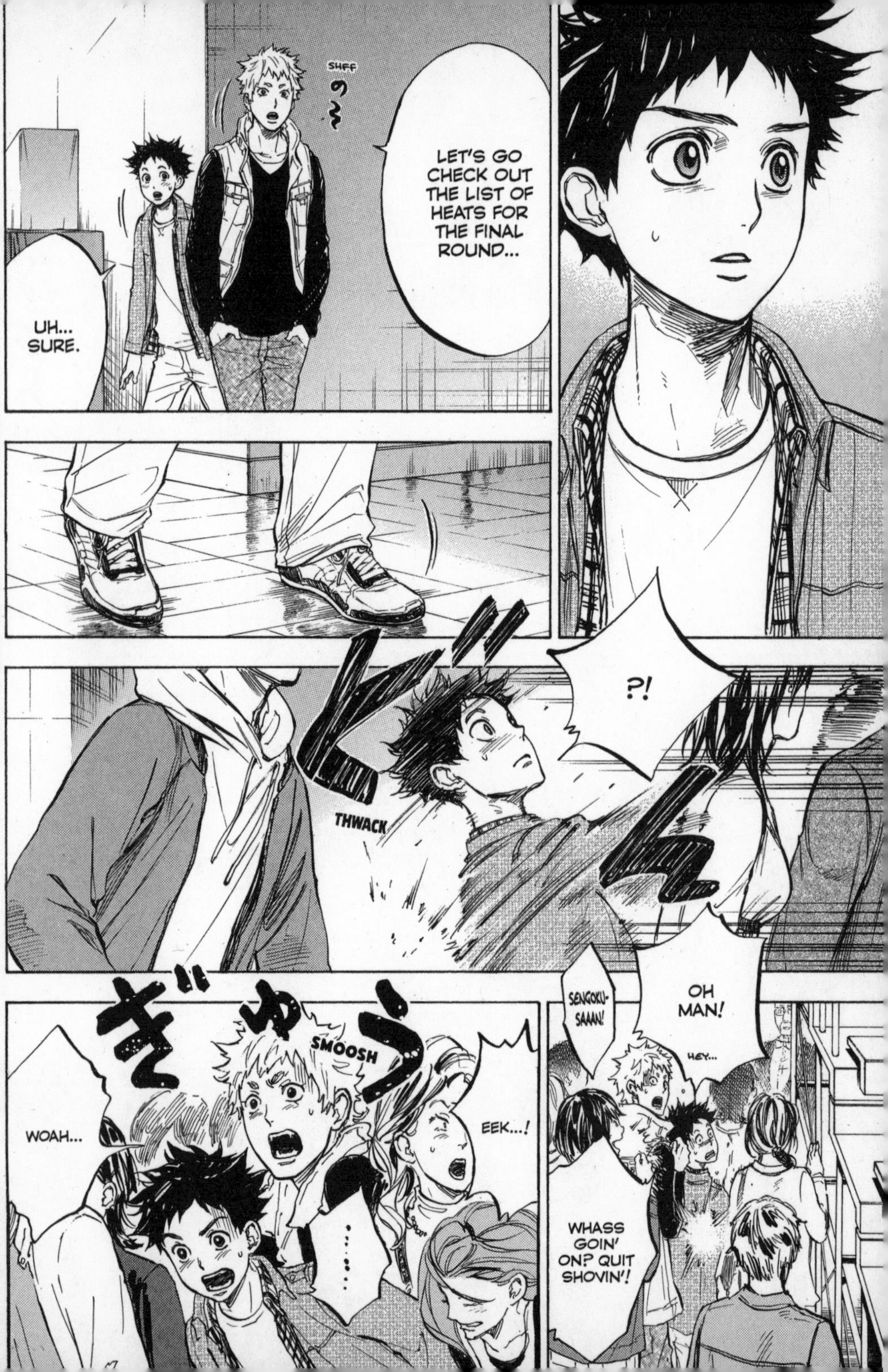

SHFF
LET'S GO CHECK OUT THE LIST OF HEATS FOR THE FINAL ROUND...
UH... SURE.
?!
THWACK
OH MAN!
SENGOKU-SAAAN!
HEY...
WHASS GOIN' ON? QUIT SHOVIN'!
SMOOSH
EEK...!
WOAH...
....

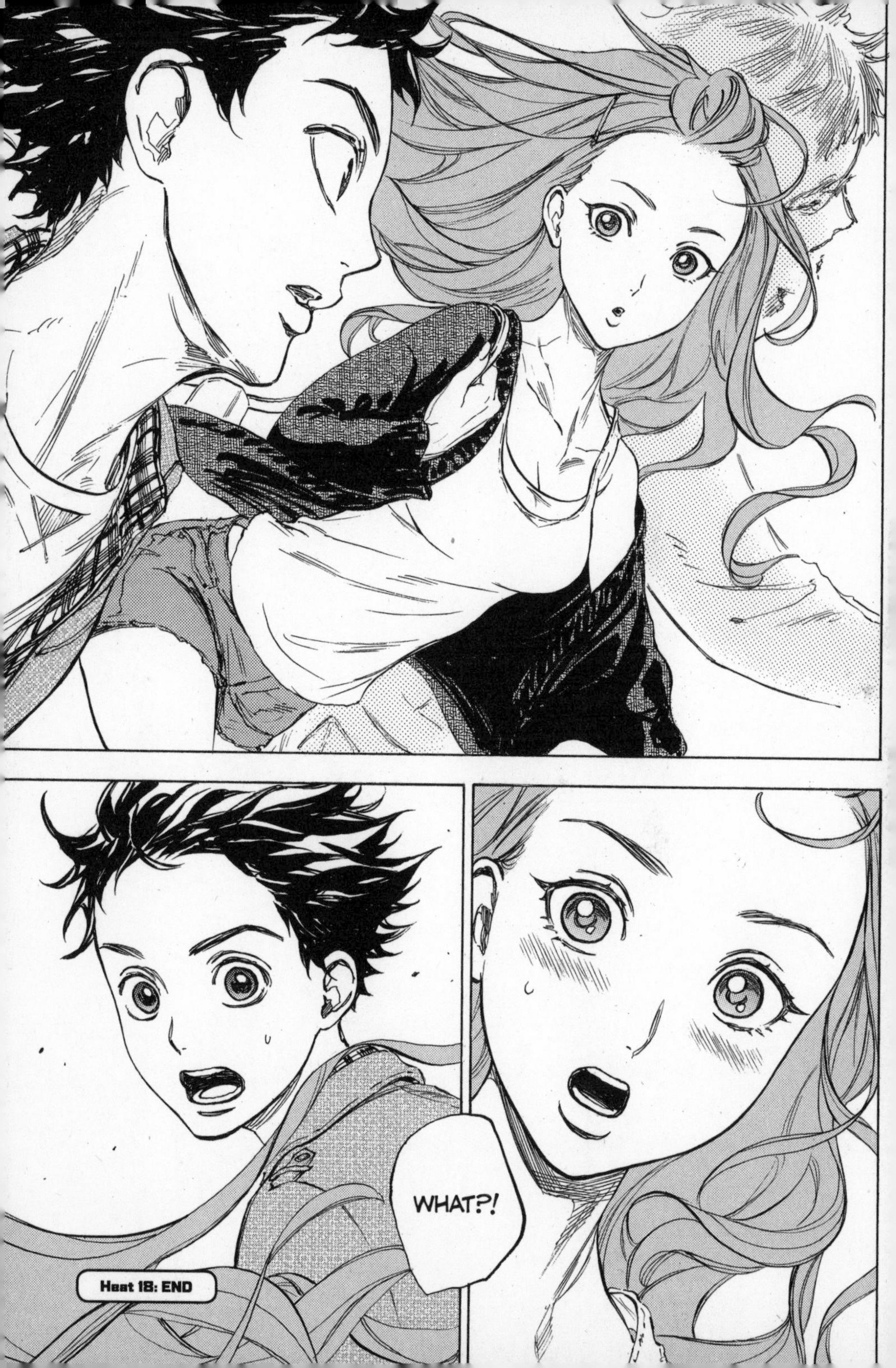
WHAT?!
Heat 18: END

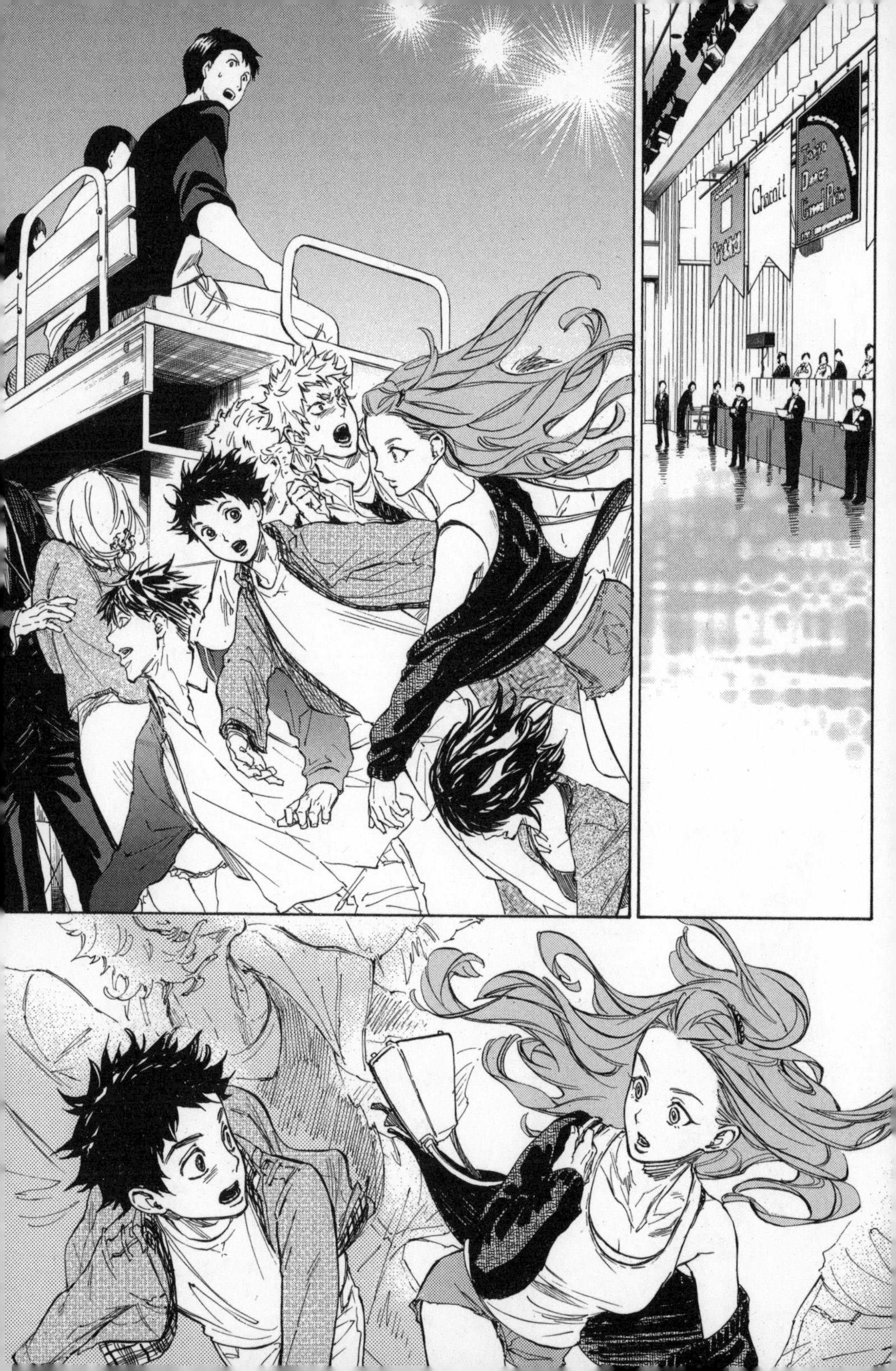
Tokyo Dance Grand Prix
Chacott

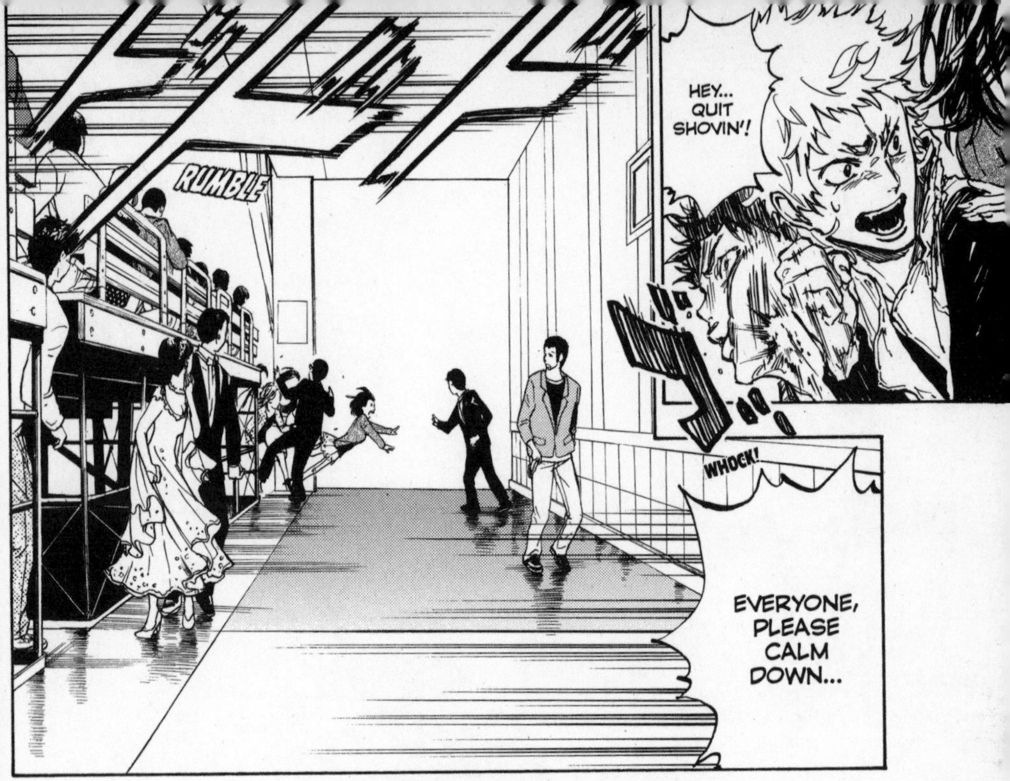
HEY... QUIT SHOVIN'!
WHOCK!
RUMBLE
EVERYONE, PLEASE CALM DOWN...

Heat 19
Lessons

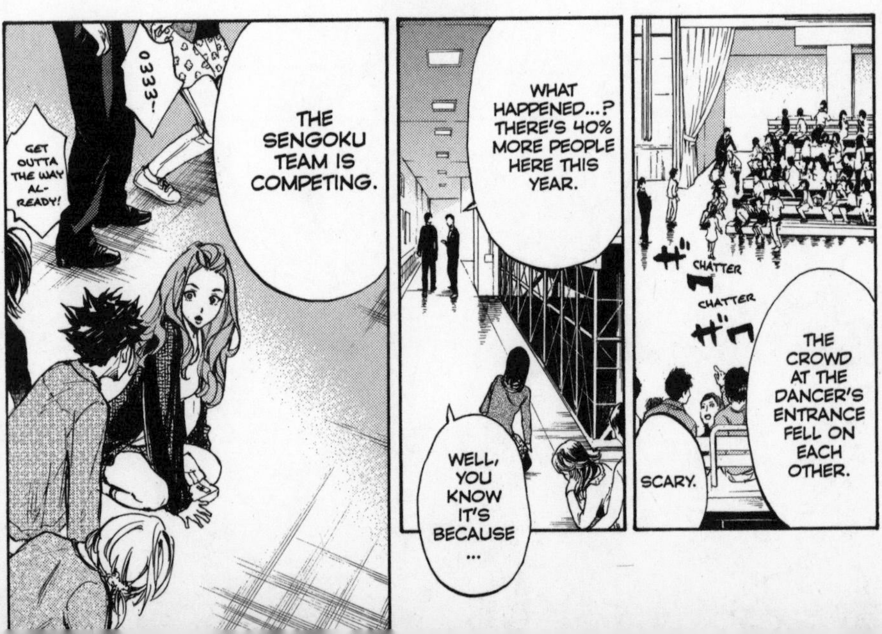
CHATTER
CHATTER
THE CROWD AT THE DANCER'S ENTRANCE FELL ON EACH OTHER.
SCARY.
WHAT HAPPENED...? THERE'S 40% MORE PEOPLE HERE THIS YEAR.
WELL, YOU KNOW IT'S BECAUSE ...
THE SENGOKU TEAM IS COMPETING.
GET OUTTA THE WAY AL-READY!

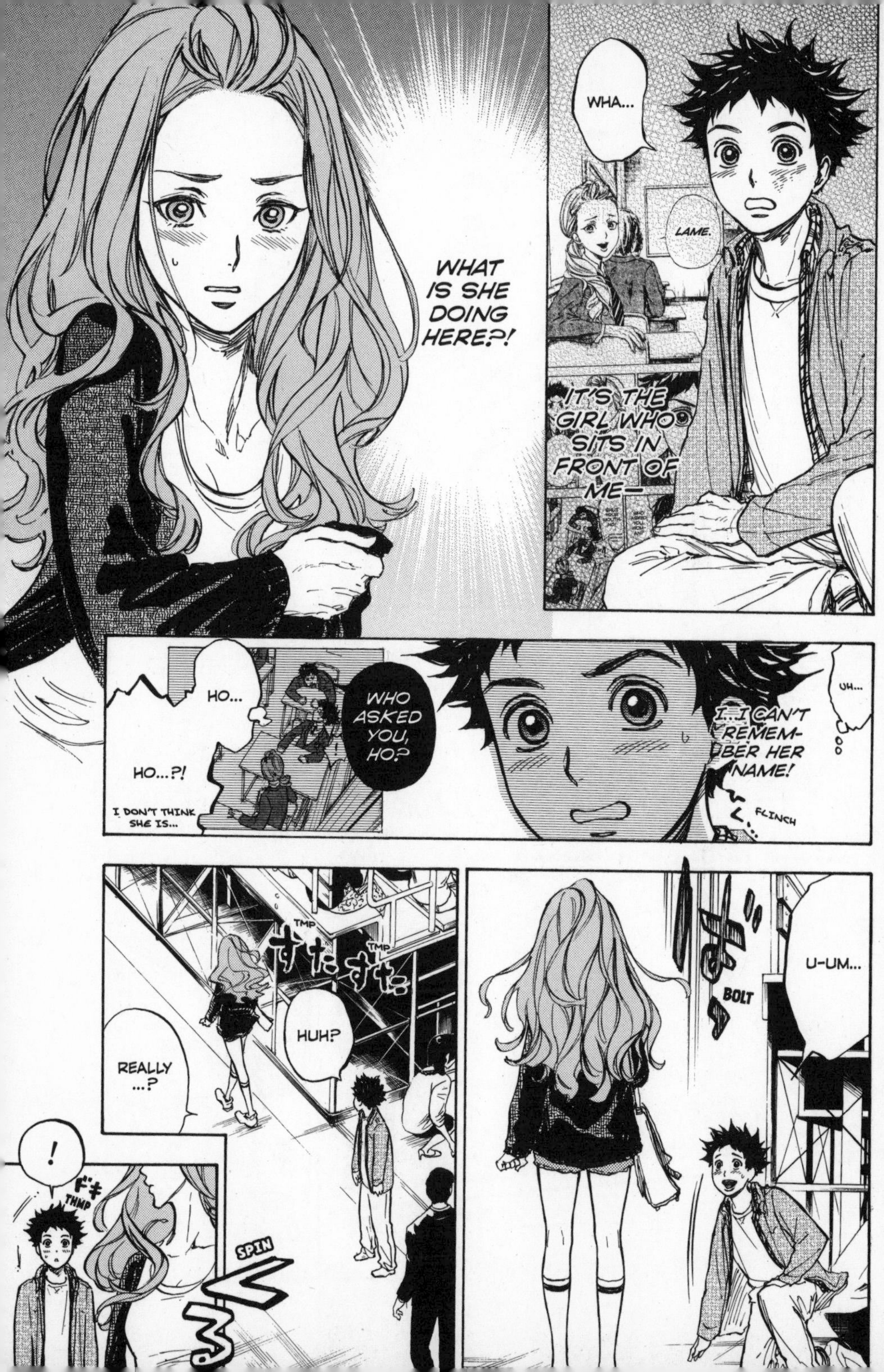
WHA...
LAME.
IT'S THE GIRL WHO SITS IN FRONT OF ME—
WHAT IS SHE DOING HERE?!
UH...
I...I CAN'T REMEMBER HER NAME!
FLINCH
WHO ASKED YOU, HO?
HO...
HO...?!
I DON'T THINK SHE IS...
U-UM...
BOLT
TMP
TMP
HUH?
REALLY ...?
!
THMP
SPIN

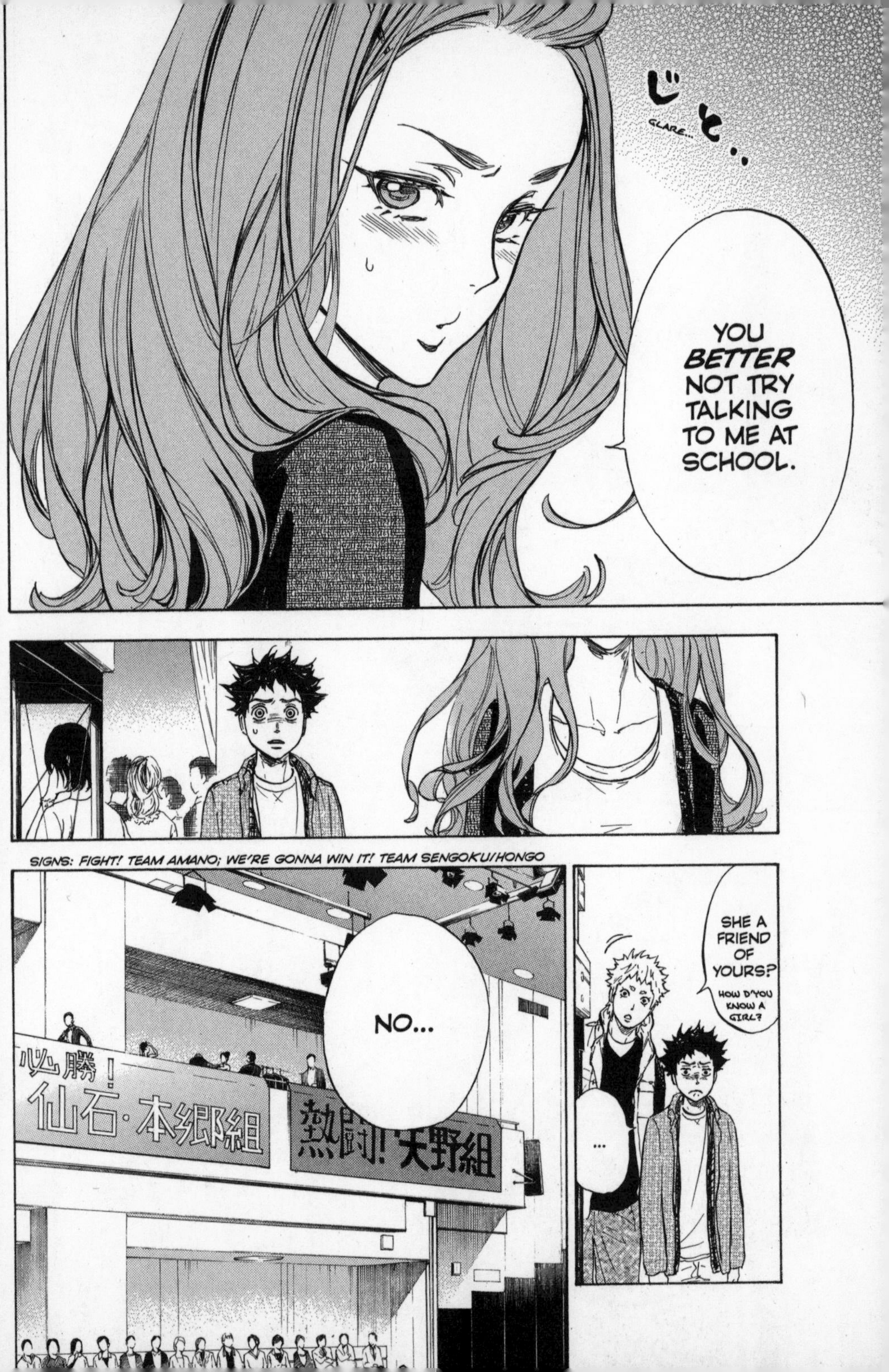
じと…
GLARE...
YOU BETTER NOT TRY TALKING TO ME AT SCHOOL.
SHE A FRIEND OF YOURS?
HOW D'YOU KNOW A GIRL?
...
SIGNS: FIGHT! TEAM AMANO; WE'RE GONNA WIN IT! TEAM SENGOKU/HONGO
必勝！仙石・本郷組
熱闘！天野組
NO...

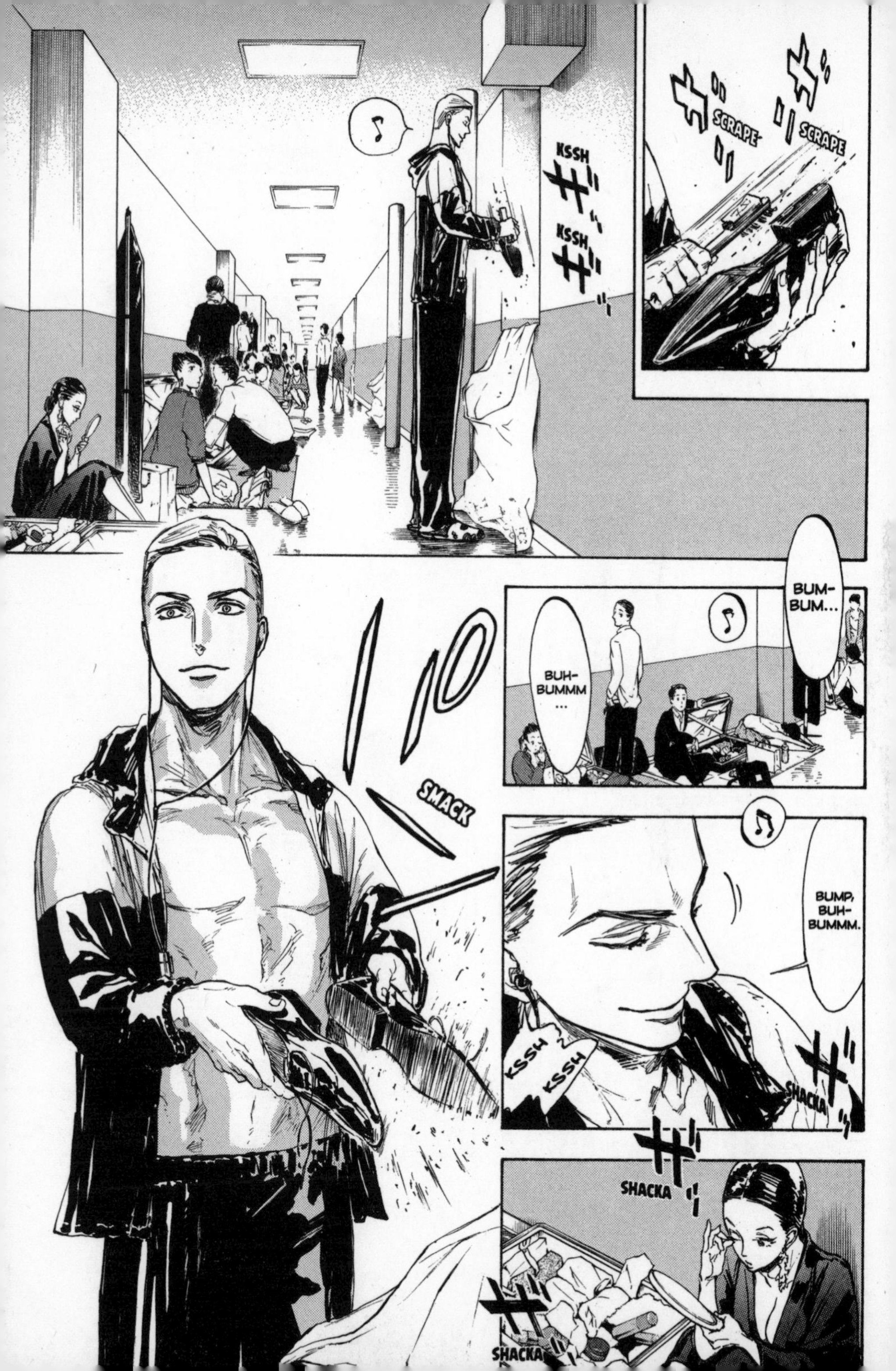
SCRAPE
SCRAPE
♪
KSSH
KSSH
BUM-BUM...
♪
BUH-BUMMM...
♫
BUMP, BUH-BUMMM.
SHACKA
KSSH
KSSH
SHACKA
SHACKA
SMACK

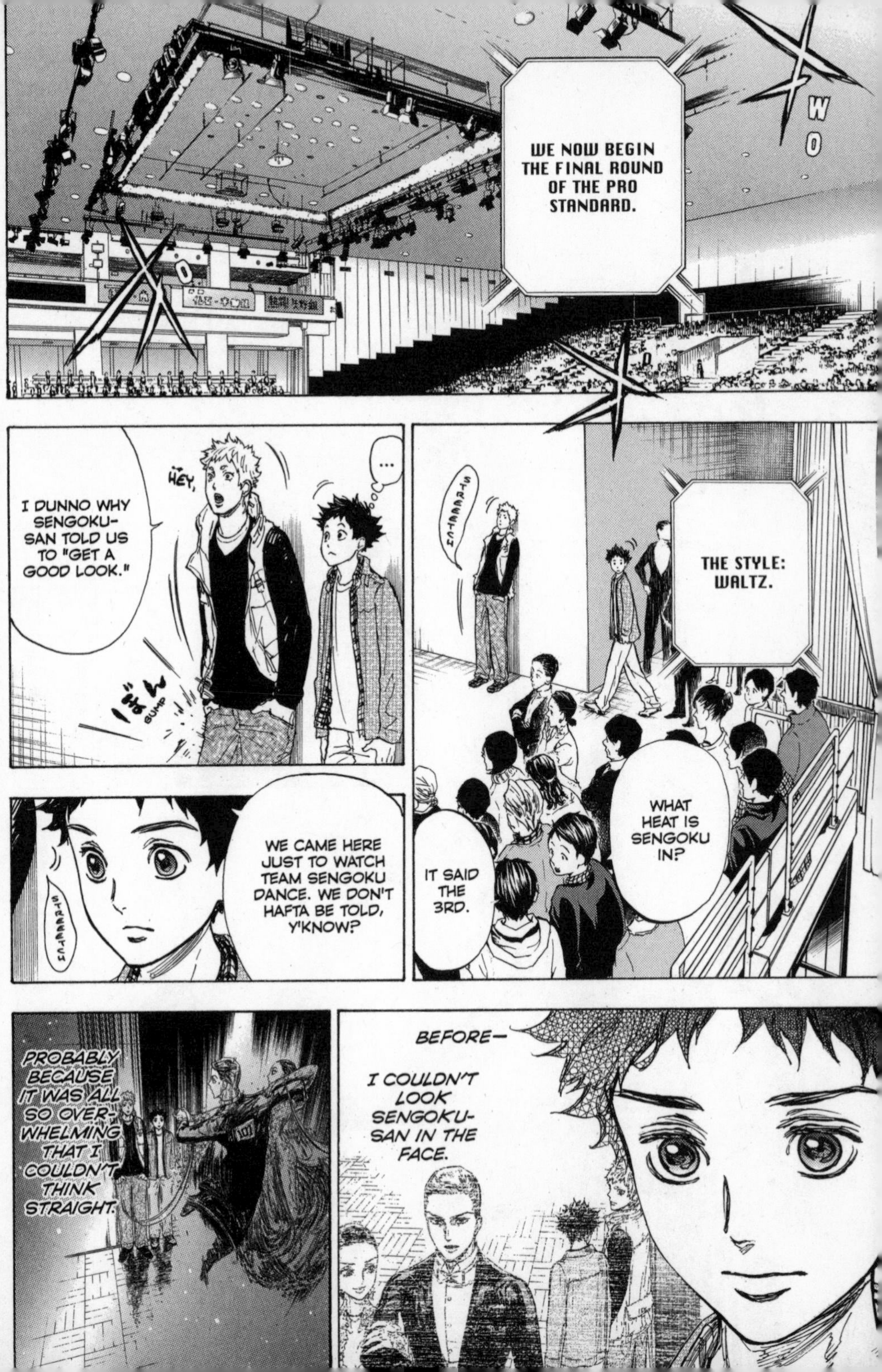
W
O
WE NOW BEGIN THE FINAL ROUND OF THE PRO STANDARD.
O
D
THE STYLE: WALTZ.
STREEETCH
...
HEY,
I DUNNO WHY SENGOKU-SAN TOLD US TO "GET A GOOD LOOK."
BUMP
WHAT HEAT IS SENGOKU IN?
IT SAID THE 3RD.
WE CAME HERE JUST TO WATCH TEAM SENGOKU DANCE. WE DON'T HAFTA BE TOLD, Y'KNOW?
STREEETCH
BEFORE—
I COULDN'T LOOK SENGOKU-SAN IN THE FACE.
PROBABLY BECAUSE IT WAS ALL SO OVER-WHELMING THAT I COULDN'T THINK STRAIGHT.

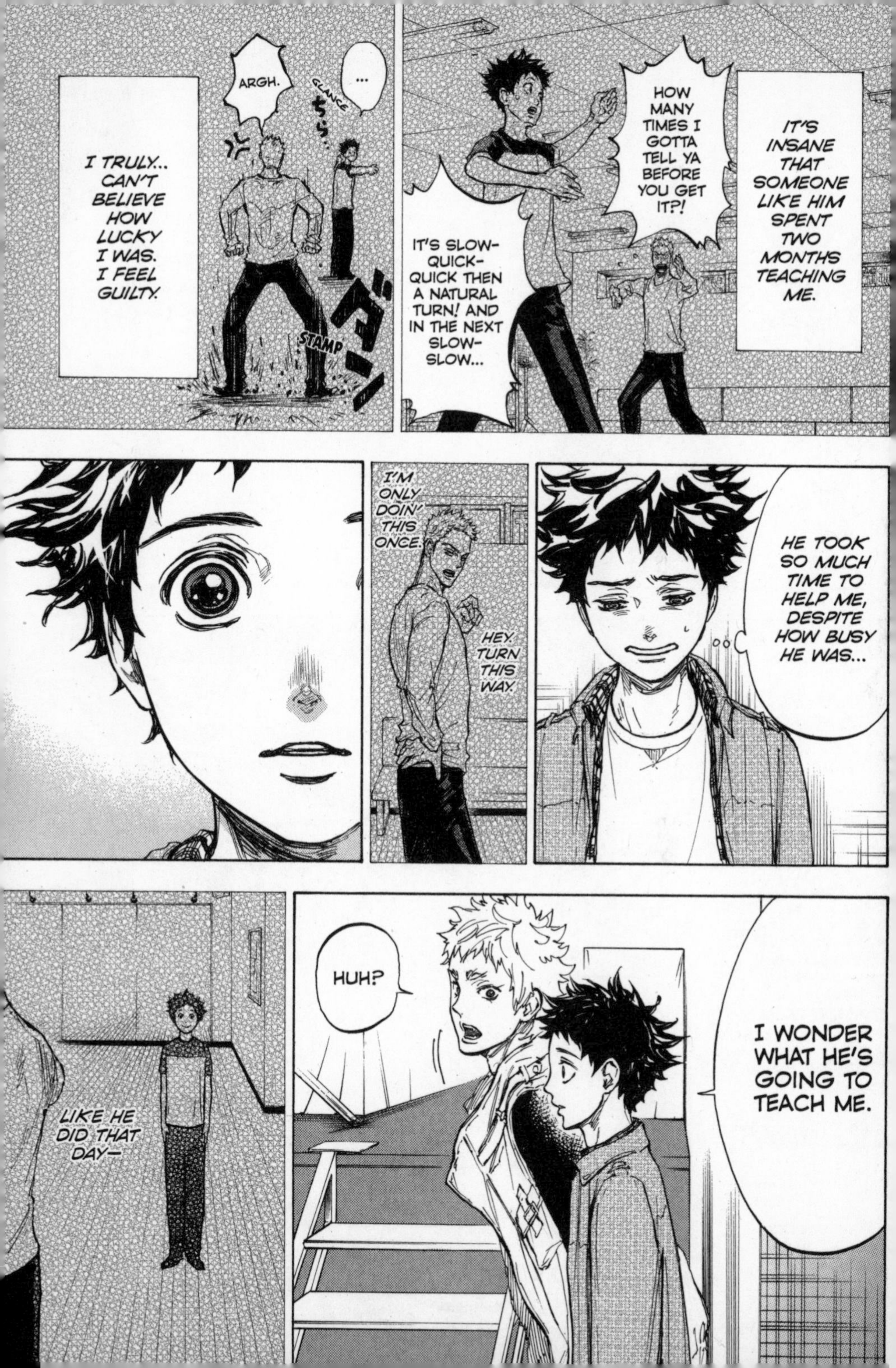
IT'S INSANE THAT SOMEONE LIKE HIM SPENT TWO MONTHS TEACHING ME.
HOW MANY TIMES I GOTTA TELL YA BEFORE YOU GET IT?!
IT'S SLOW-QUICK-QUICK THEN A NATURAL TURN! AND IN THE NEXT SLOW-SLOW...
...
GLANCE
ちら
ARGH.
STAMP
I TRULY... CAN'T BELIEVE HOW LUCKY I WAS. I FEEL GUILTY.
HE TOOK SO MUCH TIME TO HELP ME, DESPITE HOW BUSY HE WAS...
I'M ONLY DOIN' THIS ONCE.
HEY. TURN THIS WAY.
I WONDER WHAT HE'S GOING TO TEACH ME.
HUH?
LIKE HE DID THAT DAY—

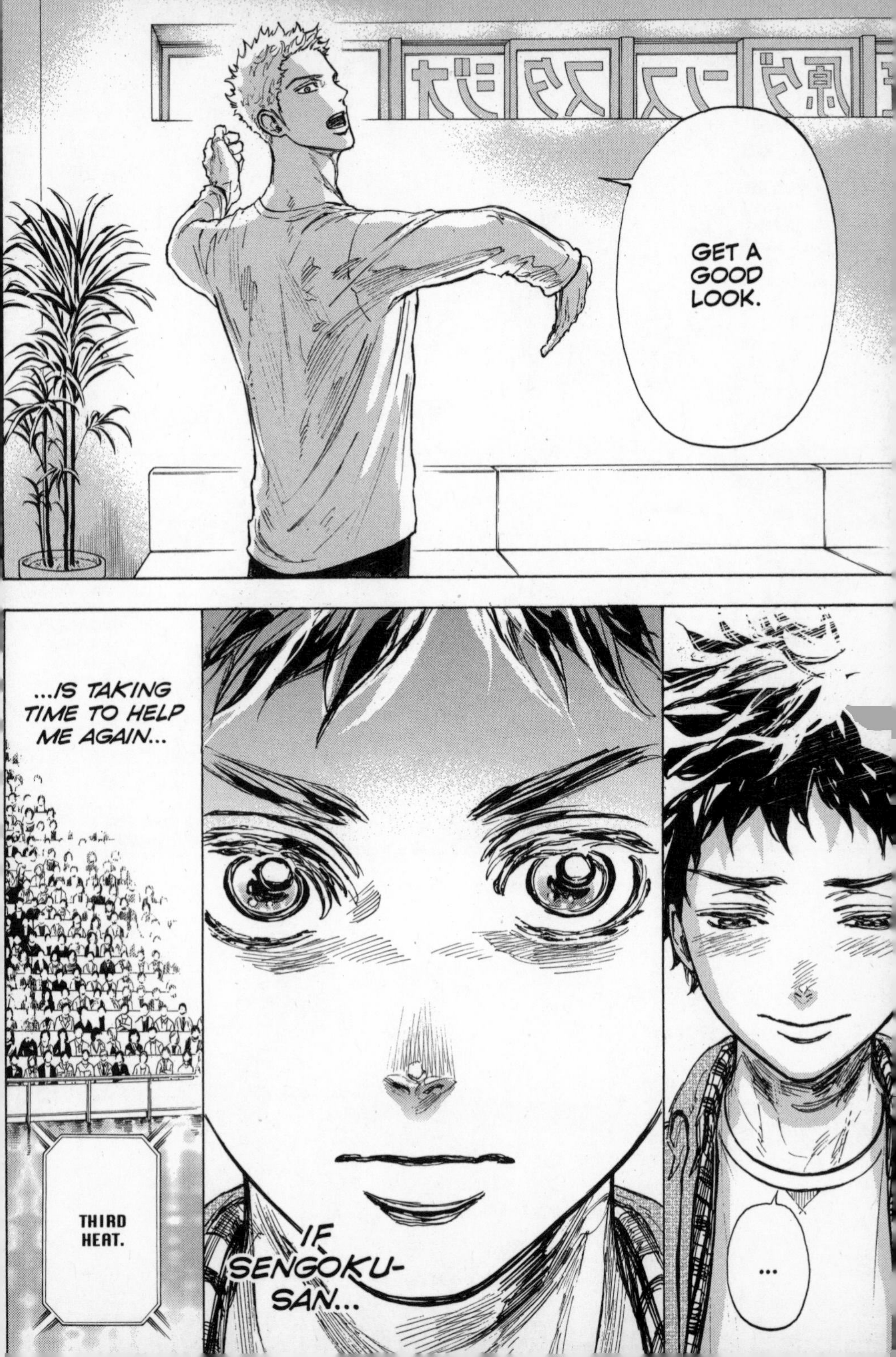
GET A GOOD LOOK.
...
IF SENGOKU-SAN...
...IS TAKING TIME TO HELP ME AGAIN...
THIRD HEAT.

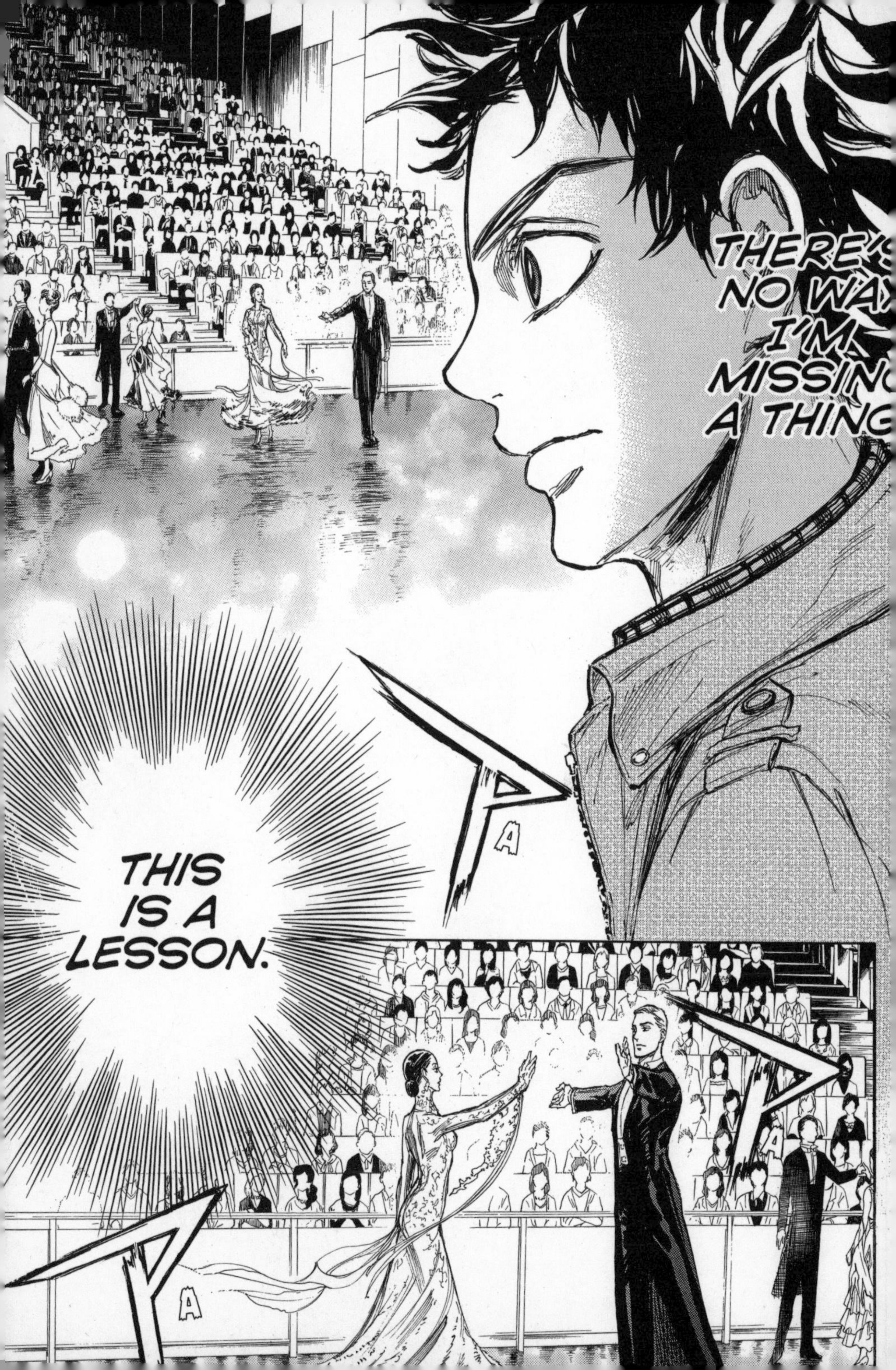
THERE'S NO WAY I'M MISSING A THING
THIS IS A LESSON.

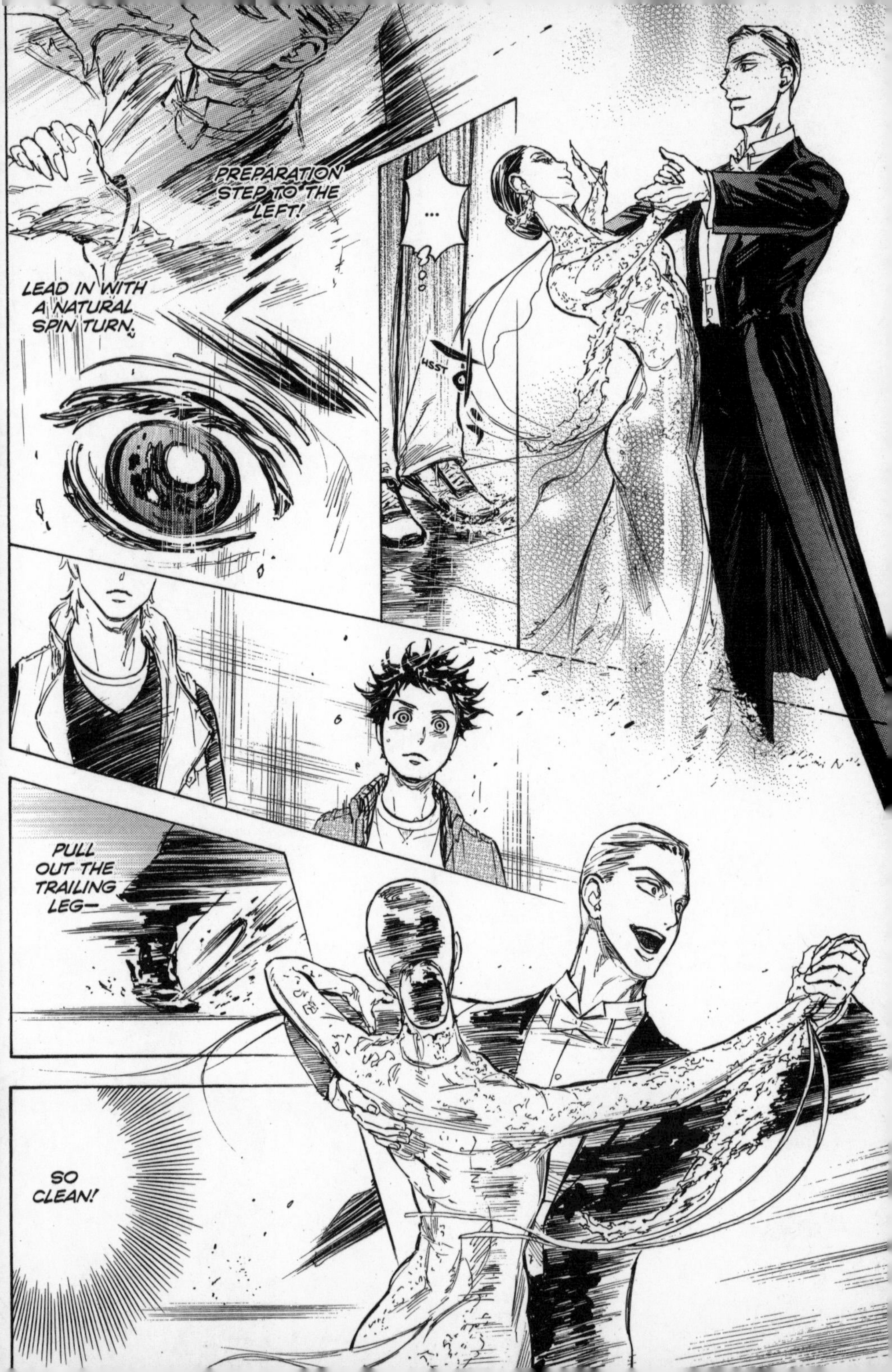
...
HSST
PREPARATION STEP TO THE LEFT!
LEAD IN WITH A NATURAL SPIN TURN.
PULL OUT THE TRAILING LEG—
SO CLEAN!

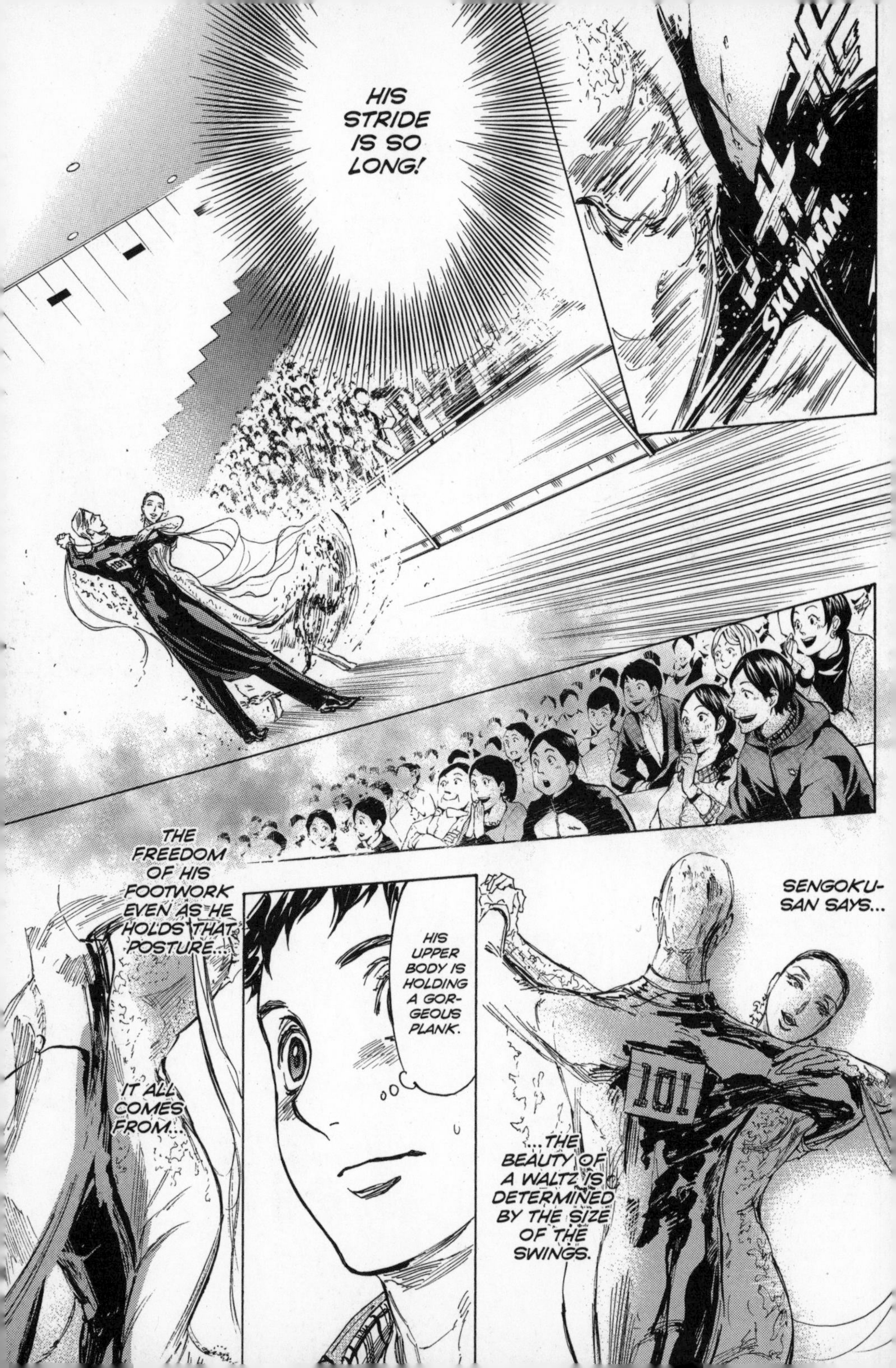
SKIMMM
HIS STRIDE IS SO LONG!
SENGOKU-SAN SAYS...
...THE BEAUTY OF A WALTZ IS DETERMINED BY THE SIZE OF THE SWINGS.
HIS UPPER BODY IS HOLDING A GORGEOUS PLANK.
THE FREEDOM OF HIS FOOTWORK EVEN AS HE HOLDS THAT POSTURE...
IT ALL COMES FROM...

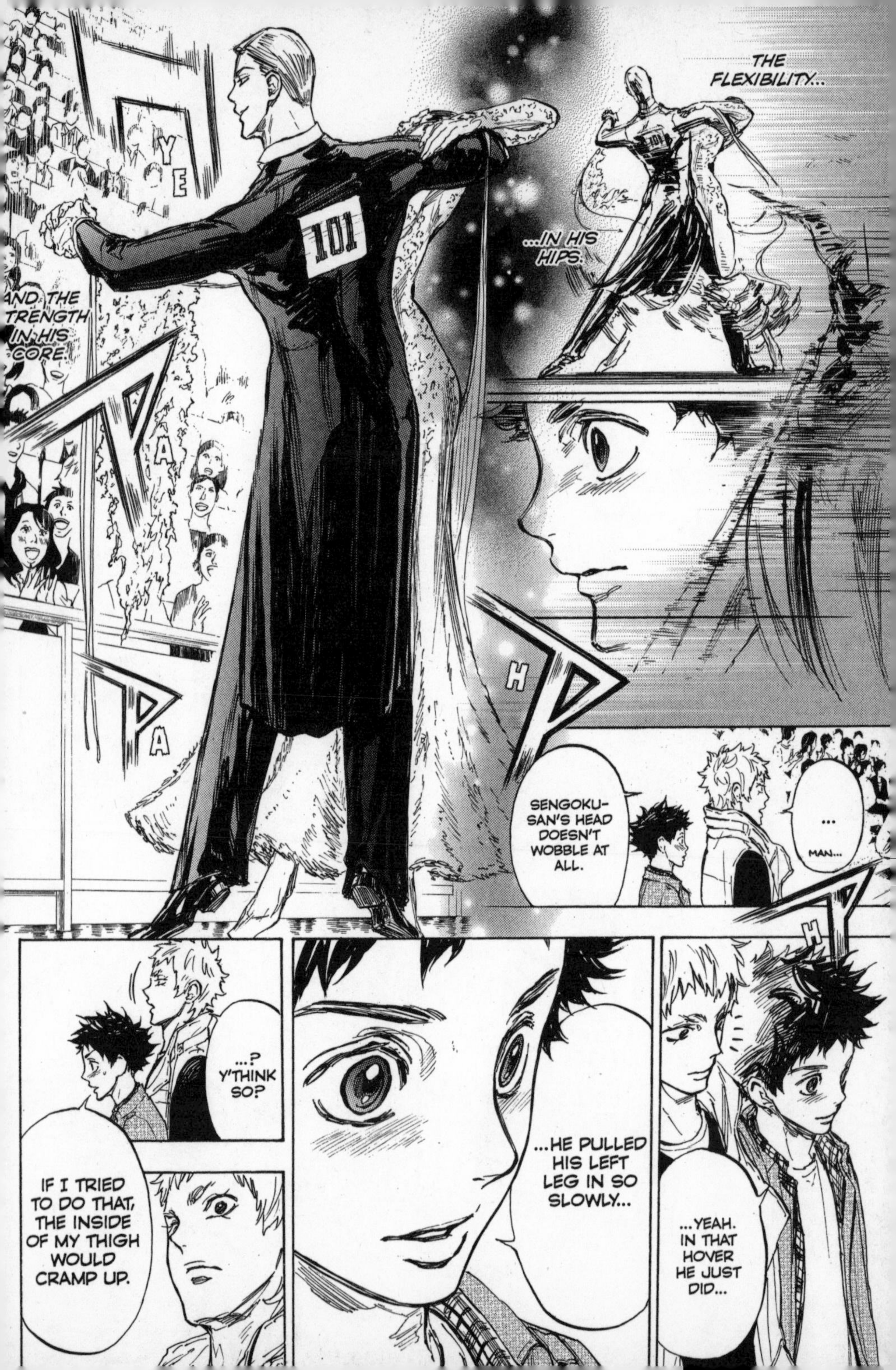
THE FLEXIBILITY...
...IN HIS HIPS.
H
...
MAN...
SENGOKU-SAN'S HEAD DOESN'T WOBBLE AT ALL.
HY
YE
AND THE TRENGTH IN HIS CORE.
PA
PA
...YEAH. IN THAT HOVER HE JUST DID...
...HE PULLED HIS LEFT LEG IN SO SLOWLY...
...? Y'THINK SO?
IF I TRIED TO DO THAT, THE INSIDE OF MY THIGH WOULD CRAMP UP.

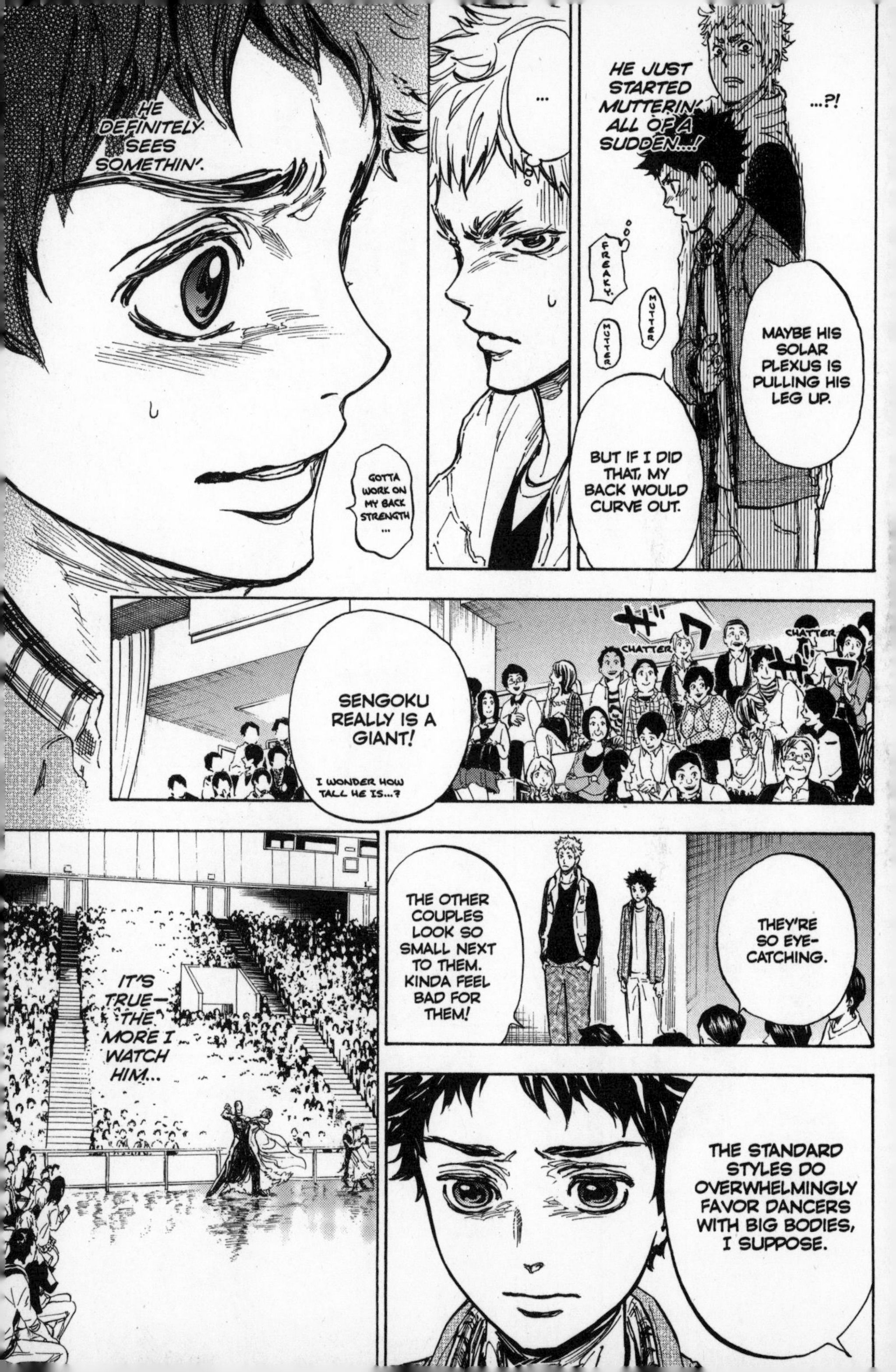
...?!
HE JUST STARTED MUTTERIN' ALL OF A SUDDEN...!
MAYBE HIS SOLAR PLEXUS IS PULLING HIS LEG UP.
MUTTER
MUTTER
FREAKY.
BUT IF I DID THAT, MY BACK WOULD CURVE OUT.
...
GOTTA WORK ON MY BACK STRENGTH...
HE DEFINITELY SEES SOMETHIN'.
CHATTER
CHATTER
SENGOKU REALLY IS A GIANT!
I WONDER HOW TALL HE IS...?
THEY'RE SO EYE-CATCHING.
THE OTHER COUPLES LOOK SO SMALL NEXT TO THEM. KINDA FEEL BAD FOR THEM!
THE STANDARD STYLES DO OVERWHELMINGLY FAVOR DANCERS WITH BIG BODIES, I SUPPOSE.
IT'S TRUE—THE MORE I WATCH HIM...

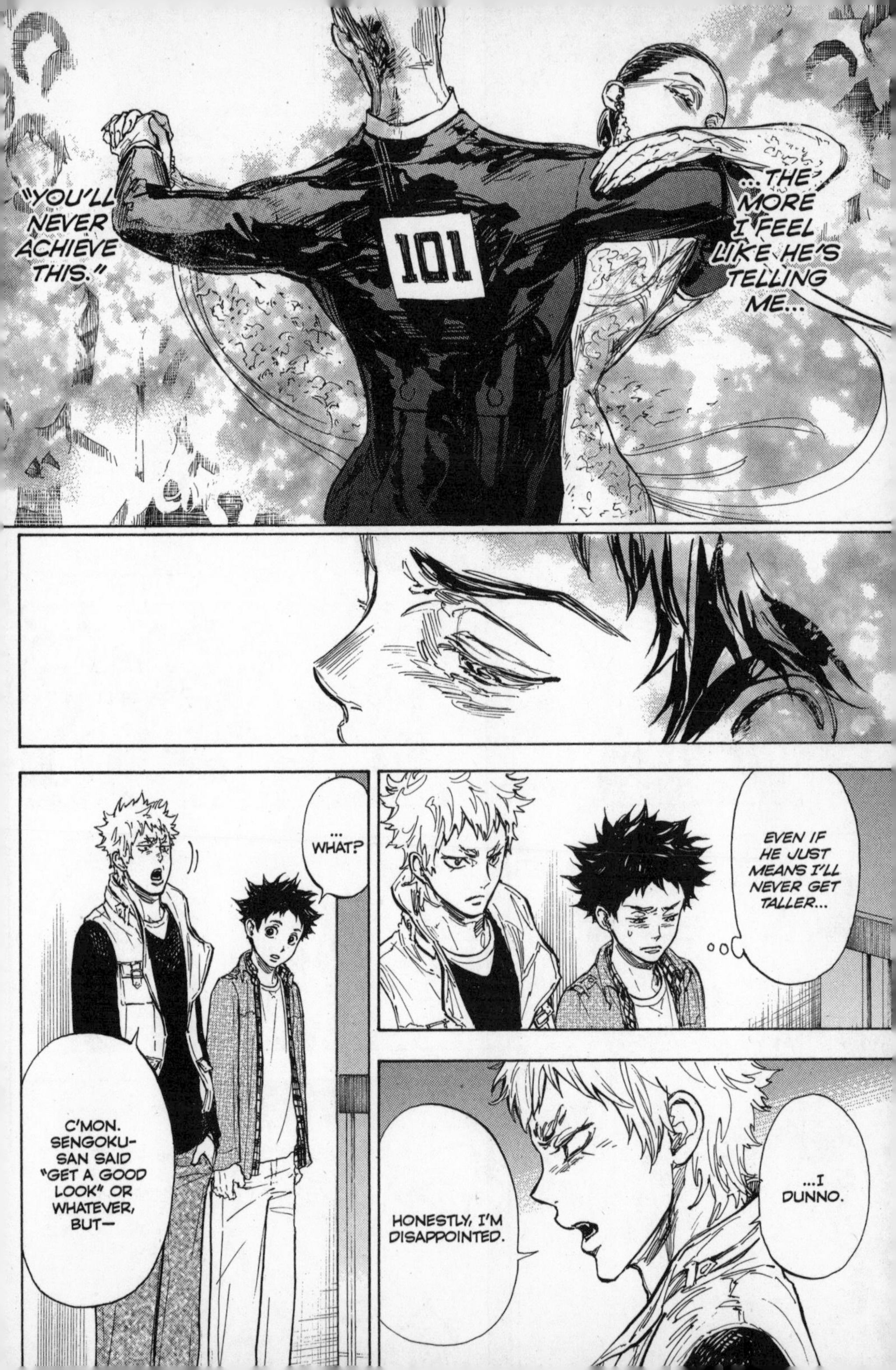
...THE MORE I FEEL LIKE HE'S TELLING ME...
"YOU'LL NEVER ACHIEVE THIS."
101
EVEN IF HE JUST MEANS I'LL NEVER GET TALLER...
...I DUNNO.
HONESTLY, I'M DISAPPOINTED.
...WHAT?
C'MON. SENGOKU-SAN SAID "GET A GOOD LOOK" OR WHATEVER, BUT—

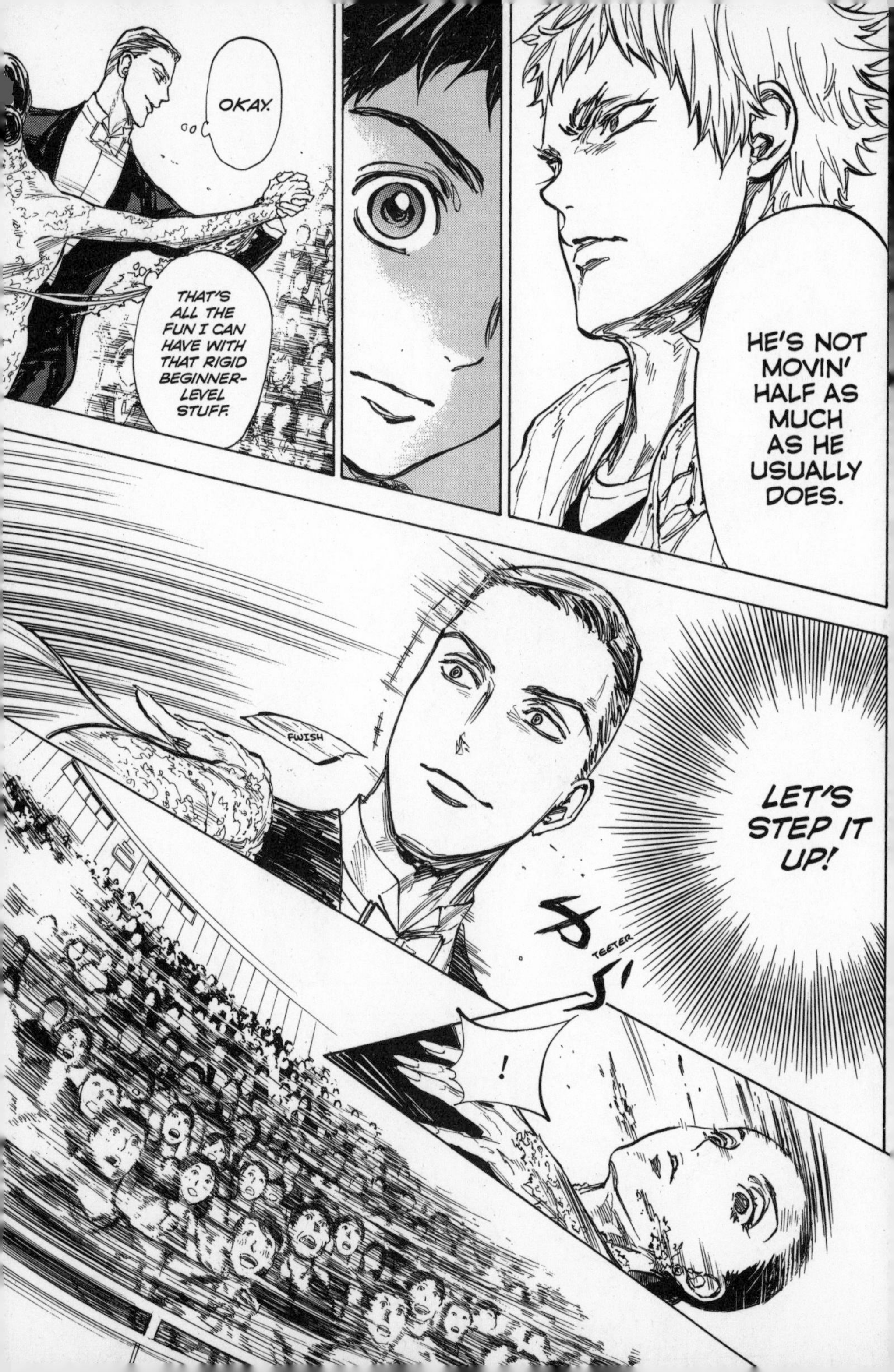
HE'S NOT MOVIN' HALF AS MUCH AS HE USUALLY DOES.
OKAY.
THAT'S ALL THE FUN I CAN HAVE WITH THAT RIGID BEGINNER-LEVEL STUFF.
LET'S STEP IT UP!
FWISH
TEETER
!

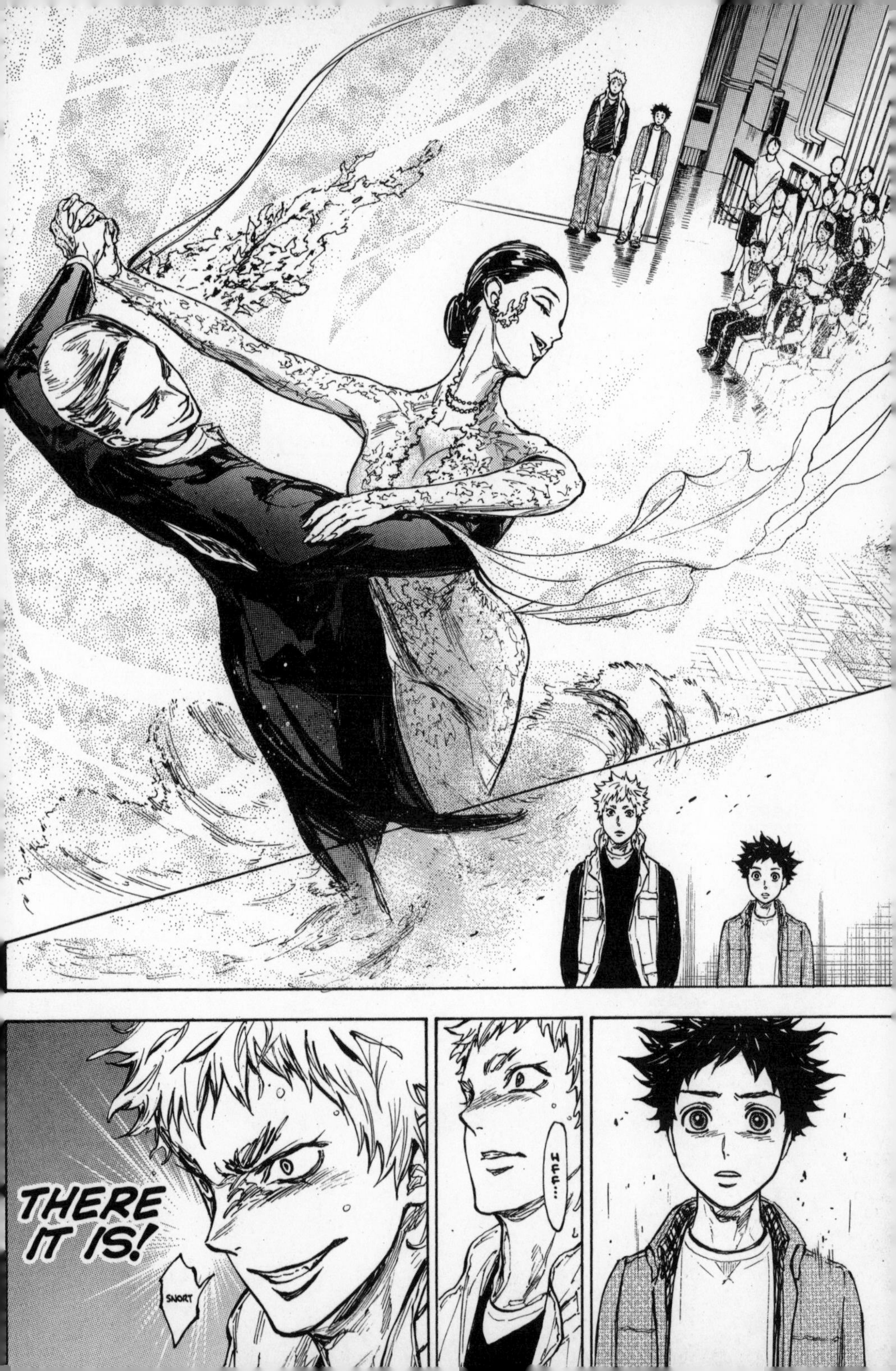
HFF...
THERE IT IS!
SNORT

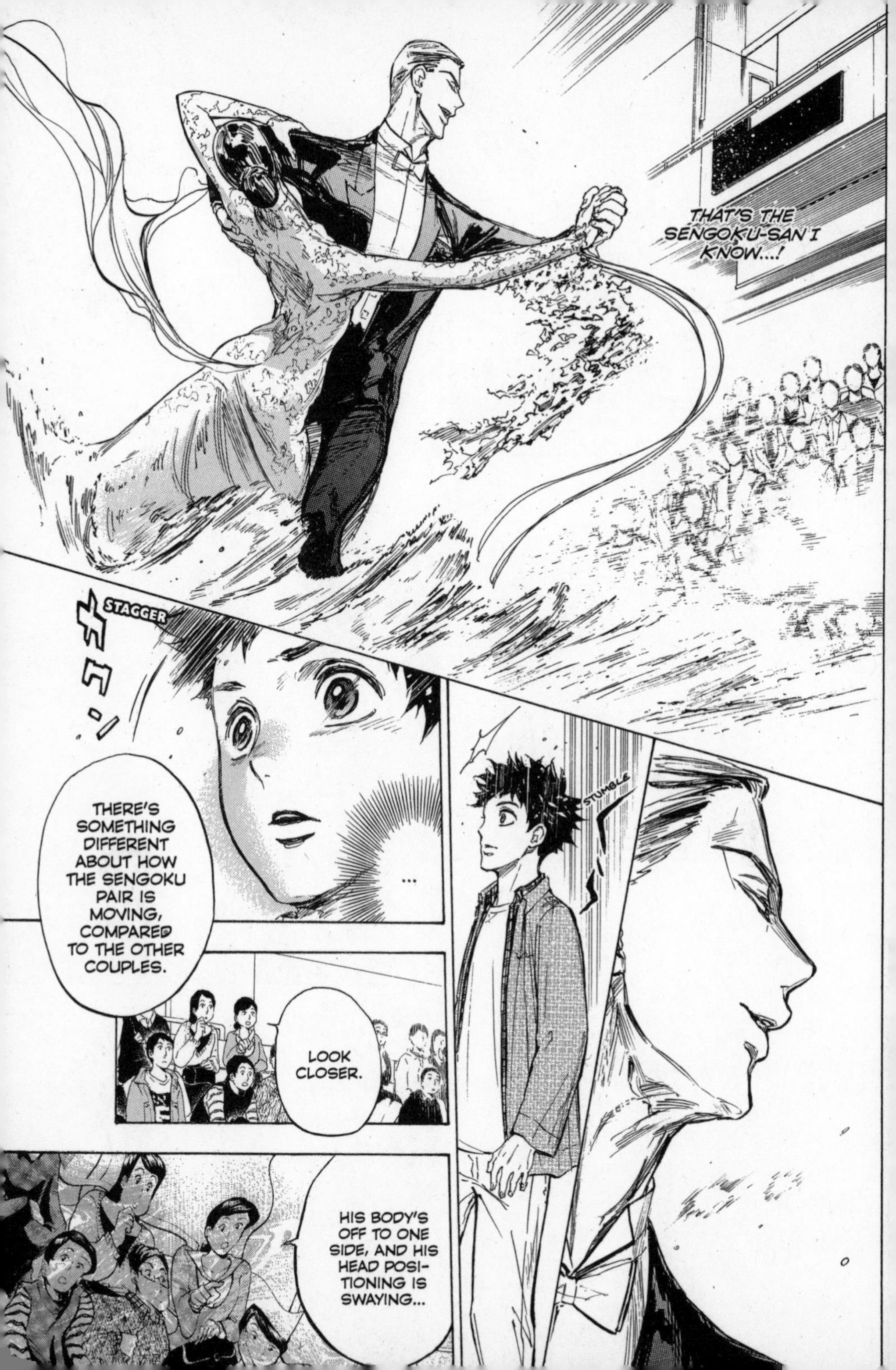
THAT'S THE SENGOKU-SAN I KNOW...!
STUMBLE
STAGGER
...
THERE'S SOMETHING DIFFERENT ABOUT HOW THE SENGOKU PAIR IS MOVING, COMPARED TO THE OTHER COUPLES.
LOOK CLOSER.
HIS BODY'S OFF TO ONE SIDE, AND HIS HEAD POSI- TIONING IS SWAYING...

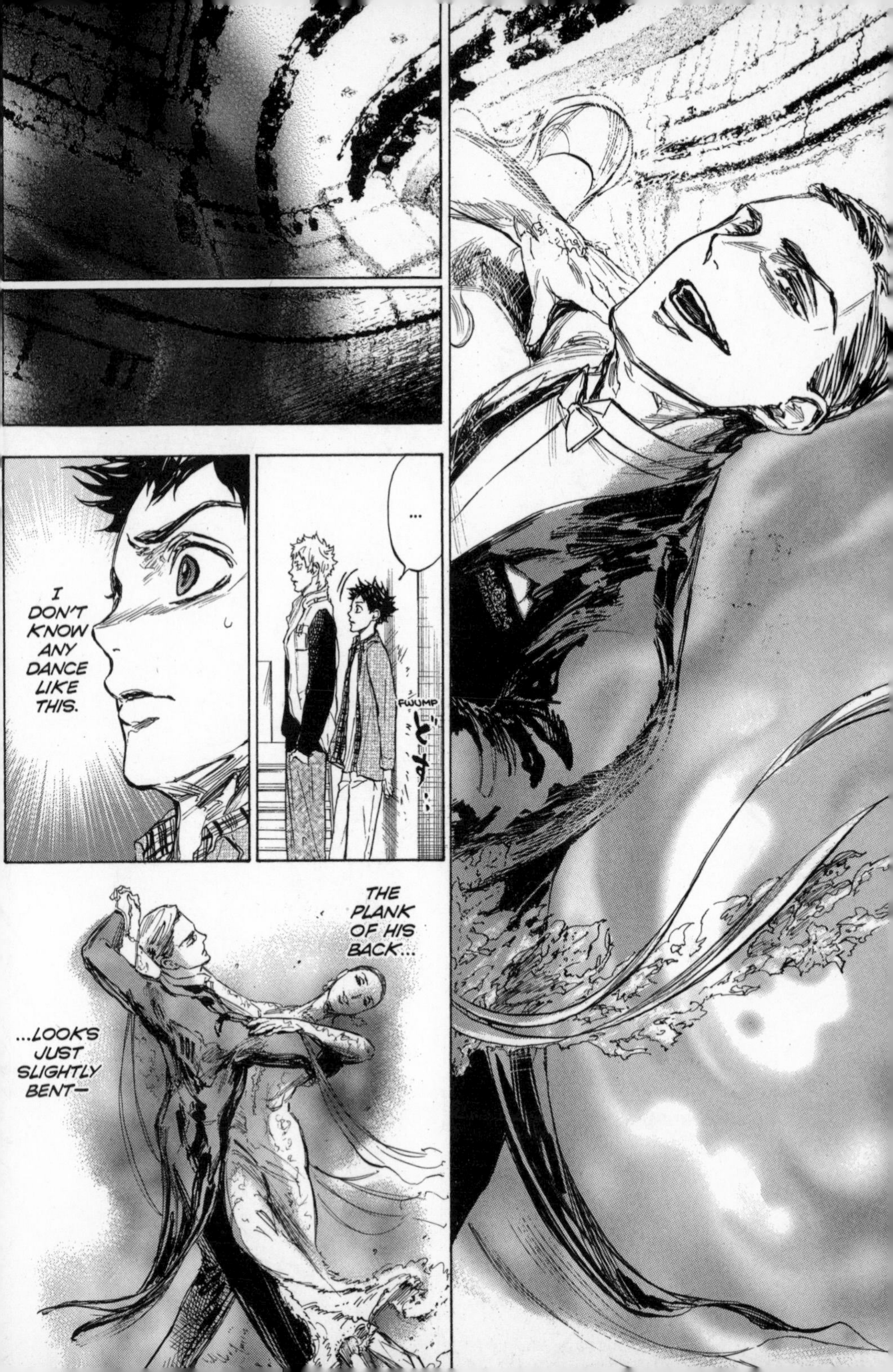
...
FWUMP
どす
I DON'T KNOW ANY DANCE LIKE THIS.
THE PLANK OF HIS BACK...
...LOOKS JUST SLIGHTLY BENT—

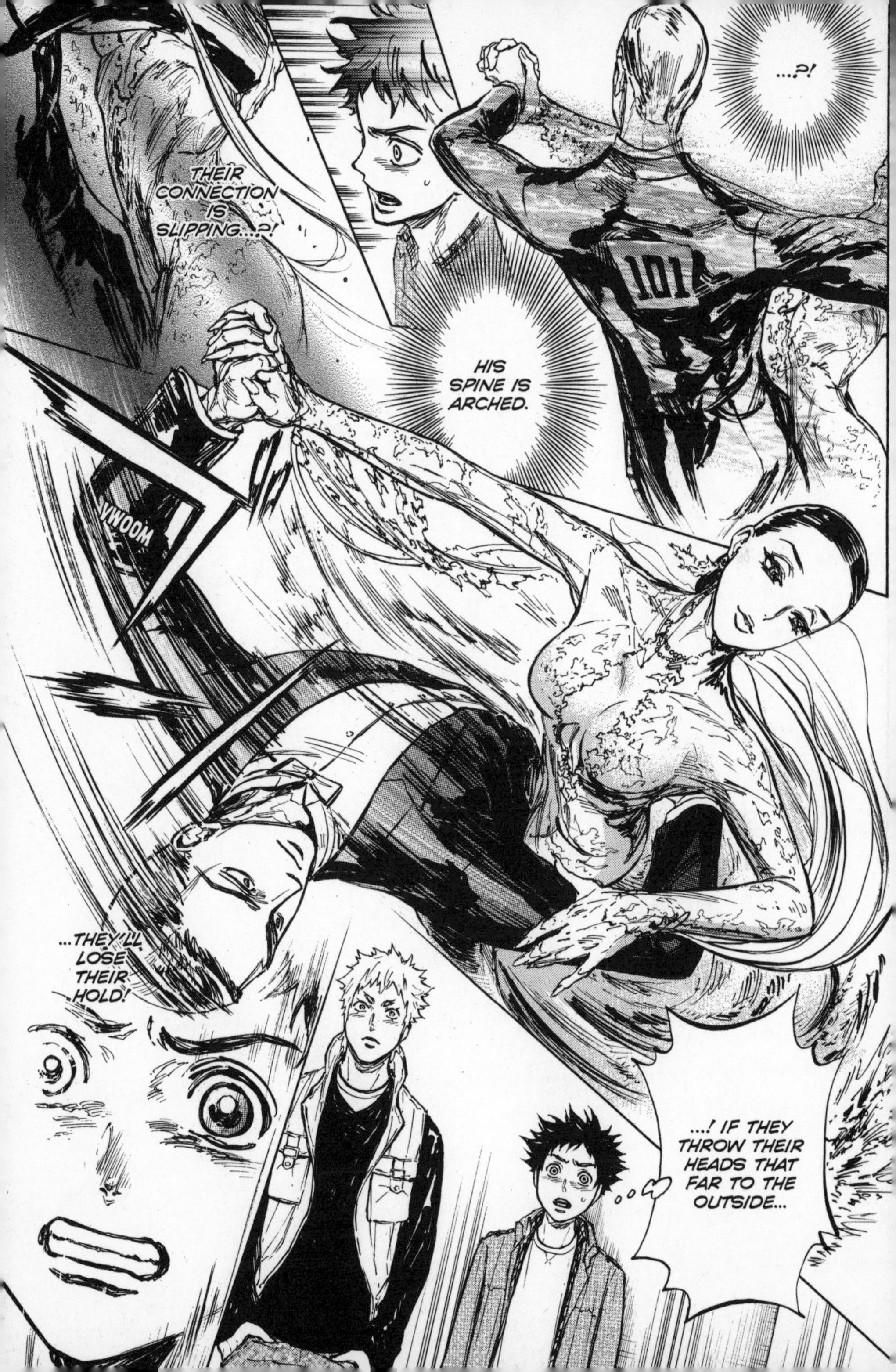
...?!
THEIR CONNECTION IS SLIPPING...?!
HIS SPINE IS ARCHED.
VWOOM
...! IF THEY THROW THEIR HEADS THAT FAR TO THE OUTSIDE...
...THEY'LL LOSE THEIR HOLD!

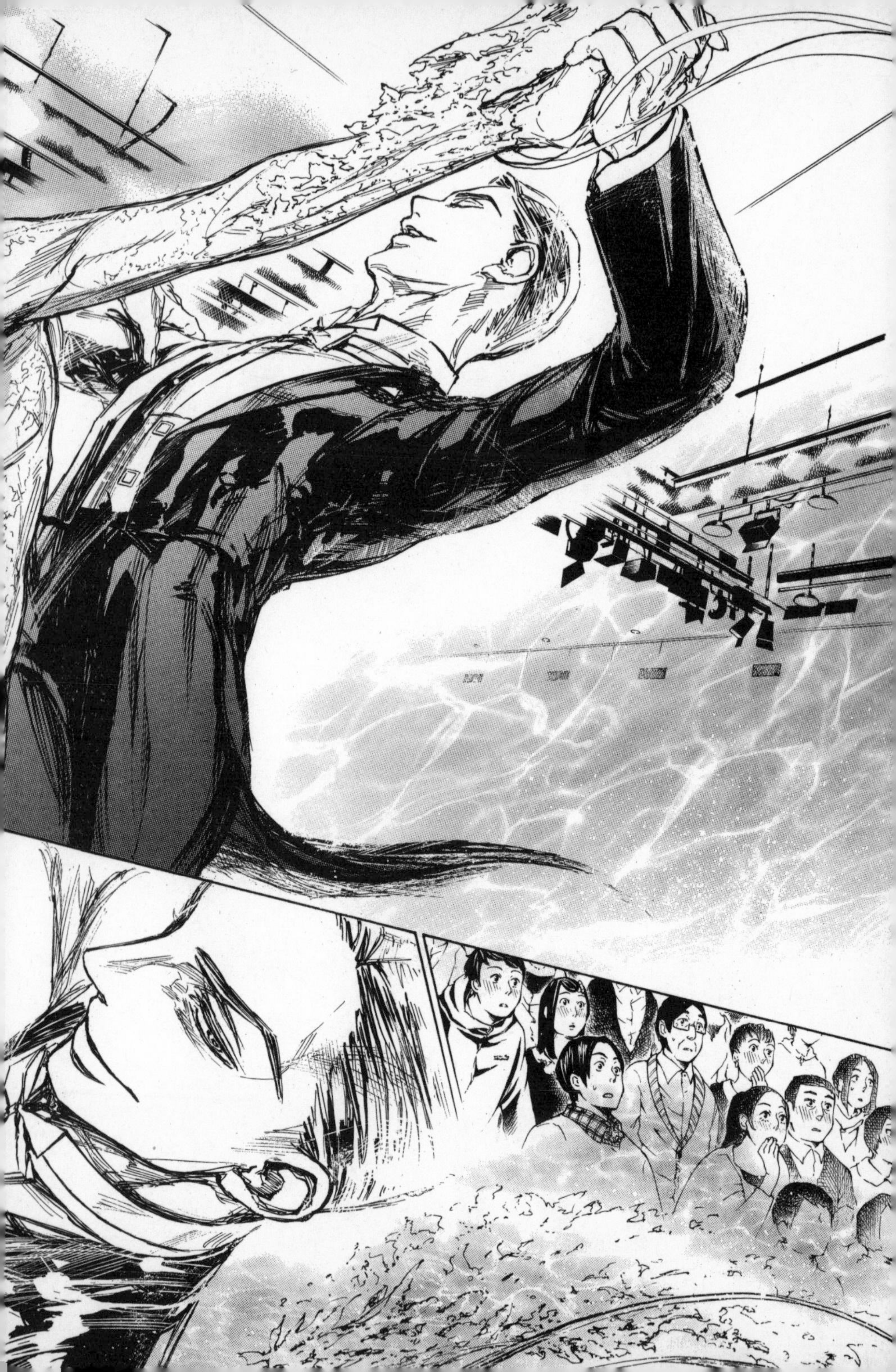

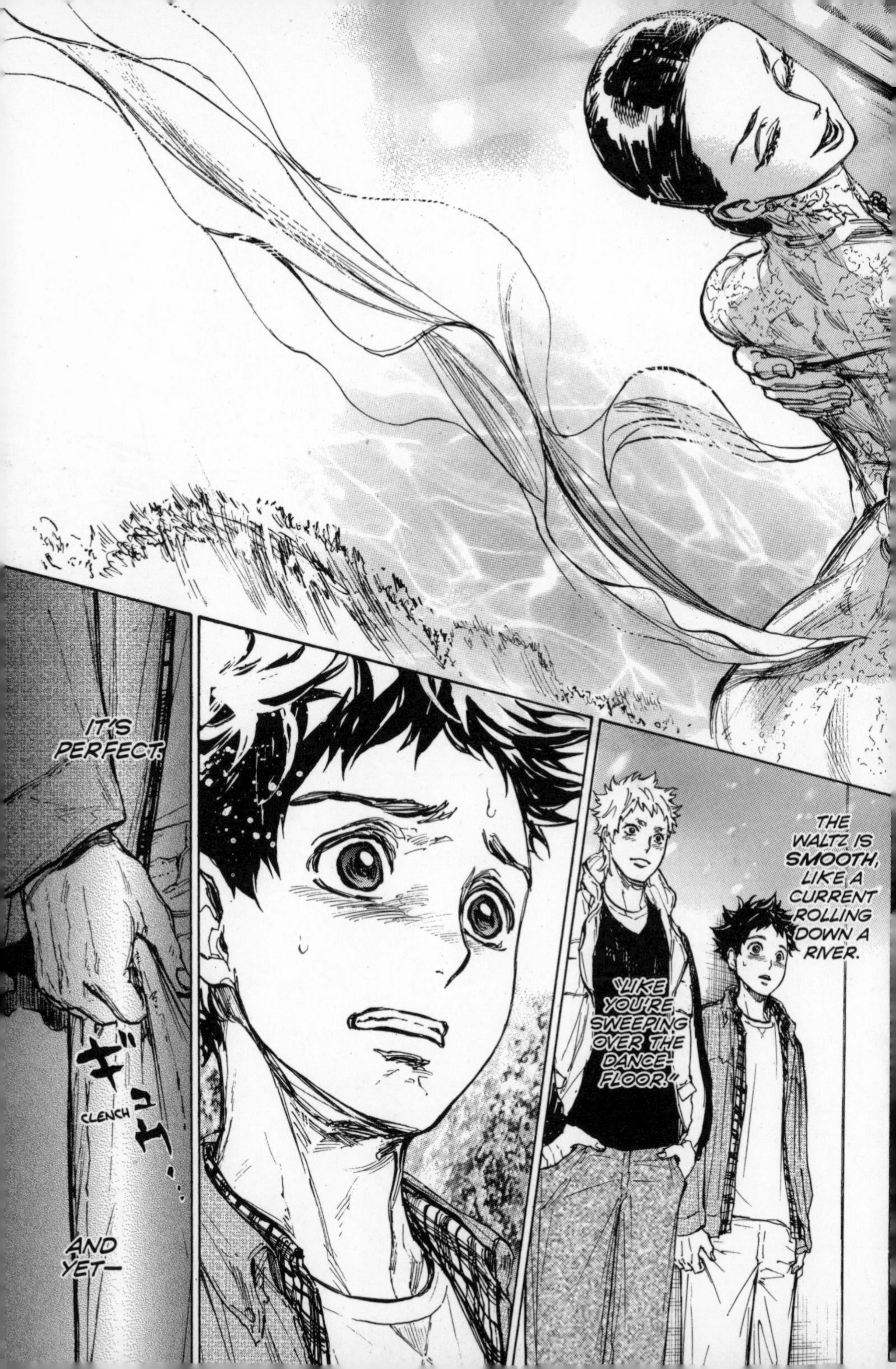
THE WALTZ IS SMOOTH, LIKE A CURRENT ROLLING DOWN A RIVER.
"LIKE YOU'RE SWEEPING OVER THE DANCE-FLOOR."
IT'S PERFECT.
ギュー…
CLENCH
AND YET—

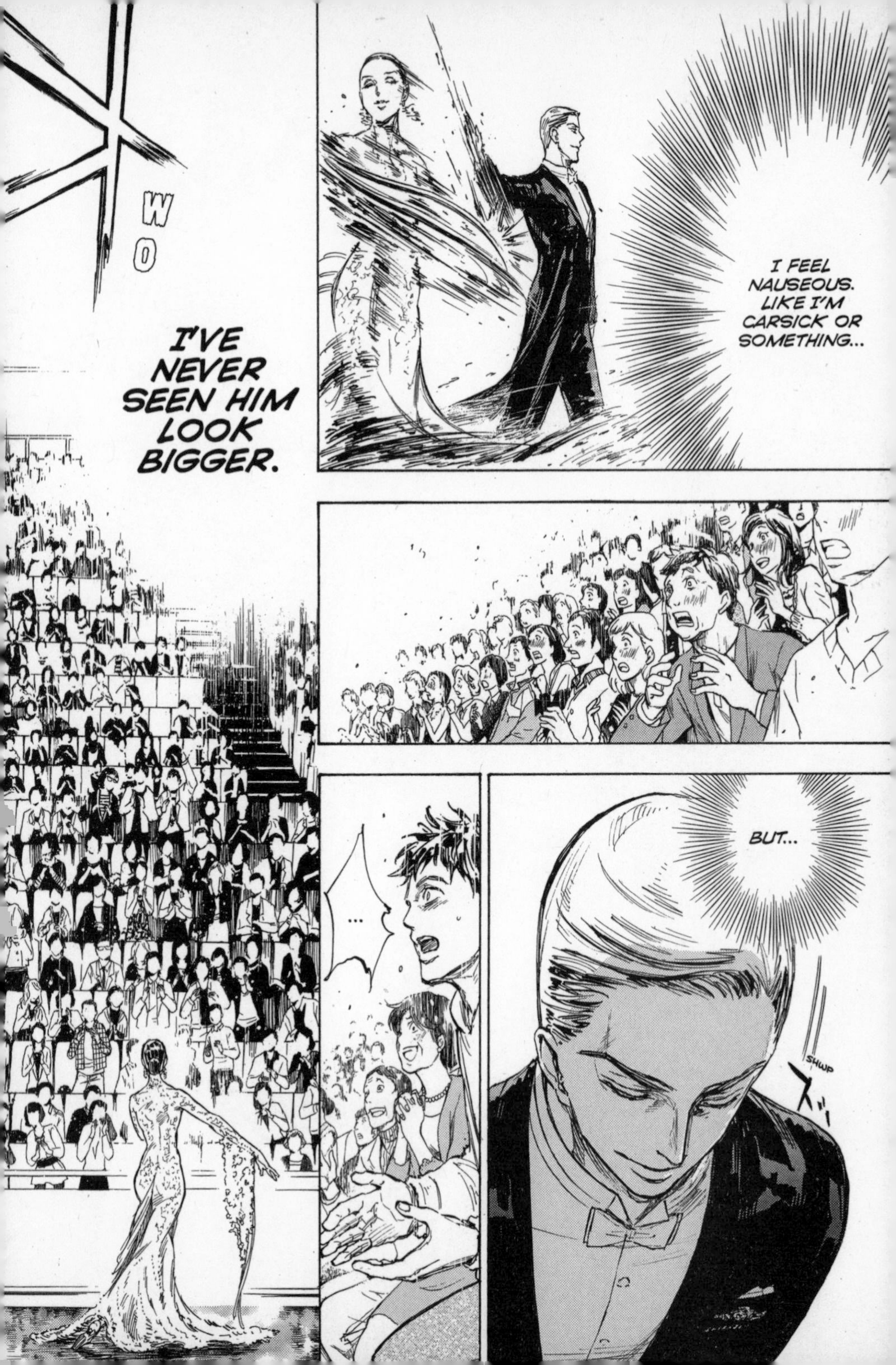
I FEEL NAUSEOUS. LIKE I'M CARSICK OR SOMETHING...
BUT...
SHWP
...
WO
I'VE NEVER SEEN HIM LOOK BIGGER.

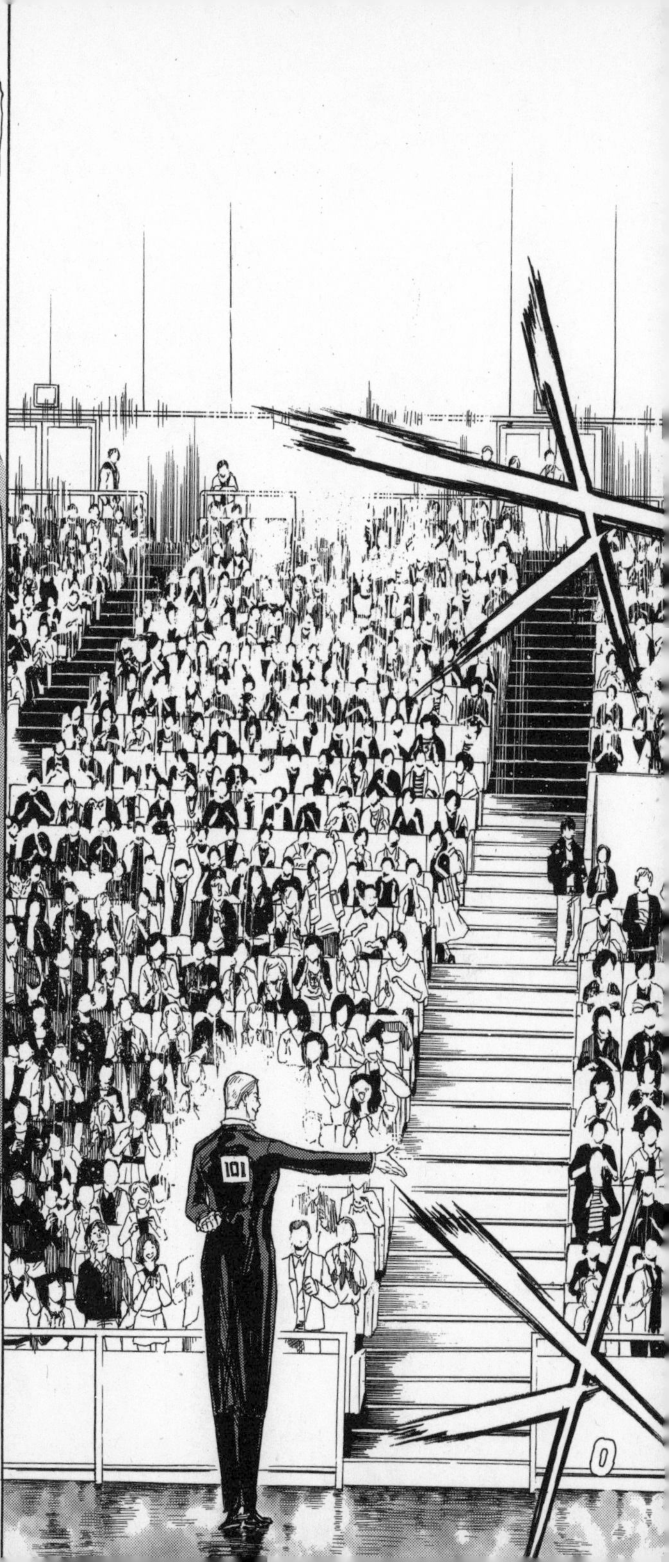

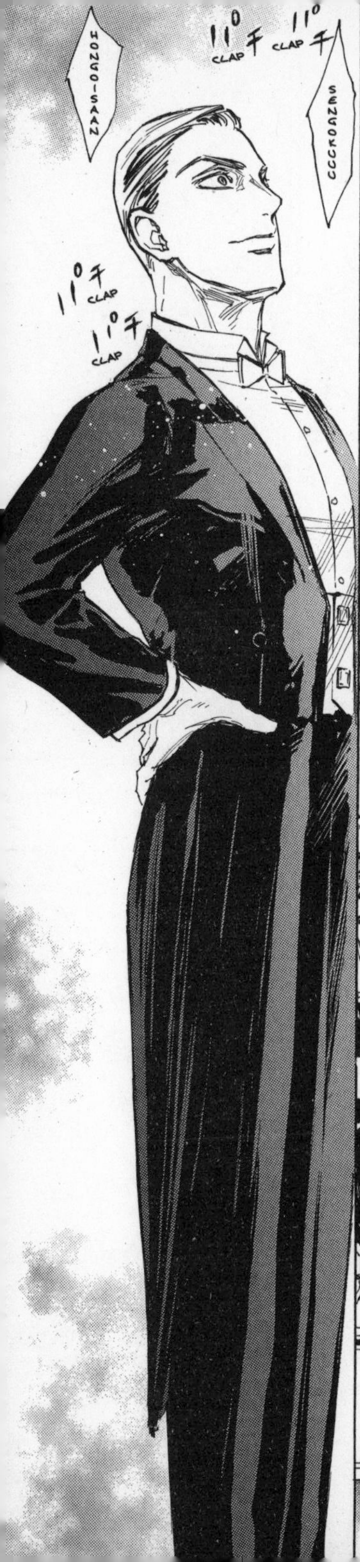
SENGOKUUUU
パチ CLAP
パチ CLAP
HONGO-SAAN
パチ CLAP
パチ CLAP

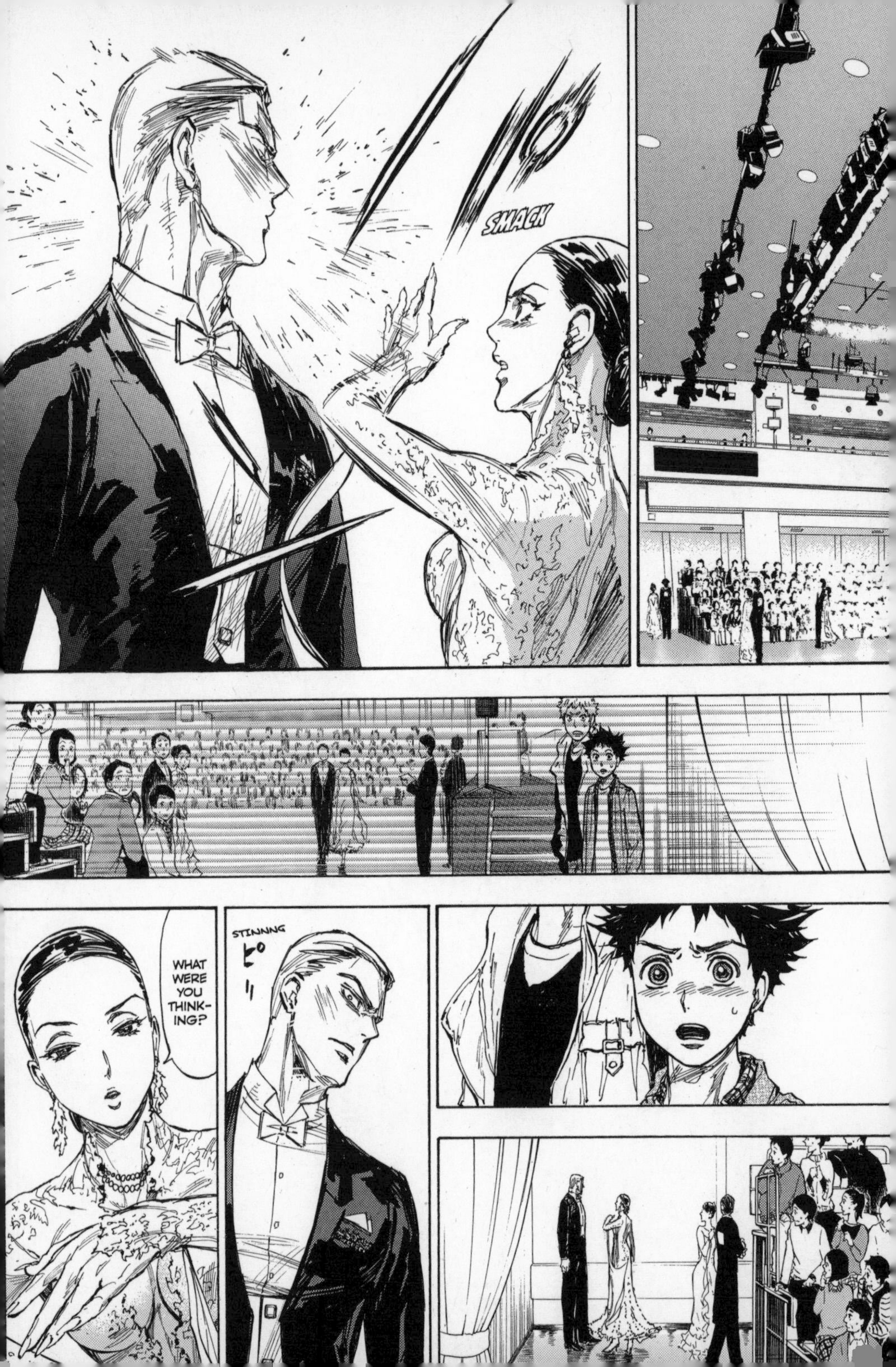
SMACK
STINNNG
WHAT WERE YOU THINKING?

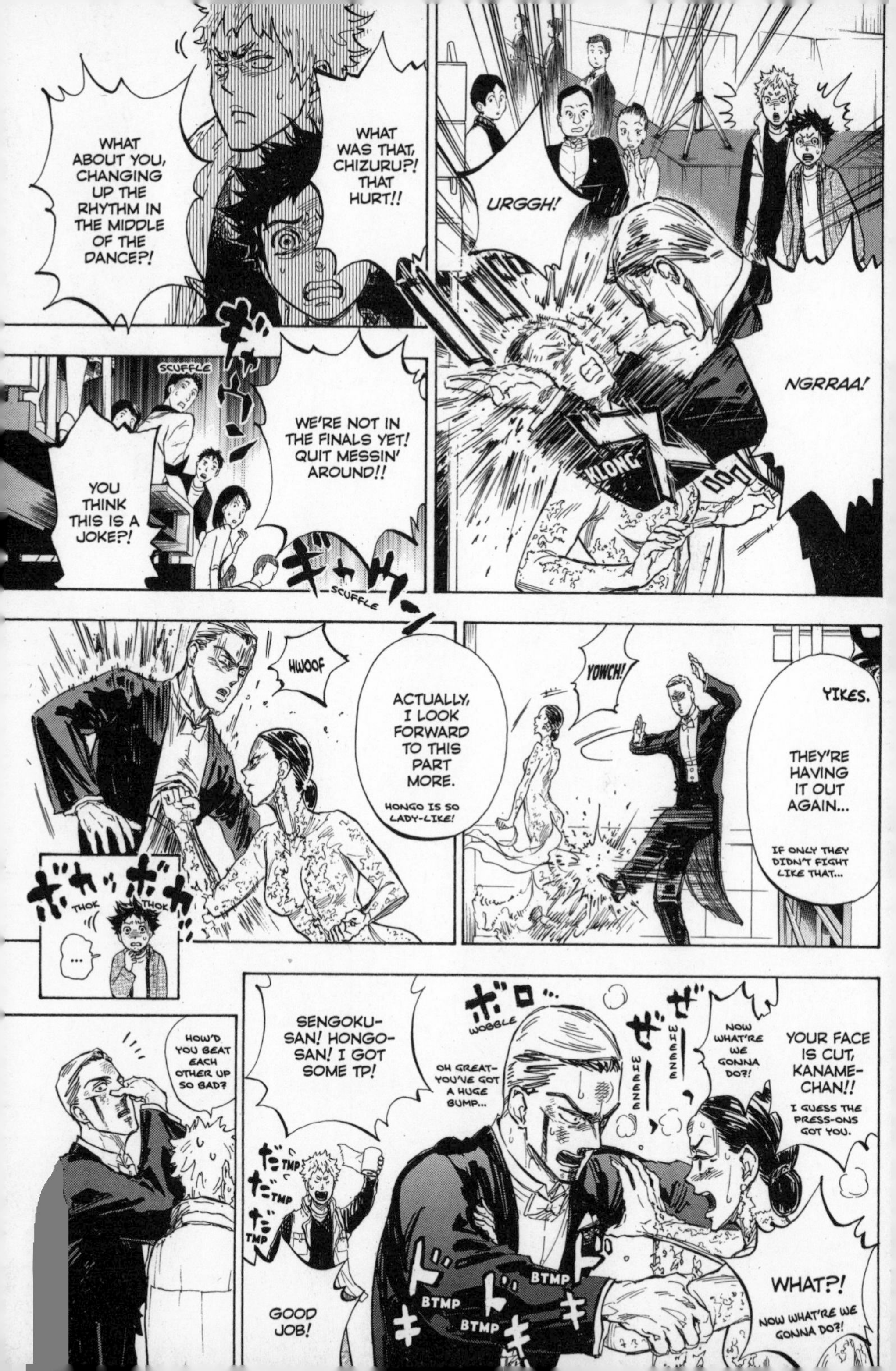

URGGH!
NGRRAA!
KLONG
WHAT WAS THAT, CHIZURU?! THAT HURT!!
WHAT ABOUT YOU, CHANGING UP THE RHYTHM IN THE MIDDLE OF THE DANCE?!
SCUFFLE
WE'RE NOT IN THE FINALS YET! QUIT MESSIN' AROUND!!
YOU THINK THIS IS A JOKE?!
SCUFFLE
YOWCH!
YIKES.
THEY'RE HAVING IT OUT AGAIN...
IF ONLY THEY DIDN'T FIGHT LIKE THAT...
HWOOF
ACTUALLY, I LOOK FORWARD TO THIS PART MORE.
HONGO IS SO LADY-LIKE!
THOK THOK
...
YOUR FACE IS CUT, KANAME-CHAN!!
I GUESS THE PRESS-ONS GOT YOU.
NOW WHAT'RE WE GONNA DO?!
WHEEZE WHEEZE
WOBBLE
OH GREAT-YOU'VE GOT A HUGE BUMP...
SENGOKU-SAN! HONGO-SAN! I GOT SOME TP!
TMP TMP TMP
GOOD JOB!
BTMP BTMP BTMP
WHAT?!
NOW WHAT'RE WE GONNA DO?!
HOW'D YOU BEAT EACH OTHER UP SO BAD?

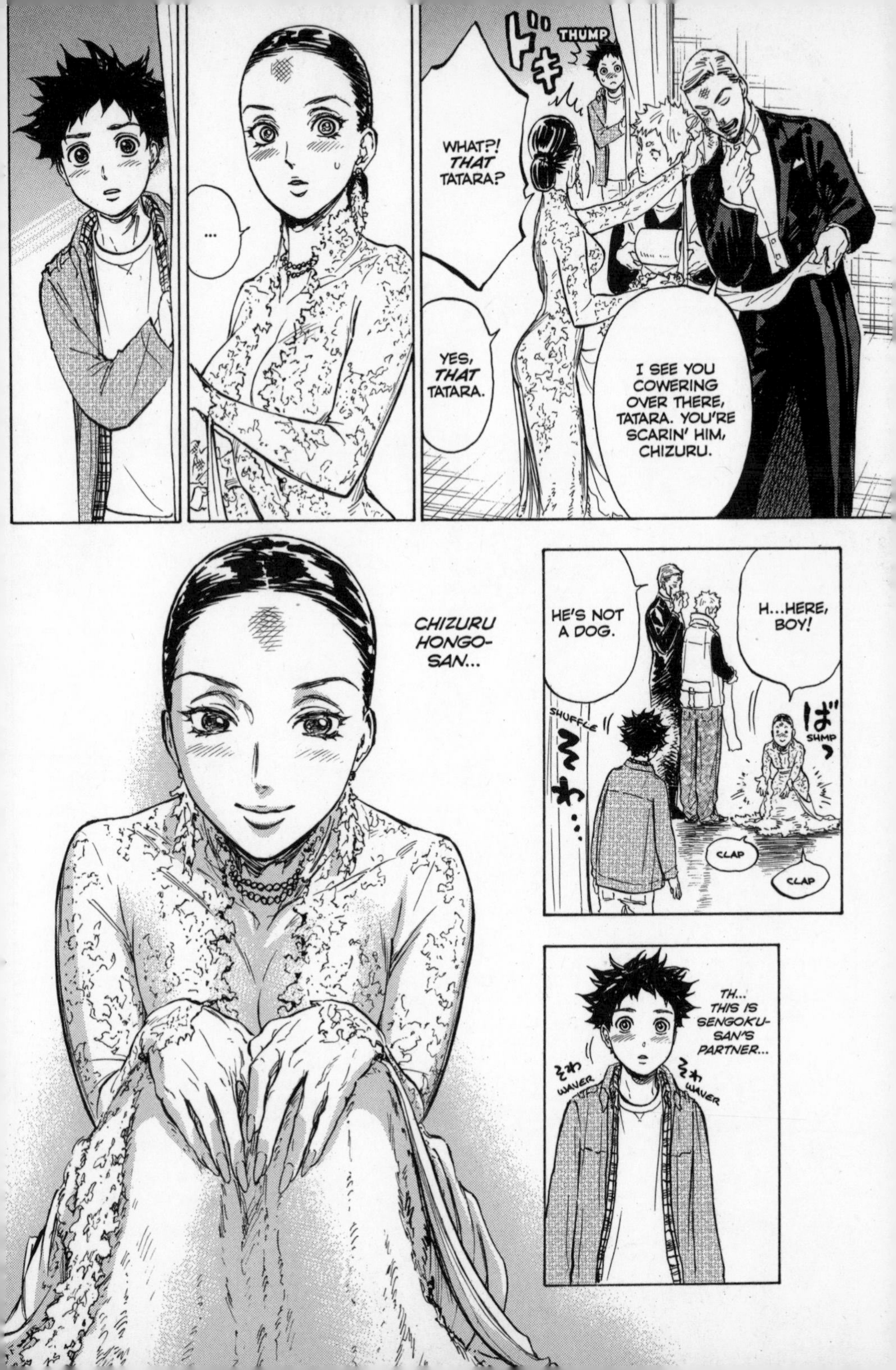
ドキ
THUMP
WHAT?! THAT TATARA?
YES, THAT TATARA.
I SEE YOU COWERING OVER THERE, TATARA. YOU'RE SCARIN' HIM, CHIZURU.
...
H...HERE, BOY!
HE'S NOT A DOG.
ばっ
SHMP
CLAP
CLAP
そわ...
SHUFFLE
TH... THIS IS SENGOKU-SAN'S PARTNER...
そわ
WAVER
そわ
WAVER
CHIZURU HONGO-SAN...

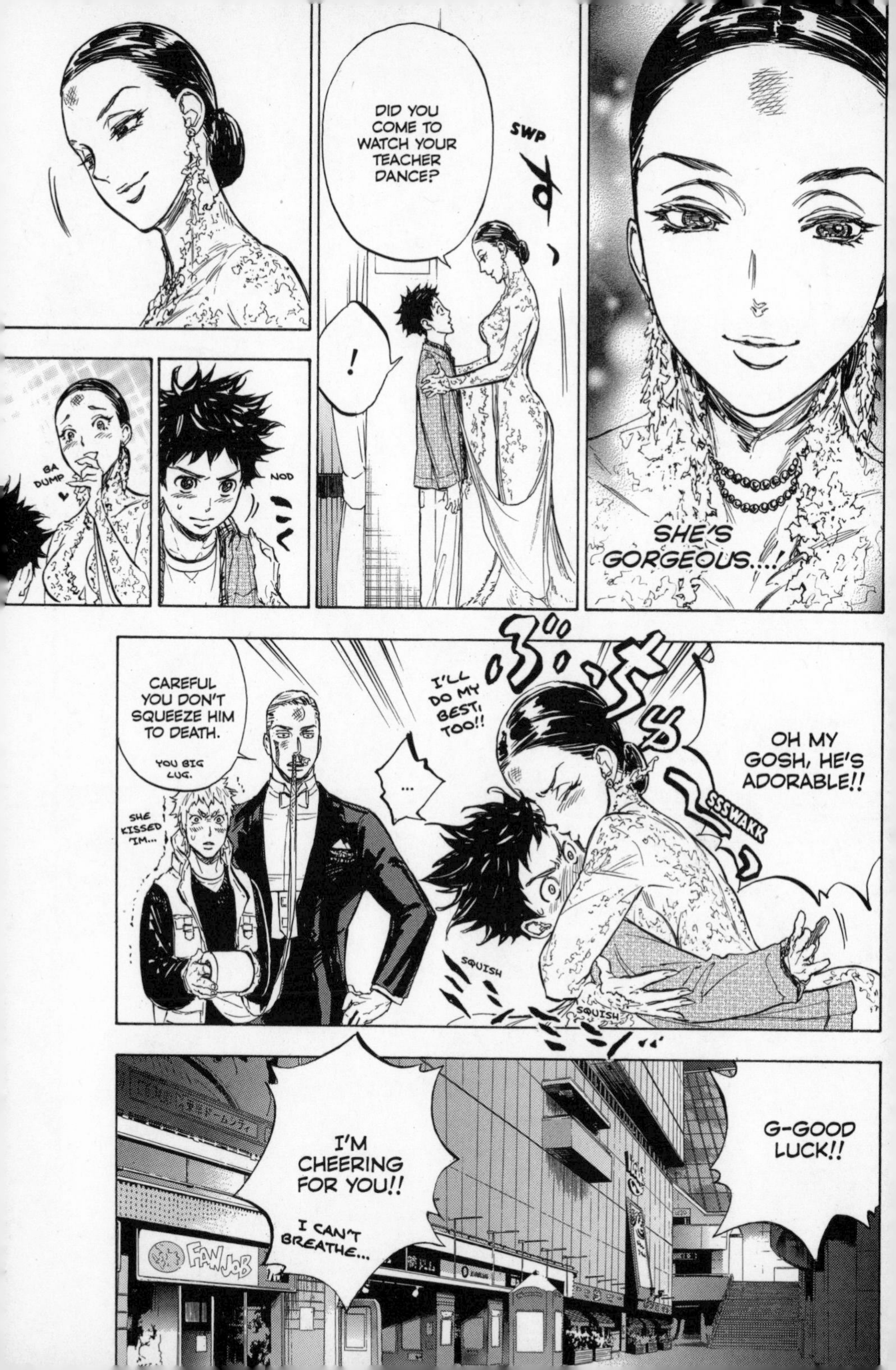
SHE'S GORGEOUS...!
DID YOU COME TO WATCH YOUR TEACHER DANCE?
SWP
!
NOD
BA DUMP
OH MY GOSH, HE'S ADORABLE!!
SSSWAKK
I'LL DO MY BEST, TOO!!
...
CAREFUL YOU DON'T SQUEEZE HIM TO DEATH.
YOU BIG LUG.
SHE KISSED 'IM...
SQUISH
SQUISH
G-GOOD LUCK!!
I'M CHEERING FOR YOU!!
I CAN'T BREATHE...
FAN JOB

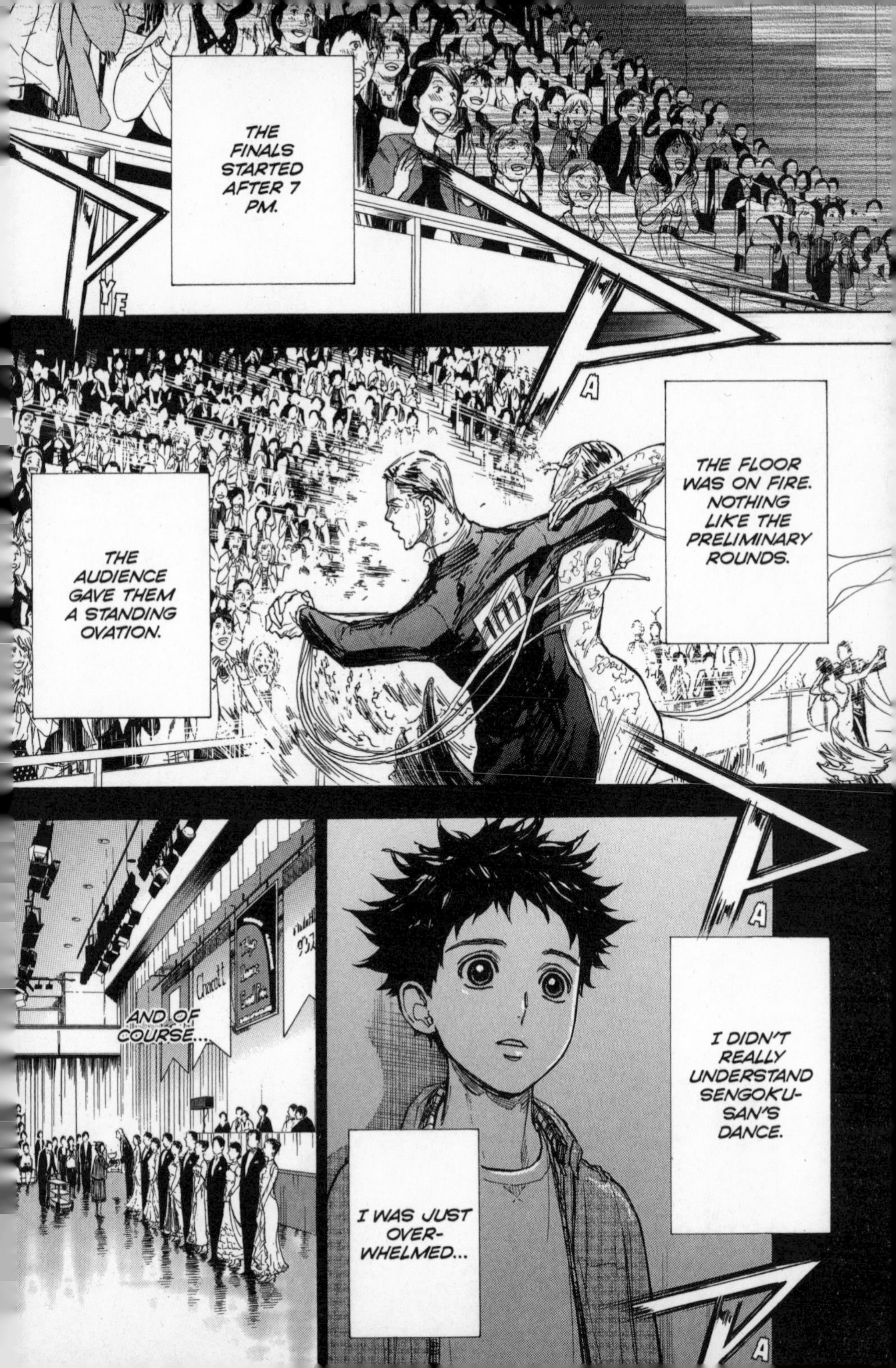
THE FINALS STARTED AFTER 7 PM.
YE
A
THE FLOOR WAS ON FIRE. NOTHING LIKE THE PRELIMINARY ROUNDS.
THE AUDIENCE GAVE THEM A STANDING OVATION.
A
I DIDN'T REALLY UNDERSTAND SENGOKU-SAN'S DANCE.
I WAS JUST OVER-WHELMED...
A
AND OF COURSE...

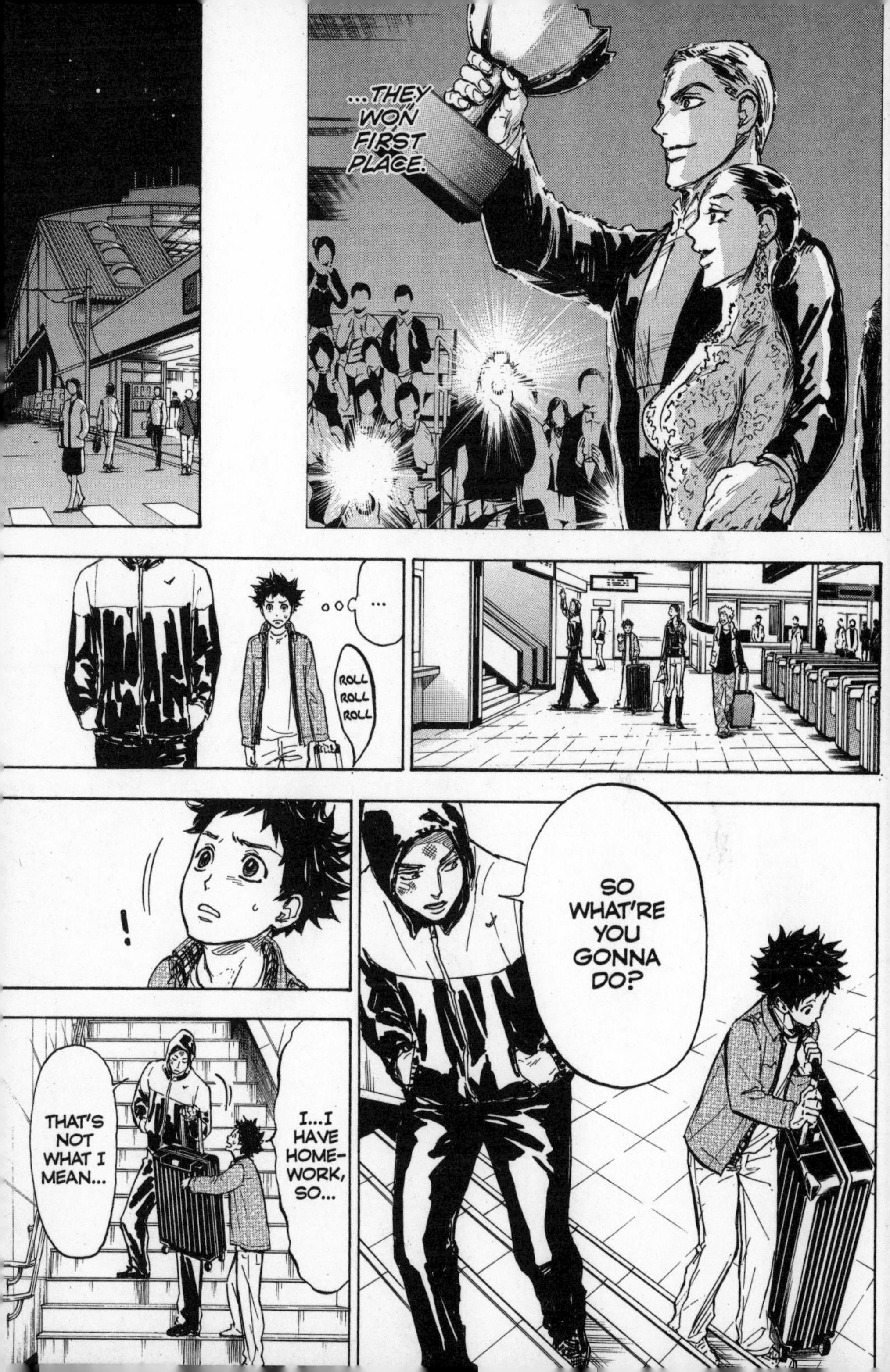
...THEY WON FIRST PLACE.
...
ROLL ROLL ROLL
SO WHAT'RE YOU GONNA DO?
!
I...I HAVE HOME-WORK, SO...
THAT'S NOT WHAT I MEAN...

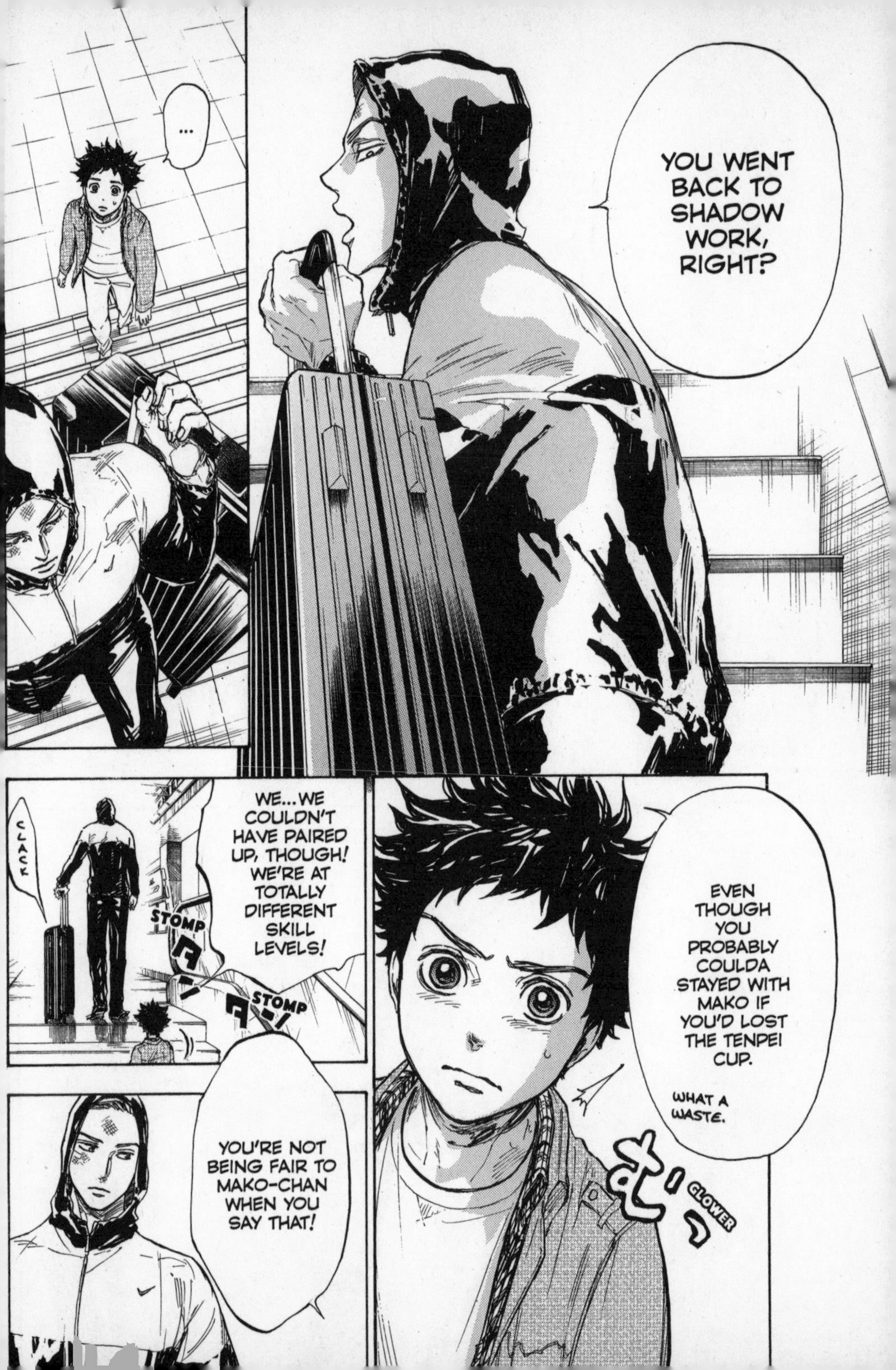
YOU WENT BACK TO SHADOW WORK, RIGHT?
...
EVEN THOUGH YOU PROBABLY COULDA STAYED WITH MAKO IF YOU'D LOST THE TENPEI CUP.
WHAT A WASTE.
むっ
GLOWER
WE...WE COULDN'T HAVE PAIRED UP, THOUGH! WE'RE AT TOTALLY DIFFERENT SKILL LEVELS!
CLACK
STOMP
STOMP
YOU'RE NOT BEING FAIR TO MAKO-CHAN WHEN YOU SAY THAT!

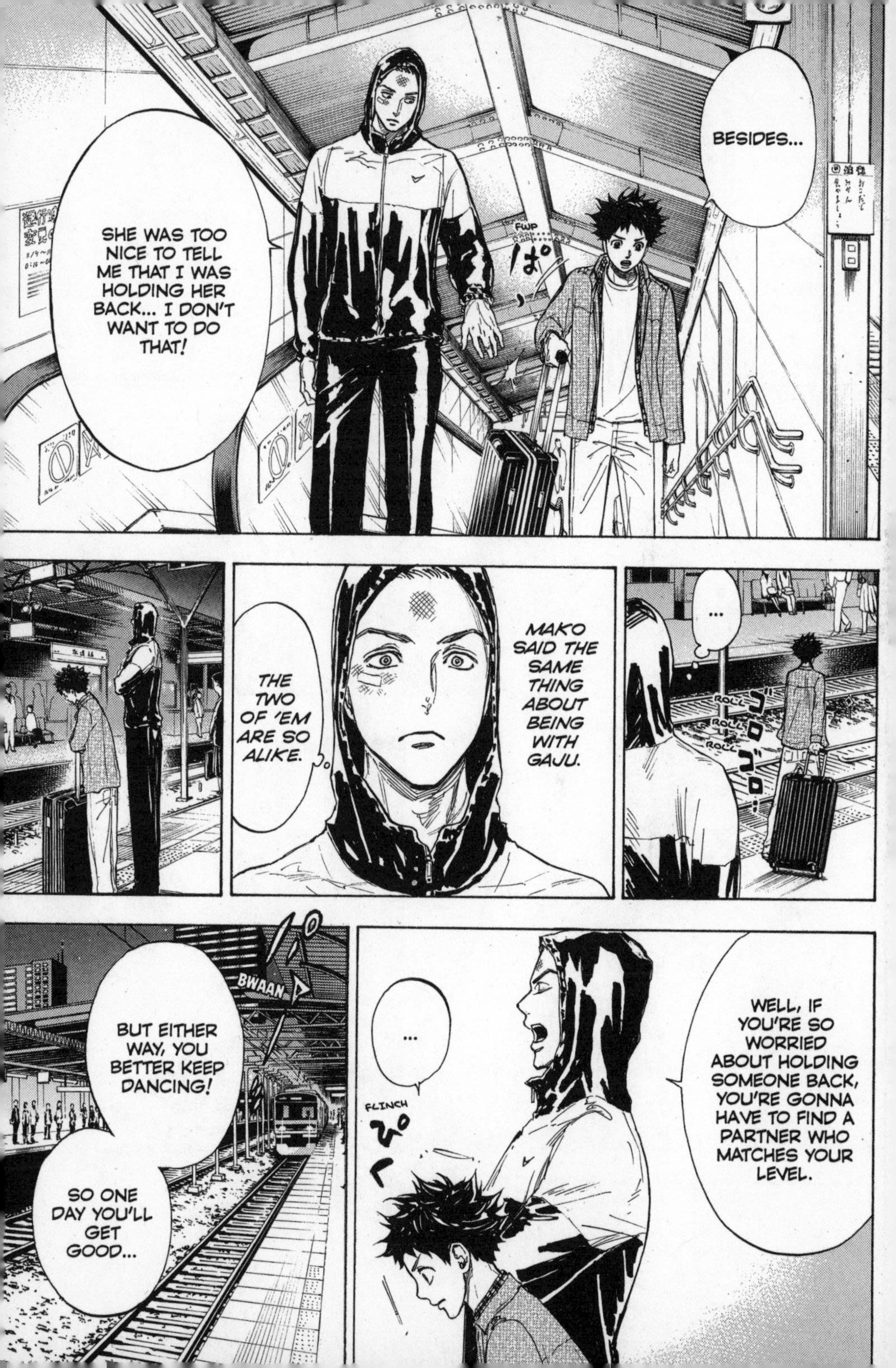
BESIDES...
SHE WAS TOO NICE TO TELL ME THAT I WAS HOLDING HER BACK... I DON'T WANT TO DO THAT!
FWP
...
ROLL
ROLL
ROLL
MAKO SAID THE SAME THING ABOUT BEING WITH GAJU.
THE TWO OF 'EM ARE SO ALIKE.
WELL, IF YOU'RE SO WORRIED ABOUT HOLDING SOMEONE BACK, YOU'RE GONNA HAVE TO FIND A PARTNER WHO MATCHES YOUR LEVEL.
...
FLINCH
BWAAN
BUT EITHER WAY, YOU BETTER KEEP DANCING!
SO ONE DAY YOU'LL GET GOOD...

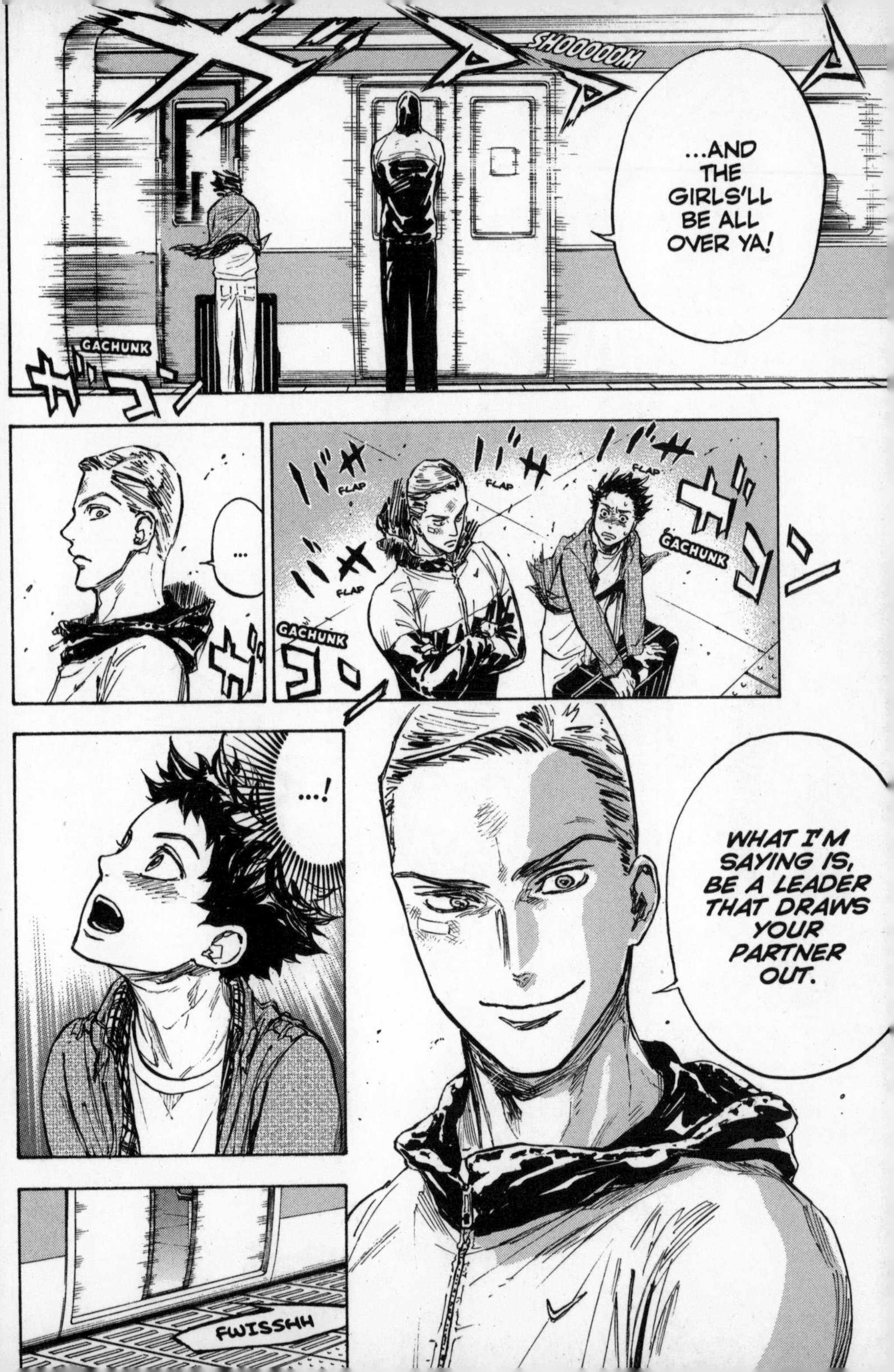
...AND THE GIRLS'LL BE ALL OVER YA!
SHOOOOOM
GACHUNK
FLAP
GACHUNK
FLAP
FLAP
GACHUNK
...
WHAT I'M SAYING IS, BE A LEADER THAT DRAWS YOUR PARTNER OUT.
...!
FWISSHH

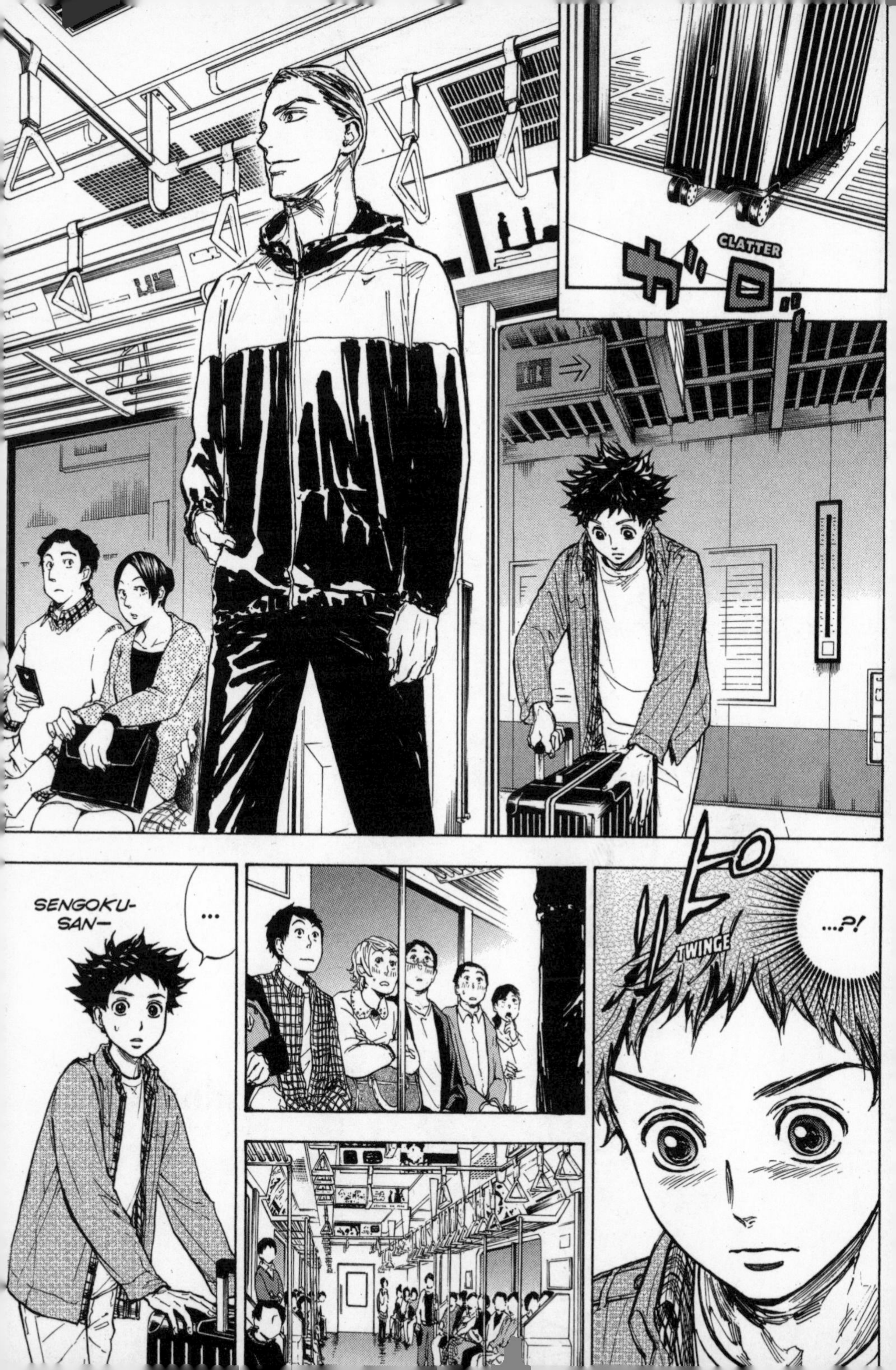
CLATTER
TWINGE
...?!
...
SENGOKU-SAN—

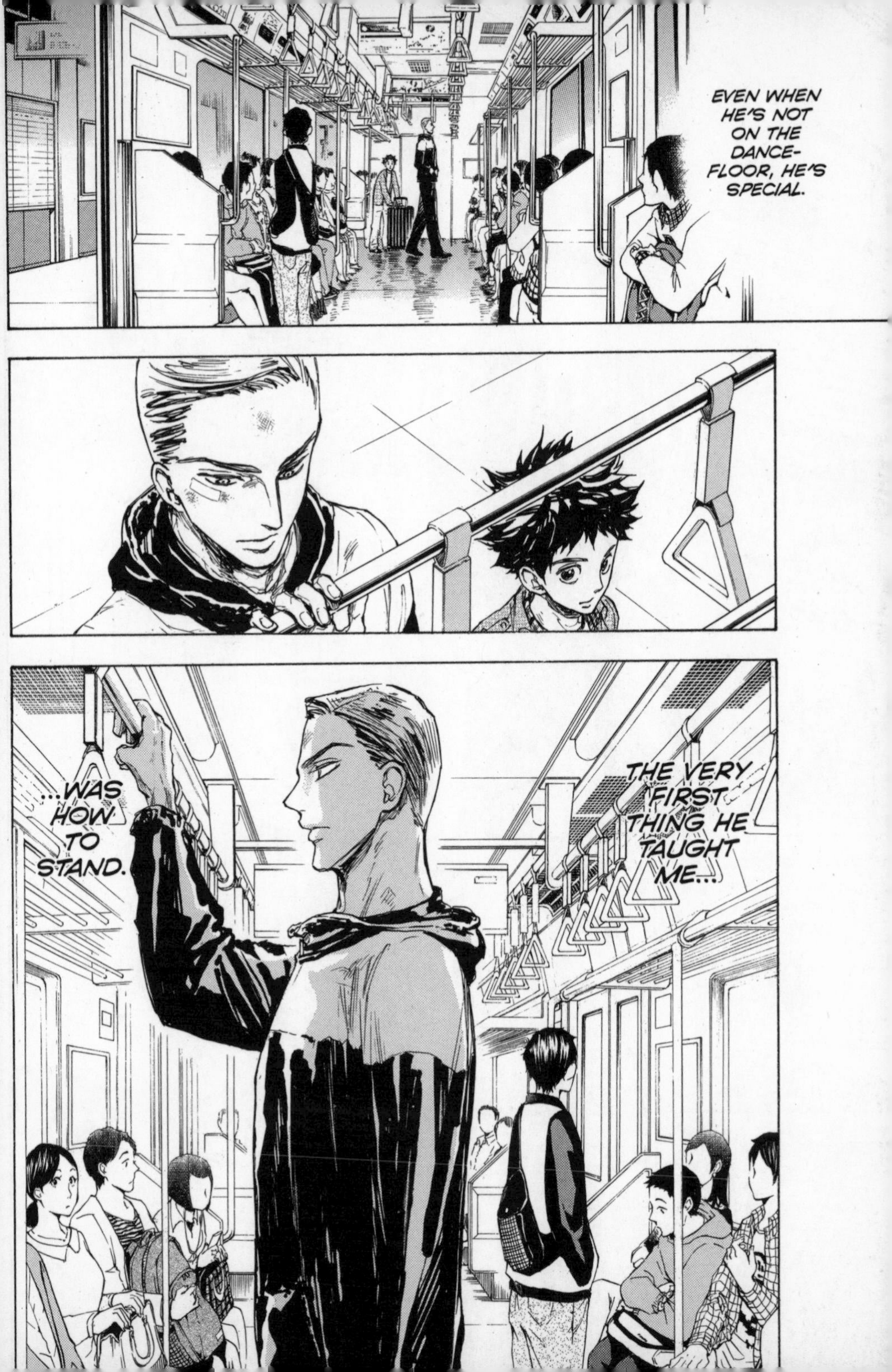
EVEN WHEN HE'S NOT ON THE DANCE-FLOOR, HE'S SPECIAL.
THE VERY FIRST THING HE TAUGHT ME...
...WAS HOW TO STAND.

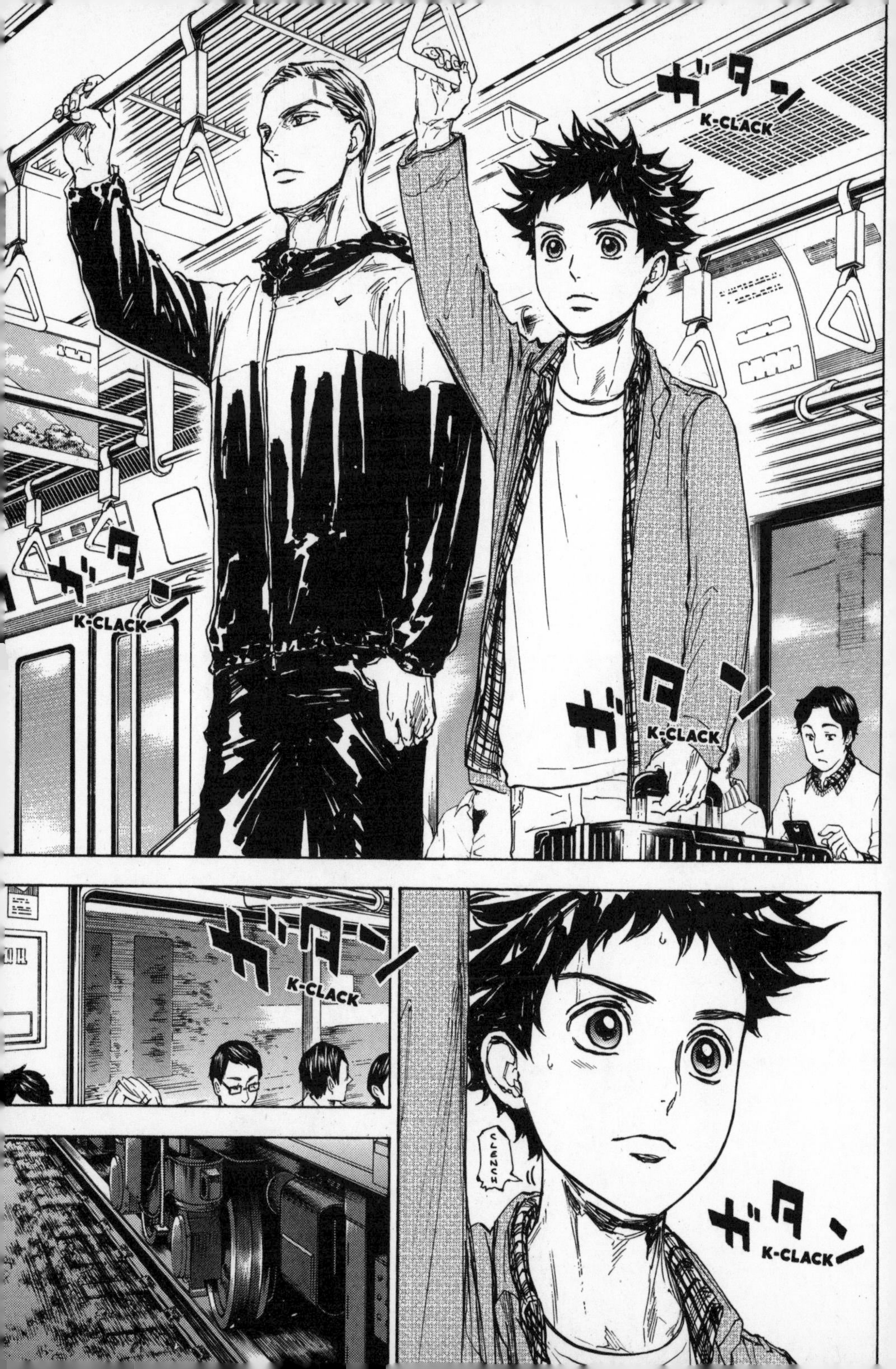

ガタン
K-CLACK
ガタン
K-CLACK
ガタ
K-CLACK
CLENCH
ガタ、
K-CLACK
ガターン
K-CLACK

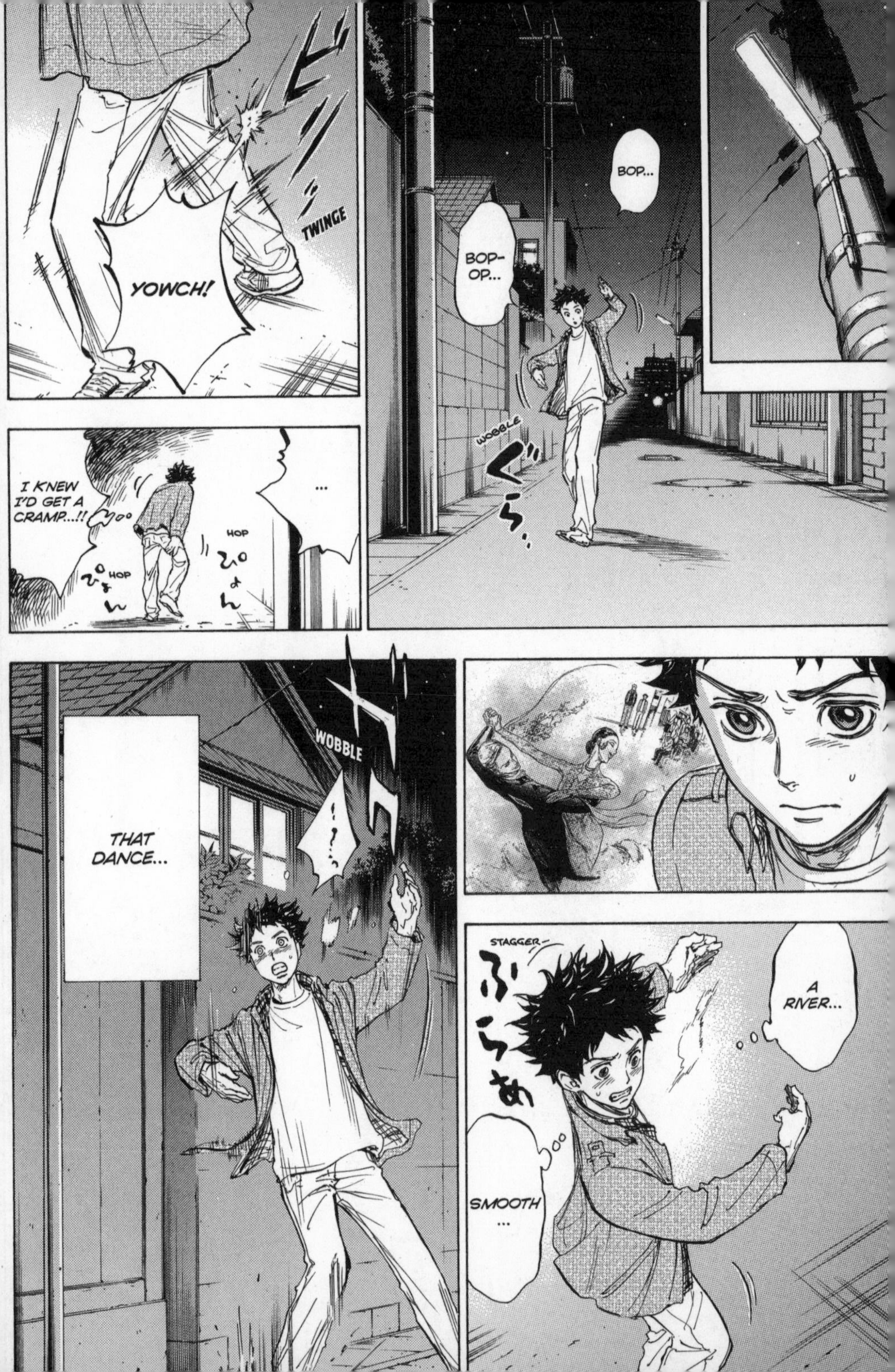
BOP...
BOP-OP...
WOBBLE
TWINGE
YOWCH!
...
I KNEW I'D GET A CRAMP...!!
HOP
HOP
A RIVER...
STAGGER
SMOOTH...
WOBBLE
!?...
THAT DANCE...

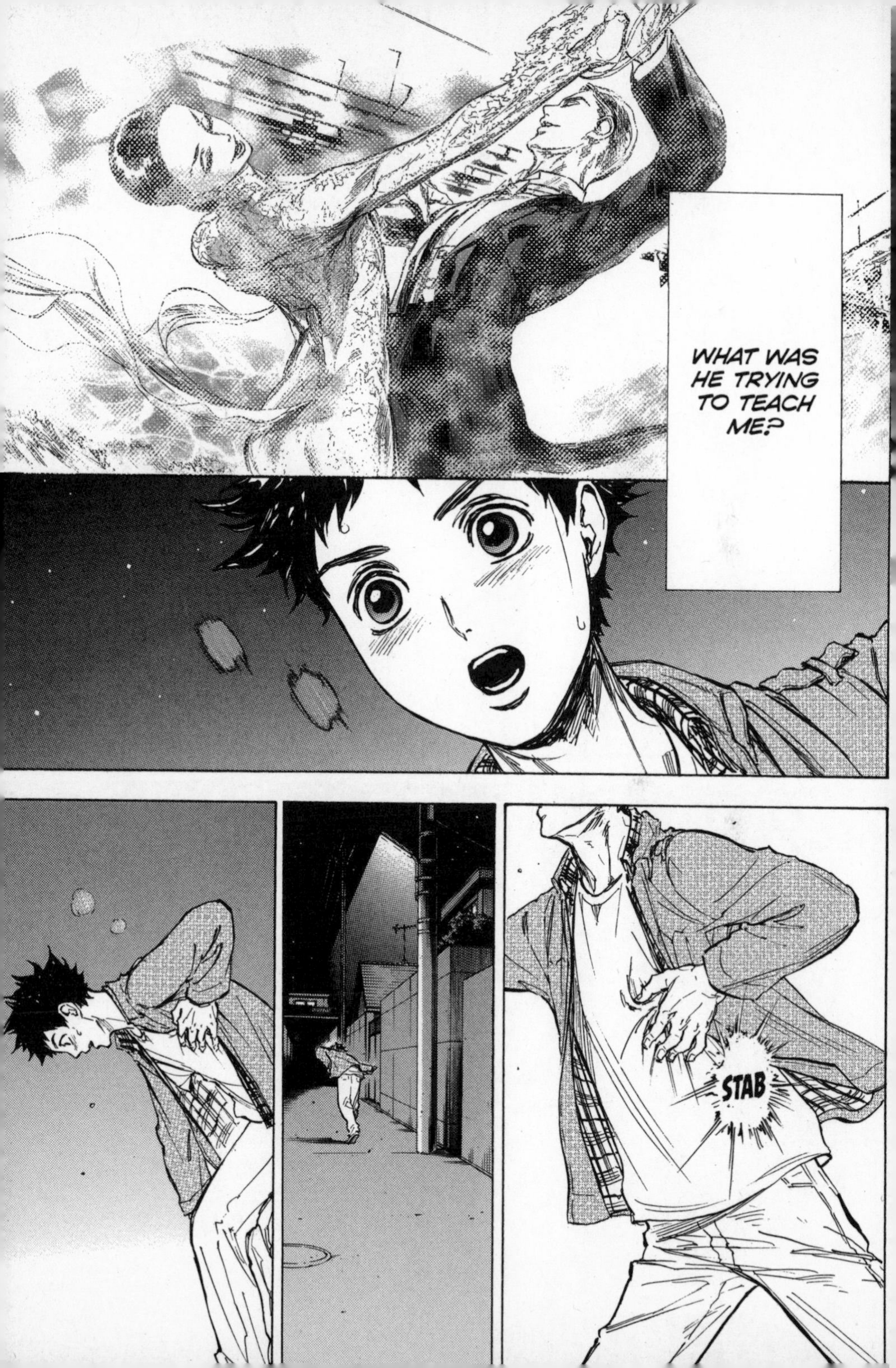
WHAT WAS HE TRYING TO TEACH ME?
STAB

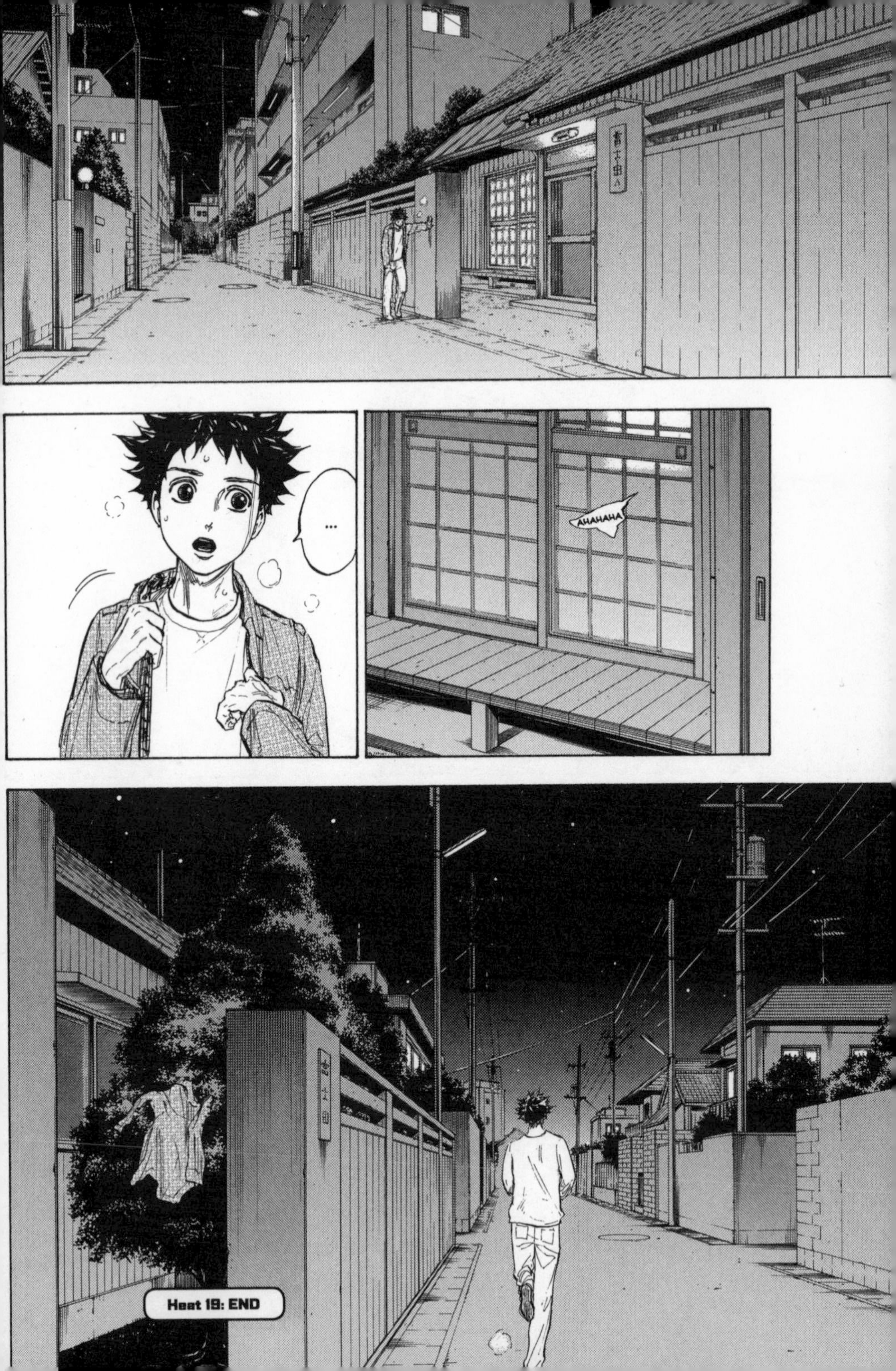
AHAHAHA
...
Heat 19: END

WELCOME TO THE BALLROOM

Heat 20
What a Weirdo

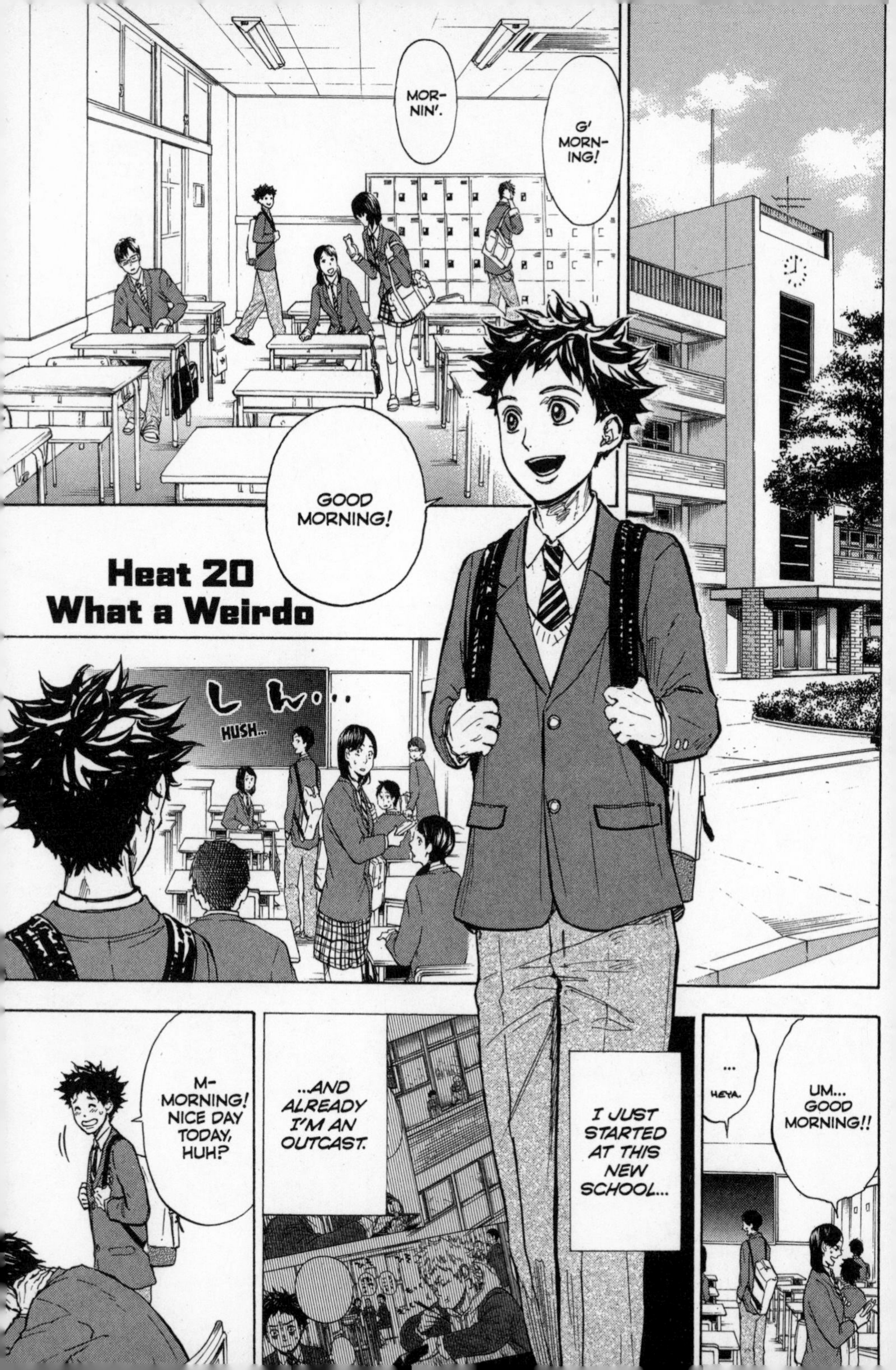
GOOD MORNING!
G' MORNING!
MOR-NIN'.
HUSH...
UM... GOOD MORNING!!
...
HEYA.
I JUST STARTED AT THIS NEW SCHOOL...
...AND ALREADY I'M AN OUTCAST.
M-MORNING! NICE DAY TODAY, HUH?

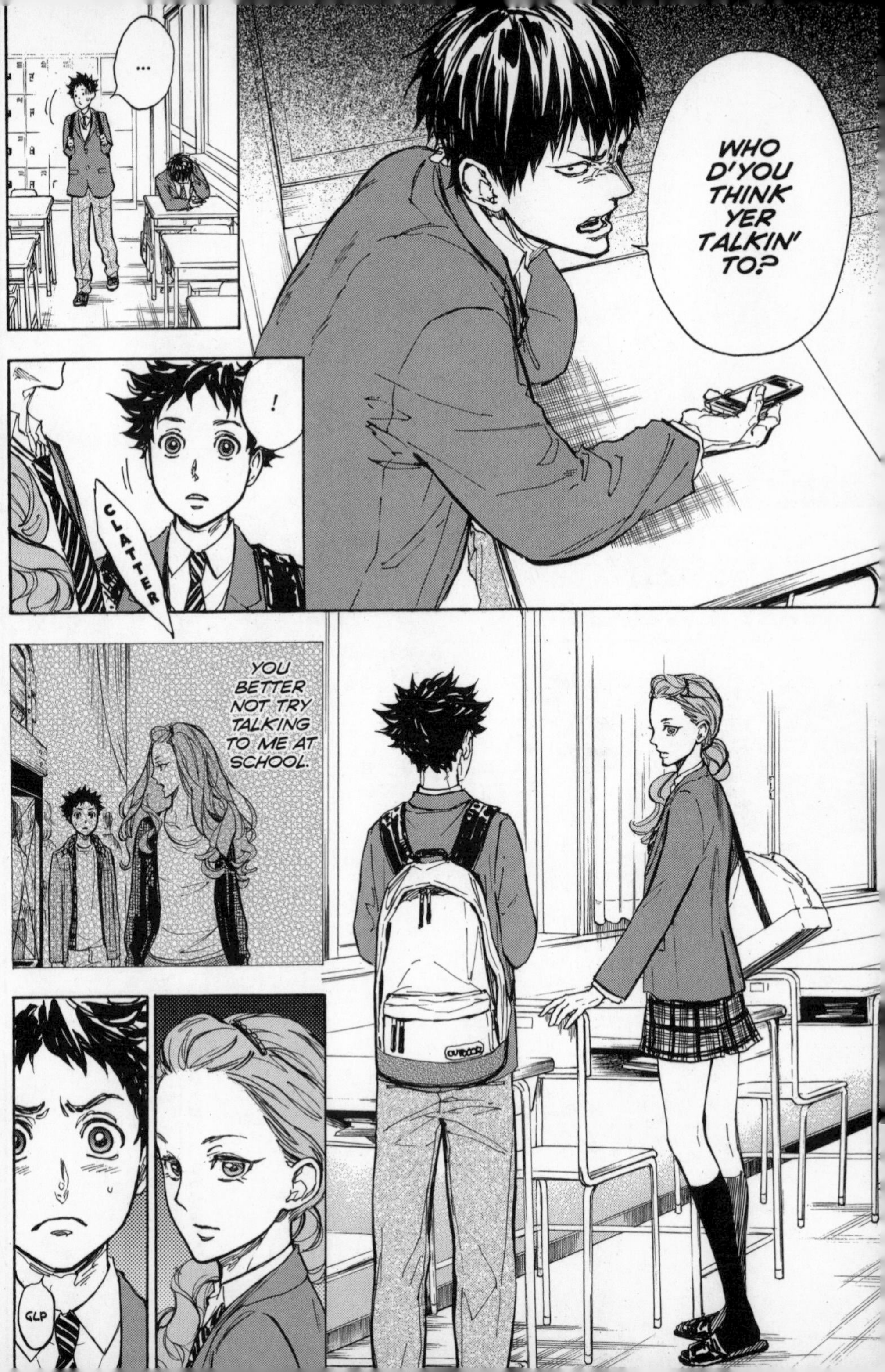
WHO D'YOU THINK YER TALKIN' TO?
...
!
CLATTER
YOU BETTER NOT TRY TALKING TO ME AT SCHOOL.
GLP

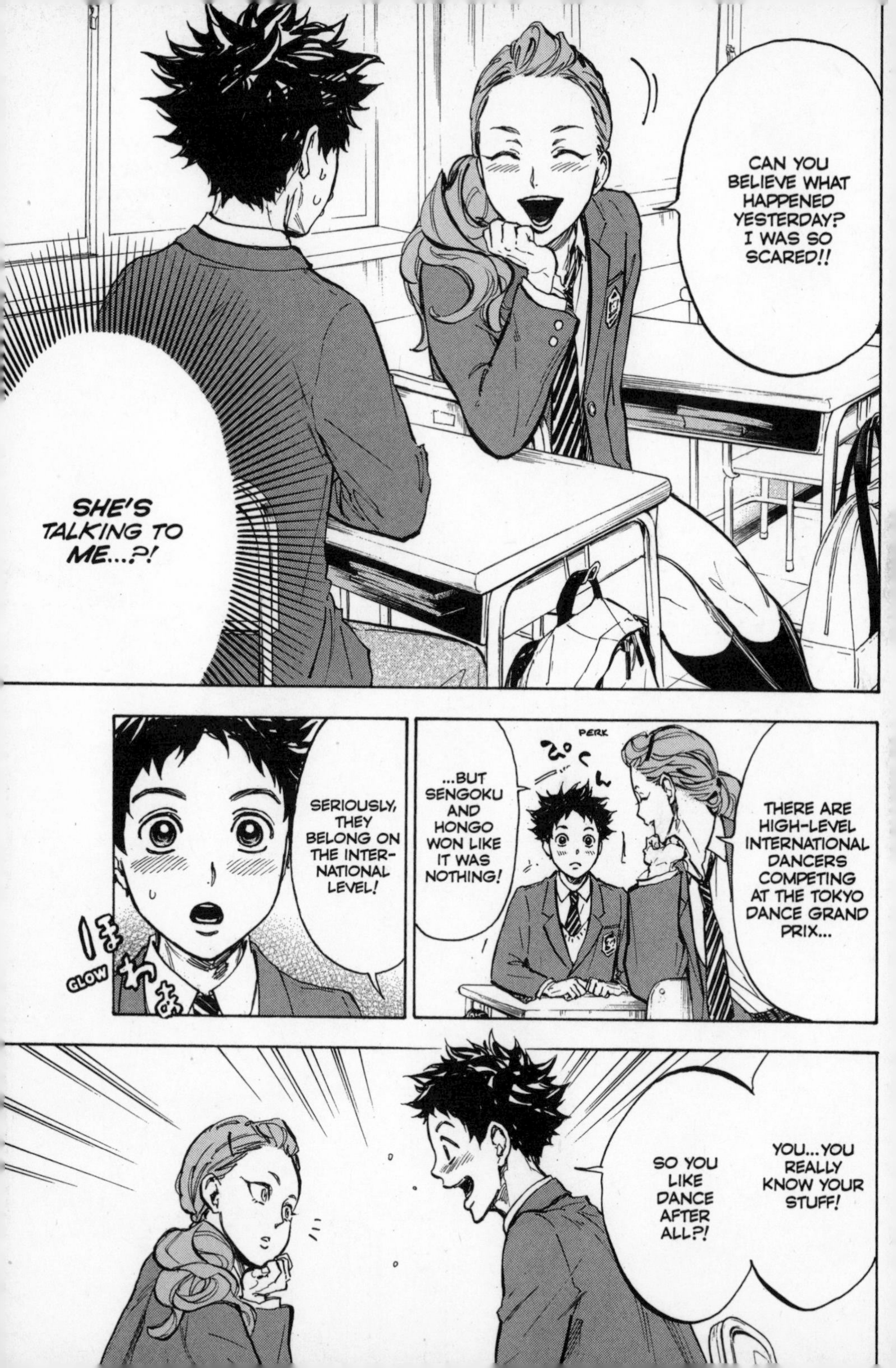
CAN YOU BELIEVE WHAT HAPPENED YESTERDAY? I WAS SO SCARED!!
SHE'S TALKING TO ME...?!
THERE ARE HIGH-LEVEL INTERNATIONAL DANCERS COMPETING AT THE TOKYO DANCE GRAND PRIX...
PERK
...BUT SENGOKU AND HONGO WON LIKE IT WAS NOTHING!
SERIOUSLY, THEY BELONG ON THE INTER-NATIONAL LEVEL!
GLOW
YOU...YOU REALLY KNOW YOUR STUFF!
SO YOU LIKE DANCE AFTER ALL?!

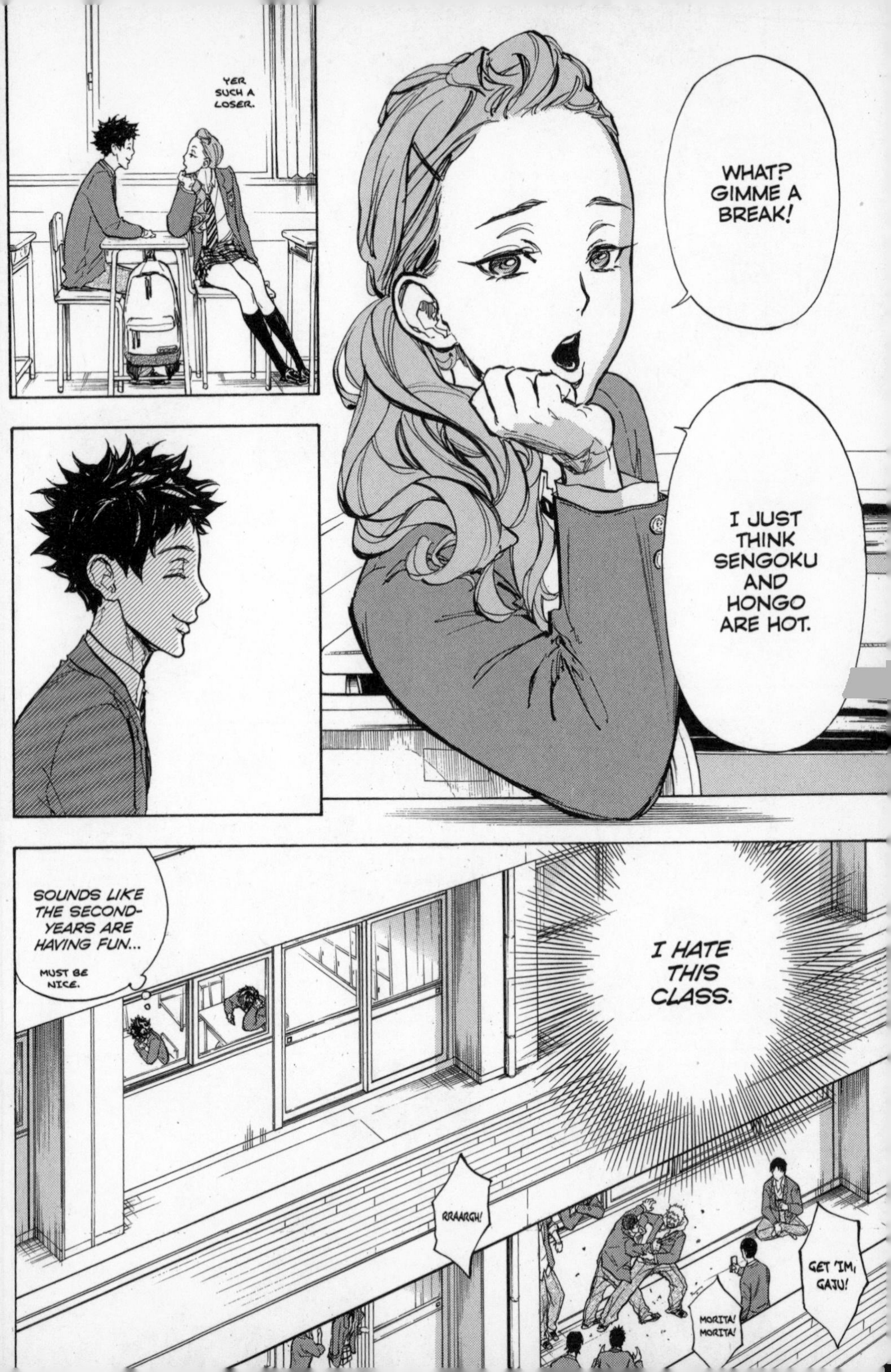
WHAT? GIMME A BREAK!
I JUST THINK SENGOKU AND HONGO ARE HOT.
YER SUCH A LOSER.
I HATE THIS CLASS.
SOUNDS LIKE THE SECOND-YEARS ARE HAVING FUN...
MUST BE NICE.
GET 'IM, GAJU!
MORITA! MORITA!
RRAARGH!

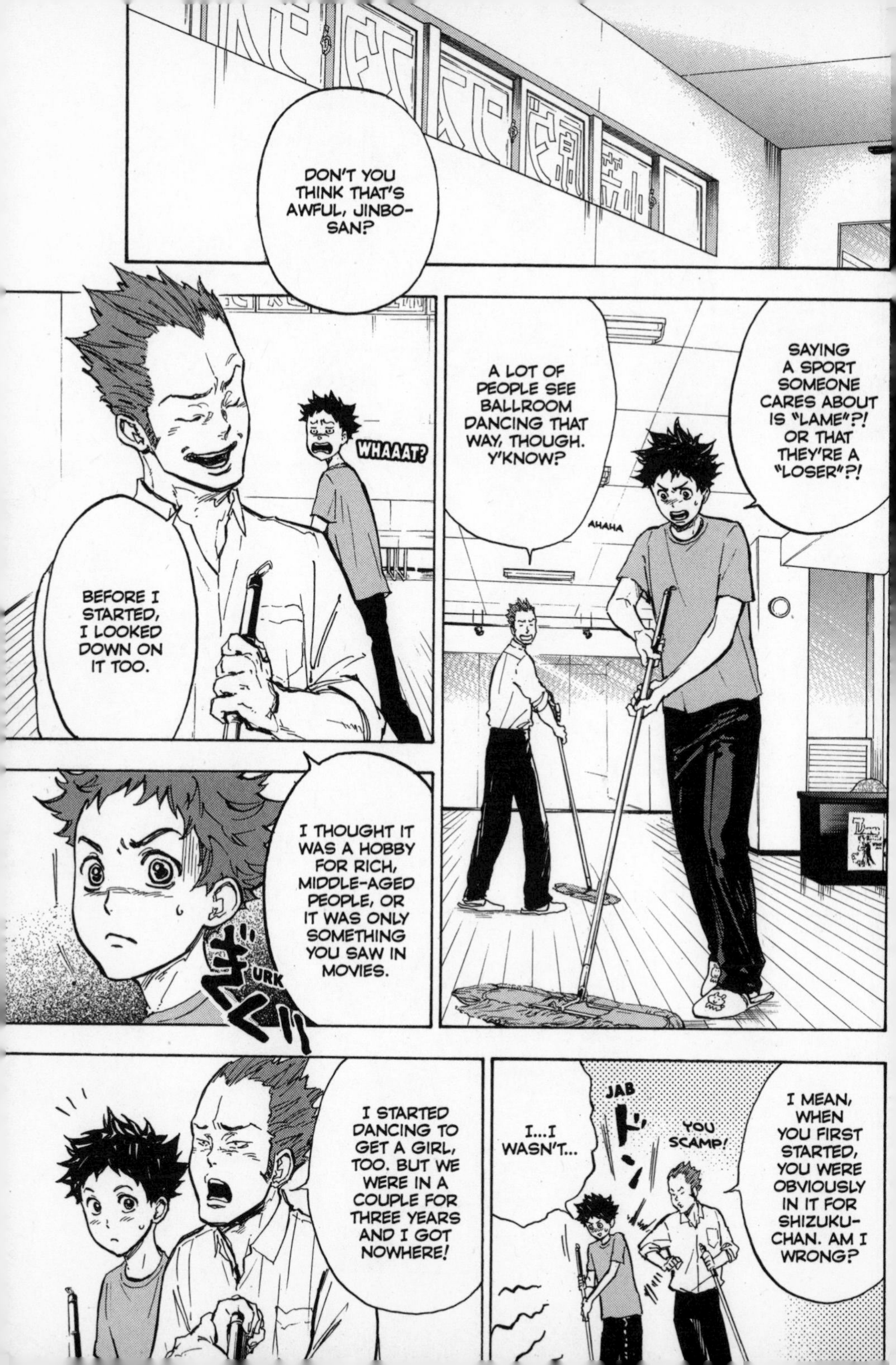
DON'T YOU THINK THAT'S AWFUL, JINBO-SAN?
SAYING A SPORT SOMEONE CARES ABOUT IS "LAME"?! OR THAT THEY'RE A "LOSER"?!
A LOT OF PEOPLE SEE BALLROOM DANCING THAT WAY, THOUGH. Y'KNOW?
AHAHA
WHAAAT?
BEFORE I STARTED, I LOOKED DOWN ON IT TOO.
I THOUGHT IT WAS A HOBBY FOR RICH, MIDDLE-AGED PEOPLE, OR IT WAS ONLY SOMETHING YOU SAW IN MOVIES.
URK
I MEAN, WHEN YOU FIRST STARTED, YOU WERE OBVIOUSLY IN IT FOR SHIZUKU-CHAN. AM I WRONG?
YOU SCAMP!
JAB
I...I WASN'T...
I STARTED DANCING TO GET A GIRL, TOO. BUT WE WERE IN A COUPLE FOR THREE YEARS AND I GOT NOWHERE!

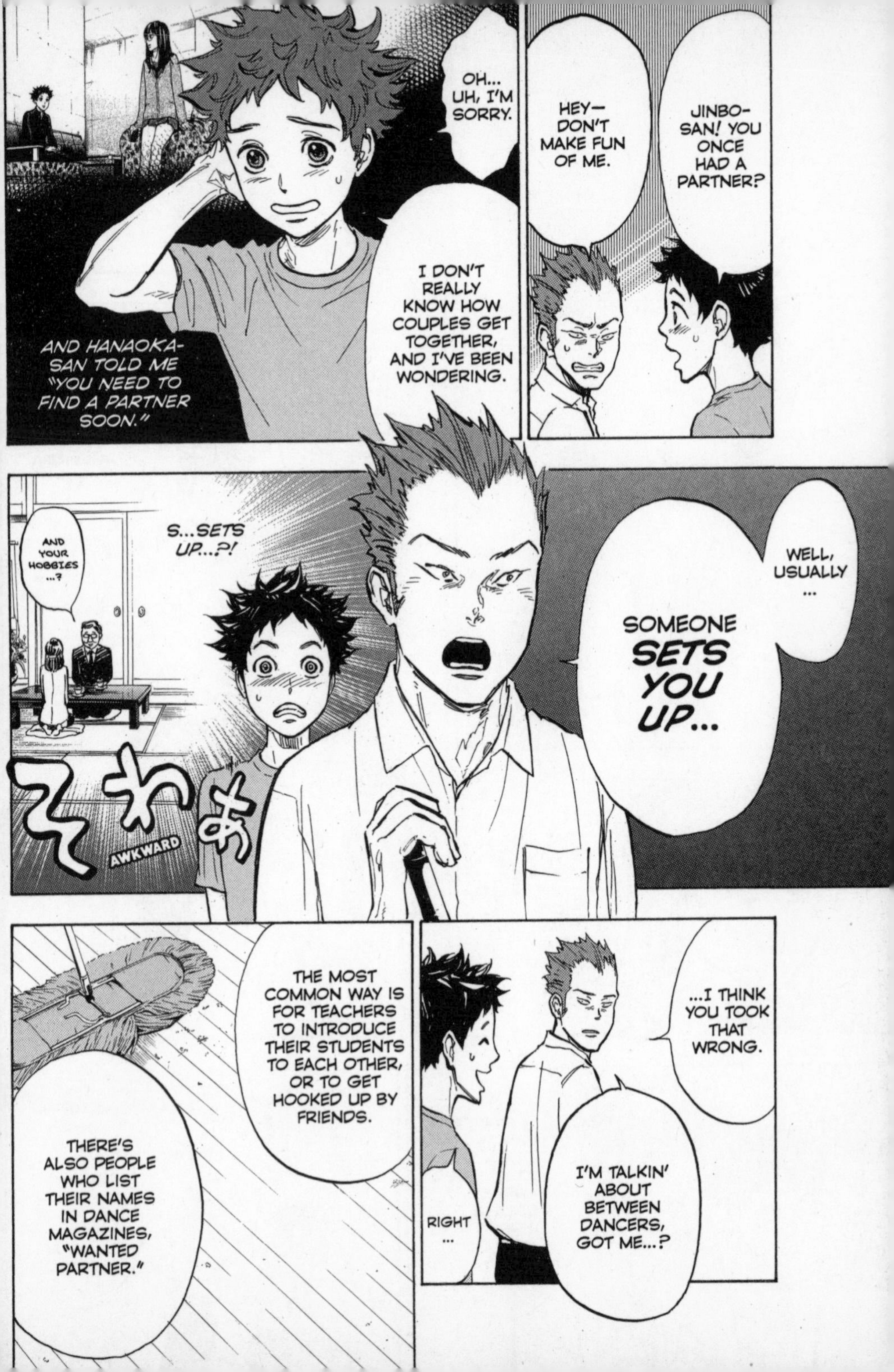
JINBO-SAN! YOU ONCE HAD A PARTNER?
HEY— DON'T MAKE FUN OF ME.
OH... UH, I'M SORRY.
I DON'T REALLY KNOW HOW COUPLES GET TOGETHER, AND I'VE BEEN WONDERING.
AND HANAOKA-SAN TOLD ME "YOU NEED TO FIND A PARTNER SOON."
WELL, USUALLY ...
SOMEONE SETS YOU UP...
S...SETS UP...?!
AND YOUR HOBBIES ...?
そわぁ
AWKWARD
...I THINK YOU TOOK THAT WRONG.
I'M TALKIN' ABOUT BETWEEN DANCERS, GOT ME...?
RIGHT ...
THE MOST COMMON WAY IS FOR TEACHERS TO INTRODUCE THEIR STUDENTS TO EACH OTHER, OR TO GET HOOKED UP BY FRIENDS.
THERE'S ALSO PEOPLE WHO LIST THEIR NAMES IN DANCE MAGAZINES, "WANTED PARTNER."

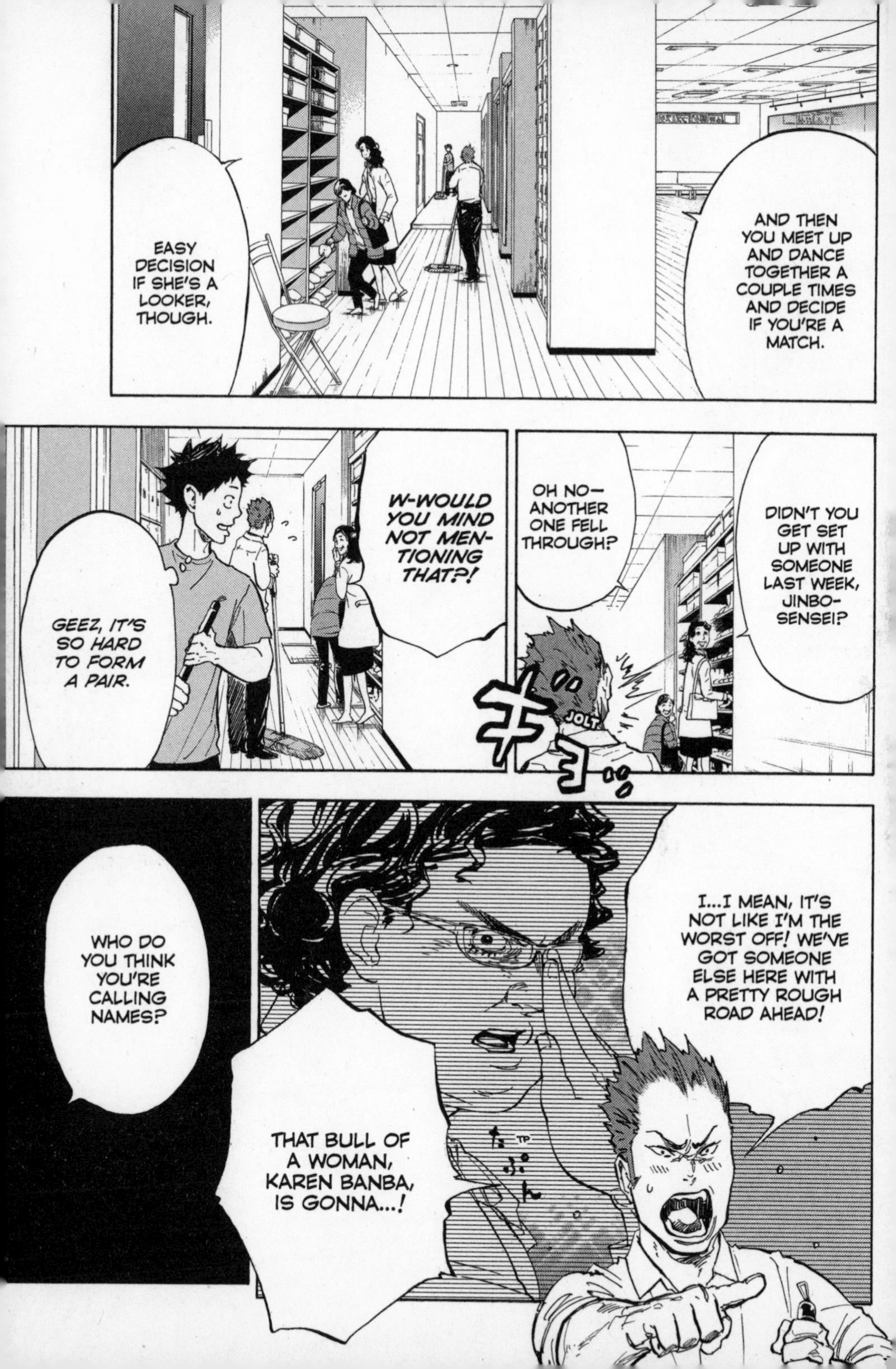
AND THEN YOU MEET UP AND DANCE TOGETHER A COUPLE TIMES AND DECIDE IF YOU'RE A MATCH.
EASY DECISION IF SHE'S A LOOKER, THOUGH.
DIDN'T YOU GET SET UP WITH SOMEONE LAST WEEK, JINBO-SENSEI?
OH NO— ANOTHER ONE FELL THROUGH?
JOLT
W-WOULD YOU MIND NOT MEN-TIONING THAT?!
GEEZ, IT'S SO HARD TO FORM A PAIR.
I...I MEAN, IT'S NOT LIKE I'M THE WORST OFF! WE'VE GOT SOMEONE ELSE HERE WITH A PRETTY ROUGH ROAD AHEAD!
THAT BULL OF A WOMAN, KAREN BANBA, IS GONNA...!
TP
WHO DO YOU THINK YOU'RE CALLING NAMES?

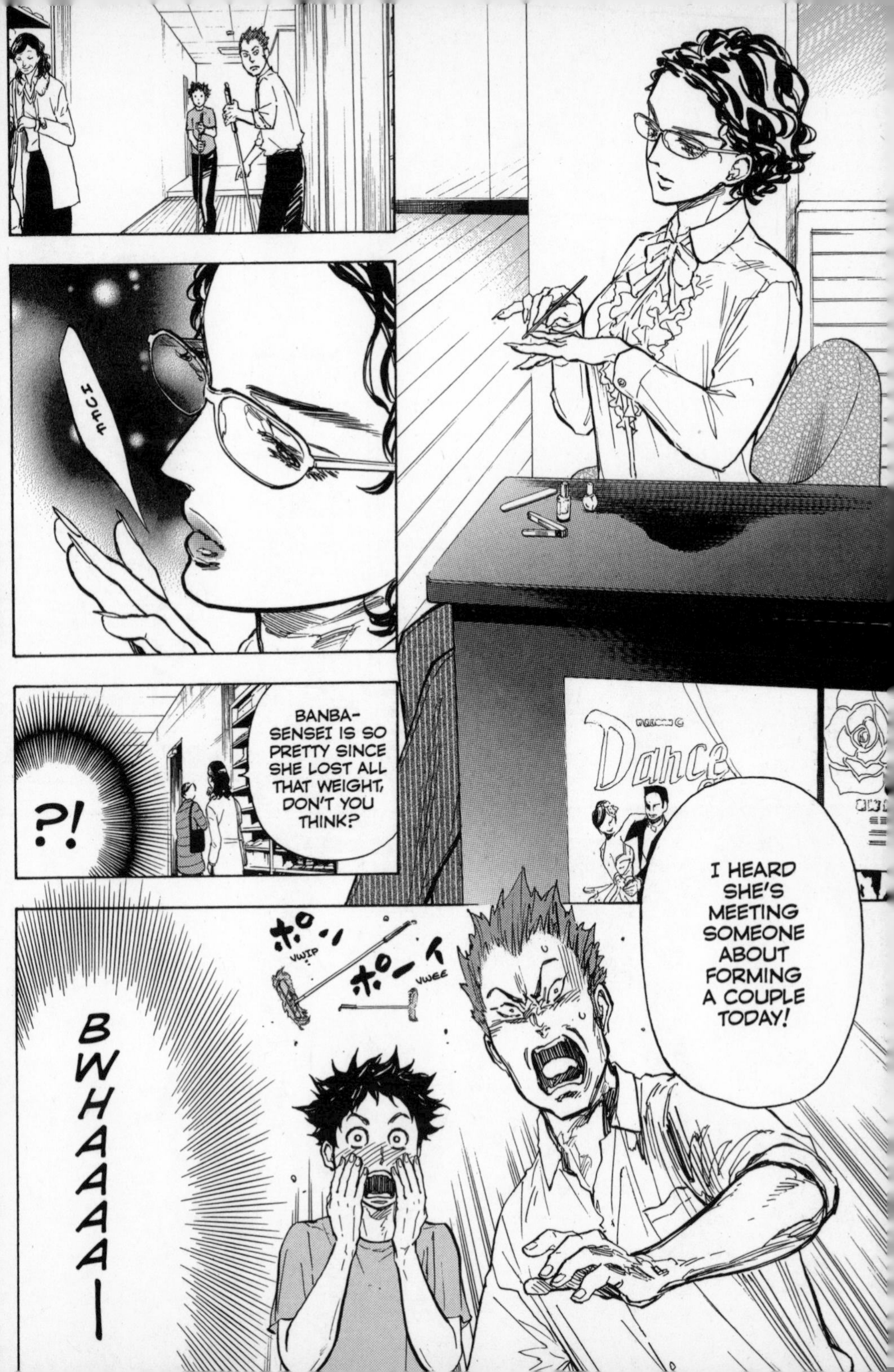
Dance
HUFF
BANBA-SENSEI IS SO PRETTY SINCE SHE LOST ALL THAT WEIGHT, DON'T YOU THINK?
?!
I HEARD SHE'S MEETING SOMEONE ABOUT FORMING A COUPLE TODAY!
ポーイ
VWIP
ポーイ
VWEE
BWHAAAAAI

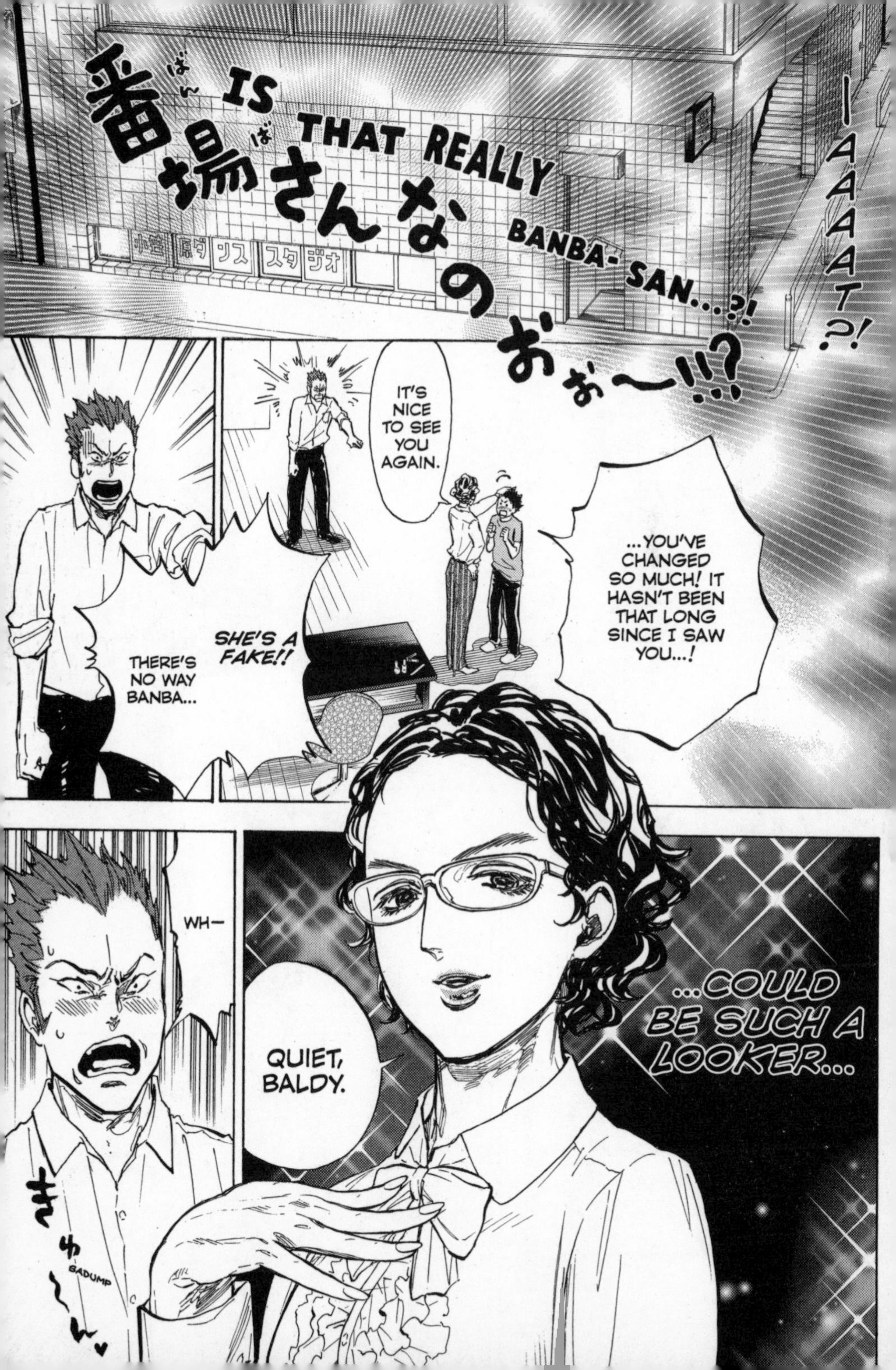

番場さんなのぉ〜!!?
IS THAT REALLY BANBA-SAN...?!
IAAAAT?!
小笠原ダンススタジオ
...YOU'VE CHANGED SO MUCH! IT HASN'T BEEN THAT LONG SINCE I SAW YOU...!
IT'S NICE TO SEE YOU AGAIN.
SHE'S A FAKE!!
THERE'S NO WAY BANBA...
...COULD BE SUCH A LOOKER...
QUIET, BALDY.
WH—
きゅ〜ん♥
BADUMP

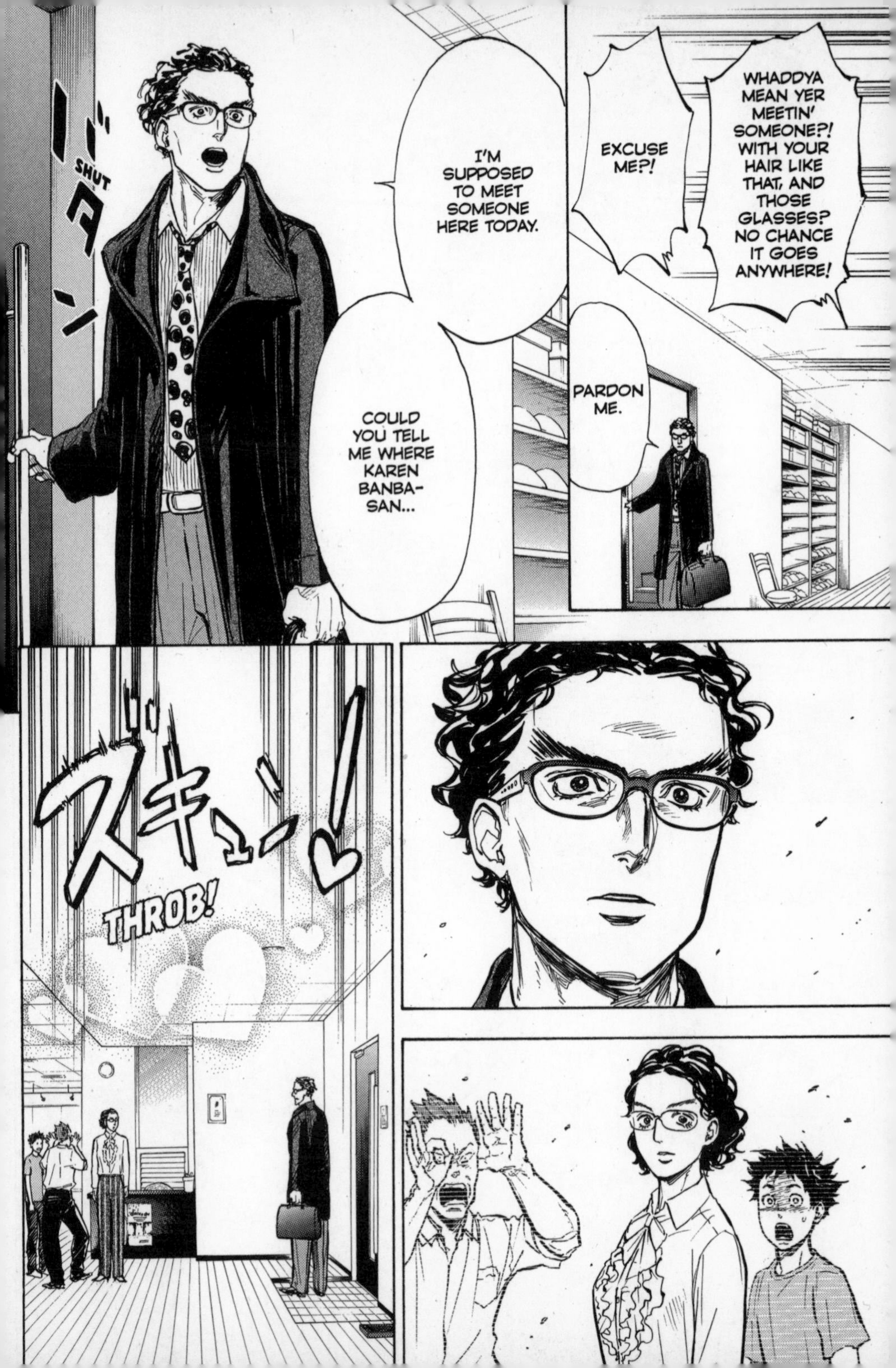
WHADDYA MEAN YER MEETIN' SOMEONE?! WITH YOUR HAIR LIKE THAT, AND THOSE GLASSES? NO CHANCE IT GOES ANYWHERE!
EXCUSE ME?!
PARDON ME.
I'M SUPPOSED TO MEET SOMEONE HERE TODAY.
COULD YOU TELL ME WHERE KAREN BANBA-SAN...
SHUT
スキュン！
THROB!

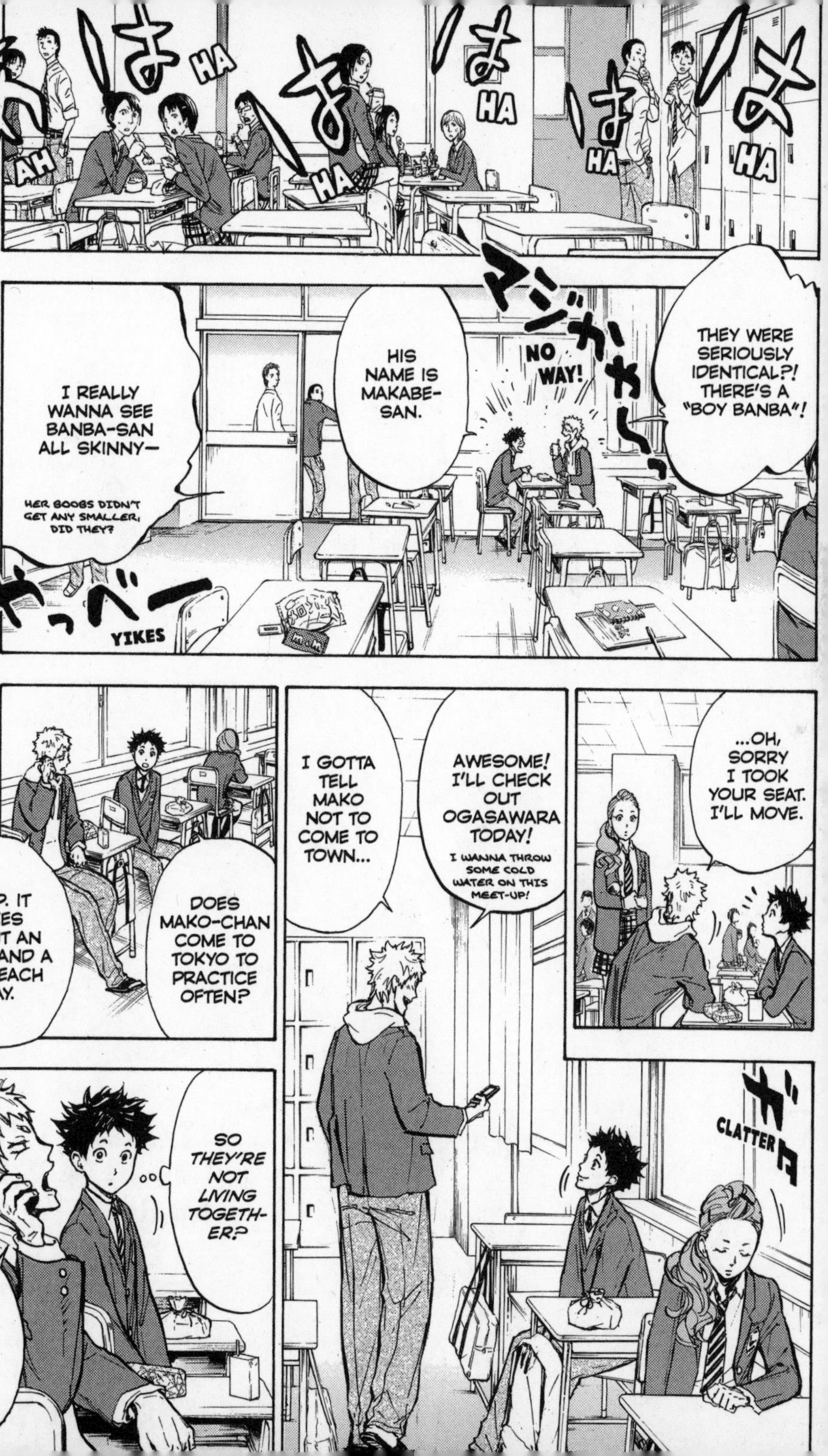
HA
HA
HA
HA
HA
AH
THEY WERE SERIOUSLY IDENTICAL?! THERE'S A "BOY BANBA"!
NO WAY!
HIS NAME IS MAKABE-SAN.
I REALLY WANNA SEE BANBA-SAN ALL SKINNY—
HER BOOBS DIDN'T GET ANY SMALLER, DID THEY?
YIKES
...OH, SORRY I TOOK YOUR SEAT. I'LL MOVE.
CLATTER
AWESOME! I'LL CHECK OUT OGASAWARA TODAY!
I WANNA THROW SOME COLD WATER ON THIS MEET-UP!
I GOTTA TELL MAKO NOT TO COME TO TOWN...
DOES MAKO-CHAN COME TO TOKYO TO PRACTICE OFTEN?
AYUP. IT TAKES ABOUT AN HOUR AND A HALF EACH WAY.
SO THEY'RE NOT LIVING TOGETHER?
HEY— MAKO. IT'S ME...

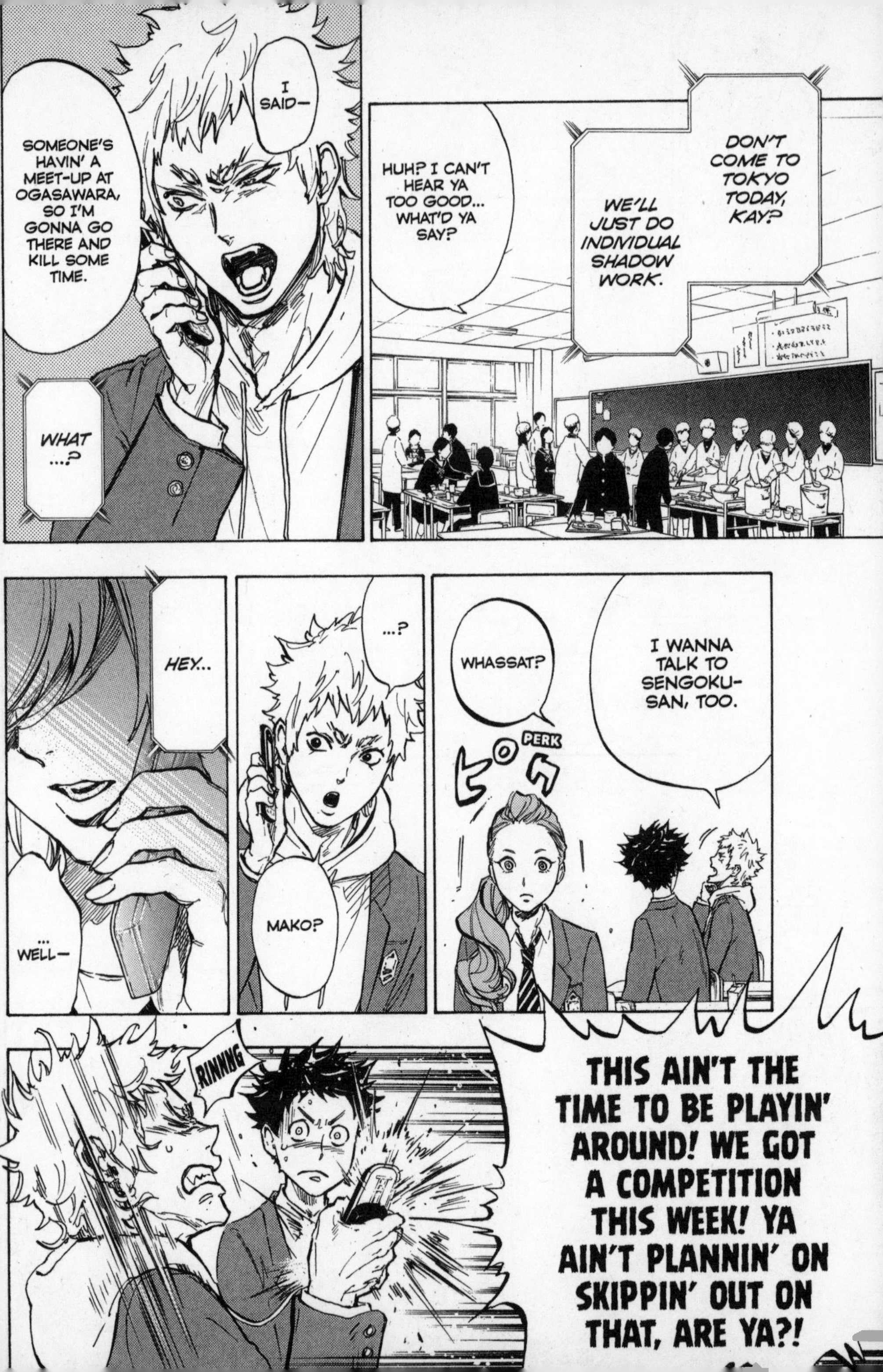

DON'T COME TO TOKYO TODAY, KAY?
WE'LL JUST DO INDIVIDUAL SHADOW WORK.
HUH? I CAN'T HEAR YA TOO GOOD... WHAT'D YA SAY?
I SAID—
SOMEONE'S HAVIN' A MEET-UP AT OGASAWARA, SO I'M GONNA GO THERE AND KILL SOME TIME.
WHAT ...?
I WANNA TALK TO SENGOKU-SAN, TOO.
WHASSAT?
PERK
...?
MAKO?
HEY...
... WELL—
THIS AIN'T THE TIME TO BE PLAYIN' AROUND! WE GOT A COMPETITION THIS WEEK! YA AIN'T PLANNIN' ON SKIPPIN' OUT ON THAT, ARE YA?!
RINNNG

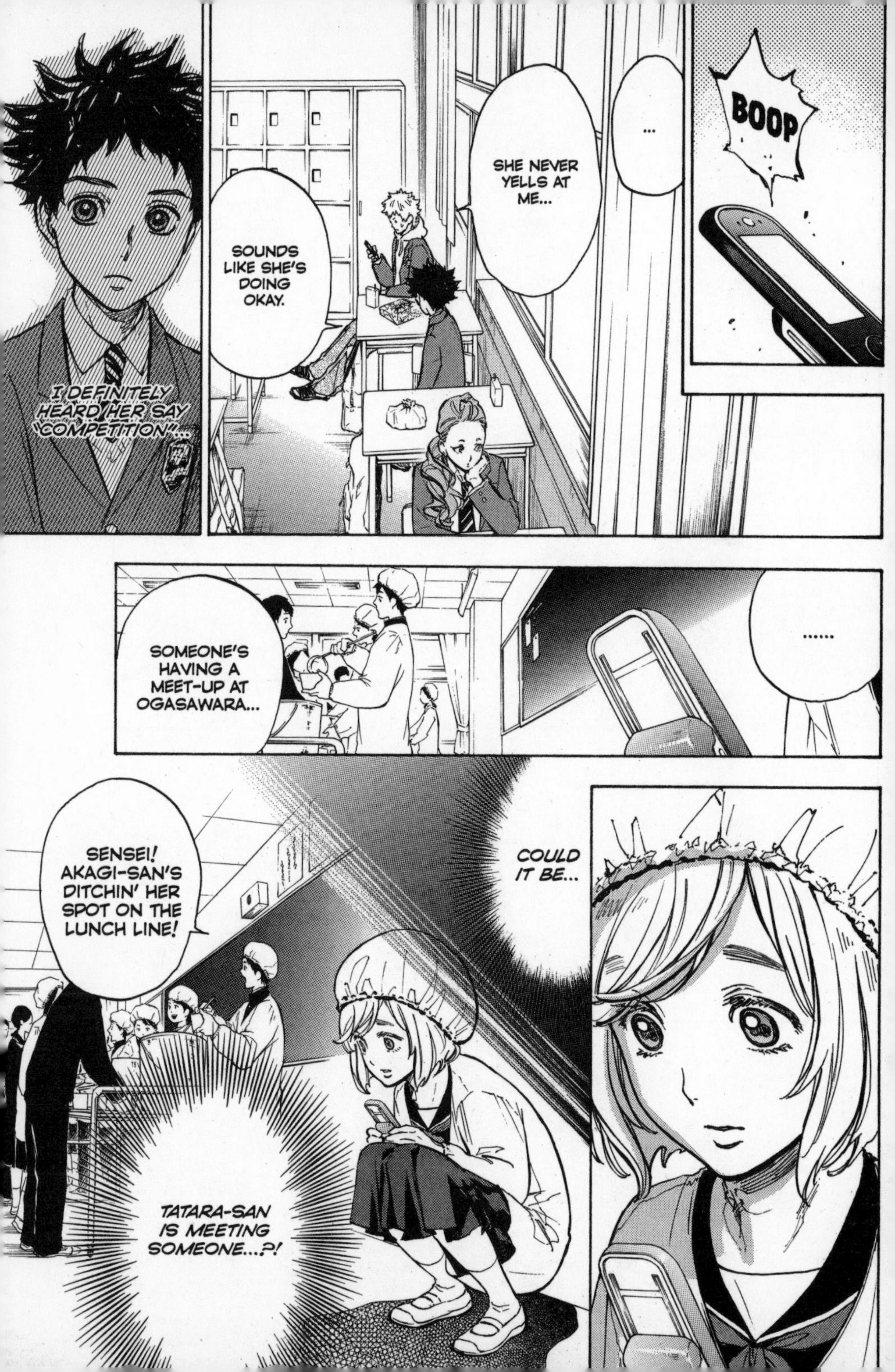
BOOP
...
SHE NEVER YELLS AT ME...
SOUNDS LIKE SHE'S DOING OKAY.
I DEFINITELY HEARD HER SAY "COMPETITION"...
......
SOMEONE'S HAVING A MEET-UP AT OGASAWARA...
COULD IT BE...
SENSEI! AKAGI-SAN'S DITCHIN' HER SPOT ON THE LUNCH LINE!
TATARA-SAN IS MEETING SOMEONE...?!

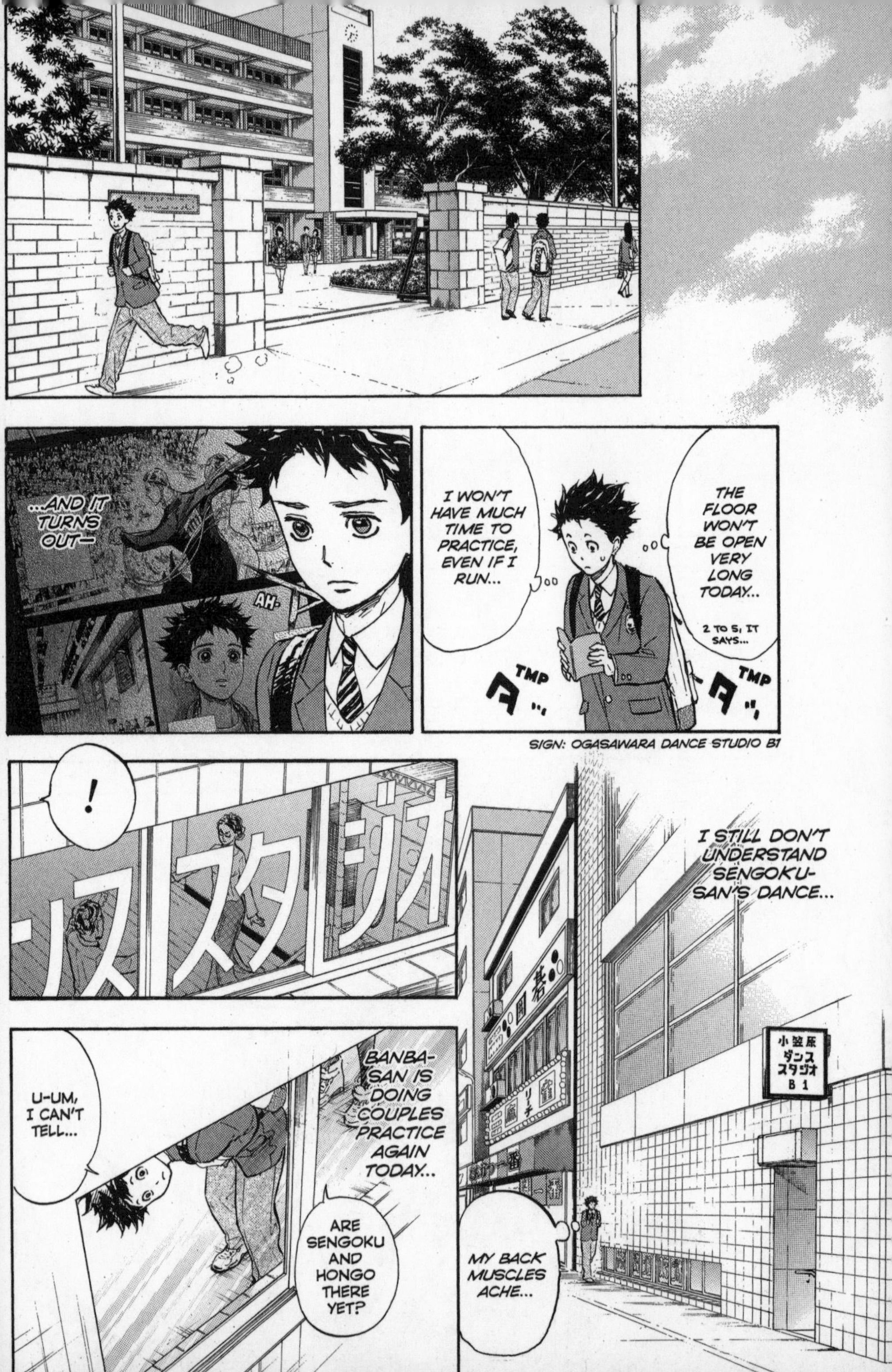
THE FLOOR WON'T BE OPEN VERY LONG TODAY...
2 TO 5, IT SAYS...
I WON'T HAVE MUCH TIME TO PRACTICE, EVEN IF I RUN...
TMP
TMP
...AND IT TURNS OUT—
AH-
SIGN: OGASAWARA DANCE STUDIO B1
I STILL DON'T UNDERSTAND SENGOKU-SAN'S DANCE...
小笠原 ダンス スタジオ B1
MY BACK MUSCLES ACHE...
!
スタジオ
BANBA-SAN IS DOING COUPLES PRACTICE AGAIN TODAY...
ARE SENGOKU AND HONGO THERE YET?
U-UM, I CAN'T TELL...

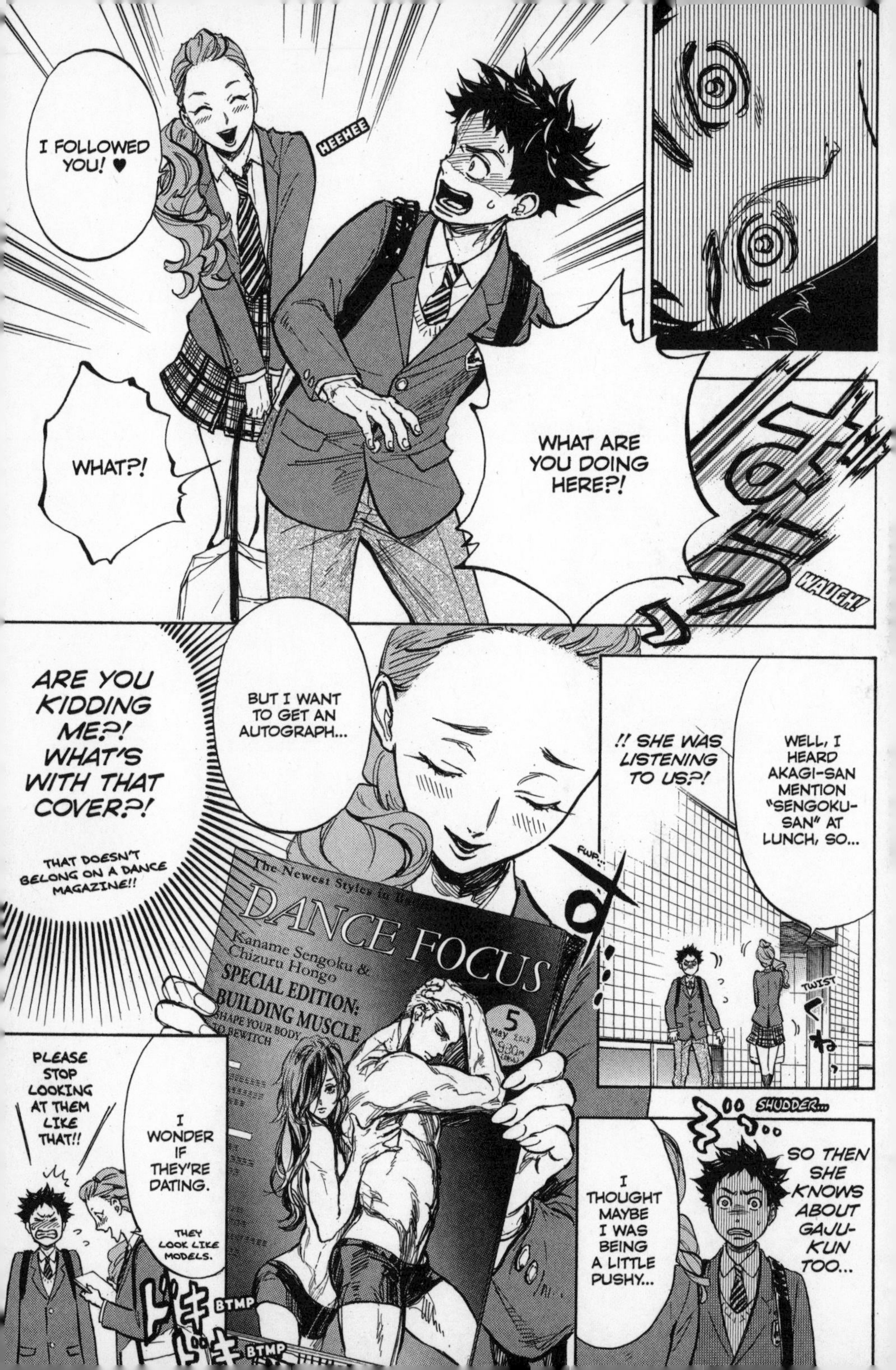
WHAT ARE YOU DOING HERE?!
WAUGH!
I FOLLOWED YOU! ♥
HEEHEE
WHAT?!
WELL, I HEARD AKAGI-SAN MENTION "SENGOKU-SAN" AT LUNCH, SO...
!! SHE WAS LISTENING TO US?!
TWIST
FWP...
BUT I WANT TO GET AN AUTOGRAPH...
ARE YOU KIDDING ME?! WHAT'S WITH THAT COVER?!
THAT DOESN'T BELONG ON A DANCE MAGAZINE!!
DANCE FOCUS
Kaname Sengoku & Chizuru Hongo
SPECIAL EDITION:
BUILDING MUSCLE
SHAPE YOUR BODY TO BEWITCH
5
May
SHUDDER...
SO THEN SHE KNOWS ABOUT GAJU-KUN TOO...
I THOUGHT MAYBE I WAS BEING A LITTLE PUSHY...
I WONDER IF THEY'RE DATING.
THEY LOOK LIKE MODELS.
PLEASE STOP LOOKING AT THEM LIKE THAT!!
BTMP
BTMP

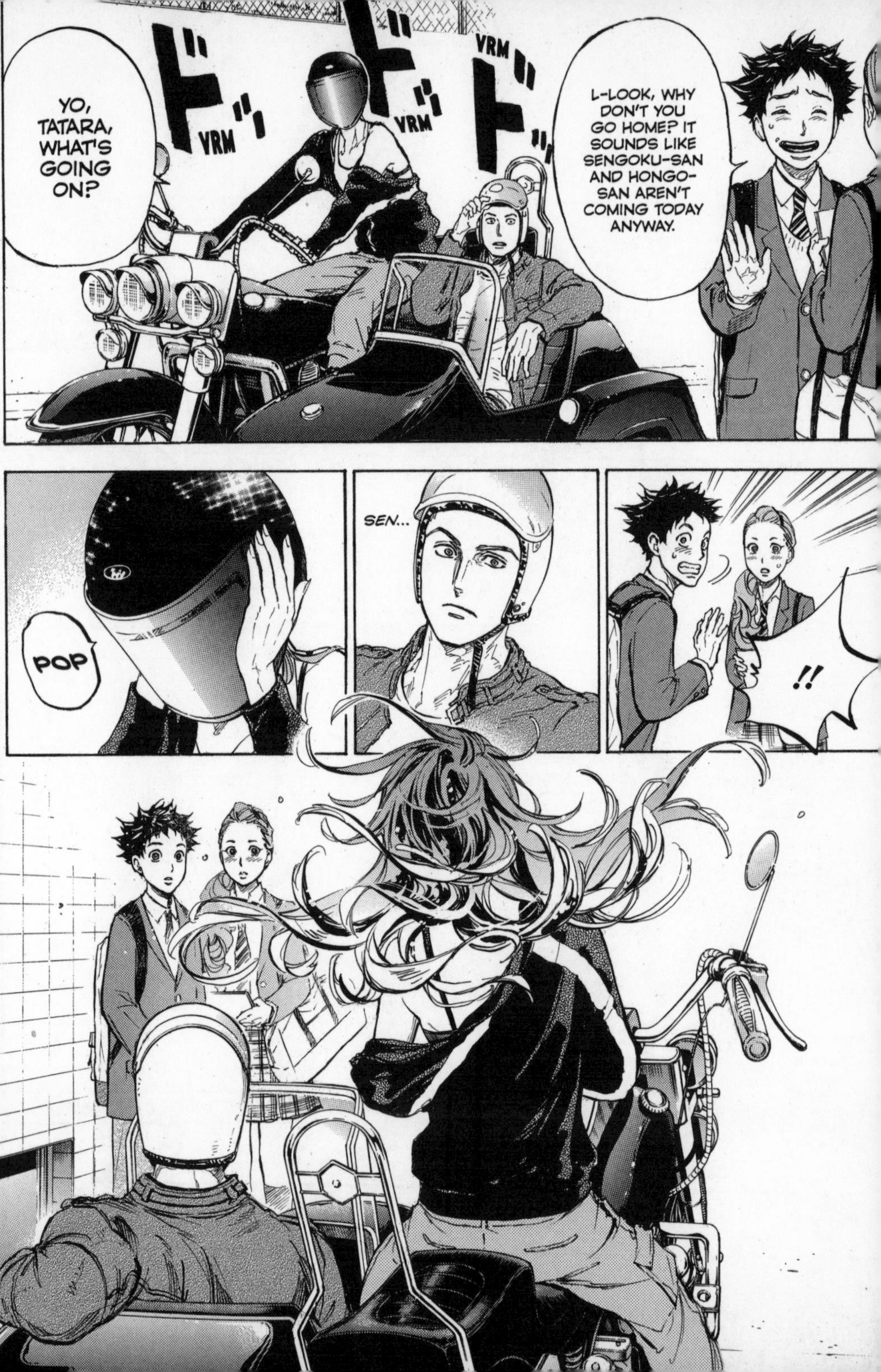
L-LOOK, WHY DON'T YOU GO HOME? IT SOUNDS LIKE SENGOKU-SAN AND HONGO-SAN AREN'T COMING TODAY ANYWAY.
VRM
VRM
VRM
YO, TATARA, WHAT'S GOING ON?
!!
SEN...
POP

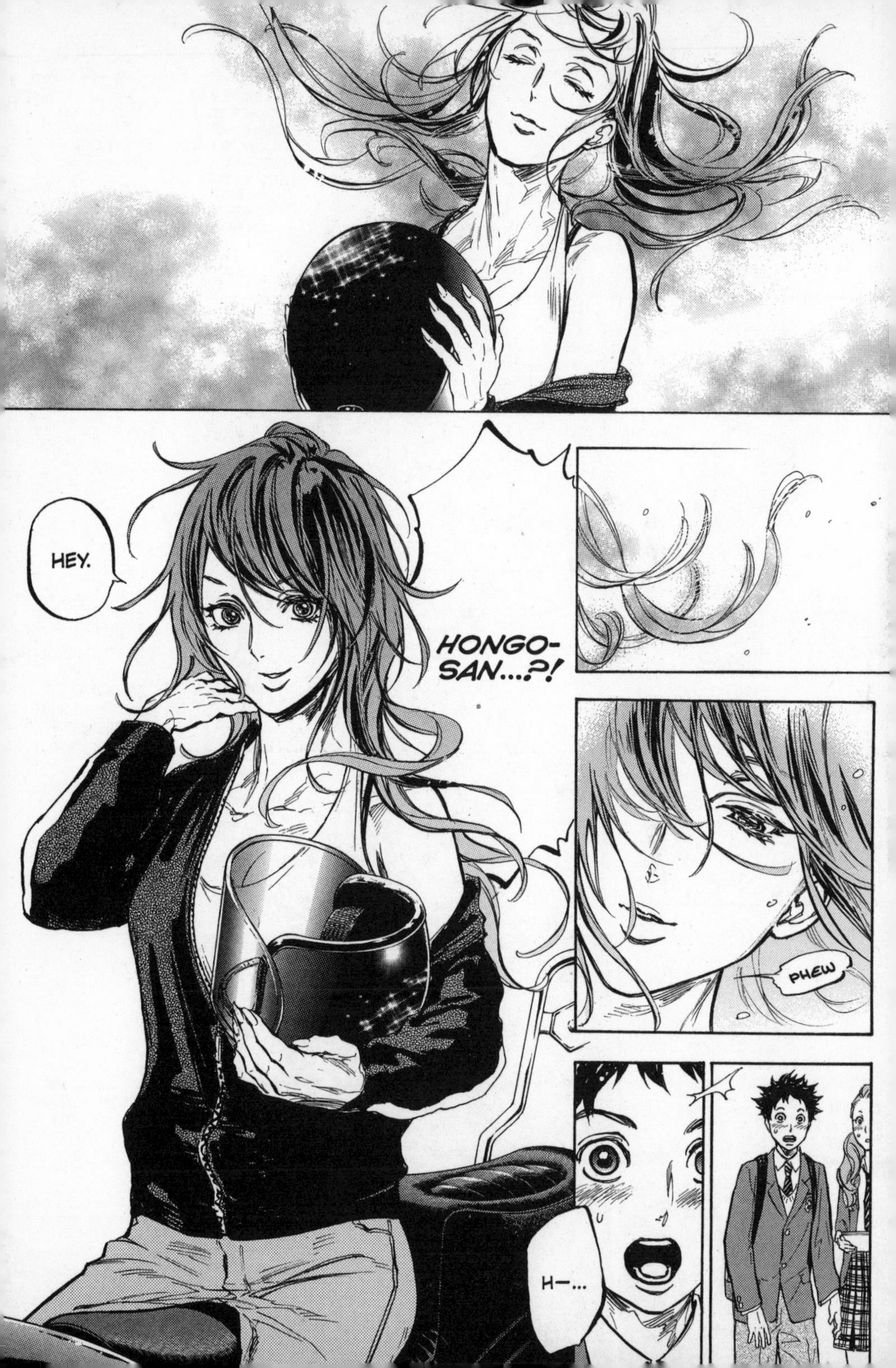
PHEW
H—...
HONGO-SAN...?!
HEY.

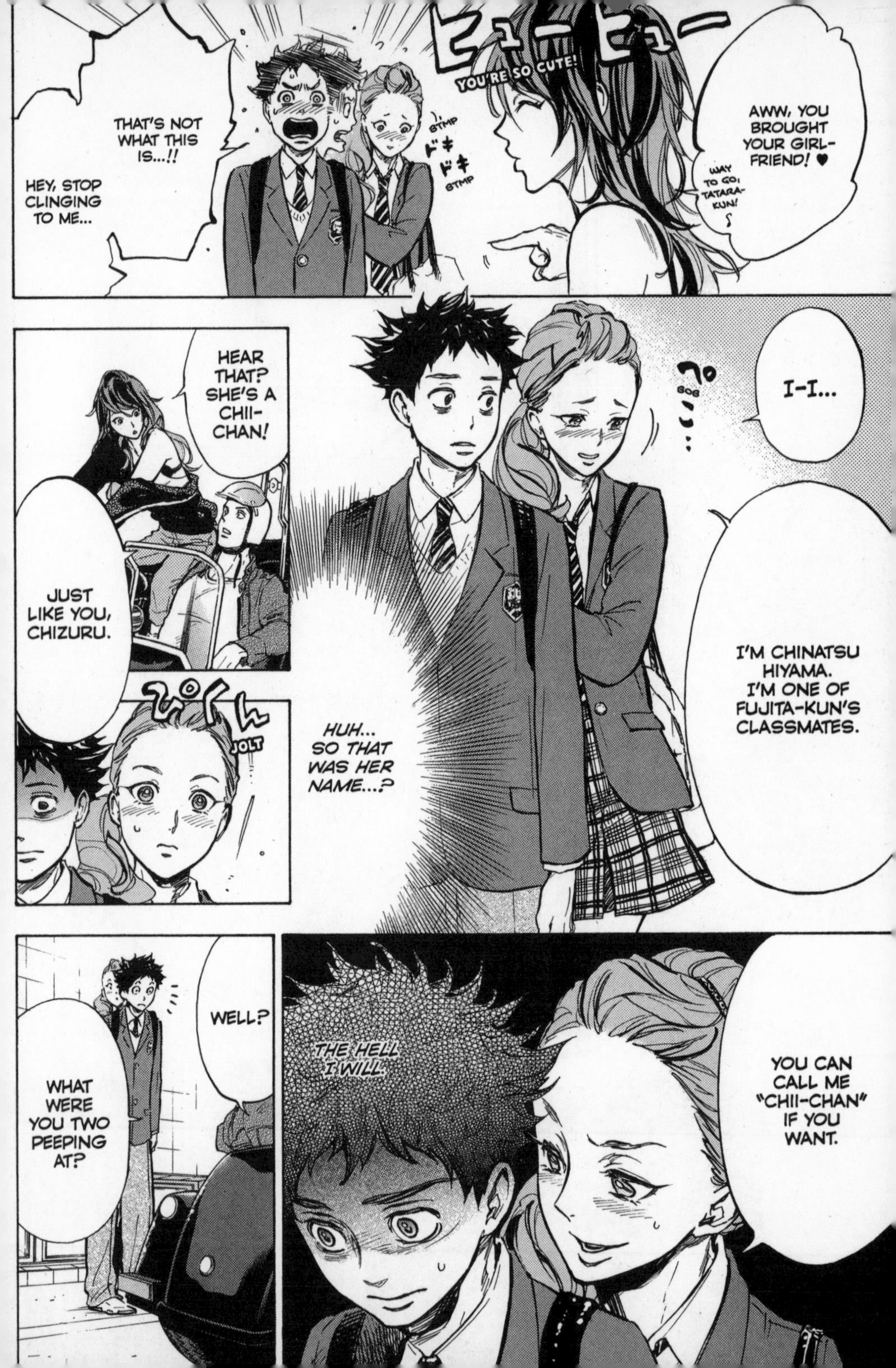
ヒューヒュー
YOU'RE SO CUTE!
AWW, YOU BROUGHT YOUR GIRL-FRIEND! ♥
WAY TO GO, TATARA-KUN!
STMP ドキドキ STMP
THAT'S NOT WHAT THIS IS...!!
HEY, STOP CLINGING TO ME...
I-I...
BOB
I'M CHINATSU HIYAMA. I'M ONE OF FUJITA-KUN'S CLASSMATES.
HUH... SO THAT WAS HER NAME...?
HEAR THAT? SHE'S A CHII-CHAN!
JUST LIKE YOU, CHIZURU.
ぴくん
JOLT
YOU CAN CALL ME "CHII-CHAN" IF YOU WANT.
THE HELL I WILL.
WELL?
WHAT WERE YOU TWO PEEPING AT?

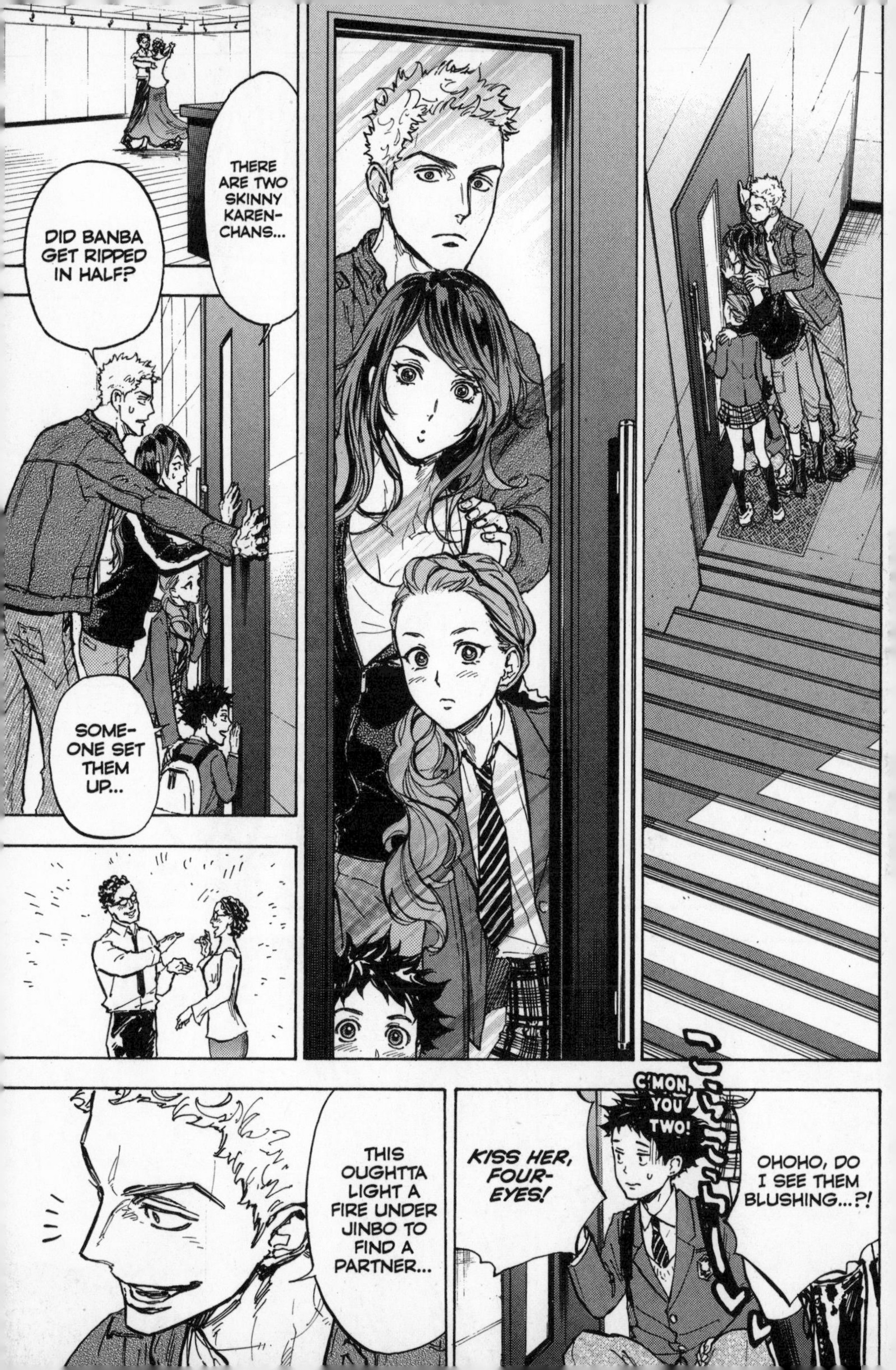

THERE ARE TWO SKINNY KAREN-CHANS...
DID BANBA GET RIPPED IN HALF?
SOME-ONE SET THEM UP...
OHOHO, DO I SEE THEM BLUSHING...?!
C'MON, YOU TWO!
KISS HER, FOUR-EYES!
THIS OUGHTTA LIGHT A FIRE UNDER JINBO TO FIND A PARTNER...

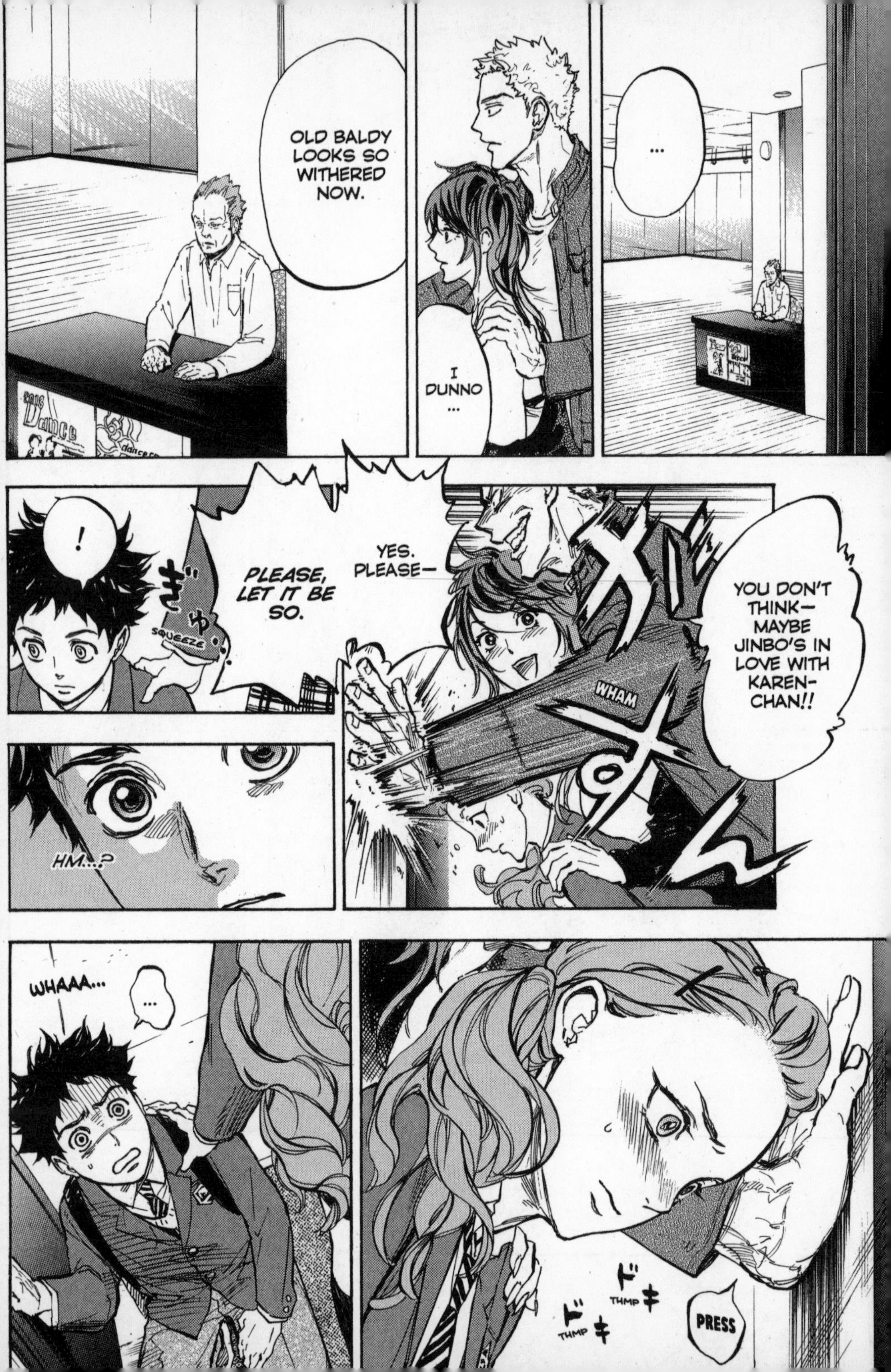
...
I DUNNO ...
OLD BALDY LOOKS SO WITHERED NOW.
YOU DON'T THINK— MAYBE JINBO'S IN LOVE WITH KAREN-CHAN!!
WHAM
YES. PLEASE—
PLEASE, LET IT BE SO.
!
ぎゅ
SQUEEZE
HM...?
ドキ
THMP
ドキ
THMP
PRESS
WHAAA...
...

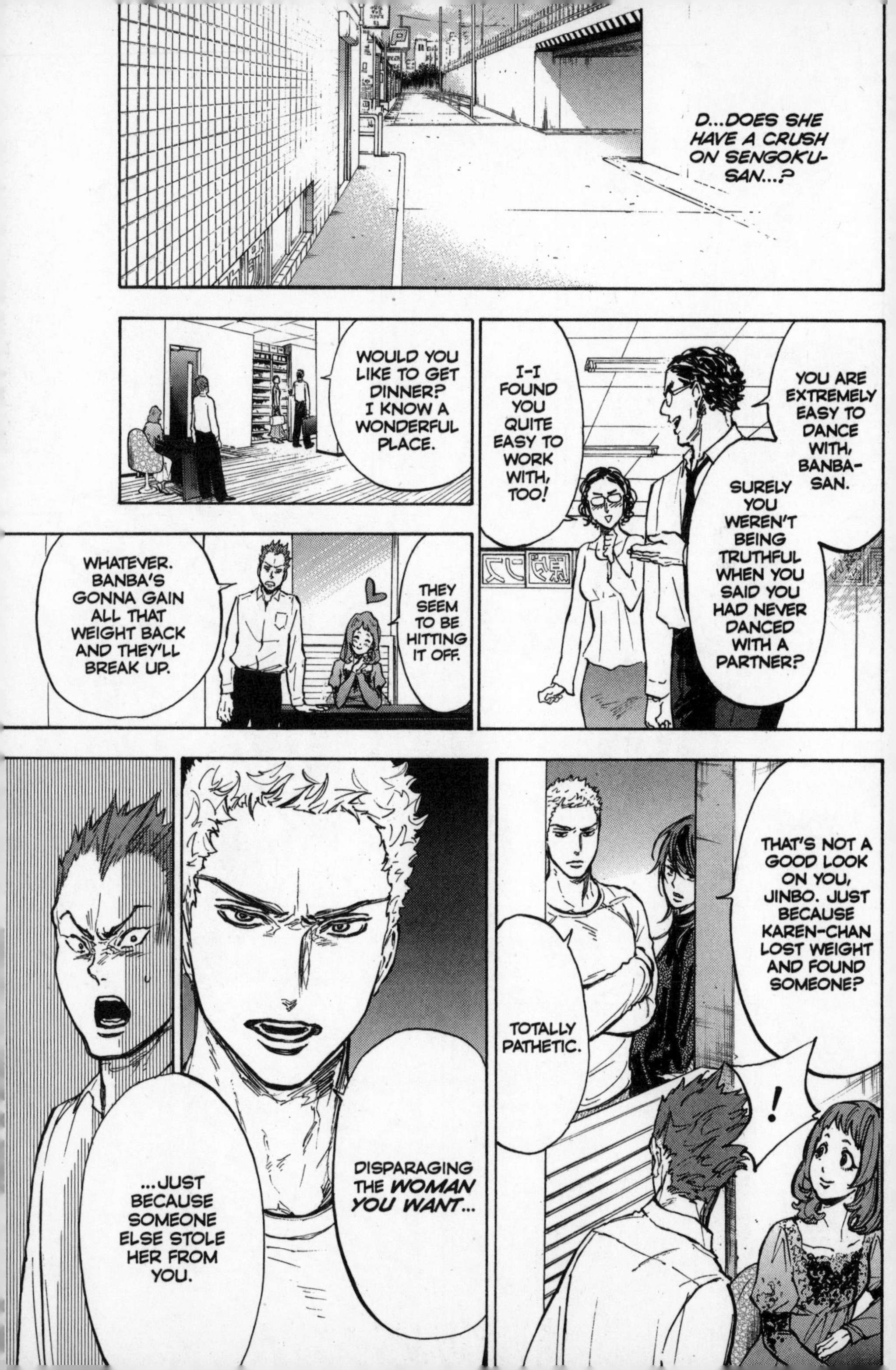
D...DOES SHE HAVE A CRUSH ON SENGOKU-SAN...?
YOU ARE EXTREMELY EASY TO DANCE WITH, BANBA-SAN.
I-I FOUND YOU QUITE EASY TO WORK WITH, TOO!
SURELY YOU WEREN'T BEING TRUTHFUL WHEN YOU SAID YOU HAD NEVER DANCED WITH A PARTNER?
WOULD YOU LIKE TO GET DINNER? I KNOW A WONDERFUL PLACE.
THEY SEEM TO BE HITTING IT OFF.
WHATEVER. BANBA'S GONNA GAIN ALL THAT WEIGHT BACK AND THEY'LL BREAK UP.
THAT'S NOT A GOOD LOOK ON YOU, JINBO. JUST BECAUSE KAREN-CHAN LOST WEIGHT AND FOUND SOMEONE?
!
TOTALLY PATHETIC.
DISPARAGING THE *WOMAN YOU WANT*...
...JUST BECAUSE SOMEONE ELSE STOLE HER FROM YOU.

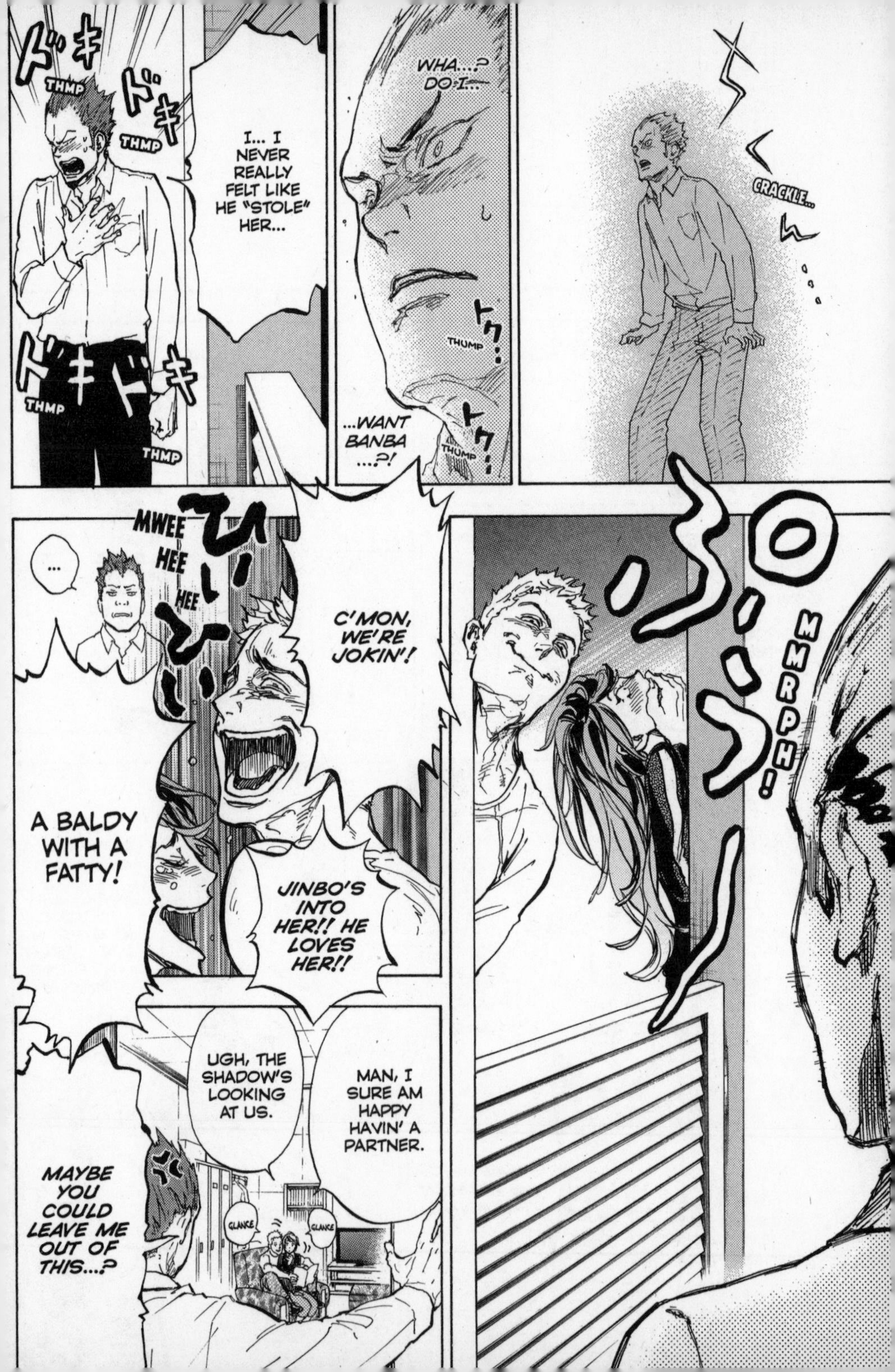
CRACKLE...
WHA...? DO I...
THUMP
THUMP
...WANT BANBA ...?!
I... I NEVER REALLY FELT LIKE HE "STOLE" HER...
THMP
THMP
THMP
THMP
MMRPH!
C'MON, WE'RE JOKIN'!
MWEE HEE HEE
...
JINBO'S INTO HER!! HE LOVES HER!!
A BALDY WITH A FATTY!
MAN, I SURE AM HAPPY HAVIN' A PARTNER.
UGH, THE SHADOW'S LOOKING AT US.
GLANCE
GLANCE
MAYBE YOU COULD LEAVE ME OUT OF THIS...?

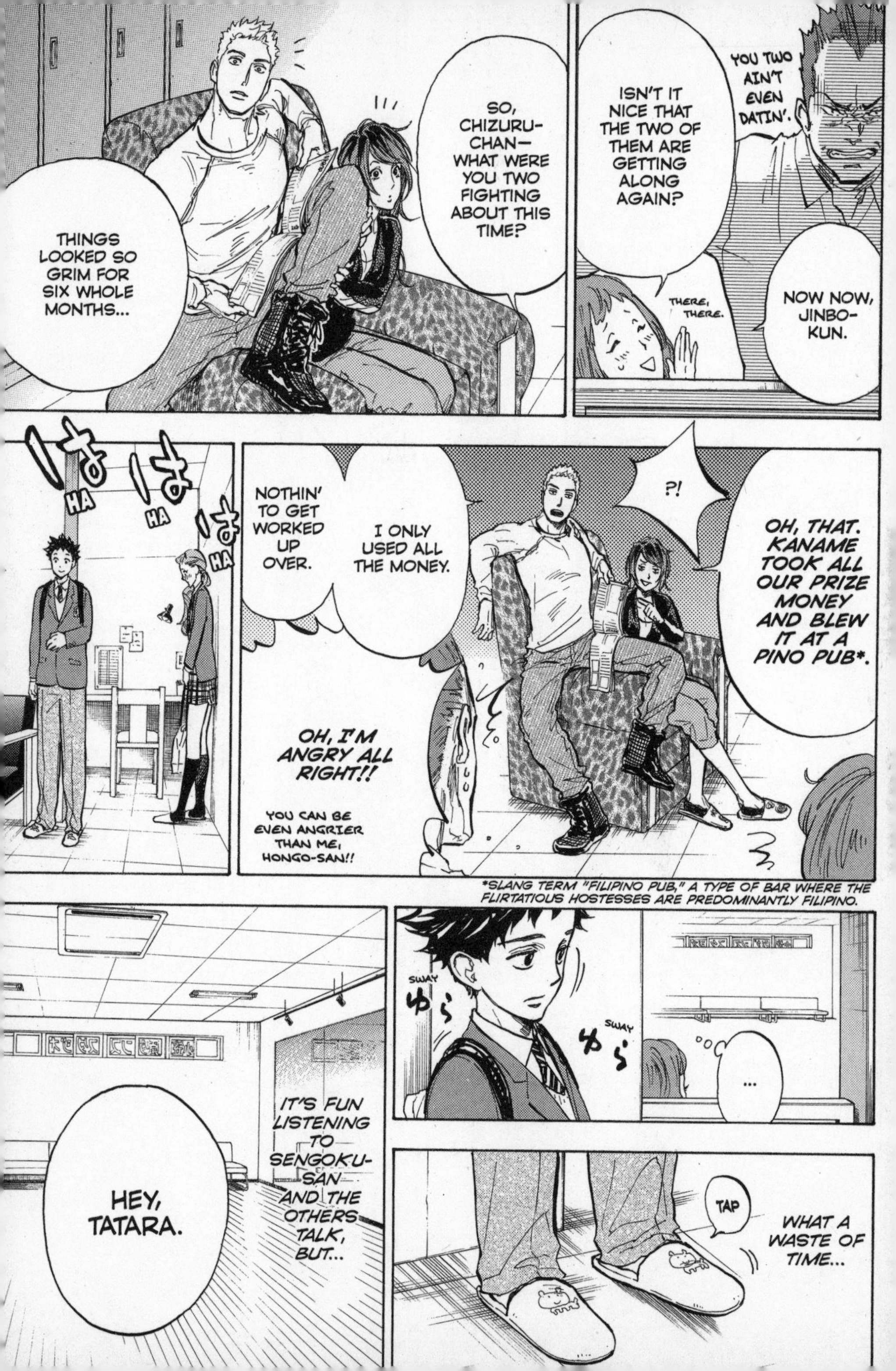
YOU TWO AIN'T EVEN DATIN'.
ISN'T IT NICE THAT THE TWO OF THEM ARE GETTING ALONG AGAIN?
NOW NOW, JINBO-KUN.
THERE, THERE.
SO, CHIZURU-CHAN—WHAT WERE YOU TWO FIGHTING ABOUT THIS TIME?
THINGS LOOKED SO GRIM FOR SIX WHOLE MONTHS...
OH, THAT. KANAME TOOK ALL OUR PRIZE MONEY AND BLEW IT AT A PINO PUB*.
?!
I ONLY USED ALL THE MONEY.
NOTHIN' TO GET WORKED UP OVER.
OH, I'M ANGRY ALL RIGHT!!
YOU CAN BE EVEN ANGRIER THAN ME, HONGO-SAN!!
HA
HA
HA
*SLANG TERM "FILIPINO PUB," A TYPE OF BAR WHERE THE FLIRTATIOUS HOSTESSES ARE PREDOMINANTLY FILIPINO.
SWAY
SWAY
...
TAP
WHAT A WASTE OF TIME...
IT'S FUN LISTENING TO SENGOKU-SAN AND THE OTHERS TALK, BUT...
HEY, TATARA.

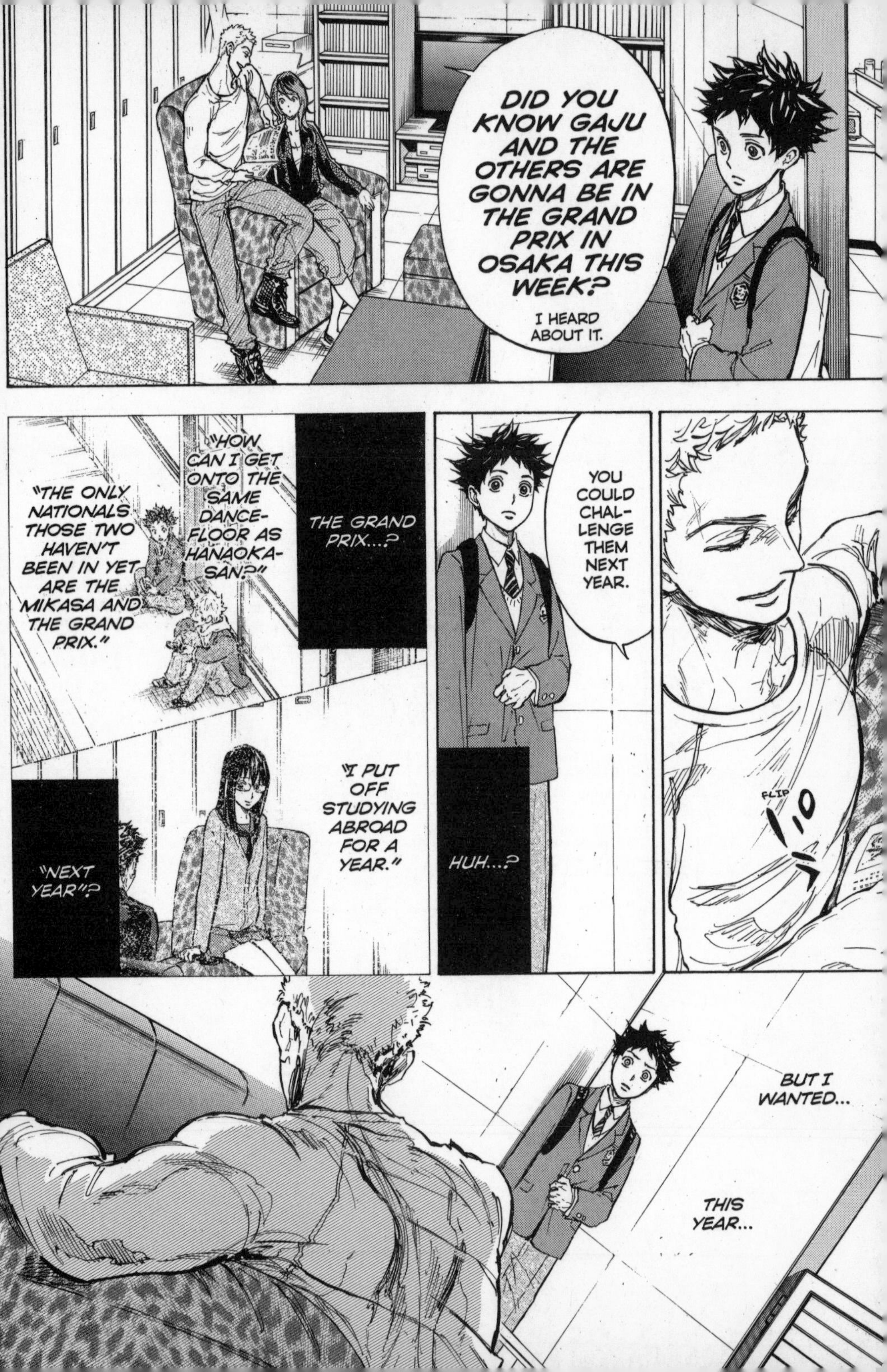
DID YOU KNOW GAJU AND THE OTHERS ARE GONNA BE IN THE GRAND PRIX IN OSAKA THIS WEEK?
I HEARD ABOUT IT.
FLIP
YOU COULD CHALLENGE THEM NEXT YEAR.
HUH...?
THE GRAND PRIX...?
"HOW CAN I GET ONTO THE SAME DANCEFLOOR AS HANAOKA-SAN?"
"THE ONLY NATIONALS THOSE TWO HAVEN'T BEEN IN YET ARE THE MIKASA AND THE GRAND PRIX."
"I PUT OFF STUDYING ABROAD FOR A YEAR."
"NEXT YEAR"?
BUT I WANTED...
THIS YEAR...

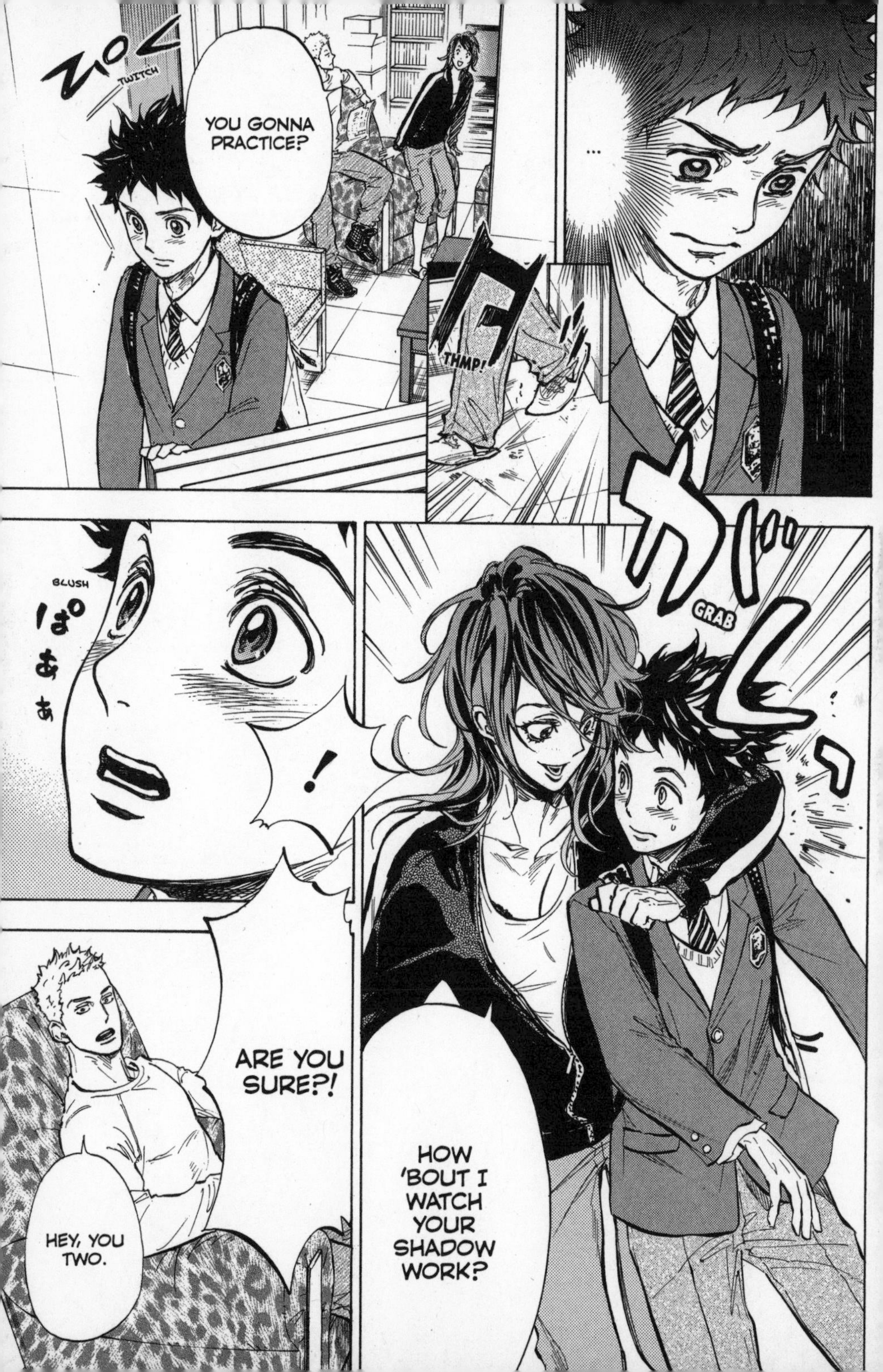
...
THMP!
TWITCH
YOU GONNA PRACTICE?
GRAB
HOW 'BOUT I WATCH YOUR SHADOW WORK?
BLUSH
!
ARE YOU SURE?!
HEY, YOU TWO.

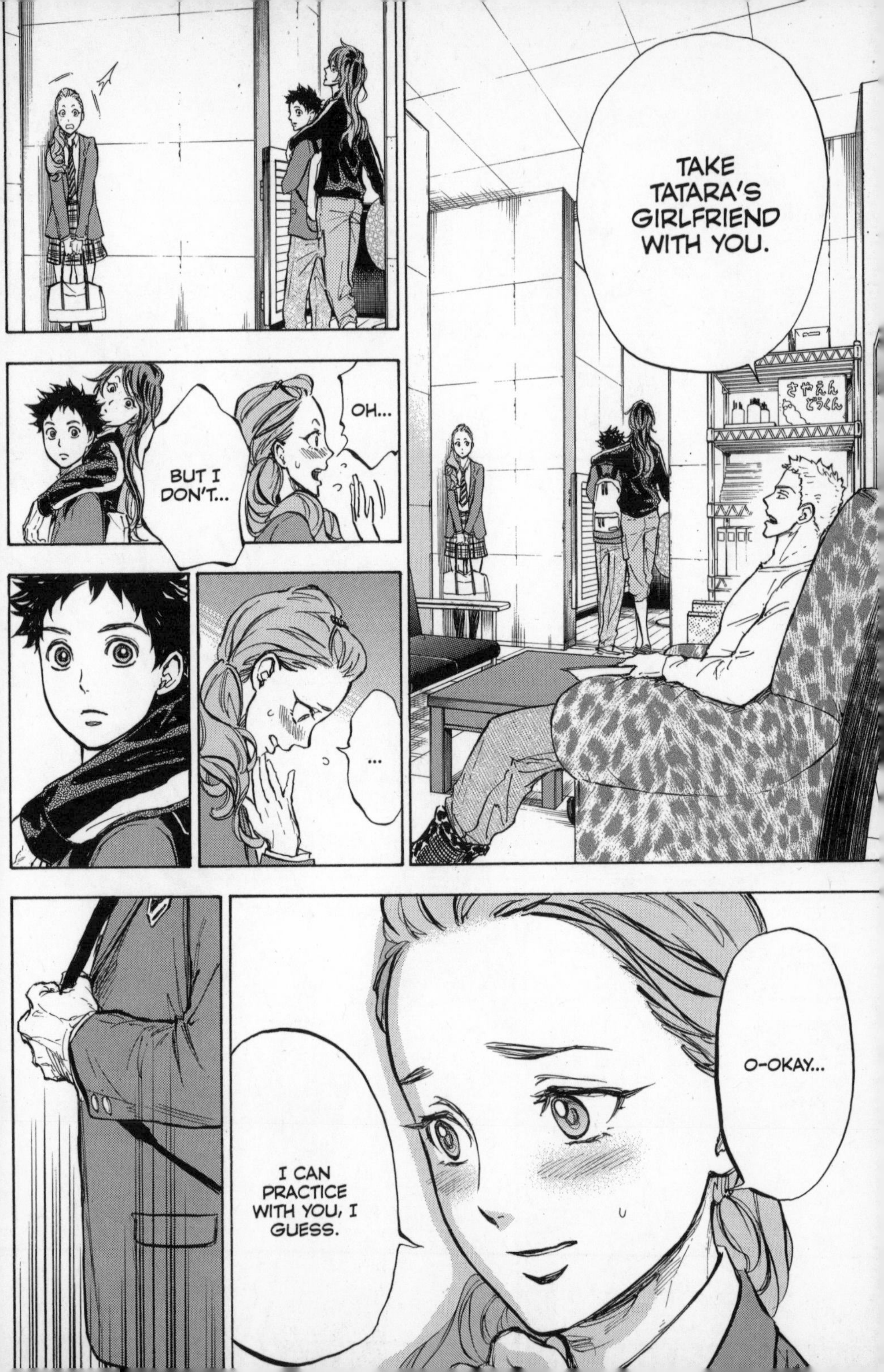
TAKE TATARA'S GIRLFRIEND WITH YOU.
さやえんどうくん
OH...
BUT I DON'T...
...
O-OKAY...
I CAN PRACTICE WITH YOU, I GUESS.

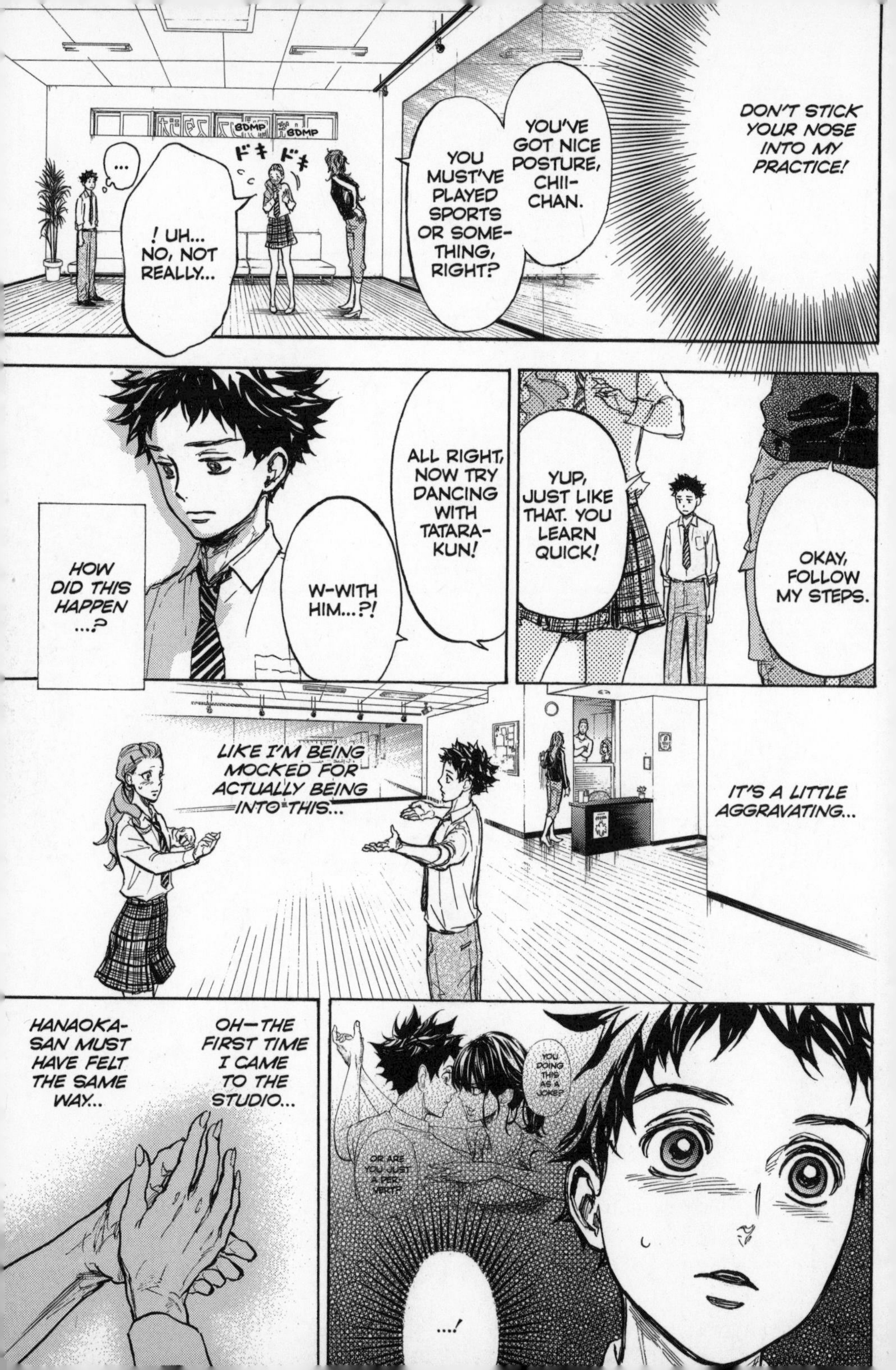
DON'T STICK YOUR NOSE INTO MY PRACTICE!
YOU'VE GOT NICE POSTURE, CHII-CHAN.
YOU MUST'VE PLAYED SPORTS OR SOME-THING, RIGHT?
ドキドキ
! UH... NO, NOT REALLY...
...
OKAY, FOLLOW MY STEPS.
YUP, JUST LIKE THAT. YOU LEARN QUICK!
ALL RIGHT, NOW TRY DANCING WITH TATARA-KUN!
W-WITH HIM...?!
HOW DID THIS HAPPEN ...?
IT'S A LITTLE AGGRAVATING...
LIKE I'M BEING MOCKED FOR ACTUALLY BEING INTO THIS...
YOU DOING THIS AS A JOKE?
OR ARE YOU JUST A PER-VERT?
...!
OH—THE FIRST TIME I CAME TO THE STUDIO...
HANAOKA-SAN MUST HAVE FELT THE SAME WAY...

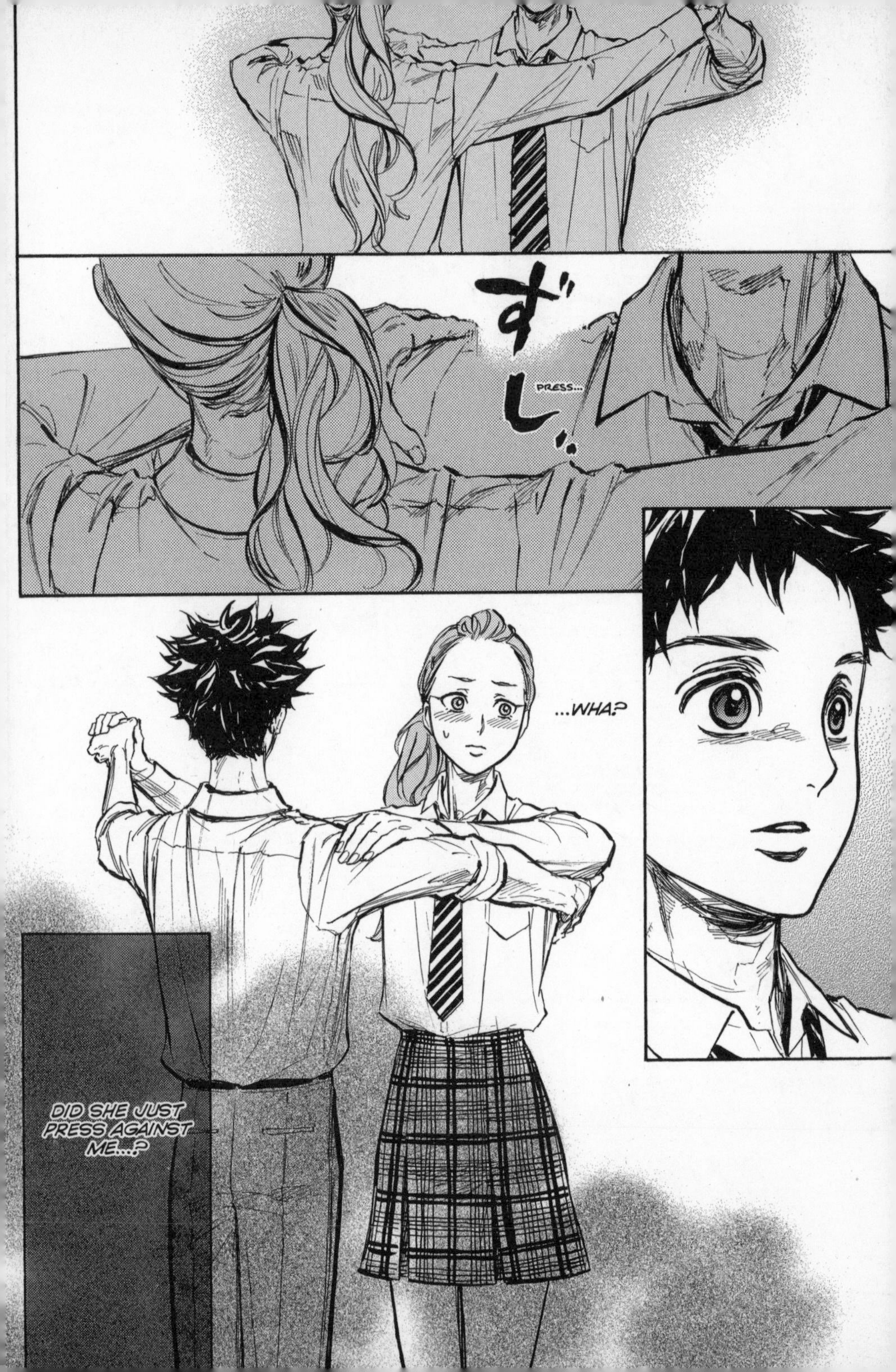
ずし
PRESS...
...WHA?
DID SHE JUST PRESS AGAINST ME...?

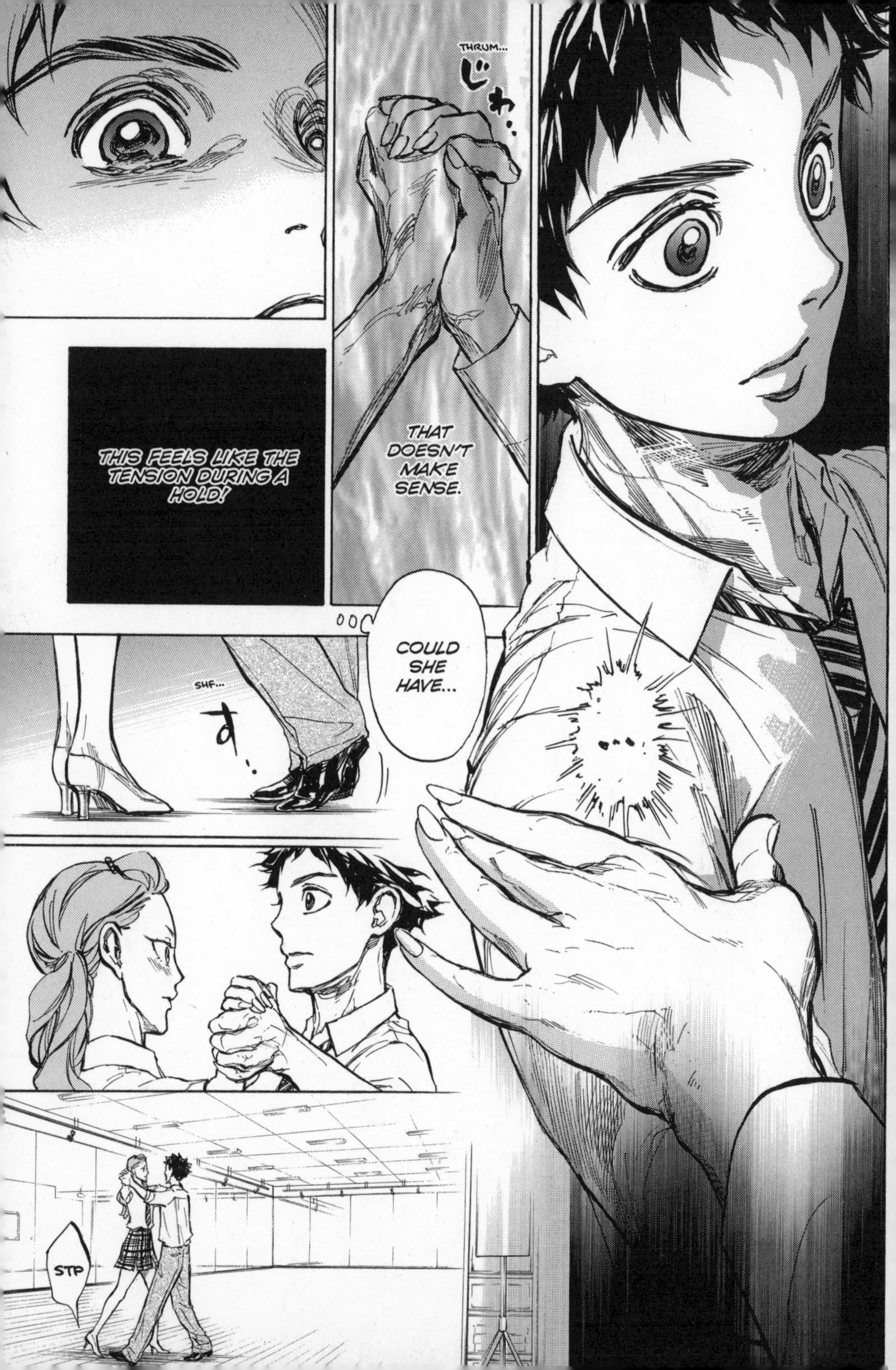
COULD SHE HAVE...
THRUM...
じわ‥
THAT DOESN'T MAKE SENSE.
THIS FEELS LIKE THE TENSION DURING A HOLD!
SHF...
す‥
STP

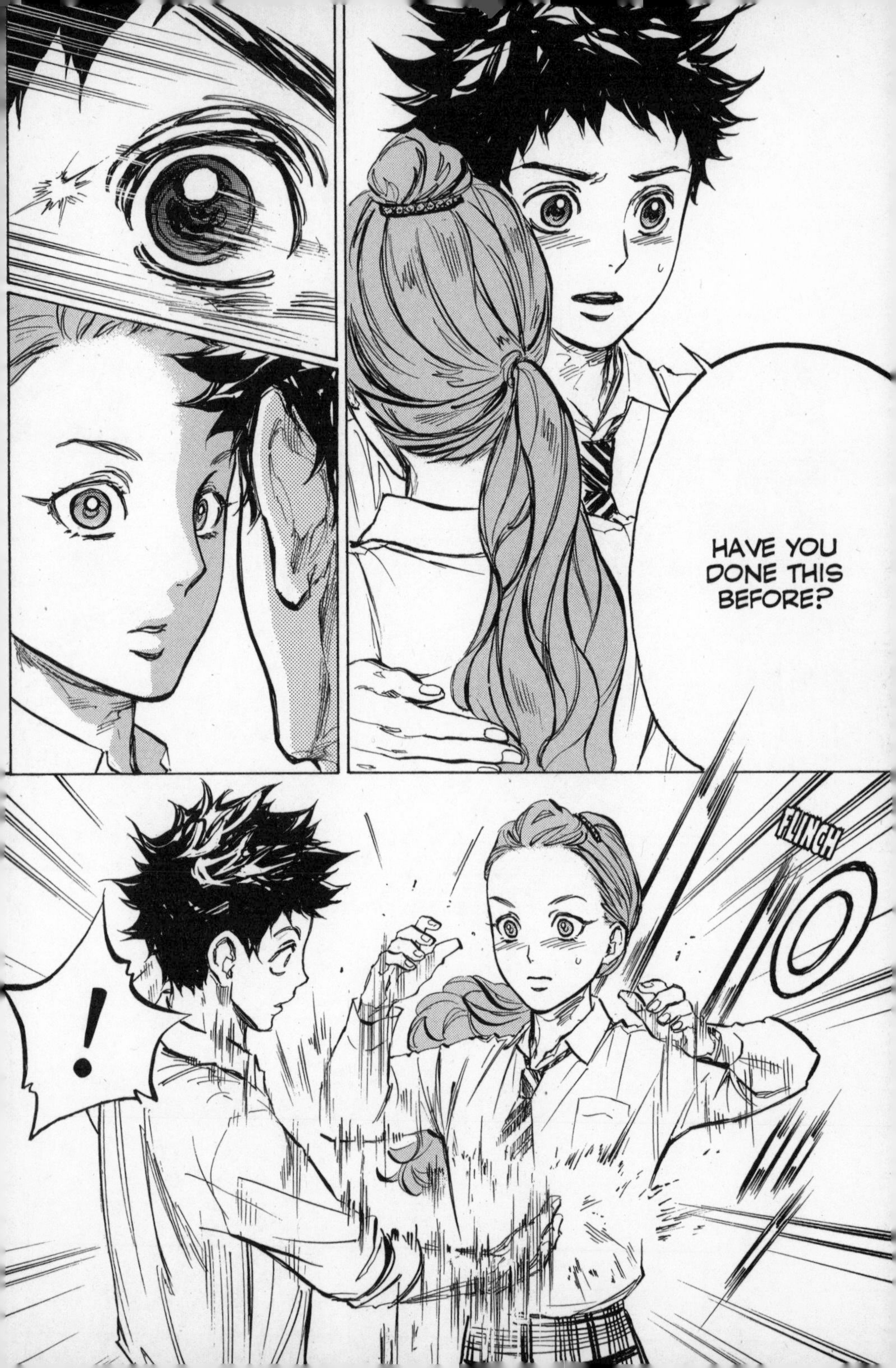
HAVE YOU DONE THIS BEFORE?
FLINCH
!

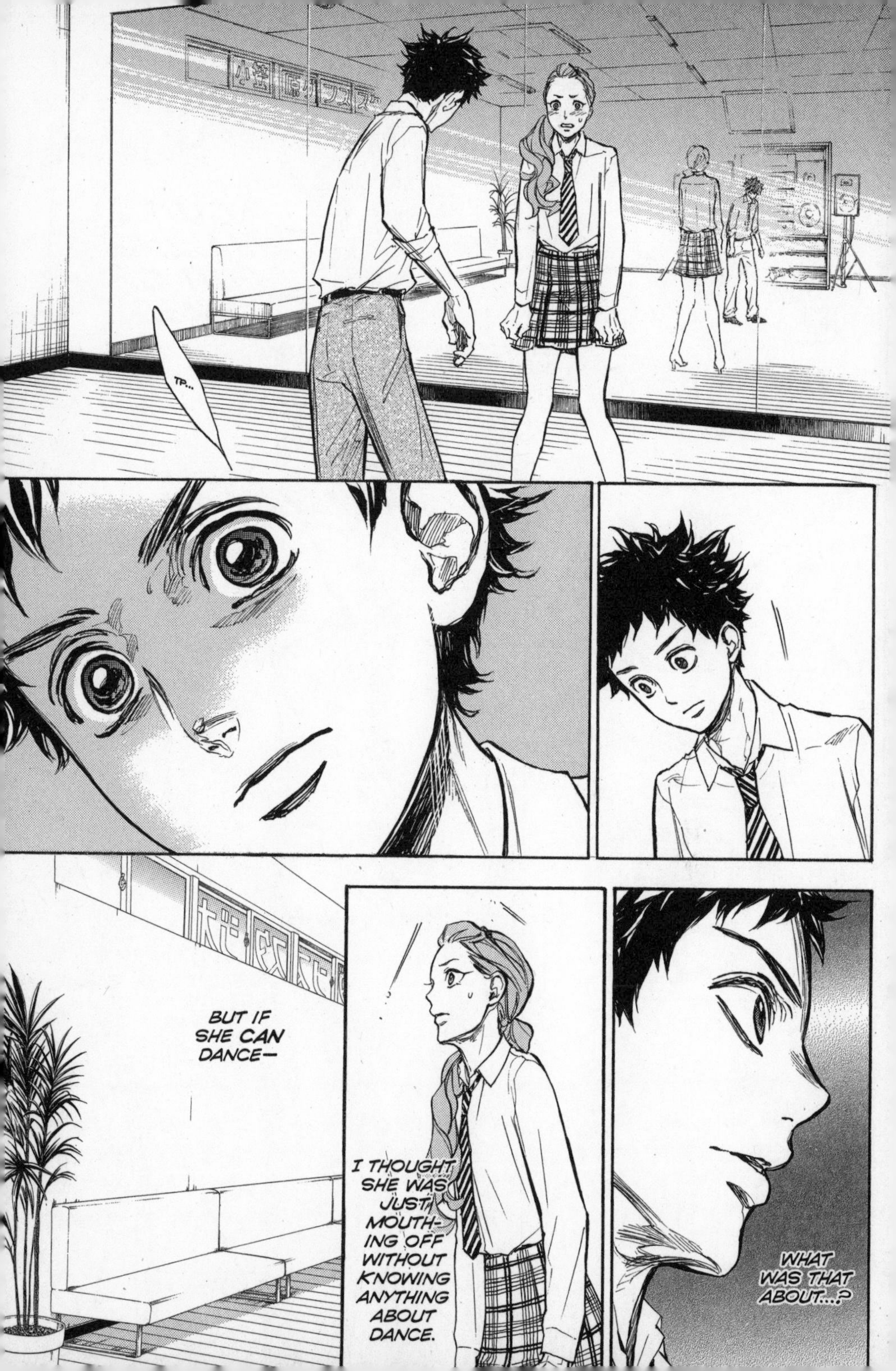
TP...
WHAT WAS THAT ABOUT...?
I THOUGHT SHE WAS JUST MOUTHING OFF WITHOUT KNOWING ANYTHING ABOUT DANCE.
BUT IF SHE CAN DANCE—

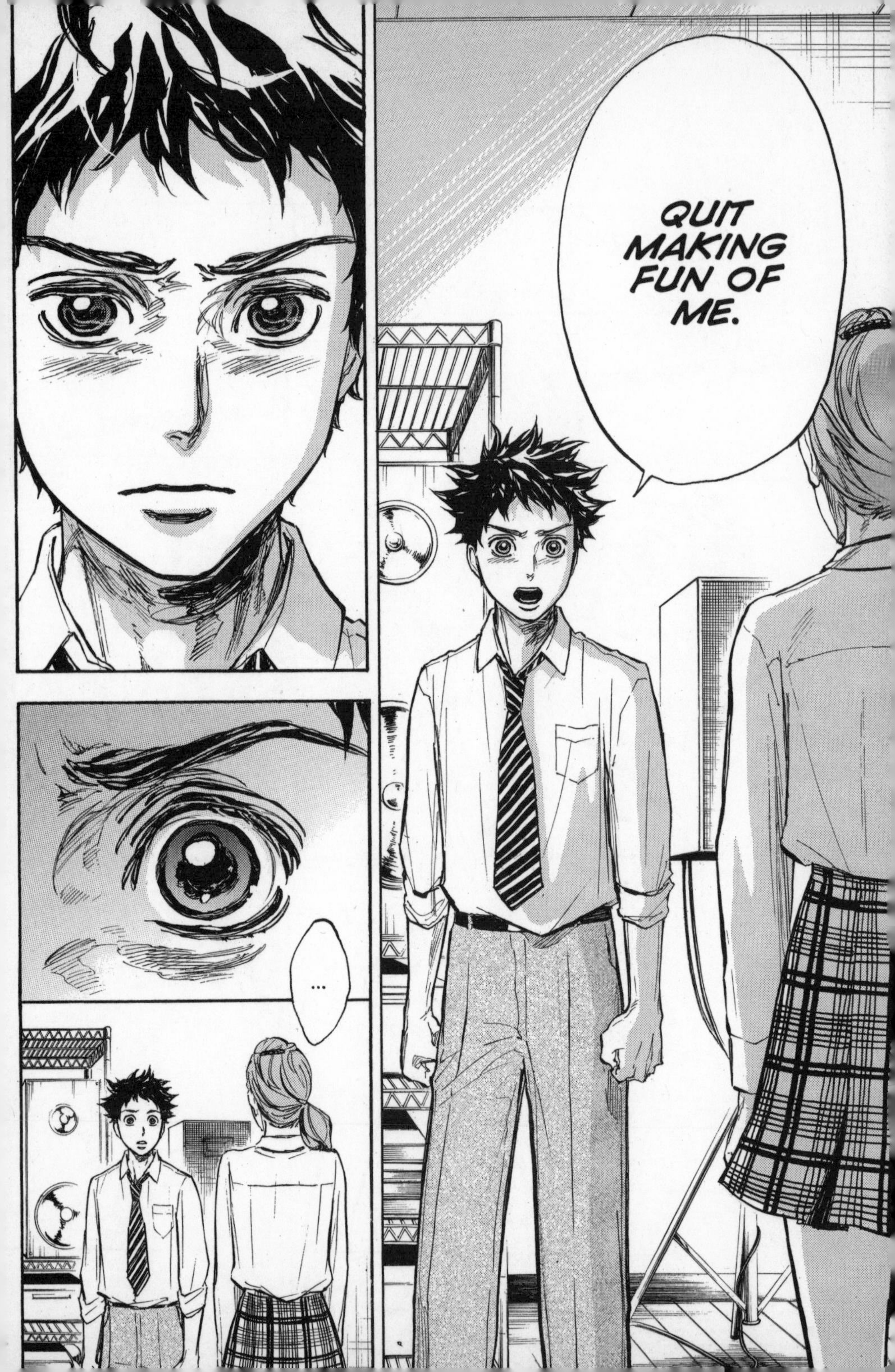
QUIT MAKING FUN OF ME.
...

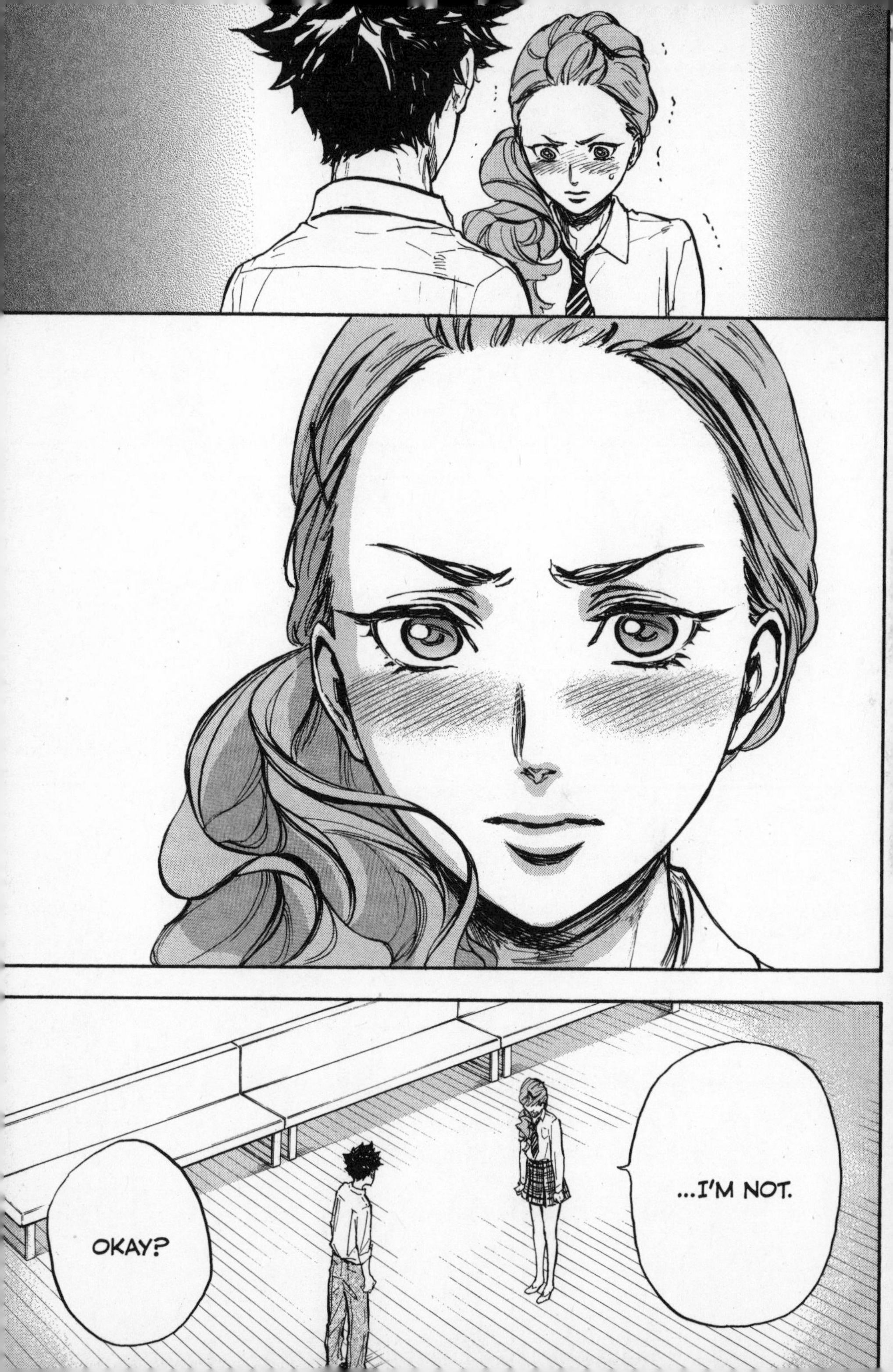
...I'M NOT.
OKAY?

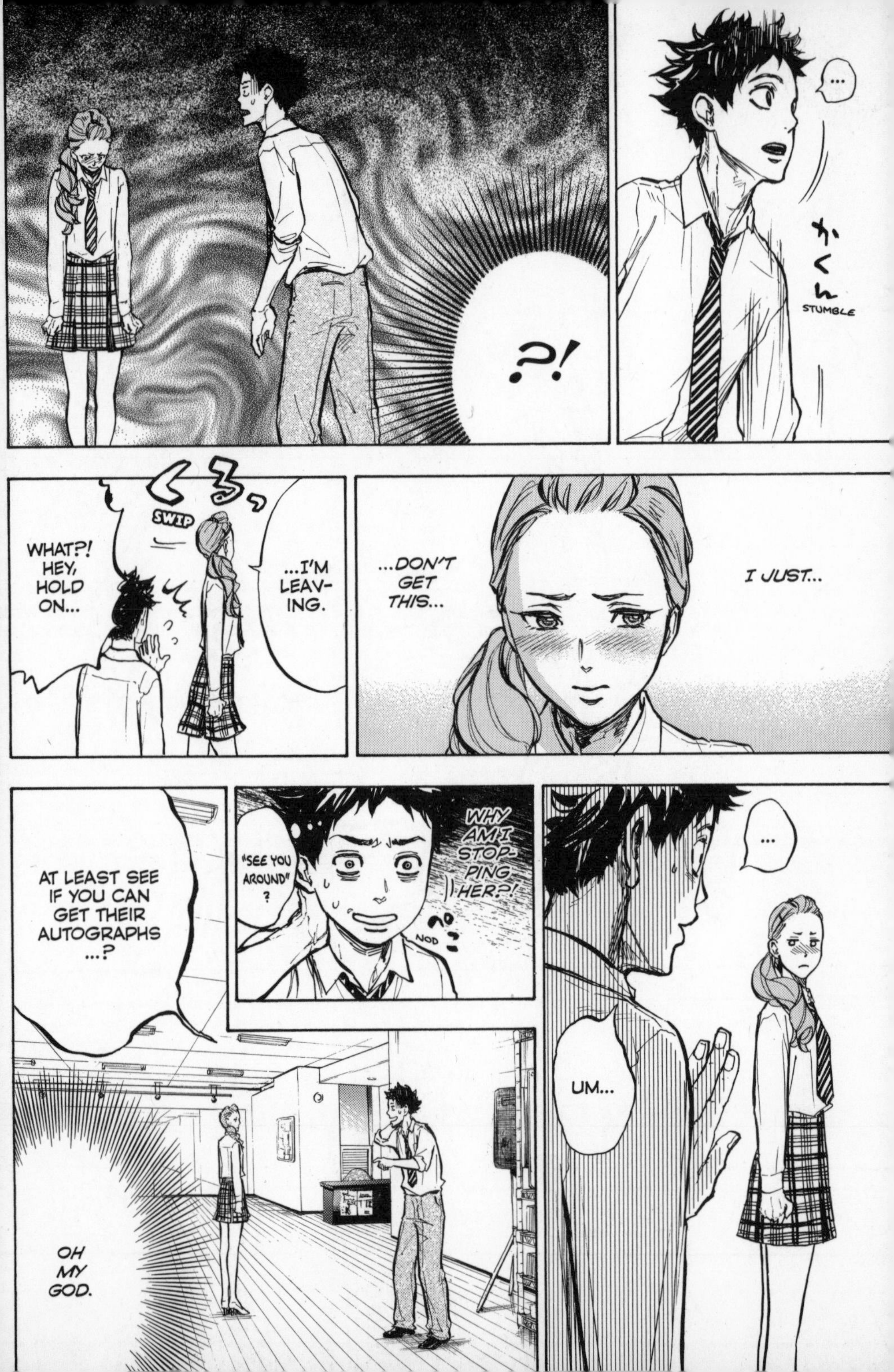

...
かくん
STUMBLE
?!
I JUST...
...DON'T GET THIS...
くるっ
SWIP
...I'M LEAVING.
WHAT?! HEY, HOLD ON...
...
UM...
WHY AM I STOPPING HER?!
"SEE YOU AROUND"?
NOD
AT LEAST SEE IF YOU CAN GET THEIR AUTOGRAPHS...?
OH MY GOD.

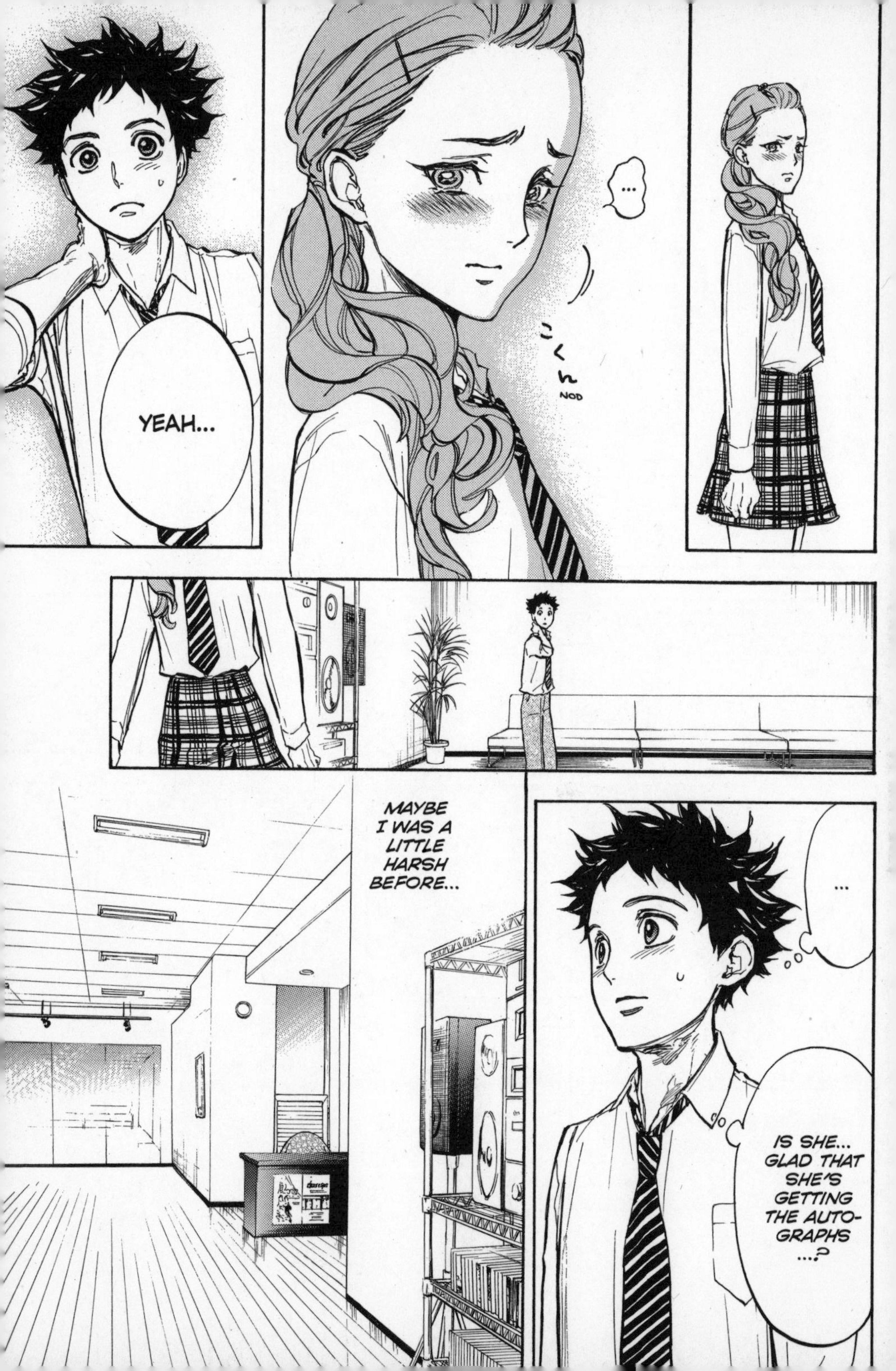
...
こくん
NOD
YEAH...
...
IS SHE... GLAD THAT SHE'S GETTING THE AUTO-GRAPHS ...?
MAYBE I WAS A LITTLE HARSH BEFORE...

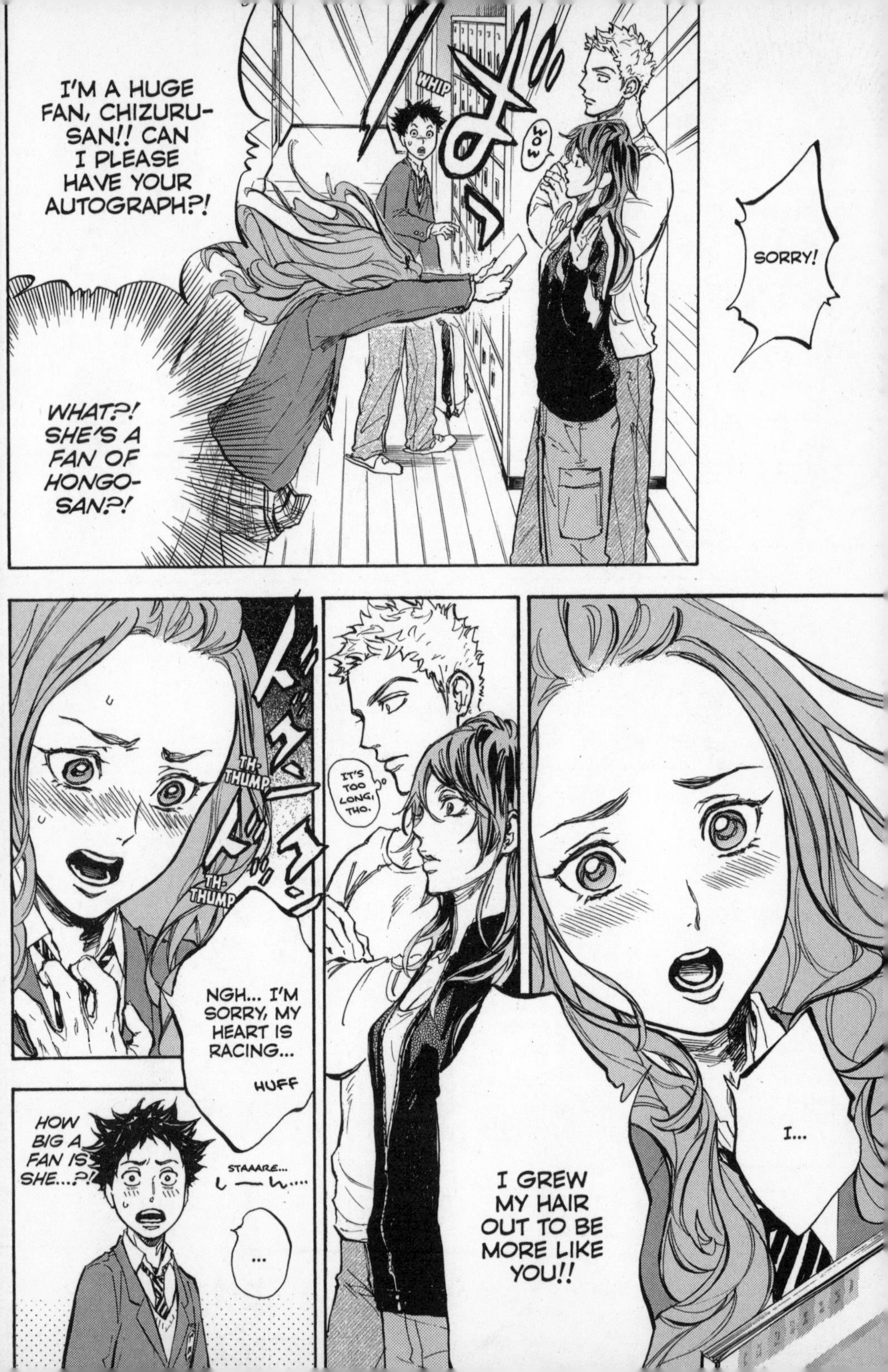
SORRY!
WOW
WHIP
I'M A HUGE FAN, CHIZURU-SAN!! CAN I PLEASE HAVE YOUR AUTOGRAPH?!
WHAT?! SHE'S A FAN OF HONGO-SAN?!
I...
I GREW MY HAIR OUT TO BE MORE LIKE YOU!!
IT'S TOO LONG, THO.
TH-THUMP
TH-THUMP
NGH... I'M SORRY, MY HEART IS RACING...
HUFF
HOW BIG A FAN IS SHE...?!
STAAARE...
...

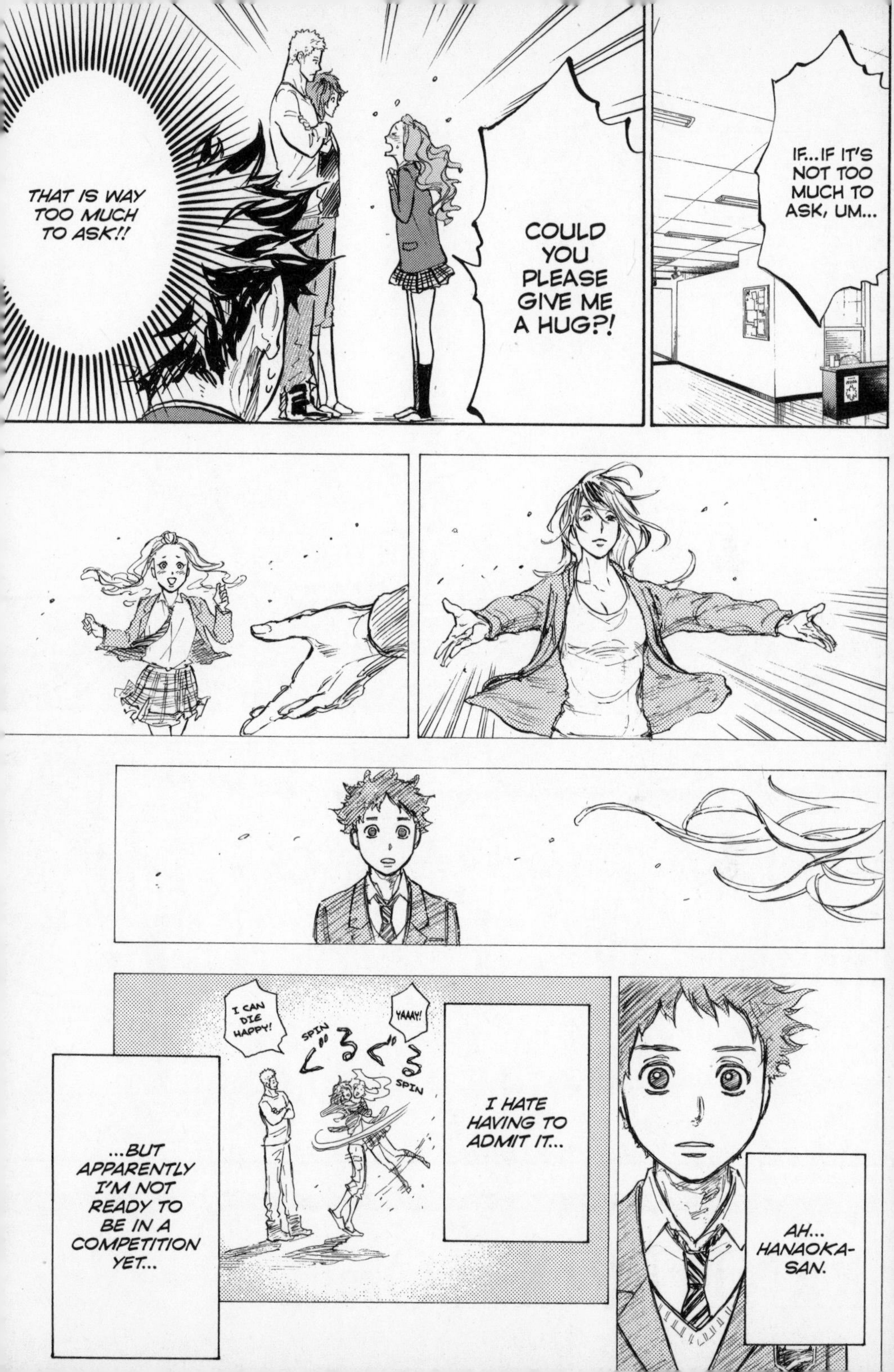
IF...IF IT'S NOT TOO MUCH TO ASK, UM...
COULD YOU PLEASE GIVE ME A HUG?!
THAT IS WAY TOO MUCH TO ASK!!
AH... HANAOKA-SAN.
YAAAY!
I CAN DIE HAPPY!
SPIN ぐるぐる SPIN
I HATE HAVING TO ADMIT IT...
...BUT APPARENTLY I'M NOT READY TO BE IN A COMPETITION YET...

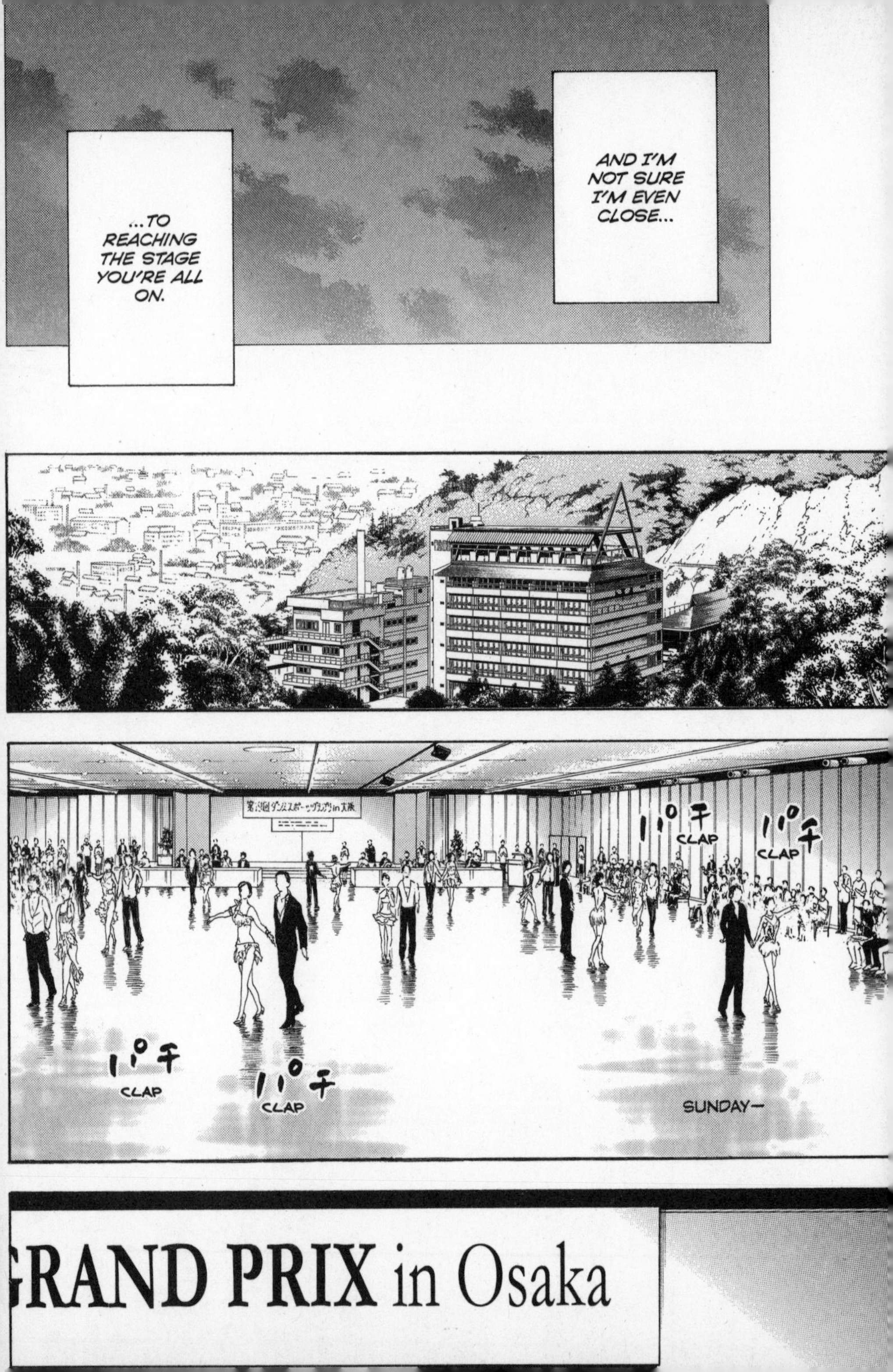
AND I'M NOT SURE I'M EVEN CLOSE...
...TO REACHING THE STAGE YOU'RE ALL ON.
パチ
CLAP
パチ
CLAP
SUNDAY—
パチ
CLAP
パチ
CLAP
GRAND PRIX in Osaka

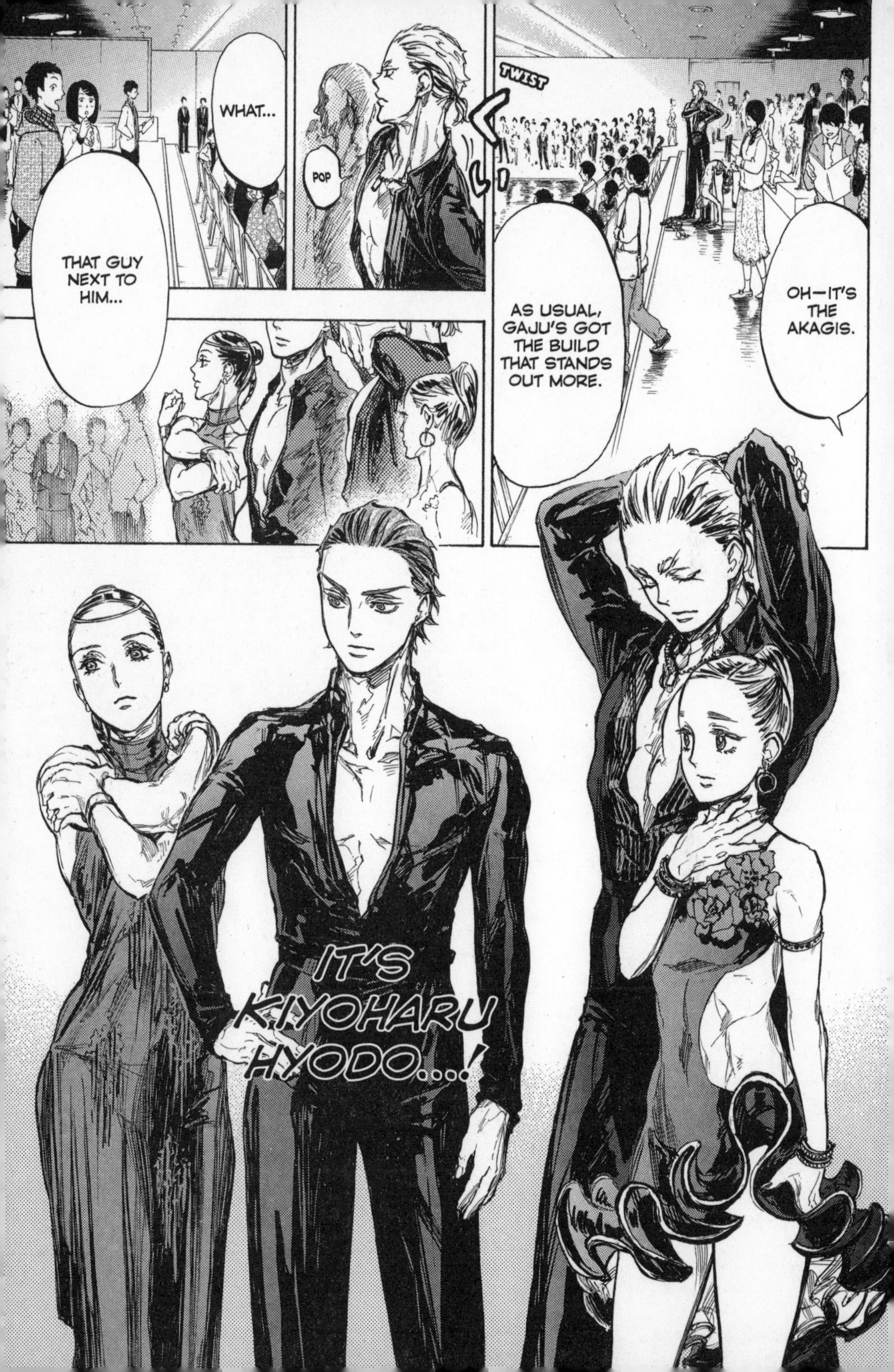
OH—IT'S THE AKAGIS.
AS USUAL, GAJU'S GOT THE BUILD THAT STANDS OUT MORE.
TWIST
WHAT...
POP
THAT GUY NEXT TO HIM...
IT'S KIYOHARU HYODO...!

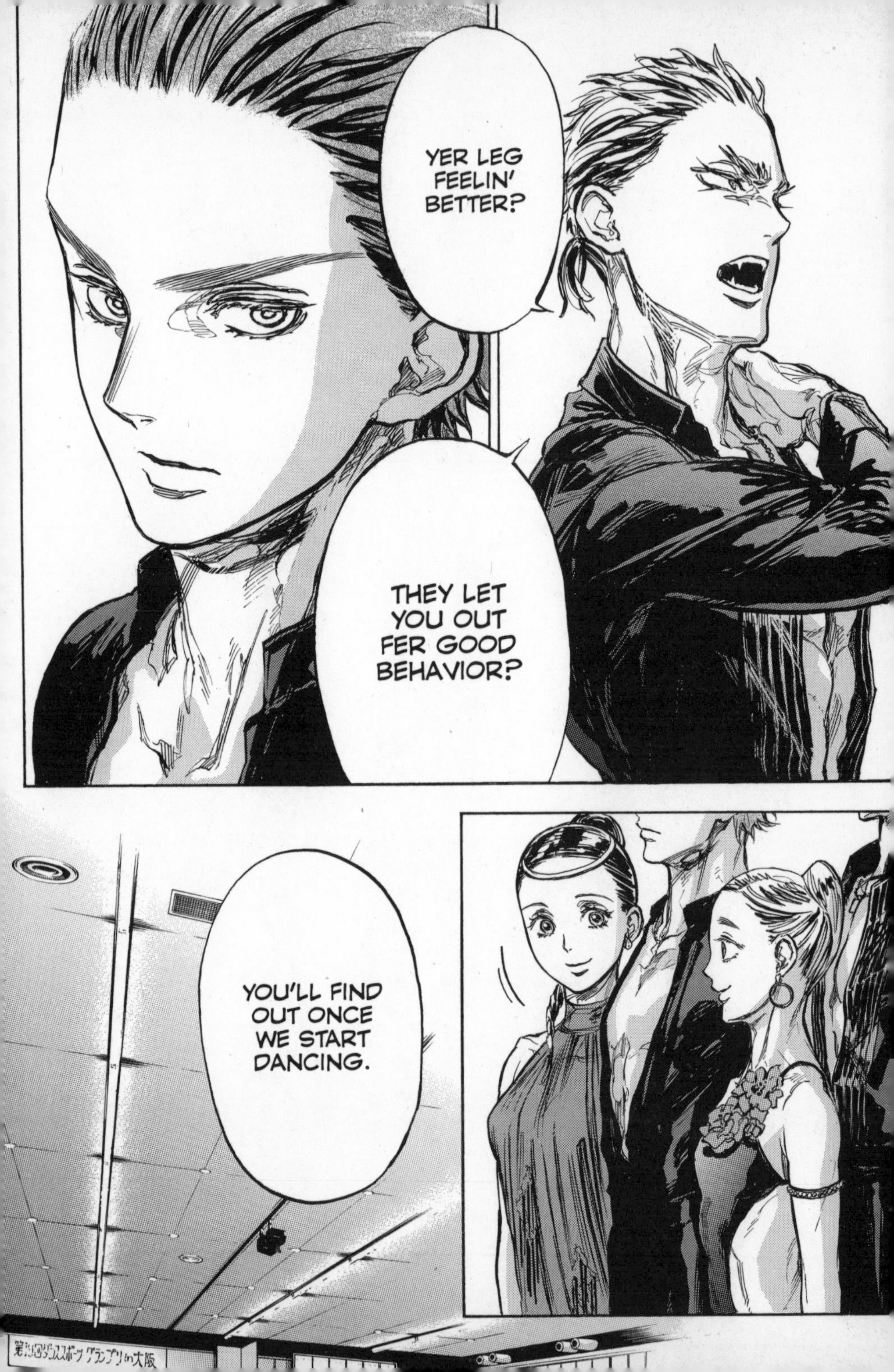
YER LEG FEELIN' BETTER?
THEY LET YOU OUT FER GOOD BEHAVIOR?
YOU'LL FIND OUT ONCE WE START DANCING.

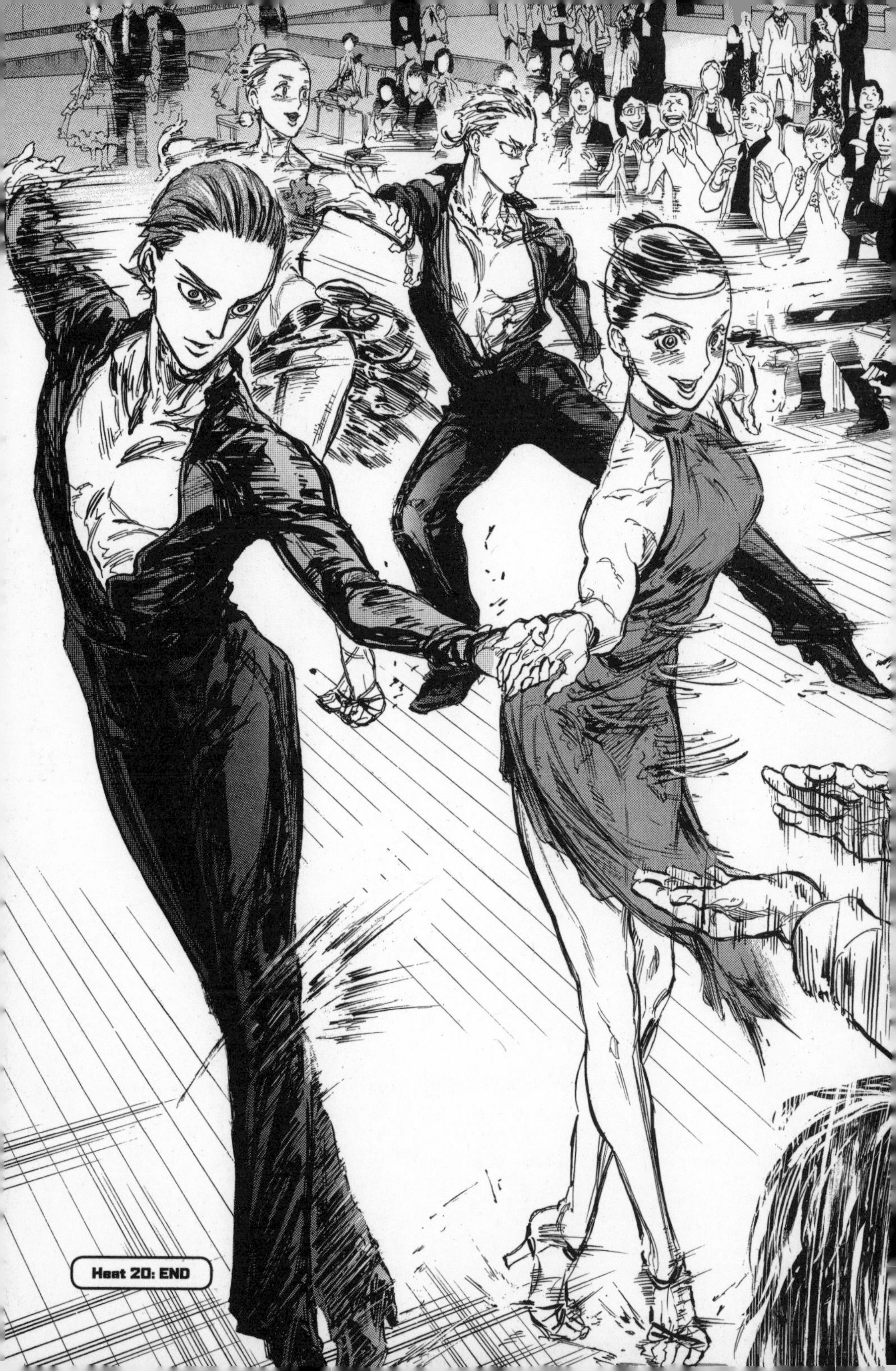
Heat 20: END

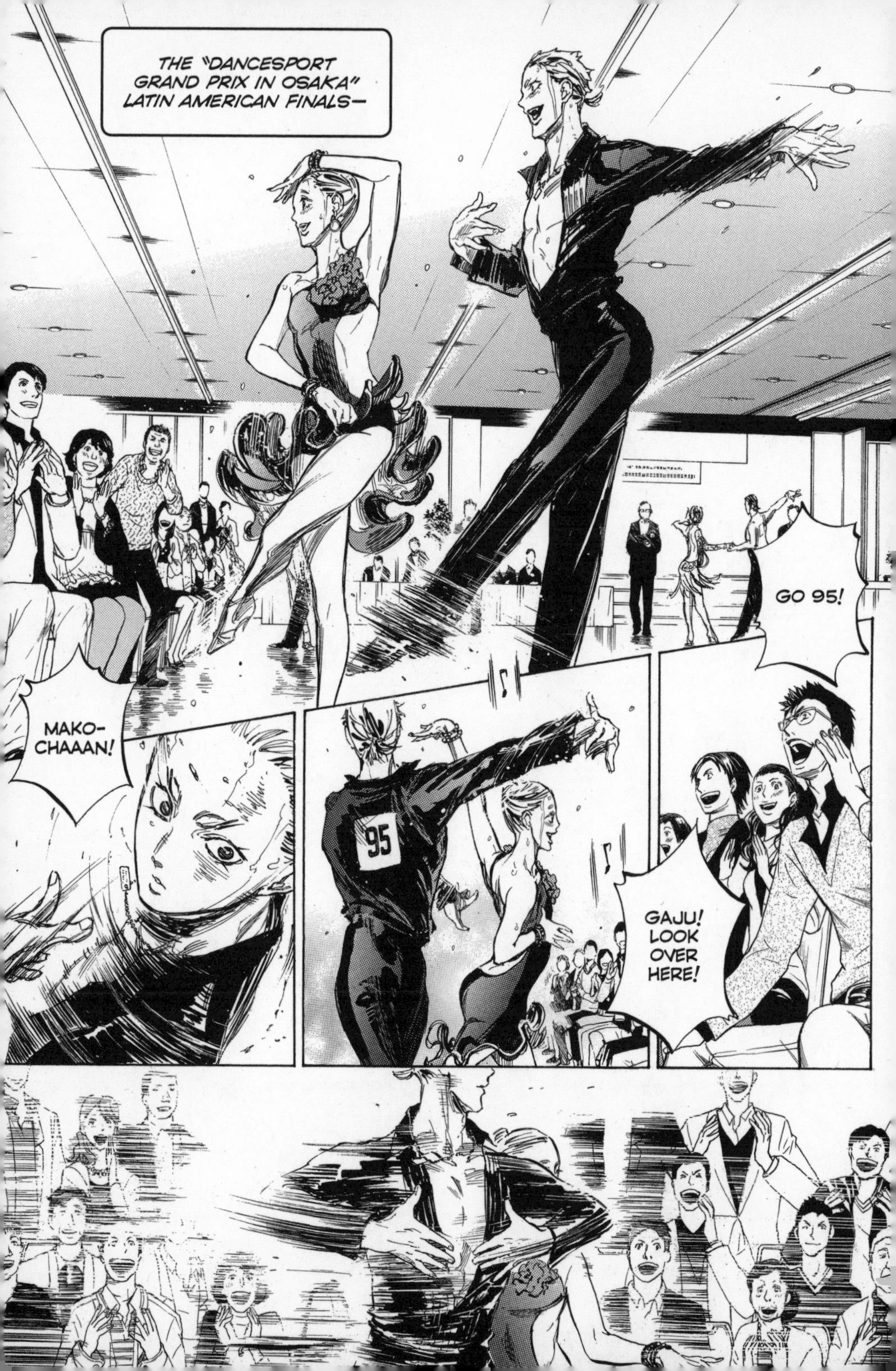
THE "DANCESPORT GRAND PRIX IN OSAKA" LATIN AMERICAN FINALS—
GO 95!
GAJU! LOOK OVER HERE!
MAKO-CHAAAN!

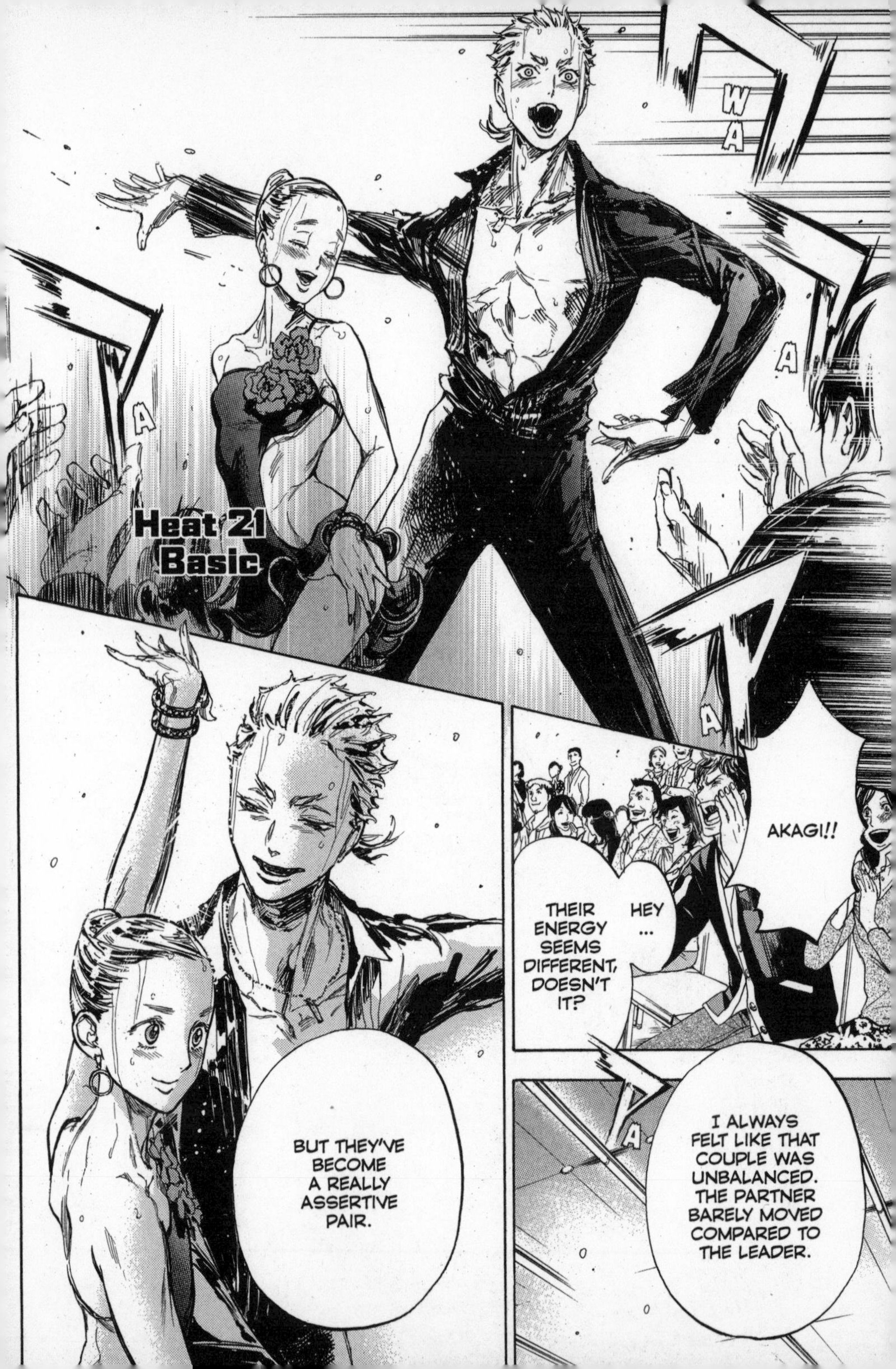
WA
A
A
Heat 21
Basic
A
AKAGI!!
HEY ...
THEIR ENERGY SEEMS DIFFERENT, DOESN'T IT?
A
I ALWAYS FELT LIKE THAT COUPLE WAS UNBALANCED. THE PARTNER BARELY MOVED COMPARED TO THE LEADER.
BUT THEY'VE BECOME A REALLY ASSERTIVE PAIR.

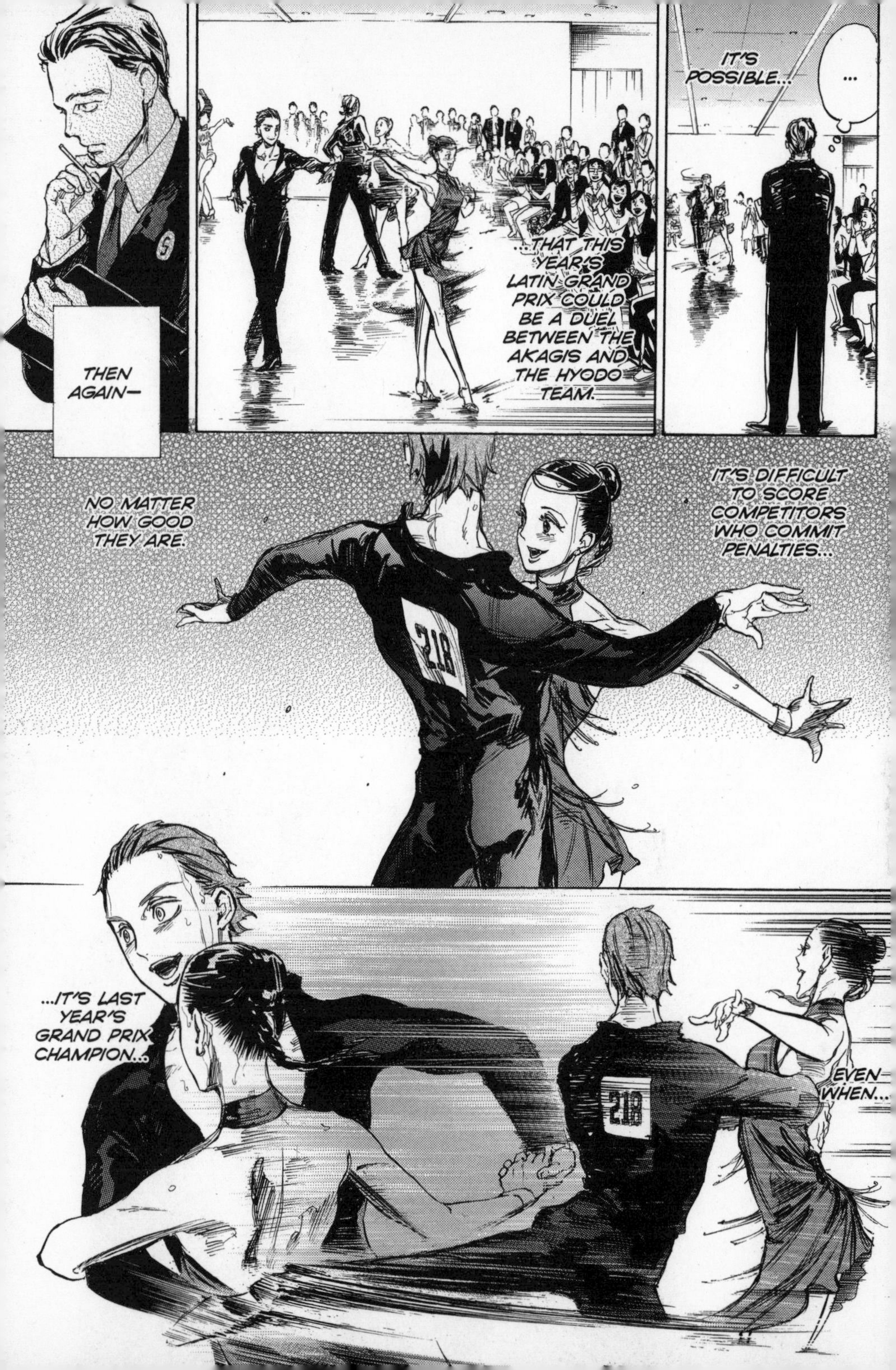
...
IT'S POSSIBLE...
...THAT THIS YEAR'S LATIN GRAND PRIX COULD BE A DUEL BETWEEN THE AKAGIS AND THE HYODO TEAM.
THEN AGAIN—
IT'S DIFFICULT TO SCORE COMPETITORS WHO COMMIT PENALTIES...
NO MATTER HOW GOOD THEY ARE.
EVEN WHEN...
...IT'S LAST YEAR'S GRAND PRIX CHAMPION...

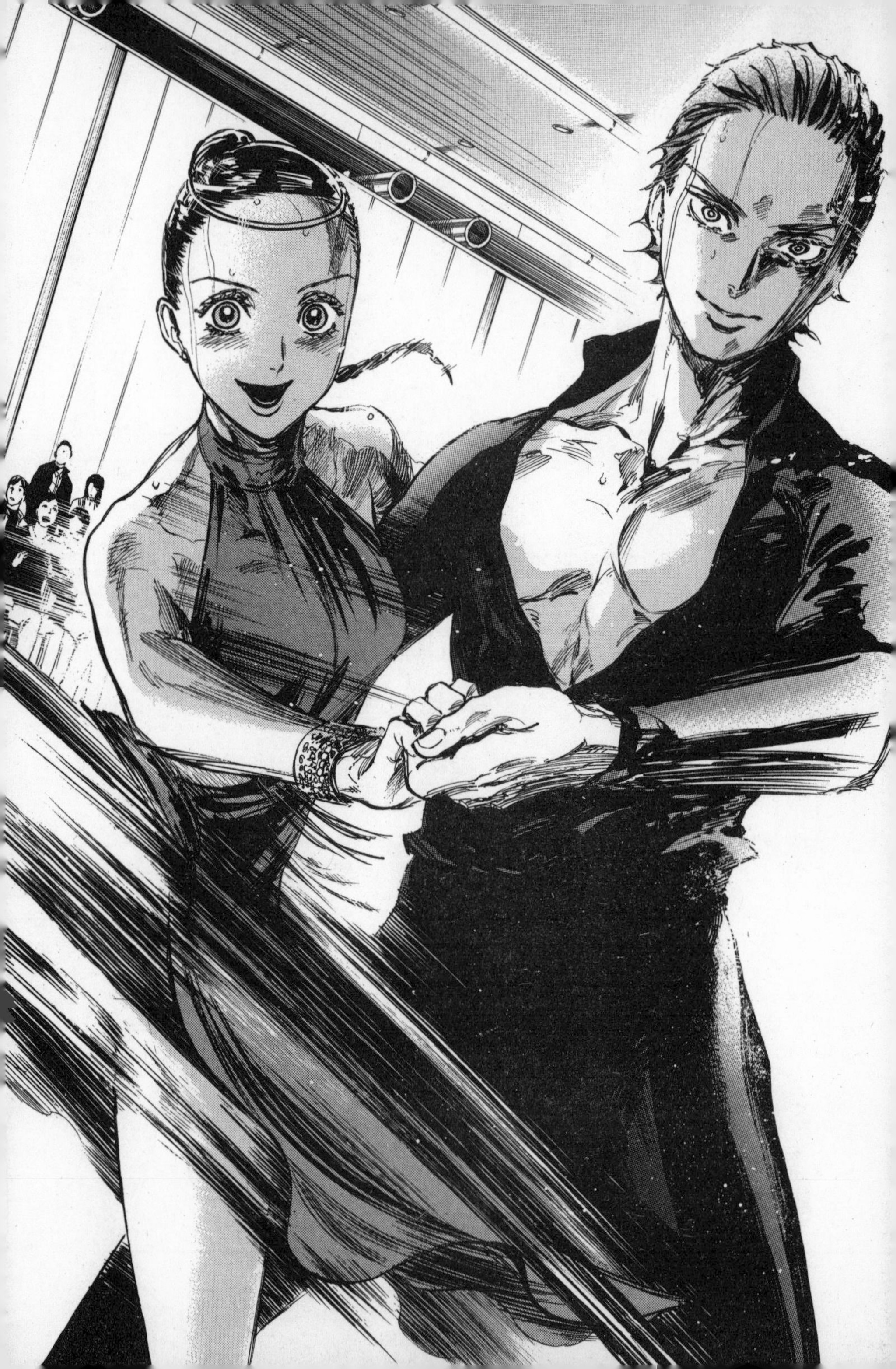

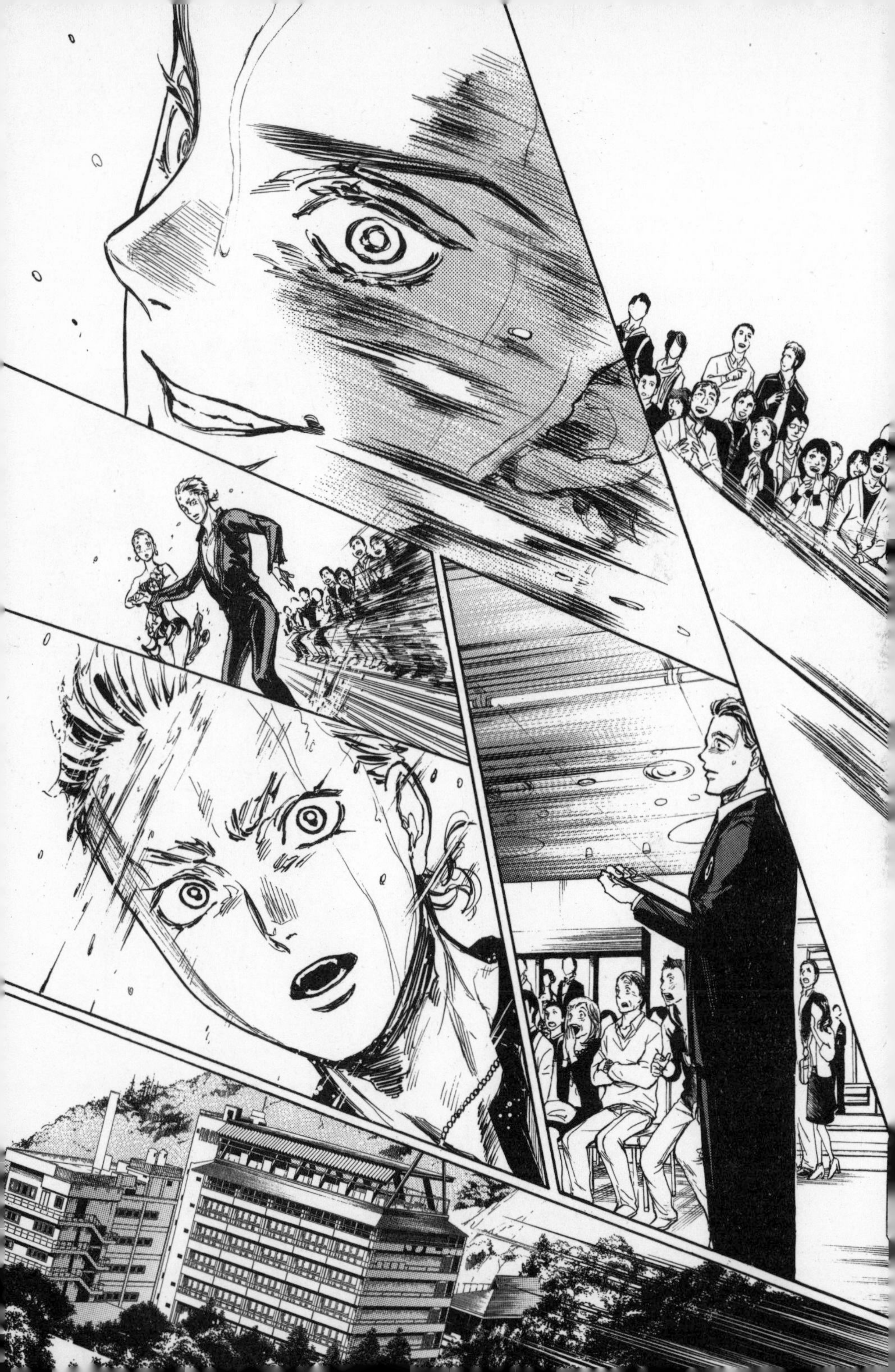

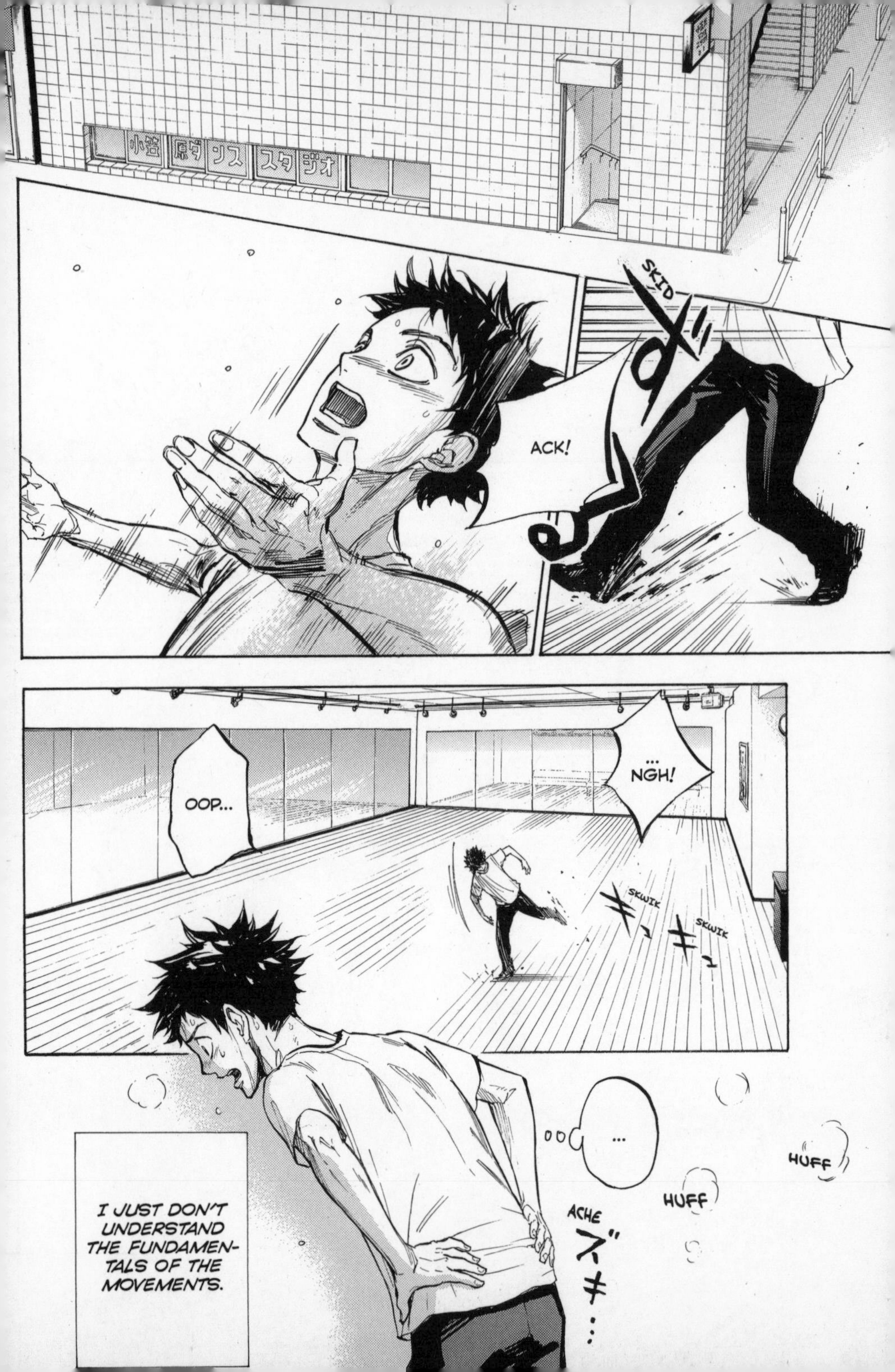

小笠原ダンススタジオ
SKID
ACK!
...NGH!
OOP...
SKWIK
SKWIK
...
HUFF
HUFF
ACHE
ズキ…
I JUST DON'T UNDERSTAND THE FUNDAMENTALS OF THE MOVEMENTS.

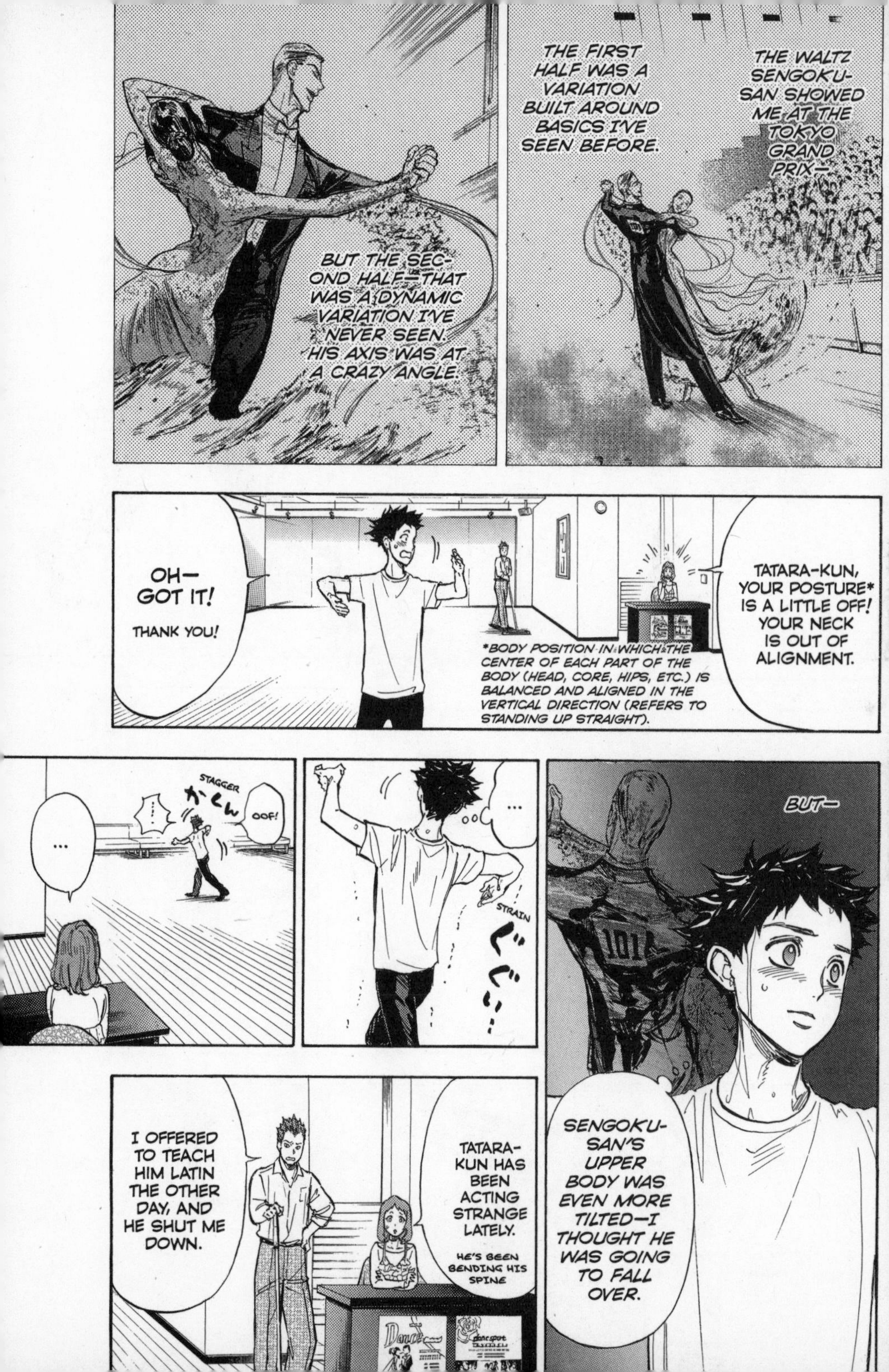
THE WALTZ SENGOKU-SAN SHOWED ME AT THE TOKYO GRAND PRIX—
THE FIRST HALF WAS A VARIATION BUILT AROUND BASICS I'VE SEEN BEFORE.
BUT THE SECOND HALF—THAT WAS A DYNAMIC VARIATION I'VE NEVER SEEN. HIS AXIS WAS AT A CRAZY ANGLE.
TATARA-KUN, YOUR POSTURE* IS A LITTLE OFF! YOUR NECK IS OUT OF ALIGNMENT.
*BODY POSITION IN WHICH THE CENTER OF EACH PART OF THE BODY (HEAD, CORE, HIPS, ETC.) IS BALANCED AND ALIGNED IN THE VERTICAL DIRECTION (REFERS TO STANDING UP STRAIGHT).
OH—GOT IT!
THANK YOU!
BUT—
SENGOKU-SAN'S UPPER BODY WAS EVEN MORE TILTED—I THOUGHT HE WAS GOING TO FALL OVER.
...
STRAIN
STAGGER
OOF!
...
TATARA-KUN HAS BEEN ACTING STRANGE LATELY.
HE'S BEEN BENDING HIS SPINE
I OFFERED TO TEACH HIM LATIN THE OTHER DAY, AND HE SHUT ME DOWN.

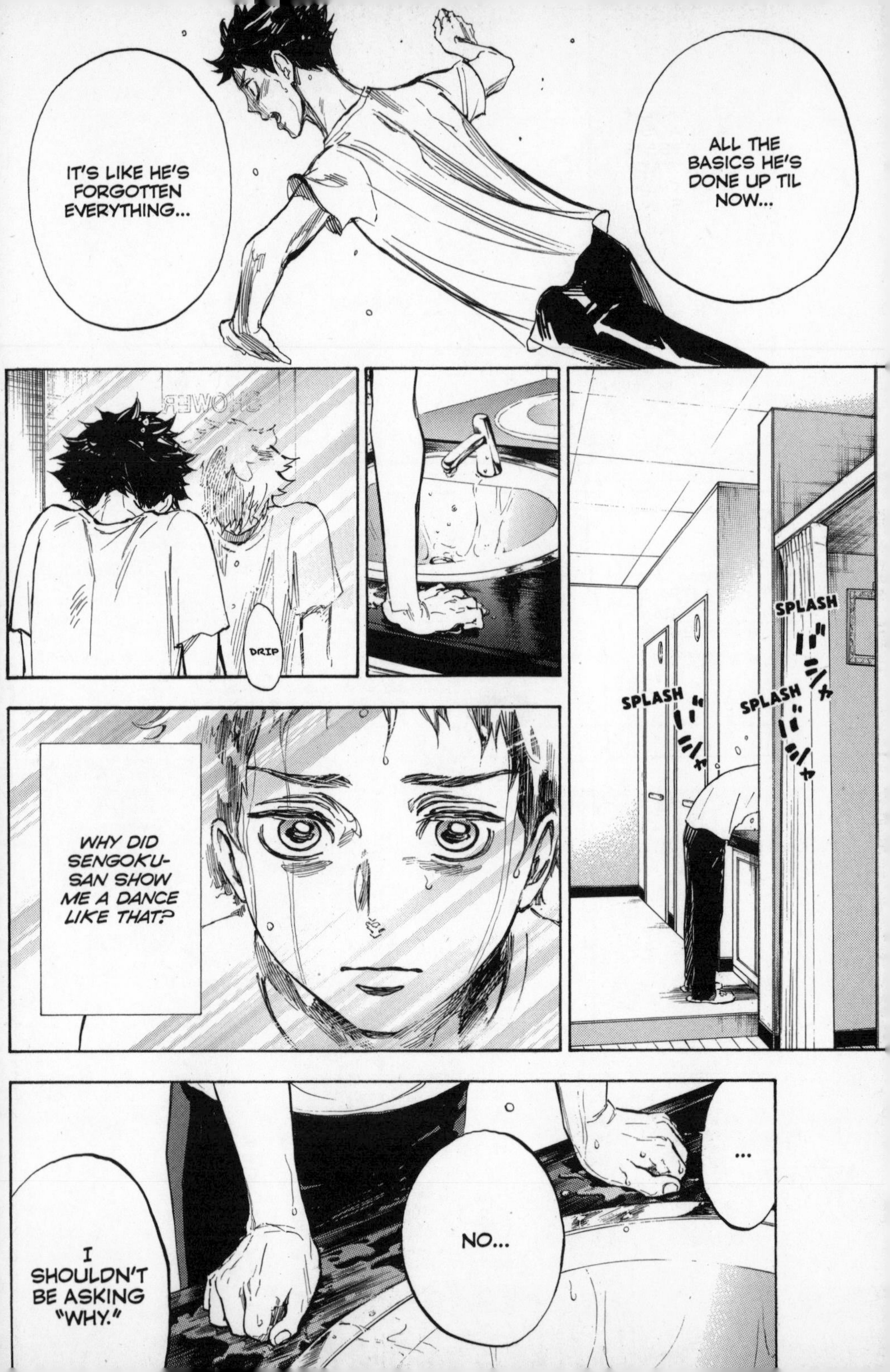
ALL THE BASICS HE'S DONE UP TIL NOW...
IT'S LIKE HE'S FORGOTTEN EVERYTHING...
SPLASH
SPLASH
SPLASH
DRIP
WHY DID SENGOKU-SAN SHOW ME A DANCE LIKE THAT?
...
NO...
I SHOULDN'T BE ASKING "WHY."

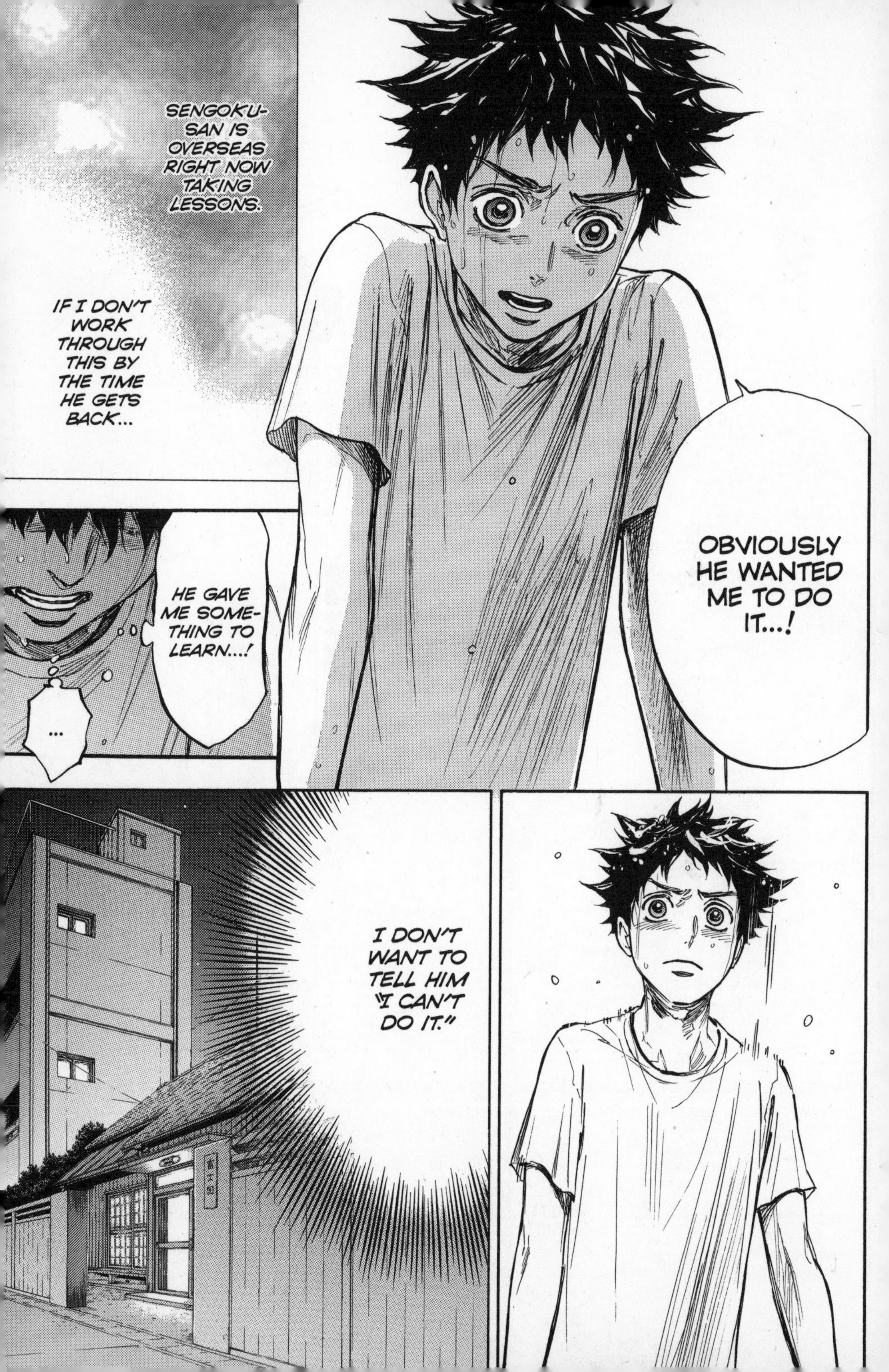
OBVIOUSLY HE WANTED ME TO DO IT...!
SENGOKU-SAN IS OVERSEAS RIGHT NOW TAKING LESSONS.
IF I DON'T WORK THROUGH THIS BY THE TIME HE GETS BACK...
HE GAVE ME SOMETHING TO LEARN...!
...
I DON'T WANT TO TELL HIM "I CAN'T DO IT."

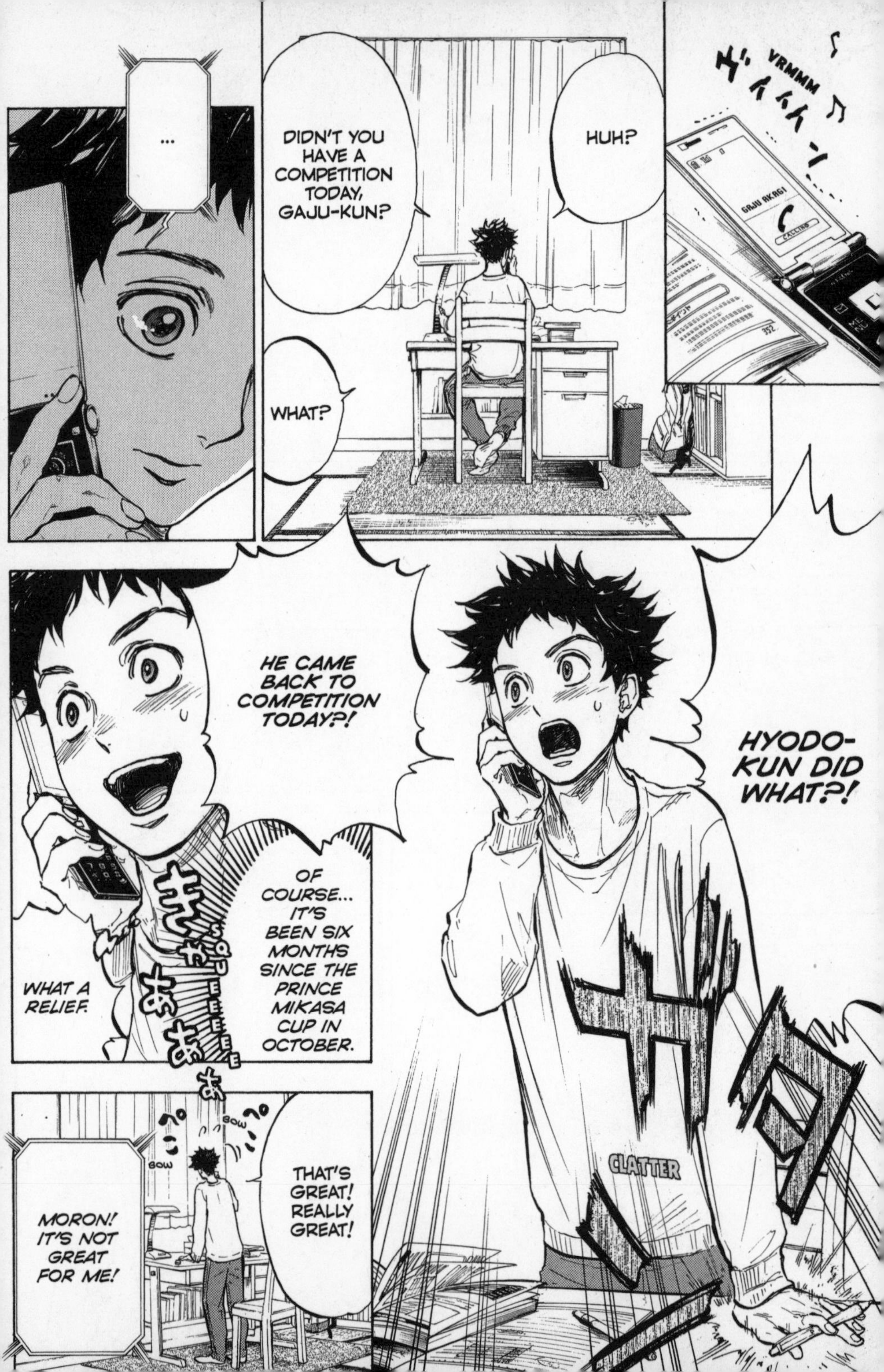
VRMMM
GAJU AKAGI
CALLING
HUH?
DIDN'T YOU HAVE A COMPETITION TODAY, GAJU-KUN?
WHAT?
...
HYODO-KUN DID WHAT?!
HE CAME BACK TO COMPETITION TODAY?!
CLATTER
OF COURSE... IT'S BEEN SIX MONTHS SINCE THE PRINCE MIKASA CUP IN OCTOBER.
SQUEEEEEE
WHAT A RELIEF.
THAT'S GREAT! REALLY GREAT!
BOW
BOW
MORON! IT'S NOT GREAT FOR ME!

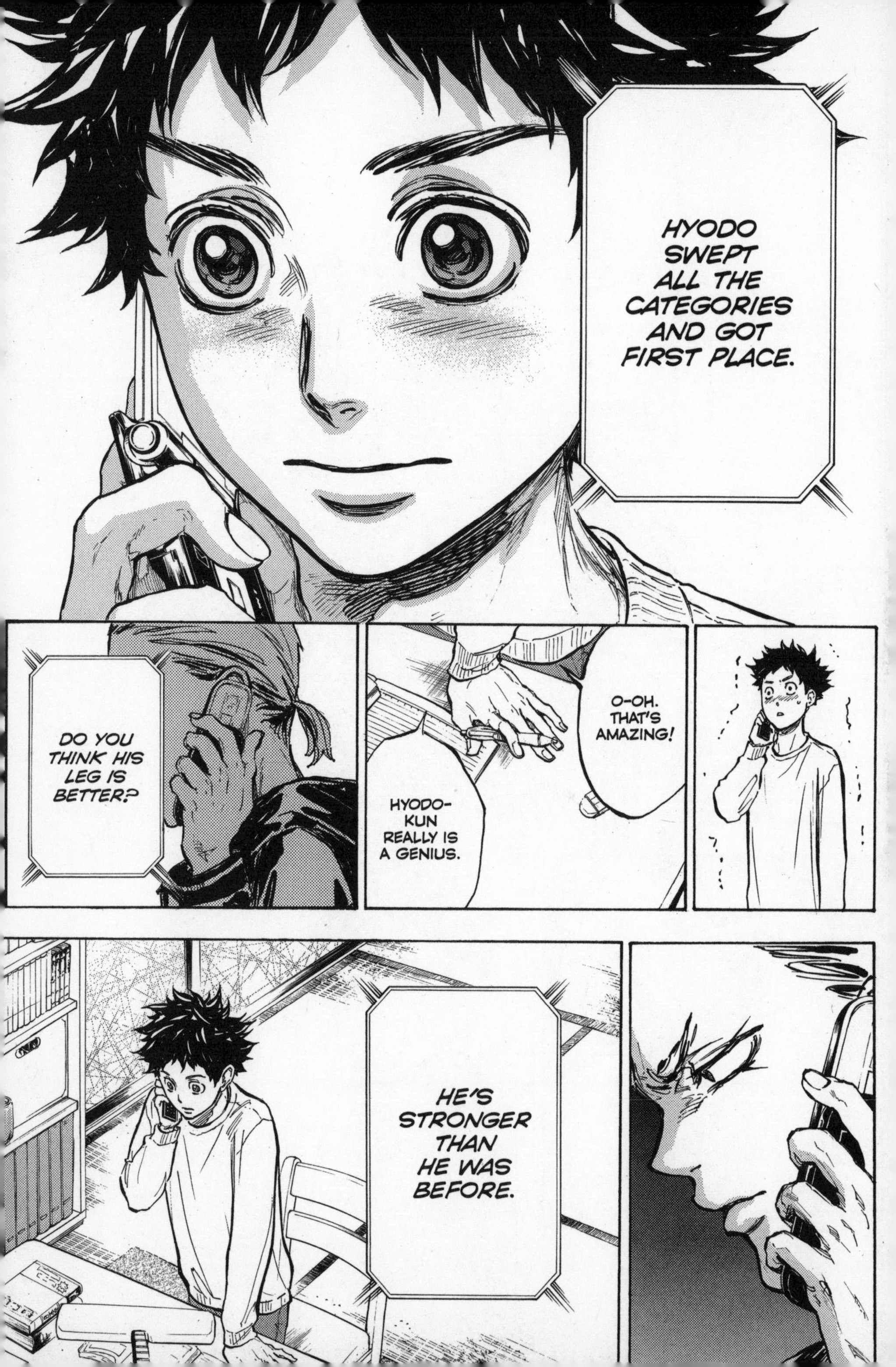
HYODO SWEPT ALL THE CATEGORIES AND GOT FIRST PLACE.
O-OH. THAT'S AMAZING!
HYODO-KUN REALLY IS A GENIUS.
DO YOU THINK HIS LEG IS BETTER?
HE'S STRONGER THAN HE WAS BEFORE.

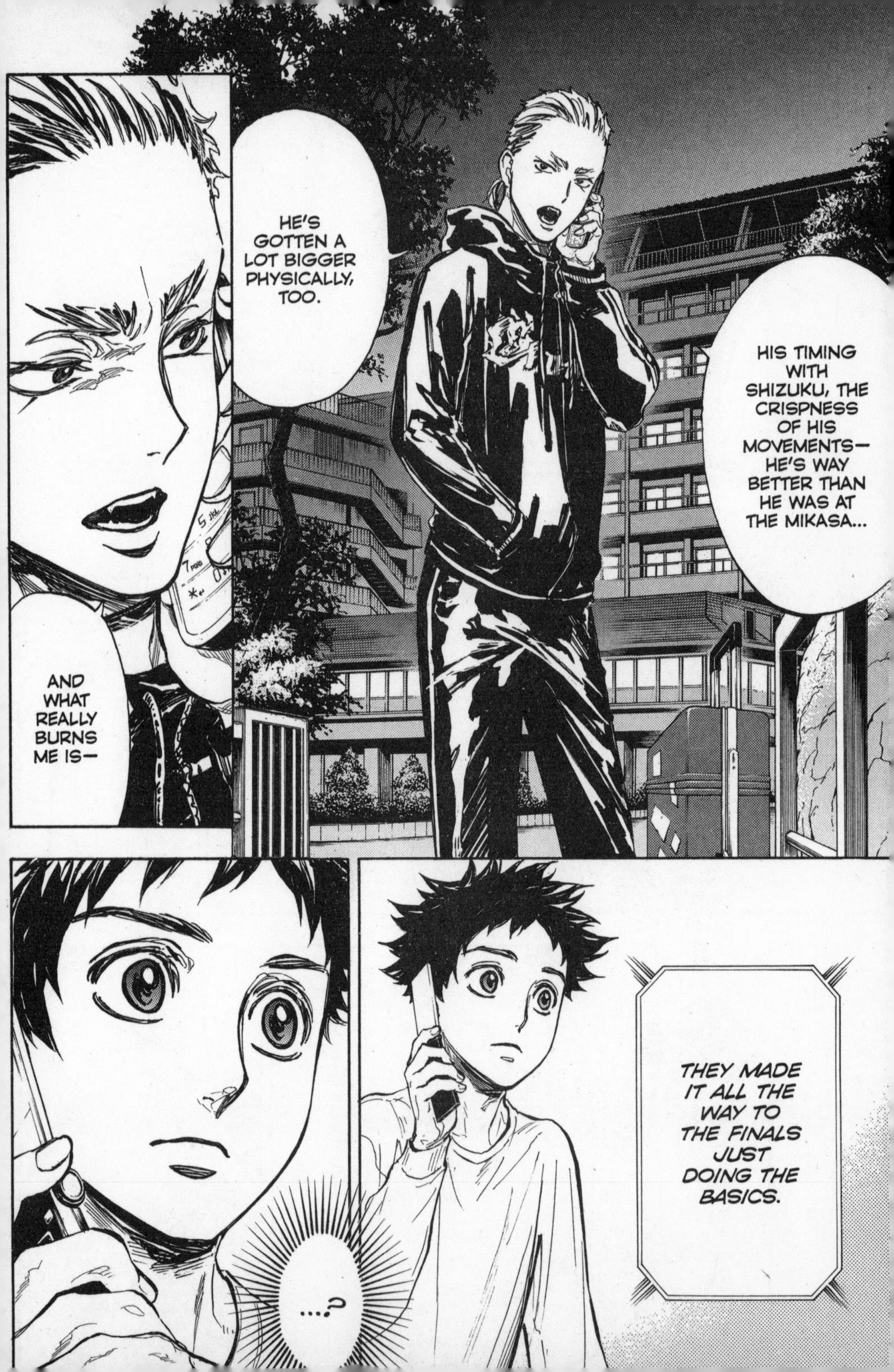
HIS TIMING WITH SHIZUKU, THE CRISPNESS OF HIS MOVEMENTS— HE'S WAY BETTER THAN HE WAS AT THE MIKASA...
HE'S GOTTEN A LOT BIGGER PHYSICALLY, TOO.
AND WHAT REALLY BURNS ME IS—
THEY MADE IT ALL THE WAY TO THE FINALS JUST DOING THE BASICS.
...?

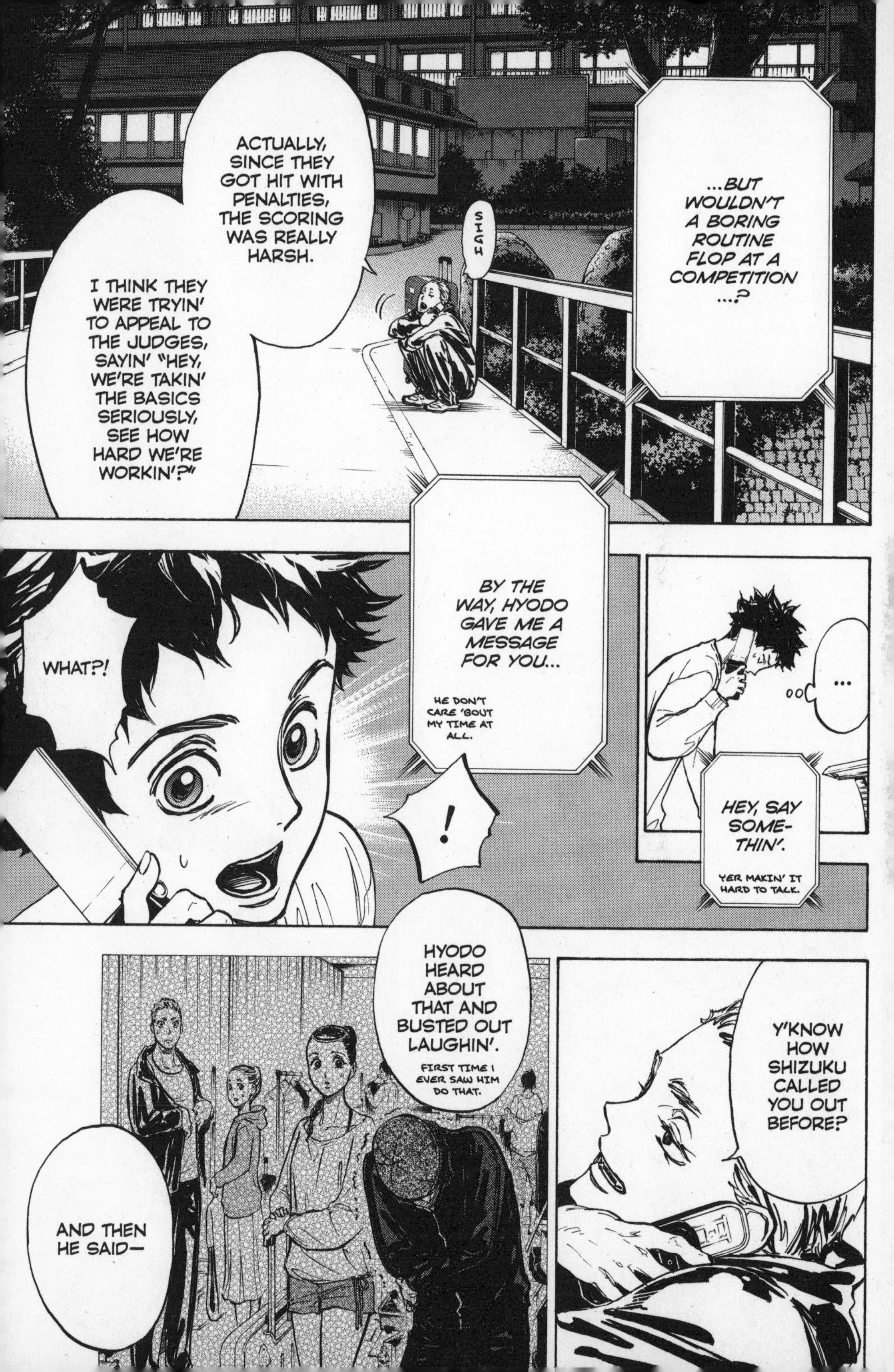
...BUT WOULDN'T A BORING ROUTINE FLOP AT A COMPETITION ...?
SIGH
ACTUALLY, SINCE THEY GOT HIT WITH PENALTIES, THE SCORING WAS REALLY HARSH.
I THINK THEY WERE TRYIN' TO APPEAL TO THE JUDGES, SAYIN' "HEY, WE'RE TAKIN' THE BASICS SERIOUSLY, SEE HOW HARD WE'RE WORKIN'?"
...
HEY, SAY SOME-THIN'.
YER MAKIN' IT HARD TO TALK.
BY THE WAY, HYODO GAVE ME A MESSAGE FOR YOU...
HE DON'T CARE 'BOUT MY TIME AT ALL.
!
WHAT?!
Y'KNOW HOW SHIZUKU CALLED YOU OUT BEFORE?
HYODO HEARD ABOUT THAT AND BUSTED OUT LAUGHIN'.
FIRST TIME I EVER SAW HIM DO THAT.
AND THEN HE SAID—

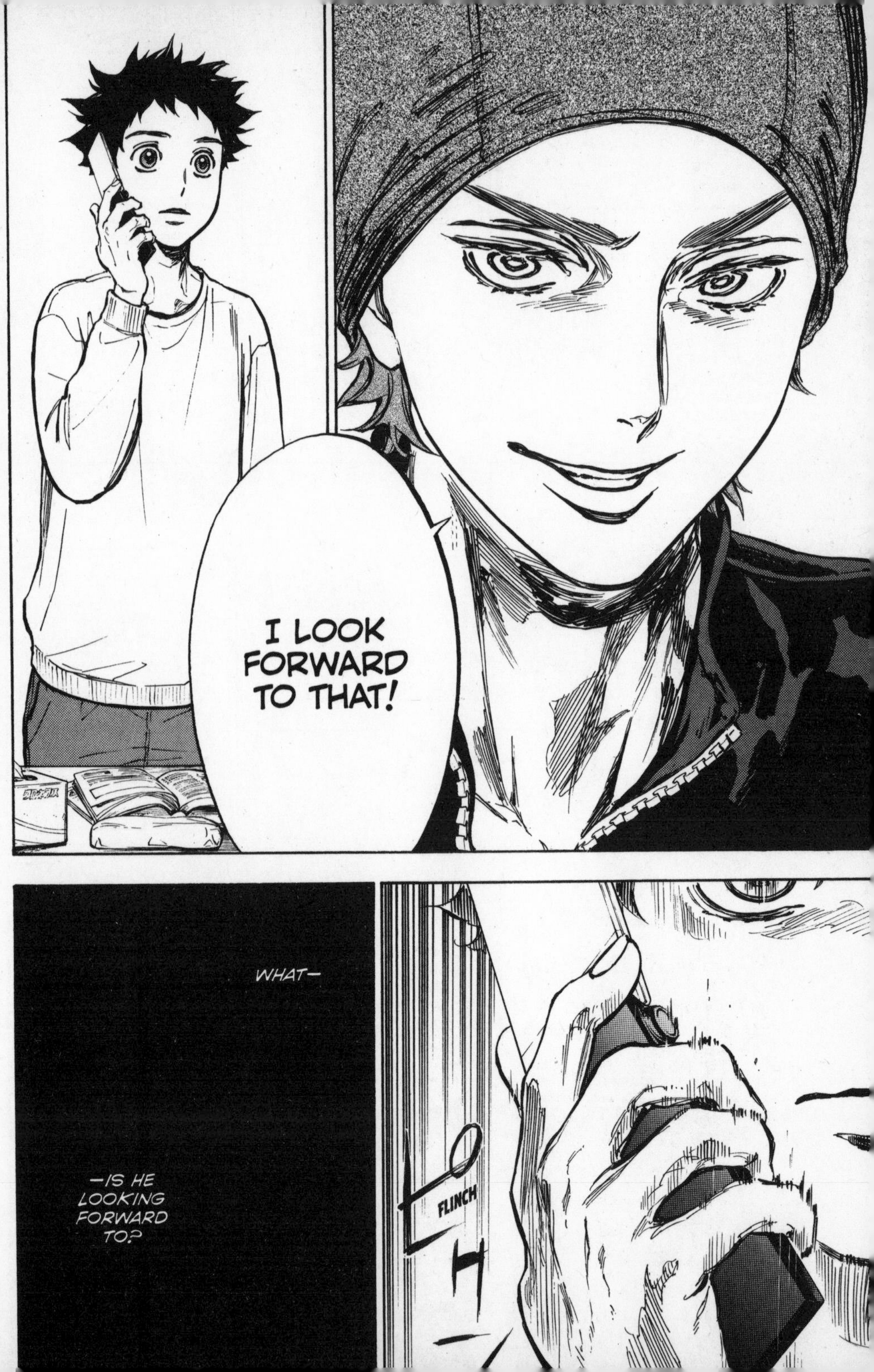
I LOOK FORWARD TO THAT!
FLINCH
WHAT—
—IS HE LOOKING FORWARD TO?

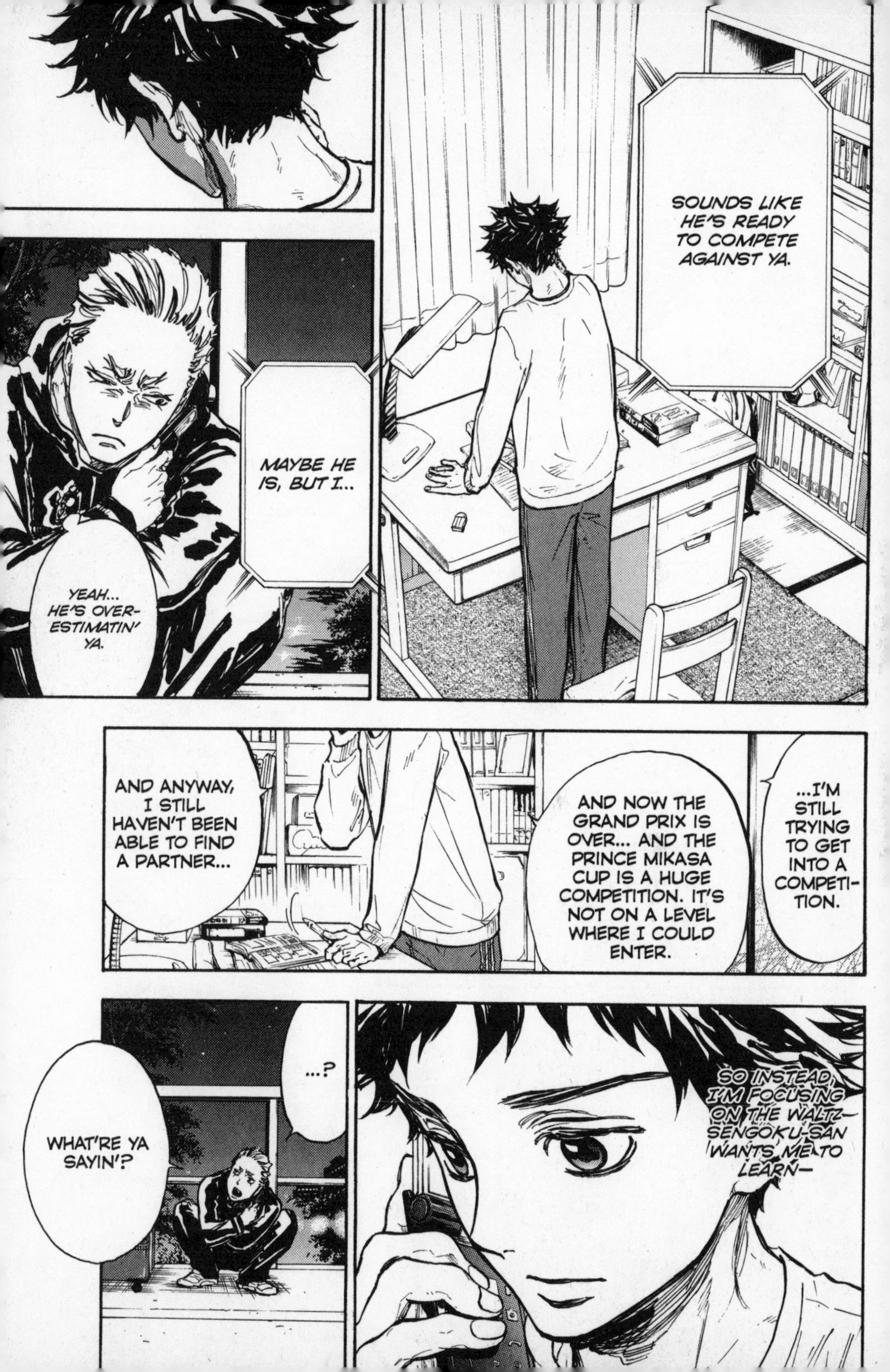
SOUNDS LIKE HE'S READY TO COMPETE AGAINST YA.
MAYBE HE IS, BUT I...
YEAH... HE'S OVER-ESTIMATIN' YA.
...I'M STILL TRYING TO GET INTO A COMPETITION.
AND NOW THE GRAND PRIX IS OVER... AND THE PRINCE MIKASA CUP IS A HUGE COMPETITION. IT'S NOT ON A LEVEL WHERE I COULD ENTER.
AND ANYWAY, I STILL HAVEN'T BEEN ABLE TO FIND A PARTNER...
SO INSTEAD, I'M FOCUSING ON THE WALTZ— SENGOKU-SAN WANTS ME TO LEARN—
...?
WHAT'RE YA SAYIN'?

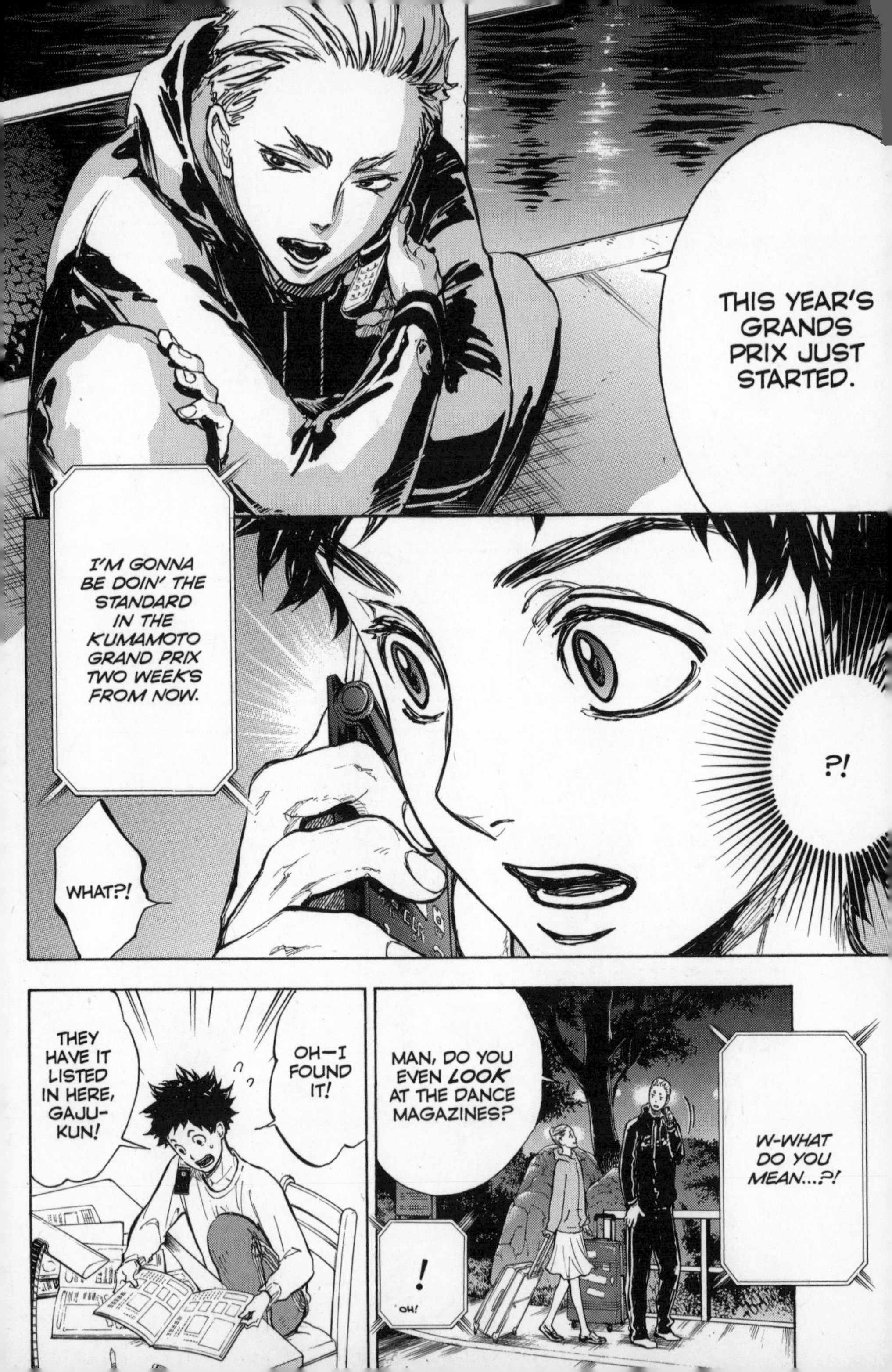
THIS YEAR'S GRANDS PRIX JUST STARTED.
I'M GONNA BE DOIN' THE STANDARD IN THE KUMAMOTO GRAND PRIX TWO WEEKS FROM NOW.
?!
WHAT?!
W-WHAT DO YOU MEAN...?!
MAN, DO YOU EVEN *LOOK* AT THE DANCE MAGAZINES?
!
OH!
OH—I FOUND IT!
THEY HAVE IT LISTED IN HERE, GAJU-KUN!

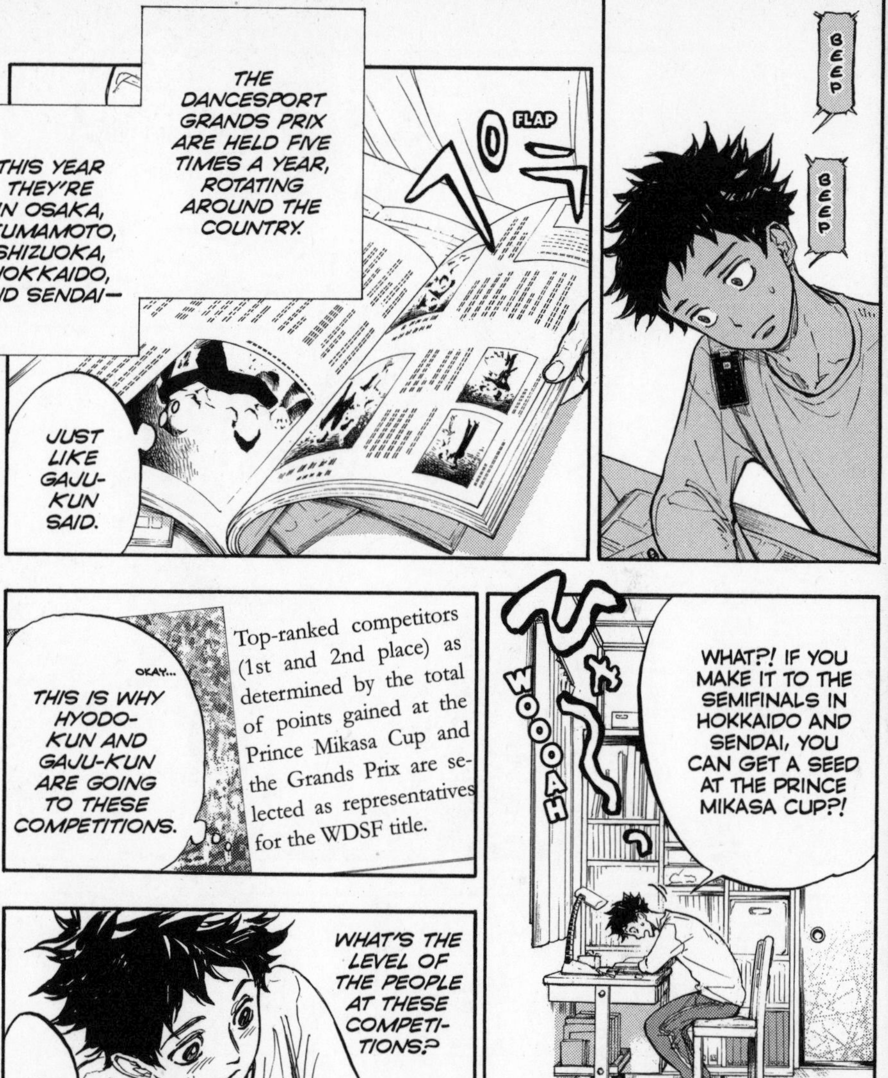
BEEP
BEEP
THE DANCESPORT GRANDS PRIX ARE HELD FIVE TIMES A YEAR, ROTATING AROUND THE COUNTRY.
THIS YEAR THEY'RE IN OSAKA, KUMAMOTO, SHIZUOKA, HOKKAIDO, AND SENDAI—
FLAP
JUST LIKE GAJU-KUN SAID.
WHAT?! IF YOU MAKE IT TO THE SEMIFINALS IN HOKKAIDO AND SENDAI, YOU CAN GET A SEED AT THE PRINCE MIKASA CUP?!
WOOOAH
Top-ranked competitors (1st and 2nd place) as determined by the total of points gained at the Prince Mikasa Cup and the Grands Prix are selected as representatives for the WDSF title.
OKAY...
THIS IS WHY HYODO-KUN AND GAJU-KUN ARE GOING TO THESE COMPETITIONS.
WHAT'S THE LEVEL OF THE PEOPLE AT THESE COMPETITIONS?
HM ...?

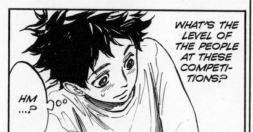

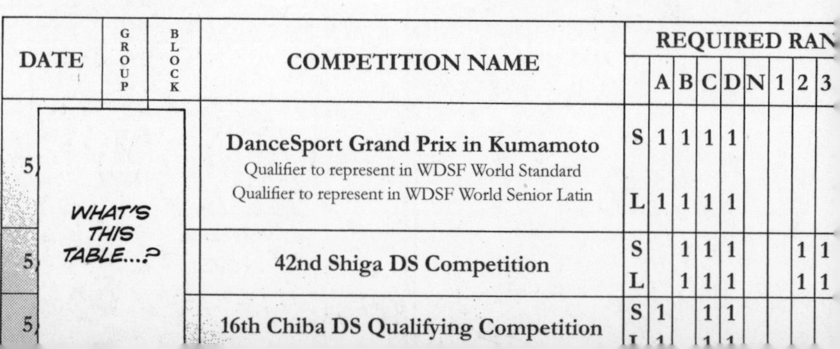
WHAT'S THIS TABLE...?

DATE	GROUP	BLOCK	COMPETITION NAME		REQUIRED RAN							
					A	B	C	D	N	1	2	3
5/			DanceSport Grand Prix in Kumamoto Qualifier to represent in WDSF World Standard Qualifier to represent in WDSF World Senior Latin	S	1	1	1	1				
				L	1	1	1	1				
5/			42nd Shiga DS Competition	S		1	1	1			1	1
				L		1	1	1			1	1
5/			16th Chiba DS Qualifying Competition	S	1		1	1				

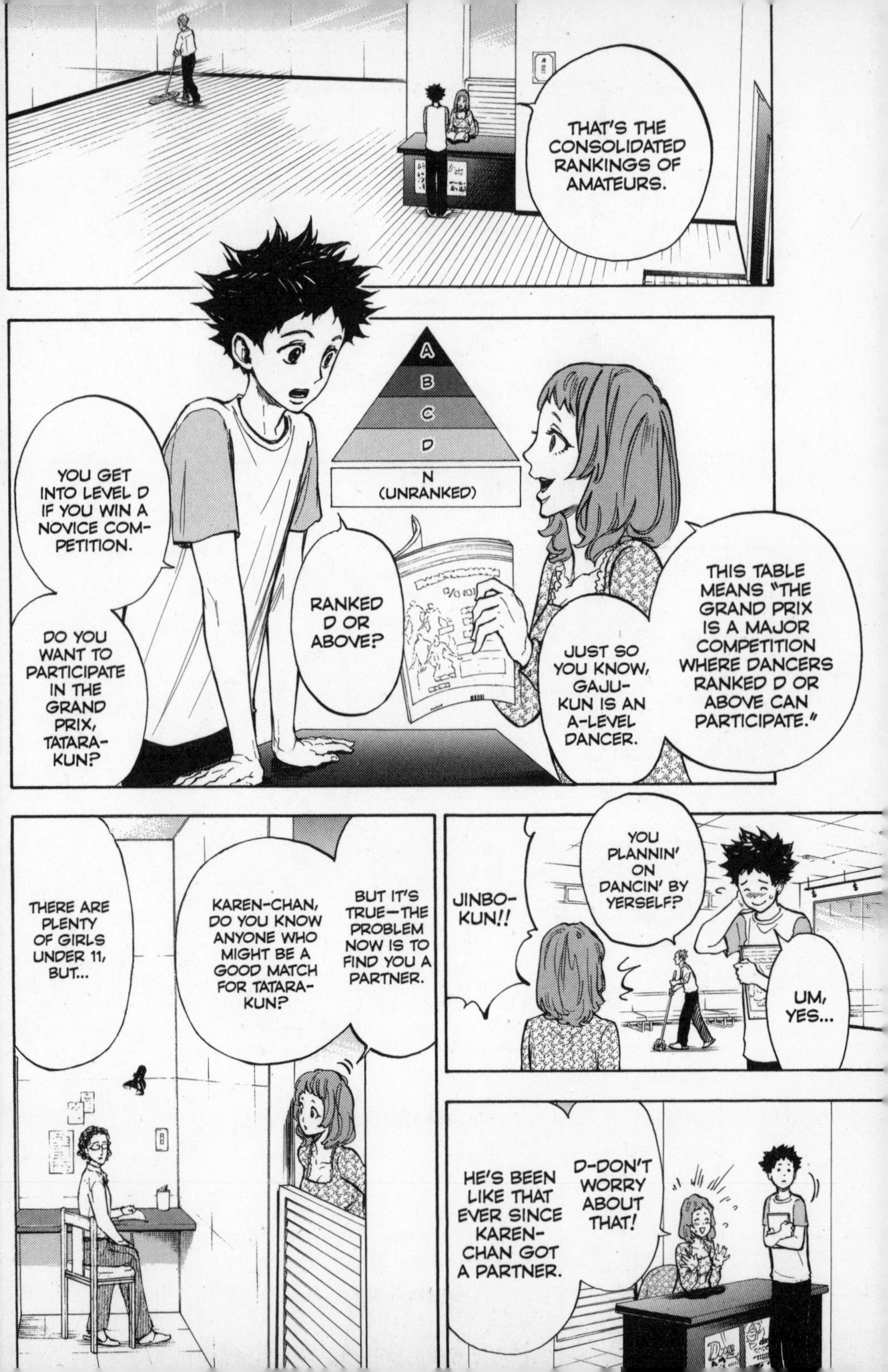
THAT'S THE CONSOLIDATED RANKINGS OF AMATEURS.
A
B
C
D
N (UNRANKED)
THIS TABLE MEANS "THE GRAND PRIX IS A MAJOR COMPETITION WHERE DANCERS RANKED D OR ABOVE CAN PARTICIPATE."
JUST SO YOU KNOW, GAJU-KUN IS AN A-LEVEL DANCER.
RANKED D OR ABOVE?
YOU GET INTO LEVEL D IF YOU WIN A NOVICE COMPETITION.
DO YOU WANT TO PARTICIPATE IN THE GRAND PRIX, TATARA-KUN?
YOU PLANNIN' ON DANCIN' BY YERSELF?
UM, YES...
JINBO-KUN!!
D-DON'T WORRY ABOUT THAT!
HE'S BEEN LIKE THAT EVER SINCE KAREN-CHAN GOT A PARTNER.
BUT IT'S TRUE—THE PROBLEM NOW IS TO FIND YOU A PARTNER.
KAREN-CHAN, DO YOU KNOW ANYONE WHO MIGHT BE A GOOD MATCH FOR TATARA-KUN?
THERE ARE PLENTY OF GIRLS UNDER 11, BUT...

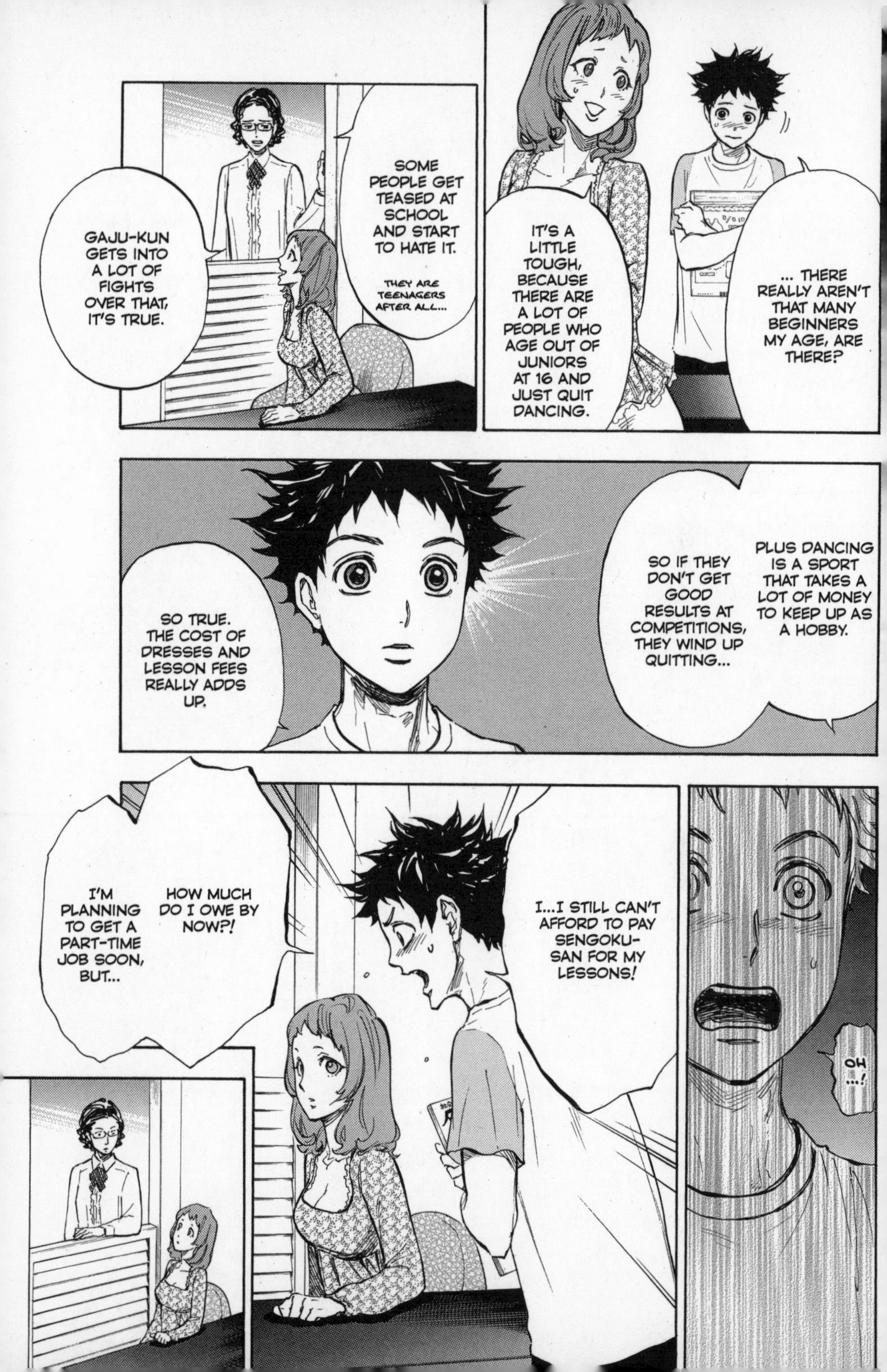
... THERE REALLY AREN'T THAT MANY BEGINNERS MY AGE, ARE THERE?
IT'S A LITTLE TOUGH, BECAUSE THERE ARE A LOT OF PEOPLE WHO AGE OUT OF JUNIORS AT 16 AND JUST QUIT DANCING.
SOME PEOPLE GET TEASED AT SCHOOL AND START TO HATE IT.
THEY ARE TEENAGERS AFTER ALL...
GAJU-KUN GETS INTO A LOT OF FIGHTS OVER THAT, IT'S TRUE.
PLUS DANCING IS A SPORT THAT TAKES A LOT OF MONEY TO KEEP UP AS A HOBBY.
SO IF THEY DON'T GET GOOD RESULTS AT COMPETITIONS, THEY WIND UP QUITTING...
SO TRUE. THE COST OF DRESSES AND LESSON FEES REALLY ADDS UP.
OH...!
I...I STILL CAN'T AFFORD TO PAY SENGOKU-SAN FOR MY LESSONS!
HOW MUCH DO I OWE BY NOW?!
I'M PLANNING TO GET A PART-TIME JOB SOON, BUT...

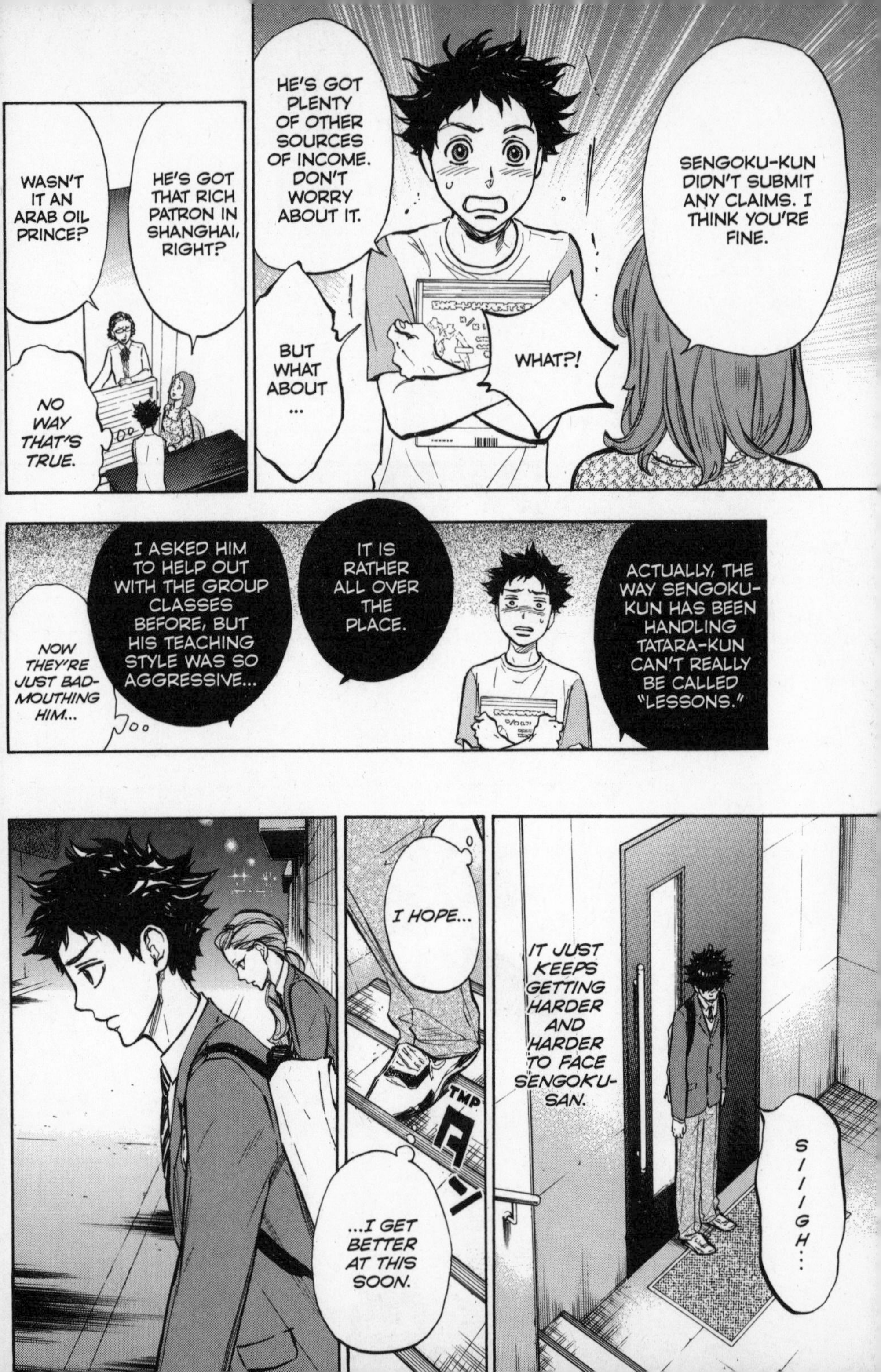
SENGOKU-KUN DIDN'T SUBMIT ANY CLAIMS. I THINK YOU'RE FINE.
WHAT?!
HE'S GOT PLENTY OF OTHER SOURCES OF INCOME. DON'T WORRY ABOUT IT.
BUT WHAT ABOUT ...
HE'S GOT THAT RICH PATRON IN SHANGHAI, RIGHT?
WASN'T IT AN ARAB OIL PRINCE?
NO WAY THAT'S TRUE.
ACTUALLY, THE WAY SENGOKU-KUN HAS BEEN HANDLING TATARA-KUN CAN'T REALLY BE CALLED "LESSONS."
IT IS RATHER ALL OVER THE PLACE.
I ASKED HIM TO HELP OUT WITH THE GROUP CLASSES BEFORE, BUT HIS TEACHING STYLE WAS SO AGGRESSIVE...
NOW THEY'RE JUST BAD-MOUTHING HIM...
S/I/I/G/H...
IT JUST KEEPS GETTING HARDER AND HARDER TO FACE SENGOKU-SAN.
I HOPE...
TMP
...I GET BETTER AT THIS SOON.

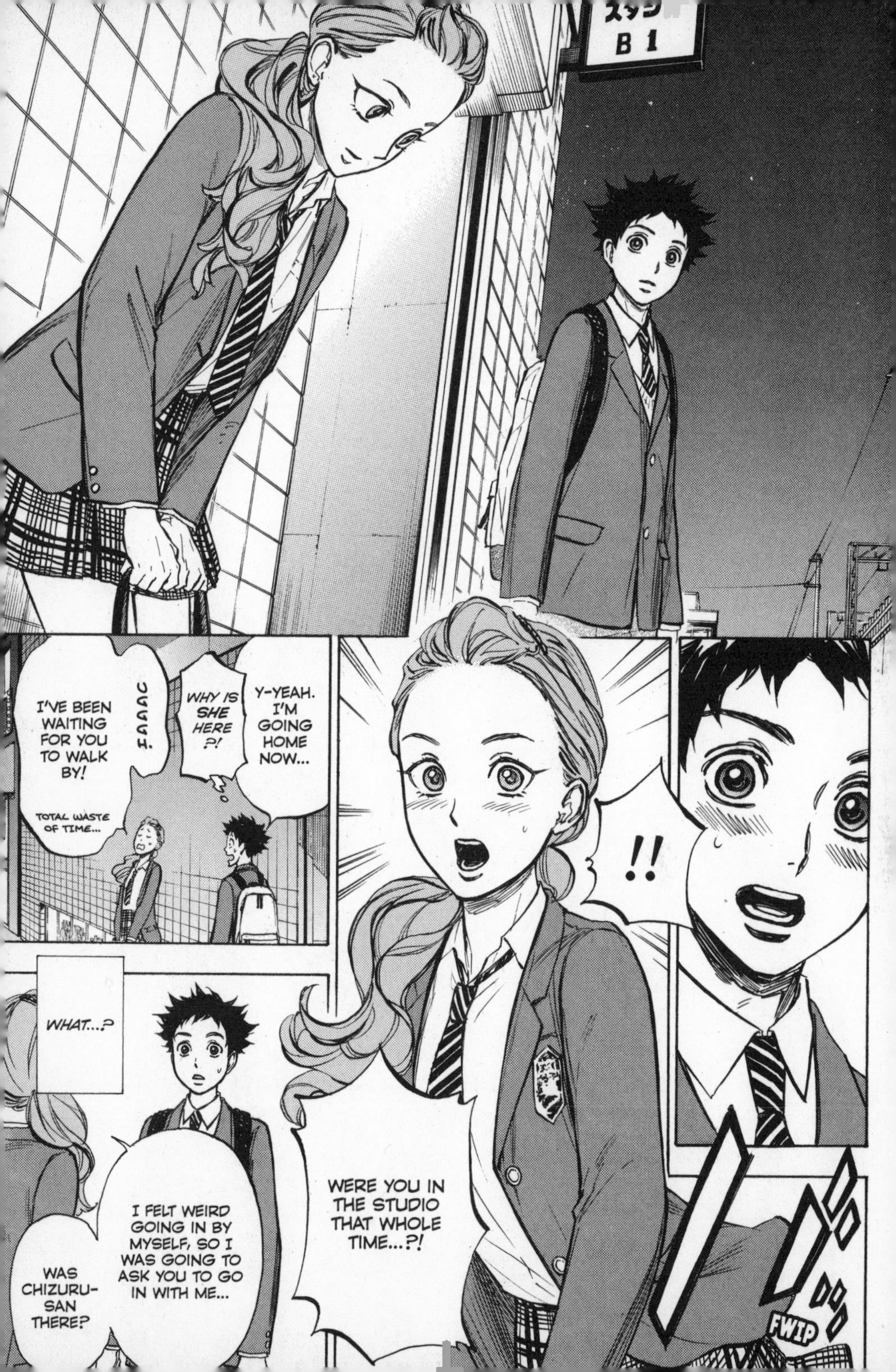
スタジ
B1
!!
WERE YOU IN THE STUDIO THAT WHOLE TIME...?!
FWIP
Y-YEAH. I'M GOING HOME NOW...
WHY IS SHE HERE?!
UGGG!
I'VE BEEN WAITING FOR YOU TO WALK BY!
TOTAL WASTE OF TIME...
WHAT...?
I FELT WEIRD GOING IN BY MYSELF, SO I WAS GOING TO ASK YOU TO GO IN WITH ME...
WAS CHIZURU-SAN THERE?

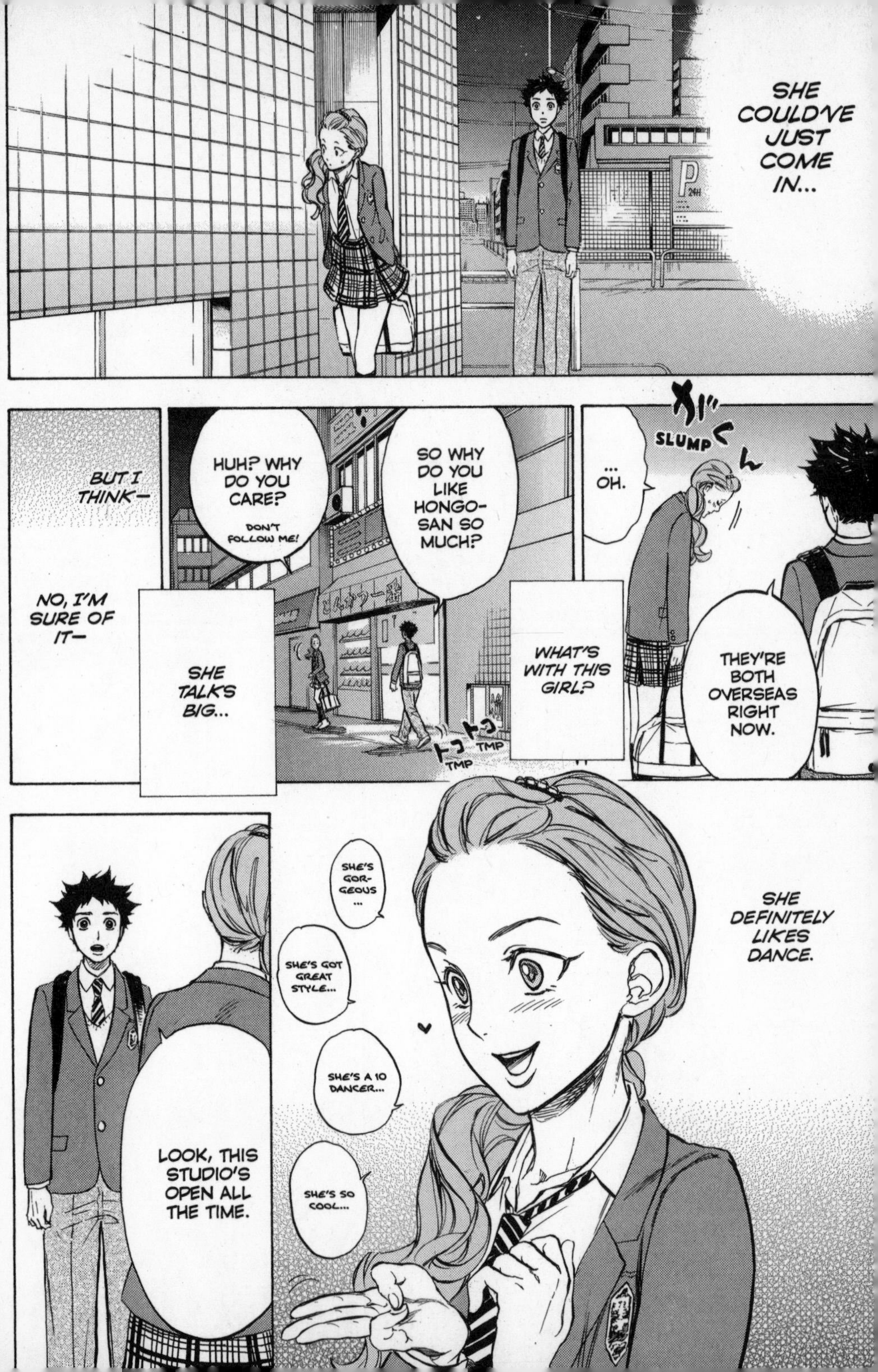
SHE COULD'VE JUST COME IN...
SLUMP
...OH.
THEY'RE BOTH OVERSEAS RIGHT NOW.
WHAT'S WITH THIS GIRL?
SO WHY DO YOU LIKE HONGO-SAN SO MUCH?
HUH? WHY DO YOU CARE?
DON'T FOLLOW ME!
TMP
TMP
SHE TALKS BIG...
BUT I THINK—
NO, I'M SURE OF IT—
SHE DEFINITELY LIKES DANCE.
SHE'S GORGEOUS...
SHE'S GOT GREAT STYLE...
SHE'S A 10 DANCER...
SHE'S SO COOL...
LOOK, THIS STUDIO'S OPEN ALL THE TIME.

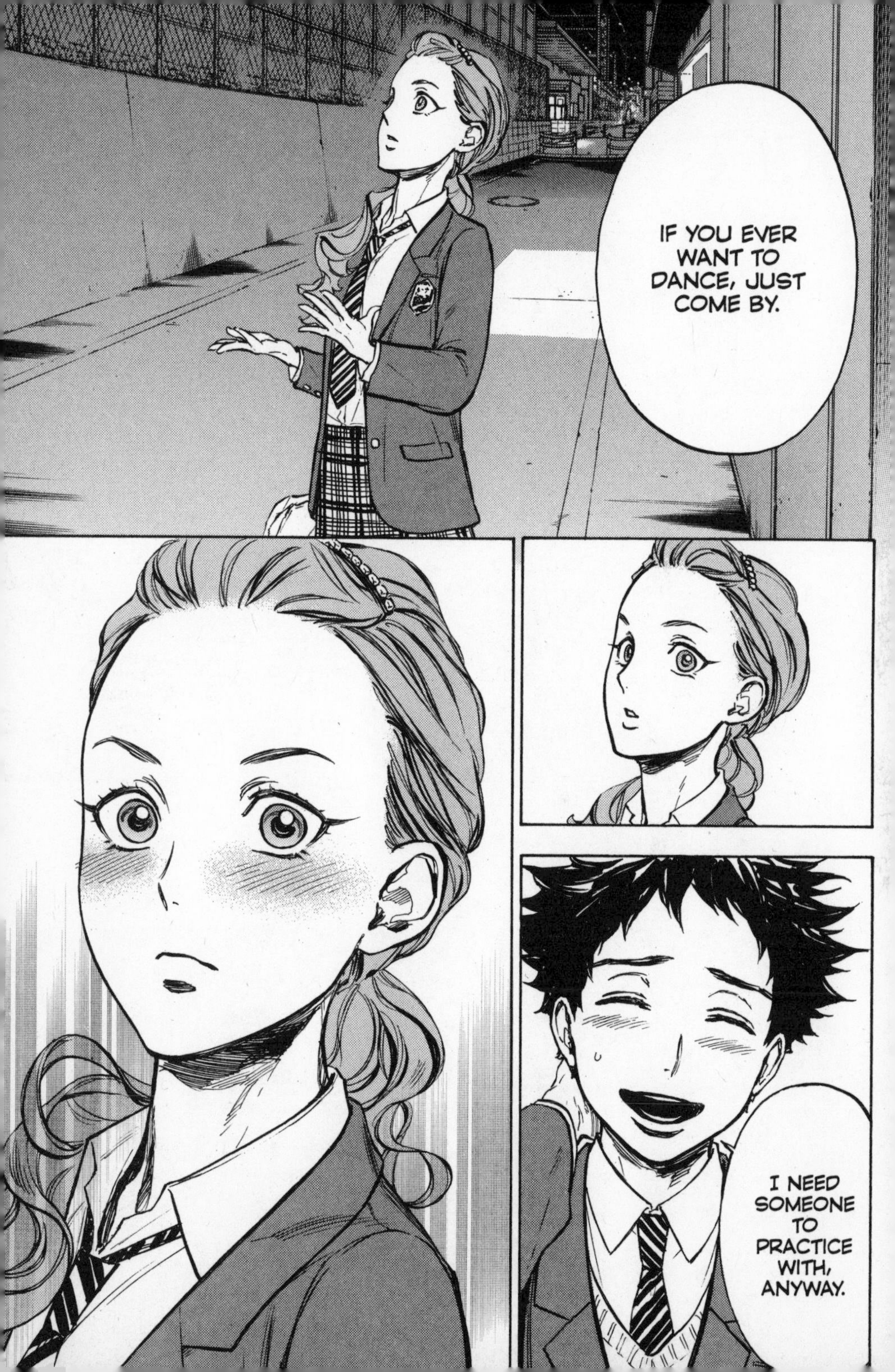
IF YOU EVER WANT TO DANCE, JUST COME BY.
I NEED SOMEONE TO PRACTICE WITH, ANYWAY.

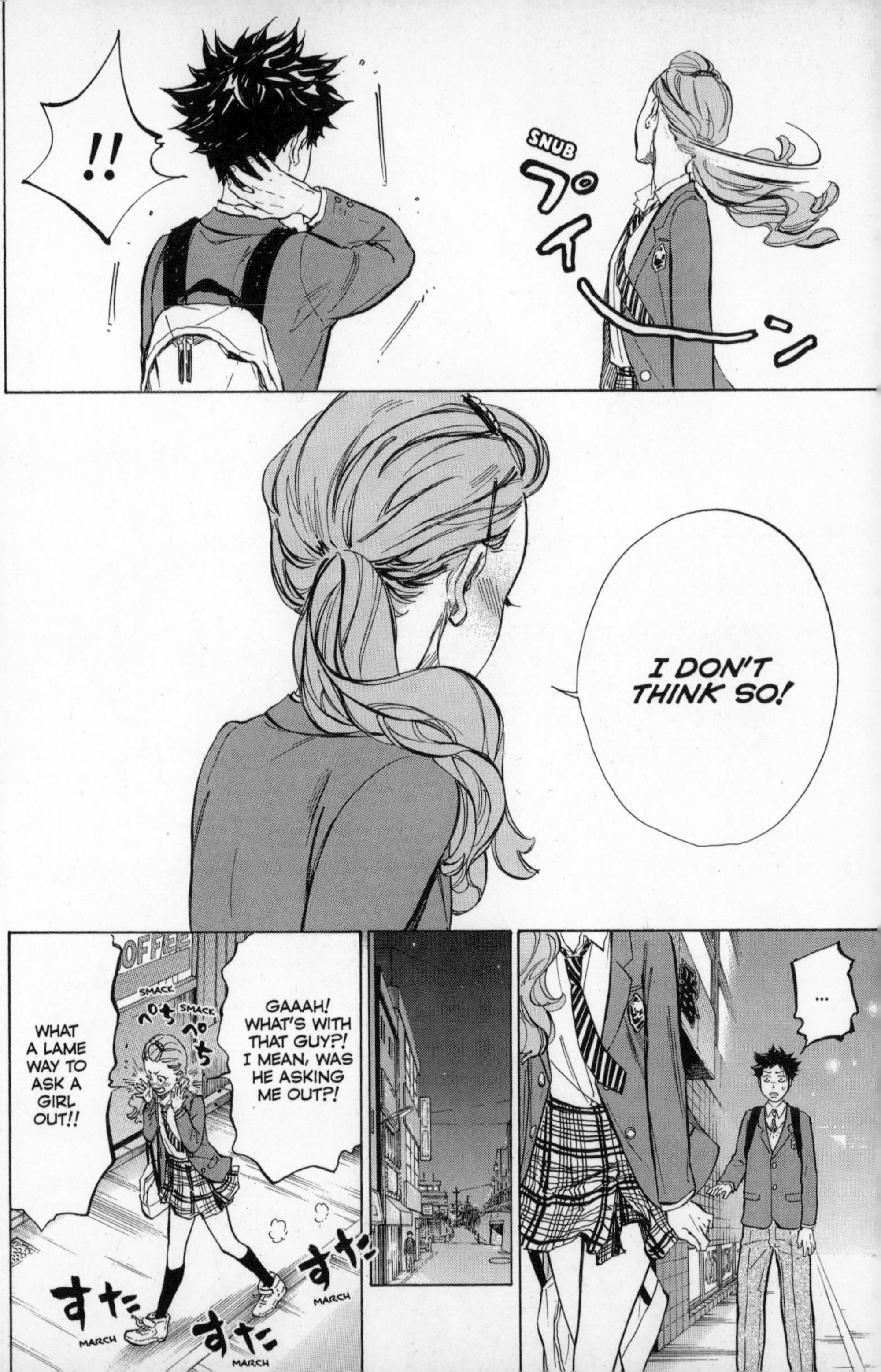
SNUB
プイーン
!!
I DON'T THINK SO!
...
GAAAH! WHAT'S WITH THAT GUY?! I MEAN, WAS HE ASKING ME OUT?!
SMACK
ぺち
SMACK
ぺち
WHAT A LAME WAY TO ASK A GIRL OUT!!
すた
MARCH
すた
MARCH
すた
MARCH

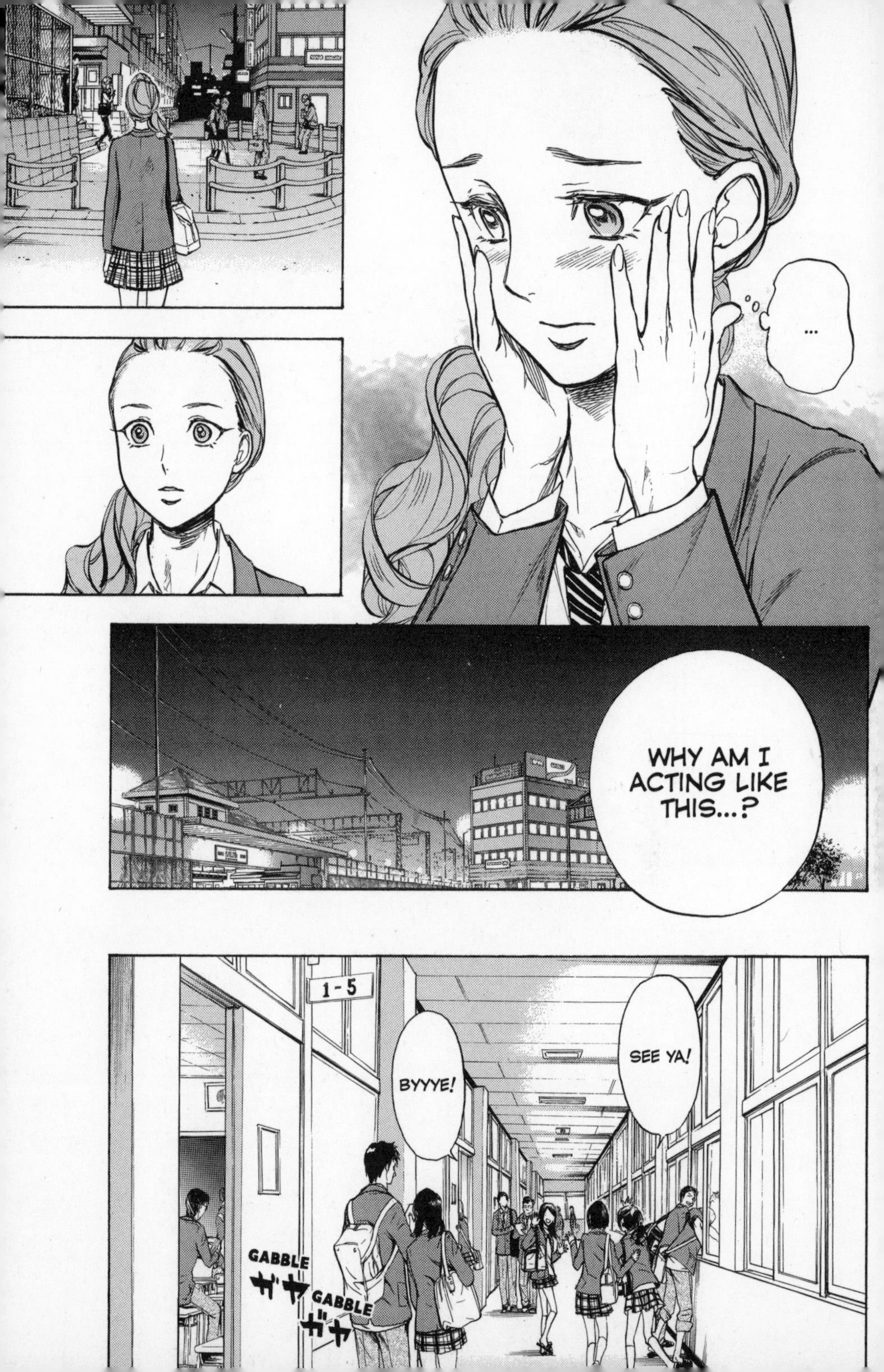
...
WHY AM I ACTING LIKE THIS...?
SEE YA!
BYYYE!
GABBLE
ガヤ
GABBLE
ガヤ

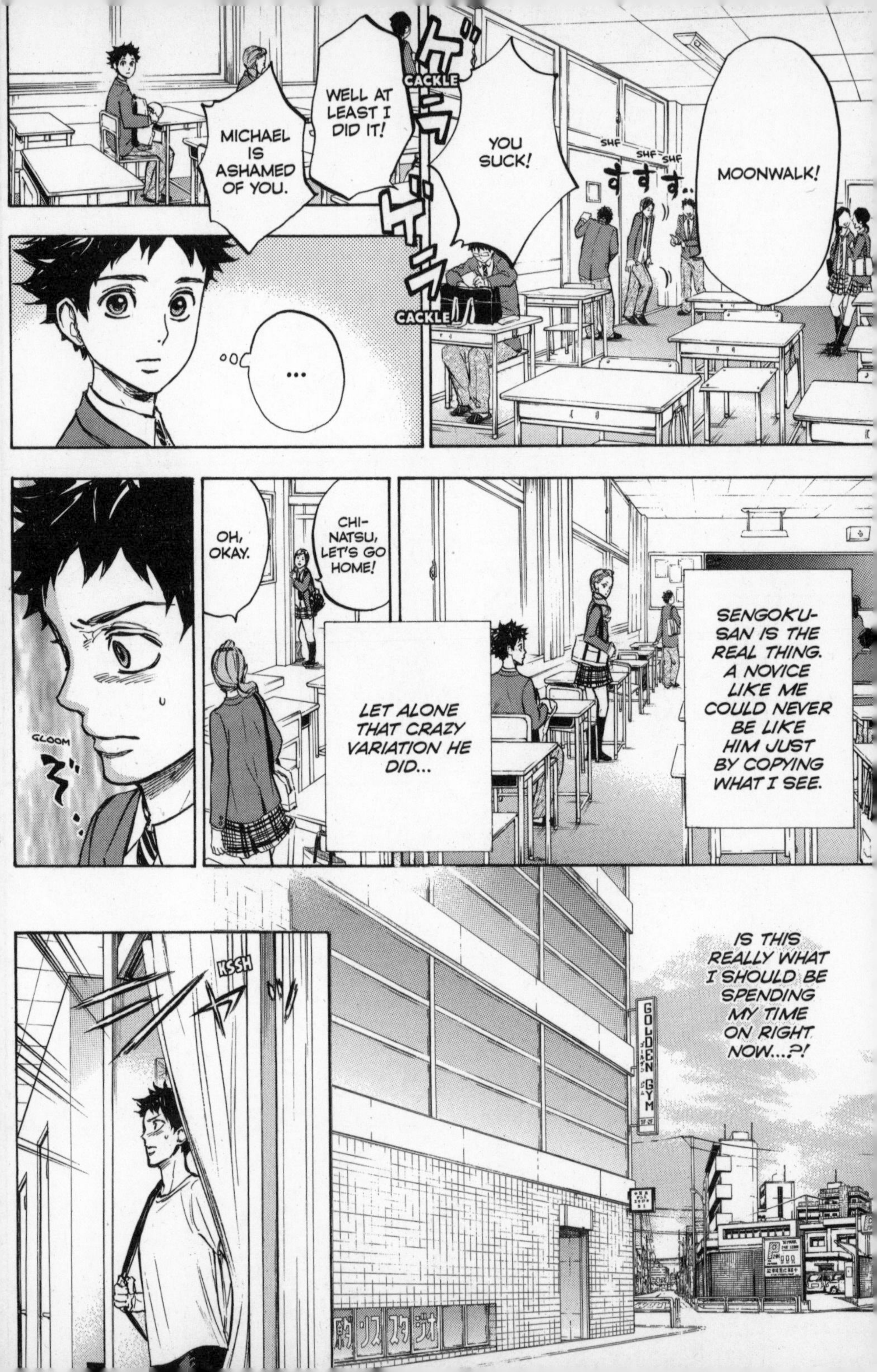
MOONWALK!
SHF SHF SHF
すすす…
YOU SUCK!
CACKLE
CACKLE
WELL AT LEAST I DID IT!
MICHAEL IS ASHAMED OF YOU.
...
SENGOKU-SAN IS THE REAL THING. A NOVICE LIKE ME COULD NEVER BE LIKE HIM JUST BY COPYING WHAT I SEE.
LET ALONE THAT CRAZY VARIATION HE DID...
CHI-NATSU, LET'S GO HOME!
OH, OKAY.
GLOOM
IS THIS REALLY WHAT I SHOULD BE SPENDING MY TIME ON RIGHT NOW...?!
GOLDEN GYM
KSSH

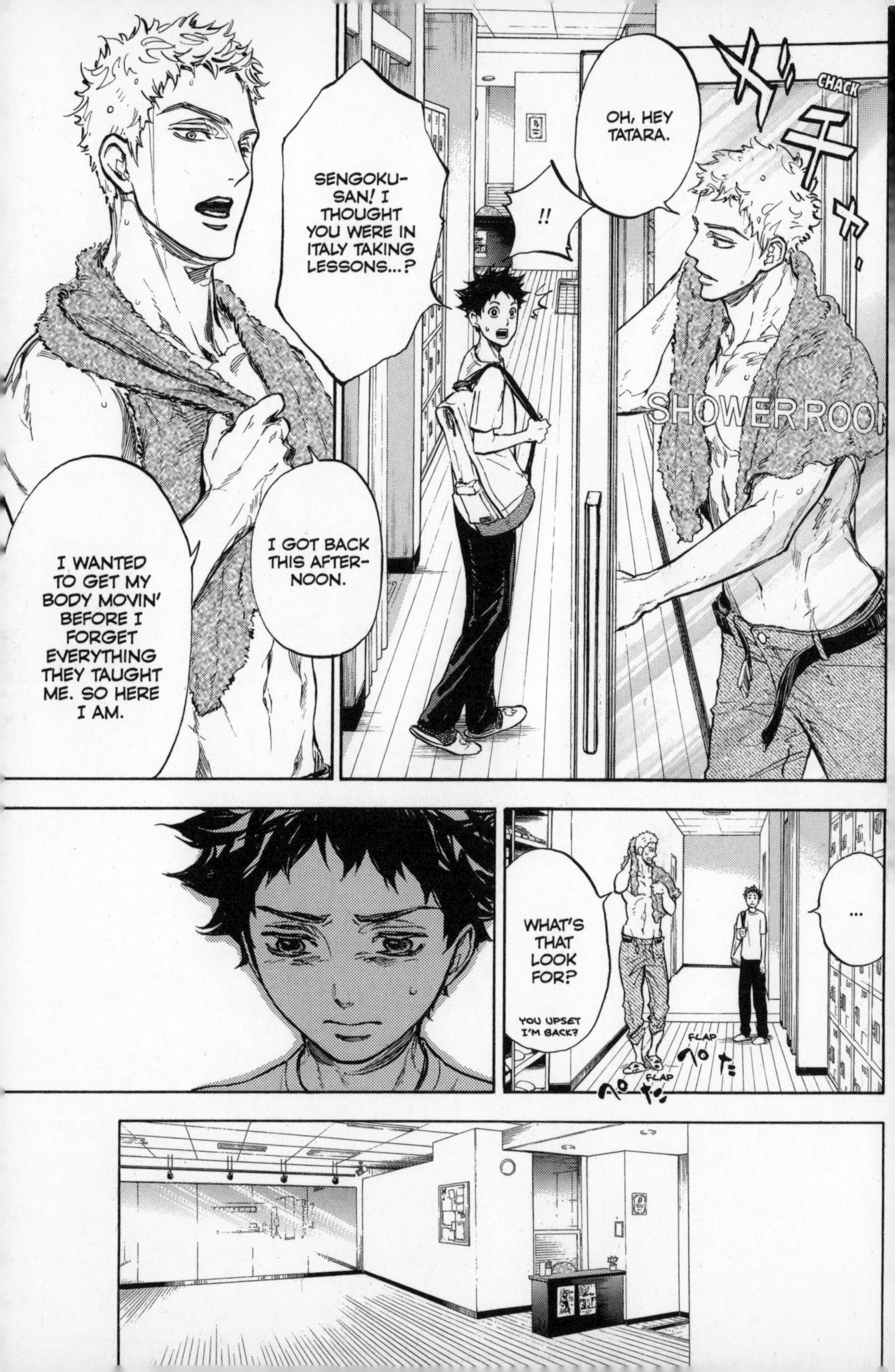
CHACK
OH, HEY TATARA.
!!
SHOWER ROO
SENGOKU-SAN! I THOUGHT YOU WERE IN ITALY TAKING LESSONS...?
I GOT BACK THIS AFTERNOON.
I WANTED TO GET MY BODY MOVIN' BEFORE I FORGET EVERYTHING THEY TAUGHT ME. SO HERE I AM.
...
WHAT'S THAT LOOK FOR?
YOU UPSET I'M BACK?
FLAP
FLAP

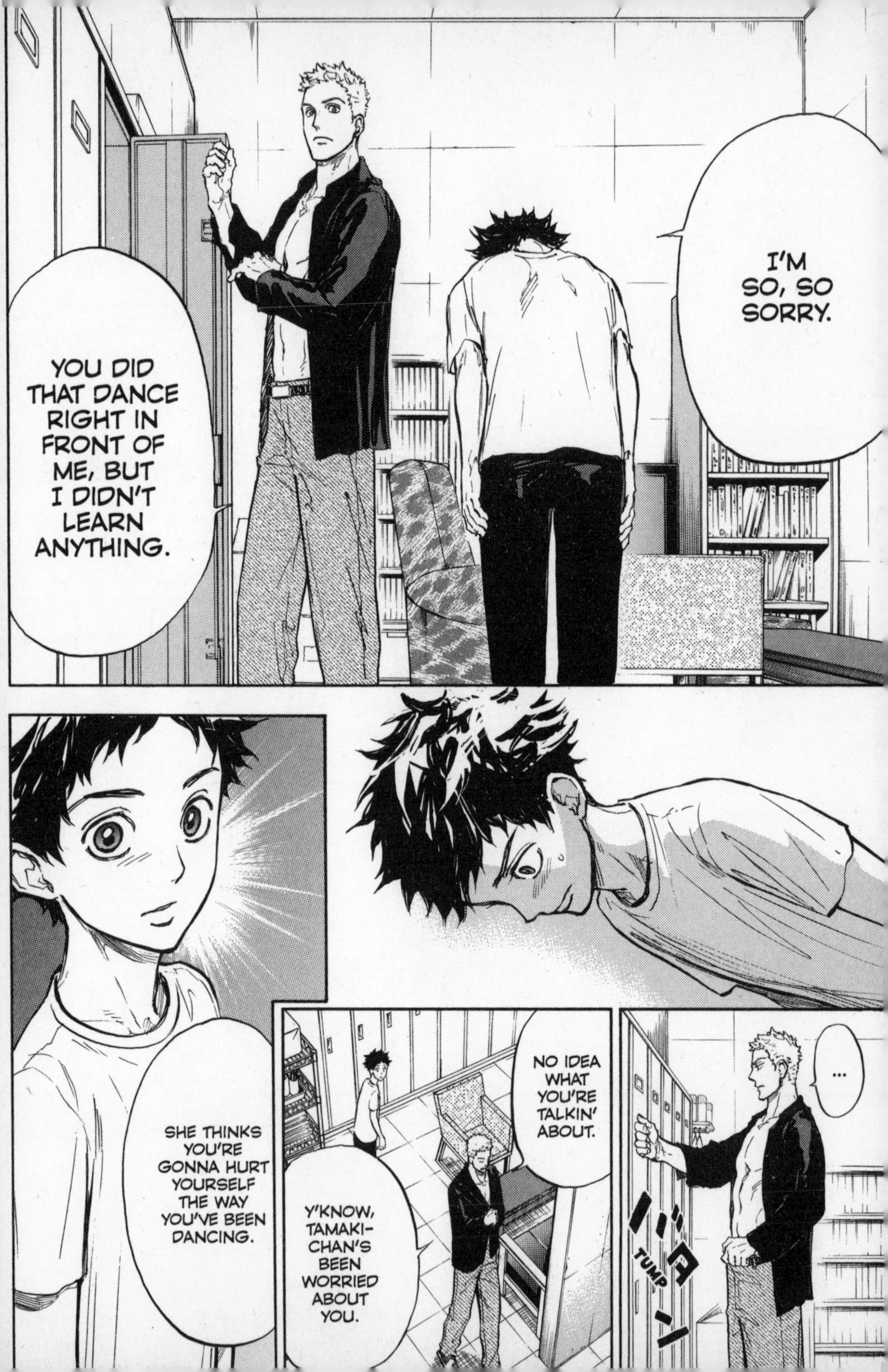
I'M SO, SO SORRY.
YOU DID THAT DANCE RIGHT IN FRONT OF ME, BUT I DIDN'T LEARN ANYTHING.
...
TUMP
NO IDEA WHAT YOU'RE TALKIN' ABOUT.
Y'KNOW, TAMAKI-CHAN'S BEEN WORRIED ABOUT YOU.
SHE THINKS YOU'RE GONNA HURT YOURSELF THE WAY YOU'VE BEEN DANCING.

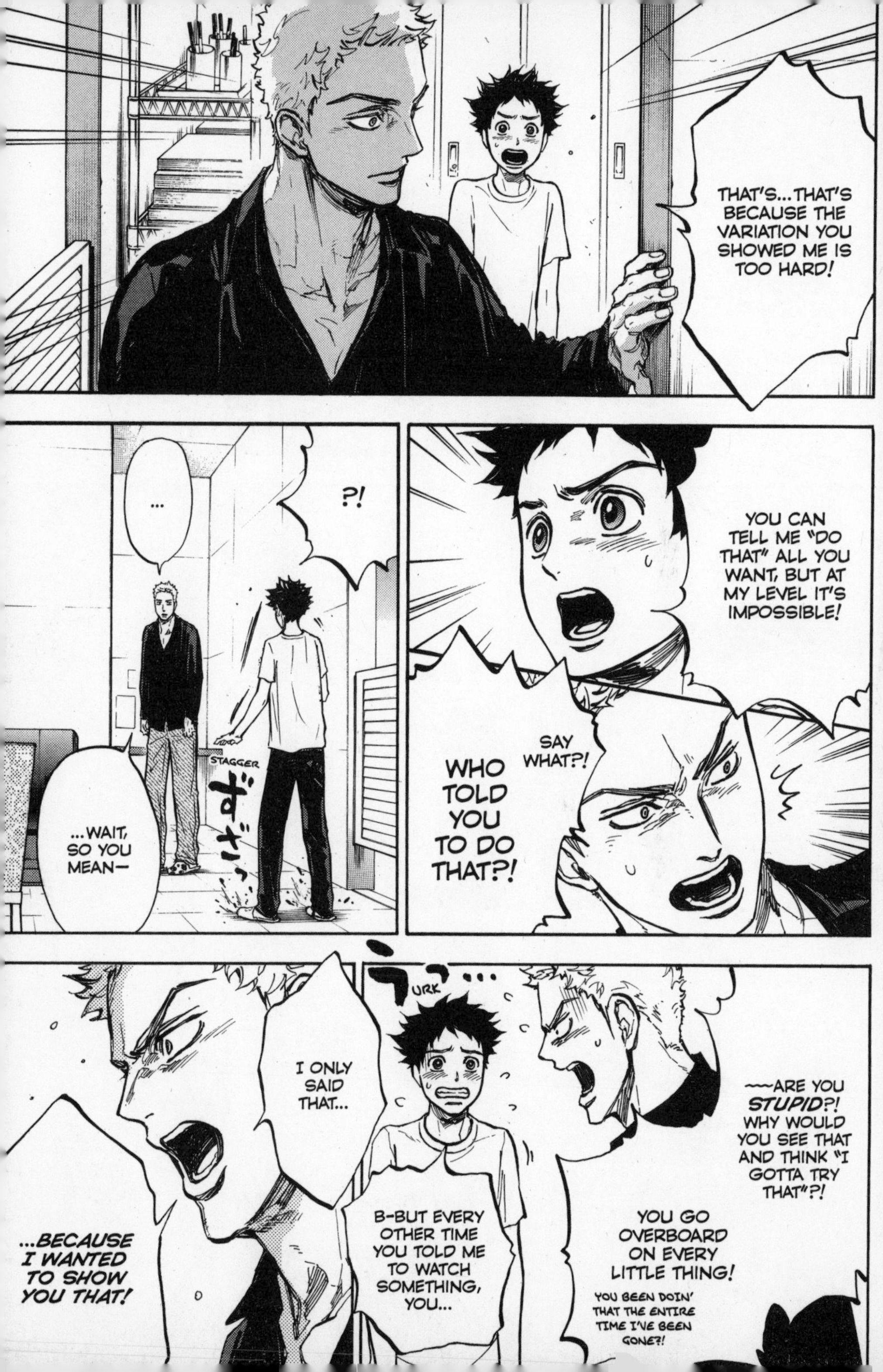
THAT'S...THAT'S BECAUSE THE VARIATION YOU SHOWED ME IS TOO HARD!
YOU CAN TELL ME "DO THAT" ALL YOU WANT, BUT AT MY LEVEL IT'S IMPOSSIBLE!
SAY WHAT?!
WHO TOLD YOU TO DO THAT?!
?!
...
STAGGER
...WAIT, SO YOU MEAN—
URK
—ARE YOU STUPID?! WHY WOULD YOU SEE THAT AND THINK "I GOTTA TRY THAT"?!
YOU GO OVERBOARD ON EVERY LITTLE THING!
YOU BEEN DOIN' THAT THE ENTIRE TIME I'VE BEEN GONE?!
B-BUT EVERY OTHER TIME YOU TOLD ME TO WATCH SOMETHING, YOU...
I ONLY SAID THAT...
...BECAUSE I WANTED TO SHOW YOU THAT!

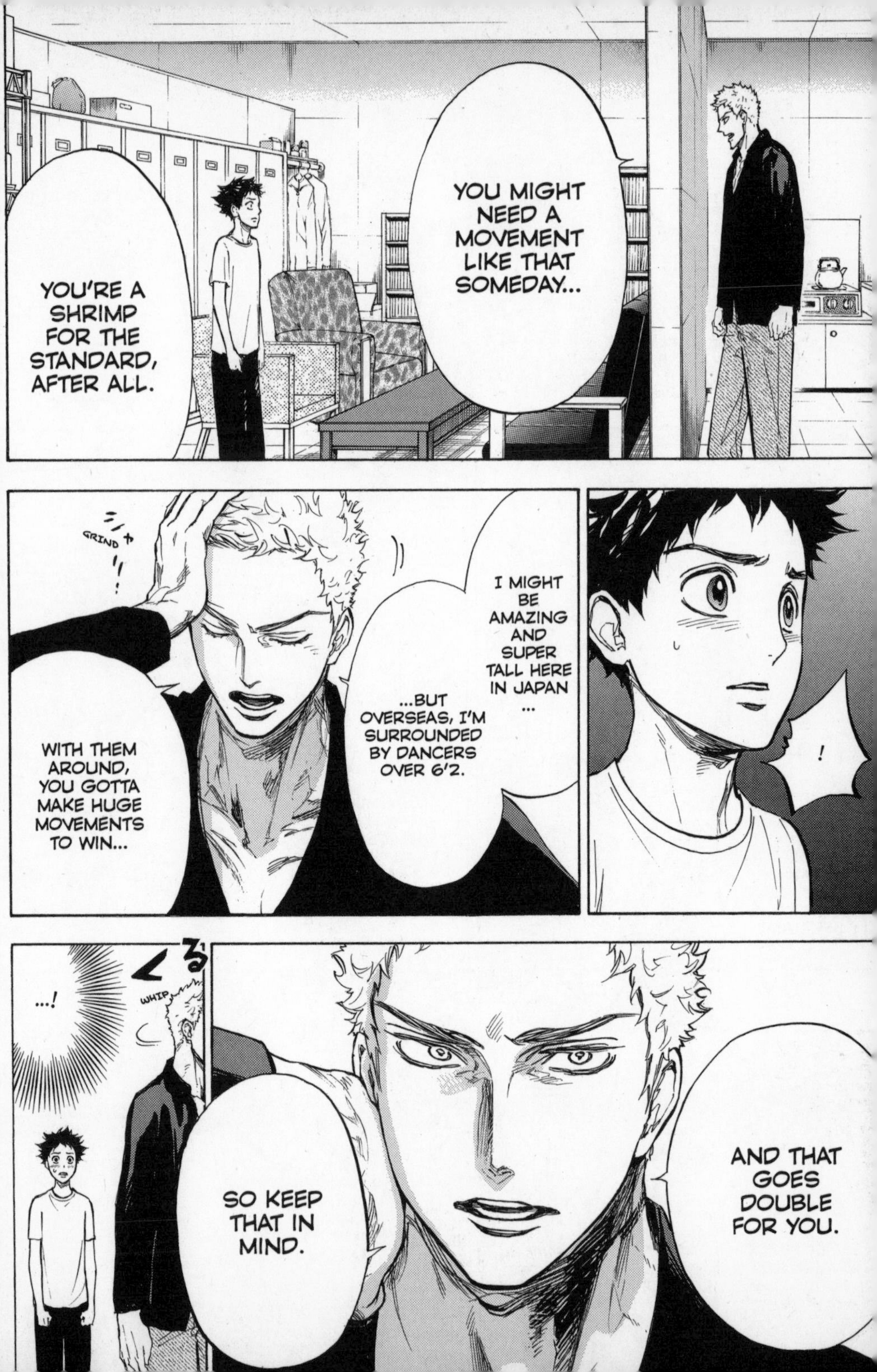
YOU MIGHT NEED A MOVEMENT LIKE THAT SOMEDAY...
YOU'RE A SHRIMP FOR THE STANDARD, AFTER ALL.
!
GRIND
I MIGHT BE AMAZING AND SUPER TALL HERE IN JAPAN ...
...BUT OVERSEAS, I'M SURROUNDED BY DANCERS OVER 6'2.
WITH THEM AROUND, YOU GOTTA MAKE HUGE MOVEMENTS TO WIN...
AND THAT GOES DOUBLE FOR YOU.
SO KEEP THAT IN MIND.
WHIP
...!

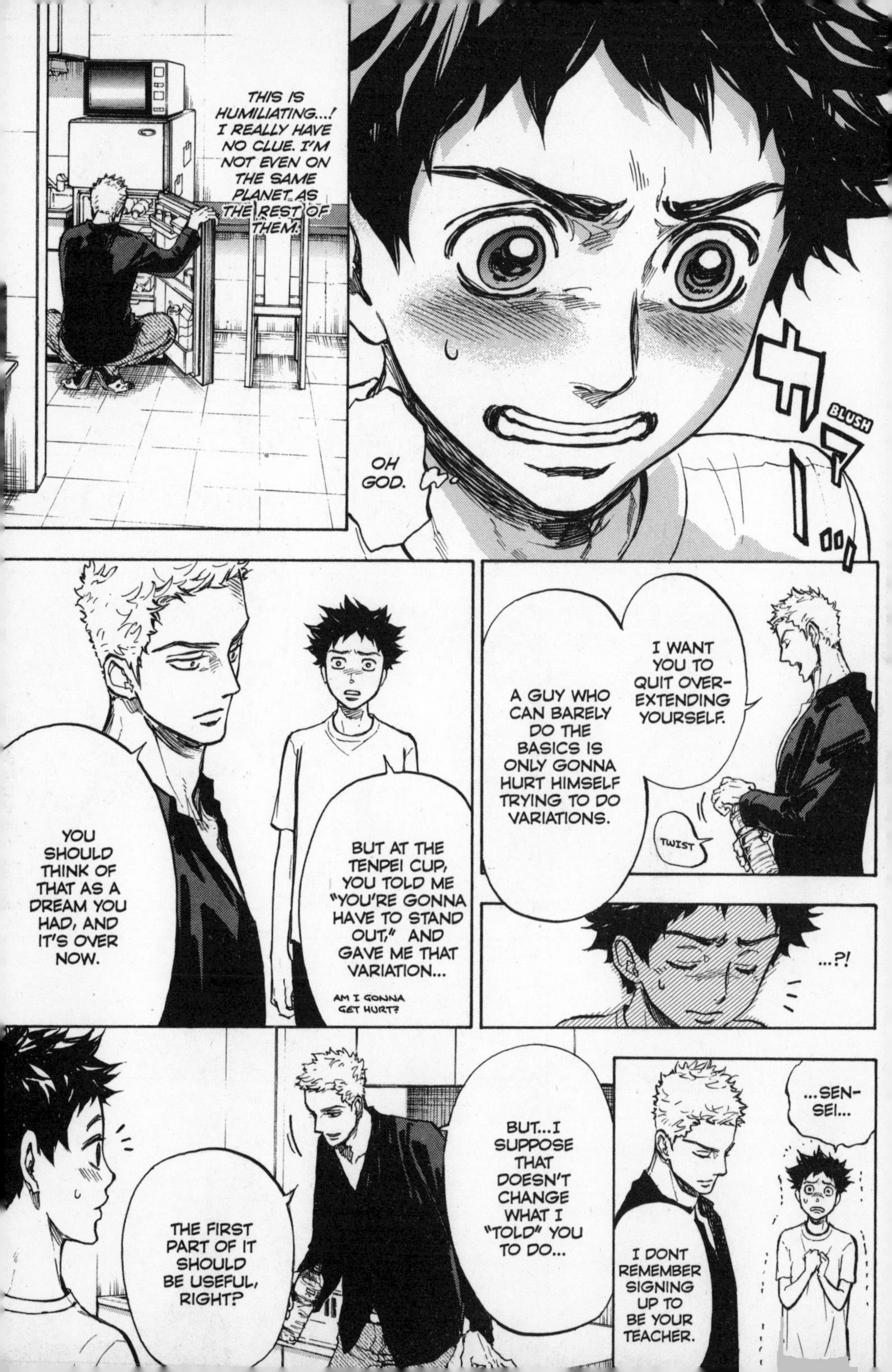
BLUSH
OH GOD.
THIS IS HUMILIATING...! I REALLY HAVE NO CLUE. I'M NOT EVEN ON THE SAME PLANET AS THE REST OF THEM.
I WANT YOU TO QUIT OVER-EXTENDING YOURSELF.
A GUY WHO CAN BARELY DO THE BASICS IS ONLY GONNA HURT HIMSELF TRYING TO DO VARIATIONS.
TWIST
...?!
BUT AT THE TENPEI CUP, YOU TOLD ME "YOU'RE GONNA HAVE TO STAND OUT," AND GAVE ME THAT VARIATION...
AM I GONNA GET HURT?
YOU SHOULD THINK OF THAT AS A DREAM YOU HAD, AND IT'S OVER NOW.
...SEN-SEI...
I DONT REMEMBER SIGNING UP TO BE YOUR TEACHER.
BUT...I SUPPOSE THAT DOESN'T CHANGE WHAT I "TOLD" YOU TO DO...
THE FIRST PART OF IT SHOULD BE USEFUL, RIGHT?

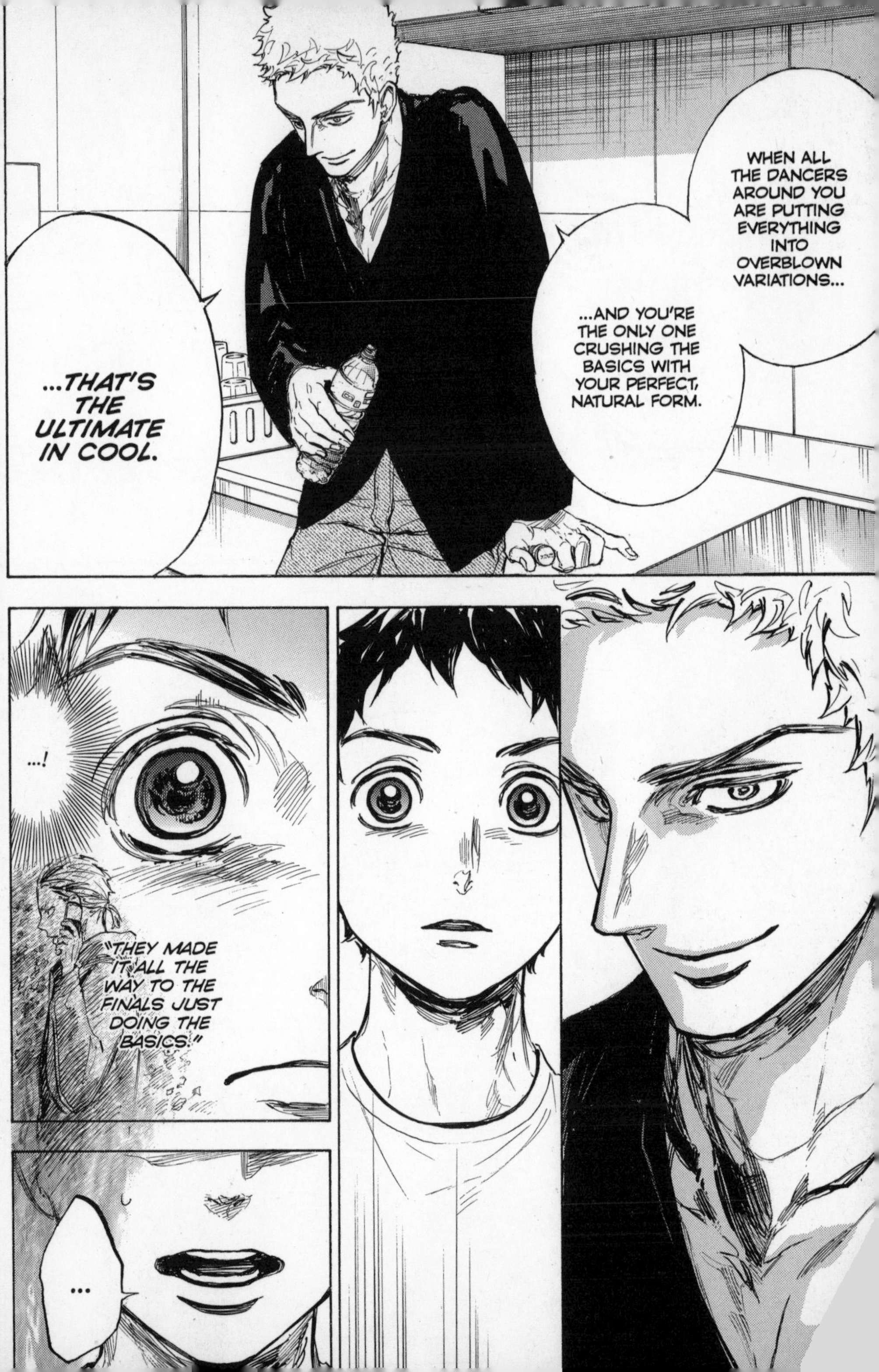
WHEN ALL THE DANCERS AROUND YOU ARE PUTTING EVERYTHING INTO OVERBLOWN VARIATIONS...
...AND YOU'RE THE ONLY ONE CRUSHING THE BASICS WITH YOUR PERFECT, NATURAL FORM.
...THAT'S THE ULTIMATE IN COOL.
...!
"THEY MADE IT ALL THE WAY TO THE FINALS JUST DOING THE BASICS."
...

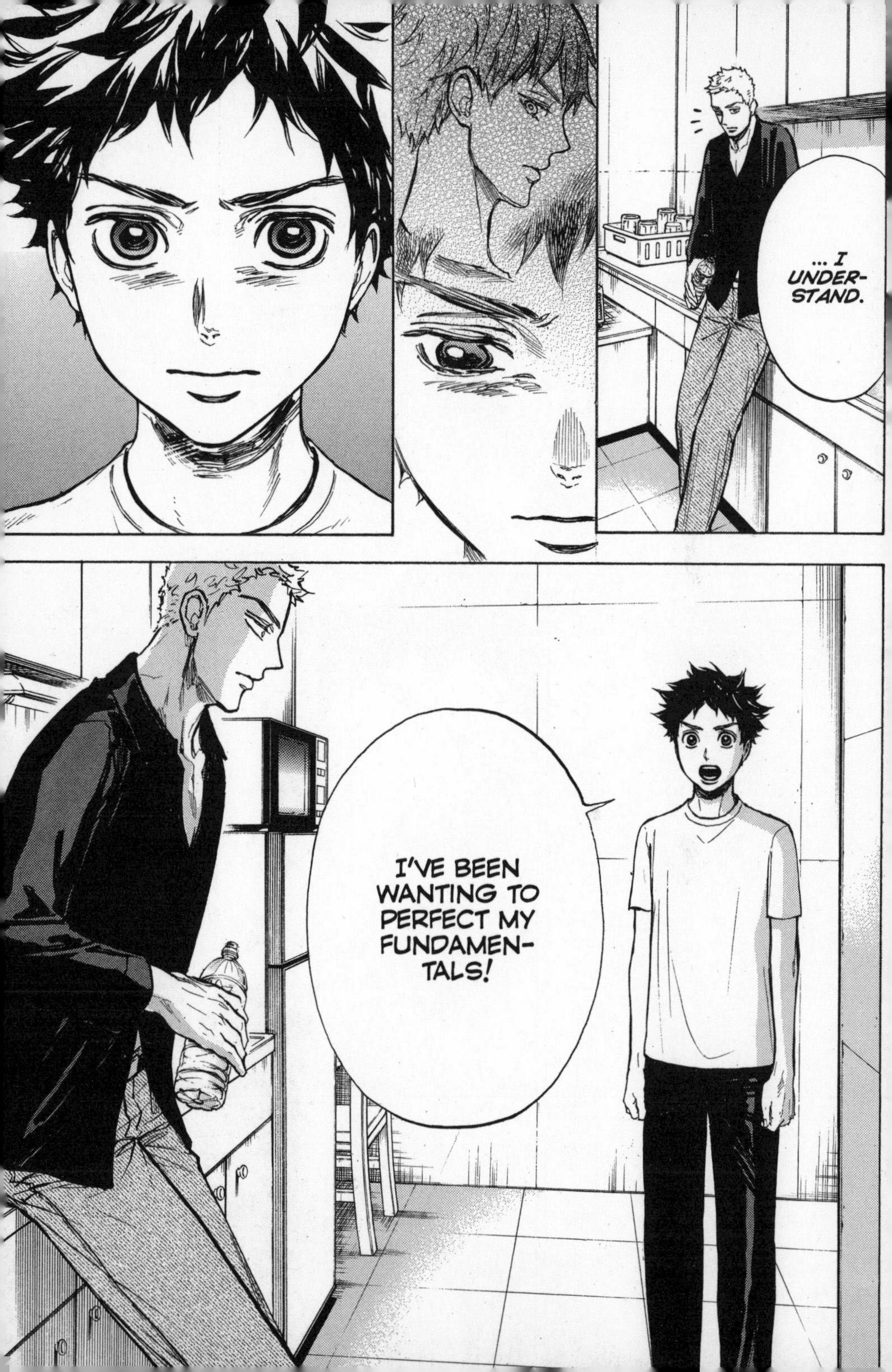

... I UNDER-STAND.
I'VE BEEN WANTING TO PERFECT MY FUNDAMEN-TALS!

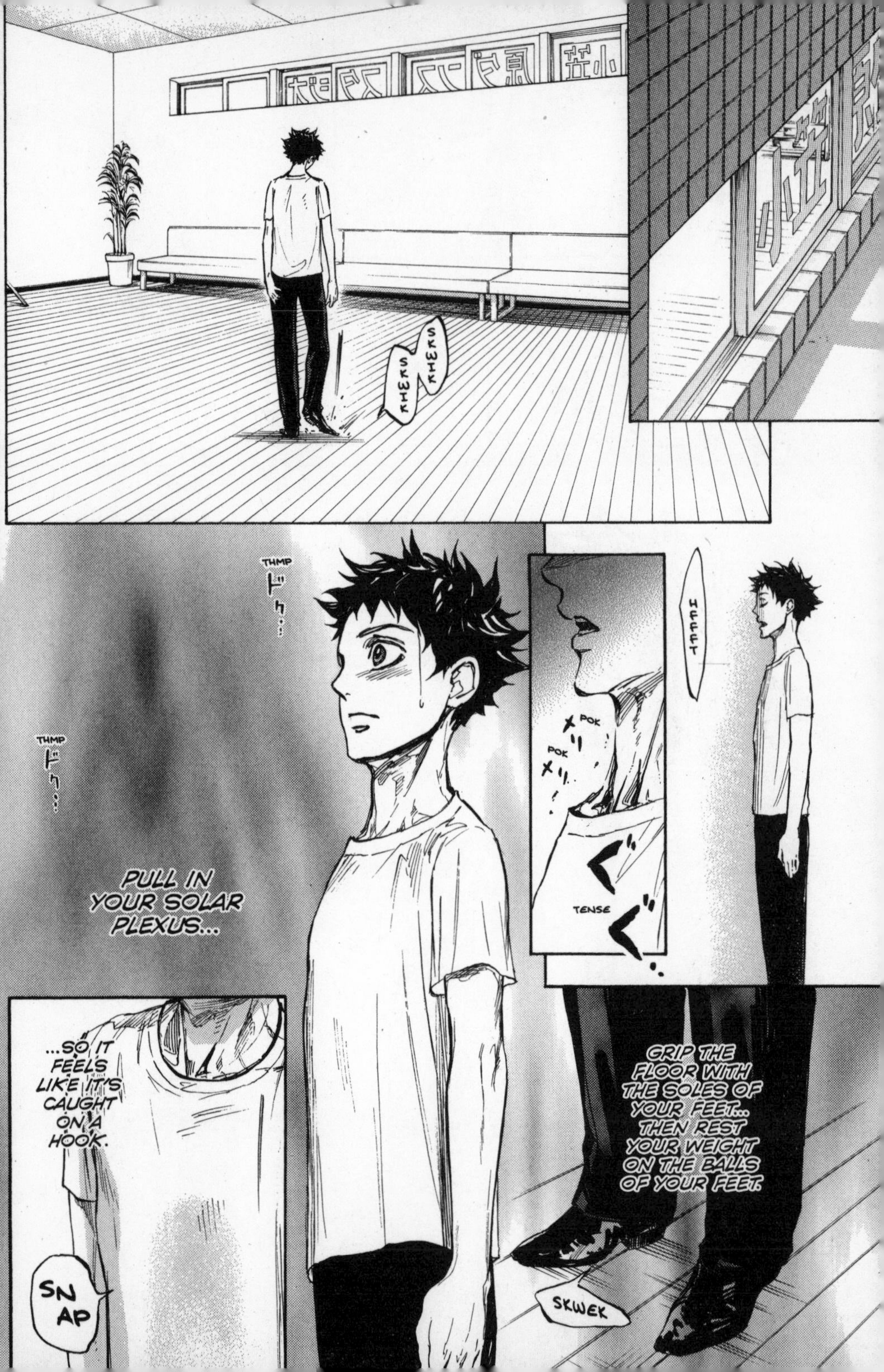
SKWIK
SKWIK
HFFFT
POK
POK
TENSE
THMP
THMP
PULL IN YOUR SOLAR PLEXUS...
GRIP THE FLOOR WITH THE SOLES OF YOUR FEET... THEN REST YOUR WEIGHT ON THE BALLS OF YOUR FEET.
SKWEK
...SO IT FEELS LIKE IT'S CAUGHT ON A HOOK.
SNAP

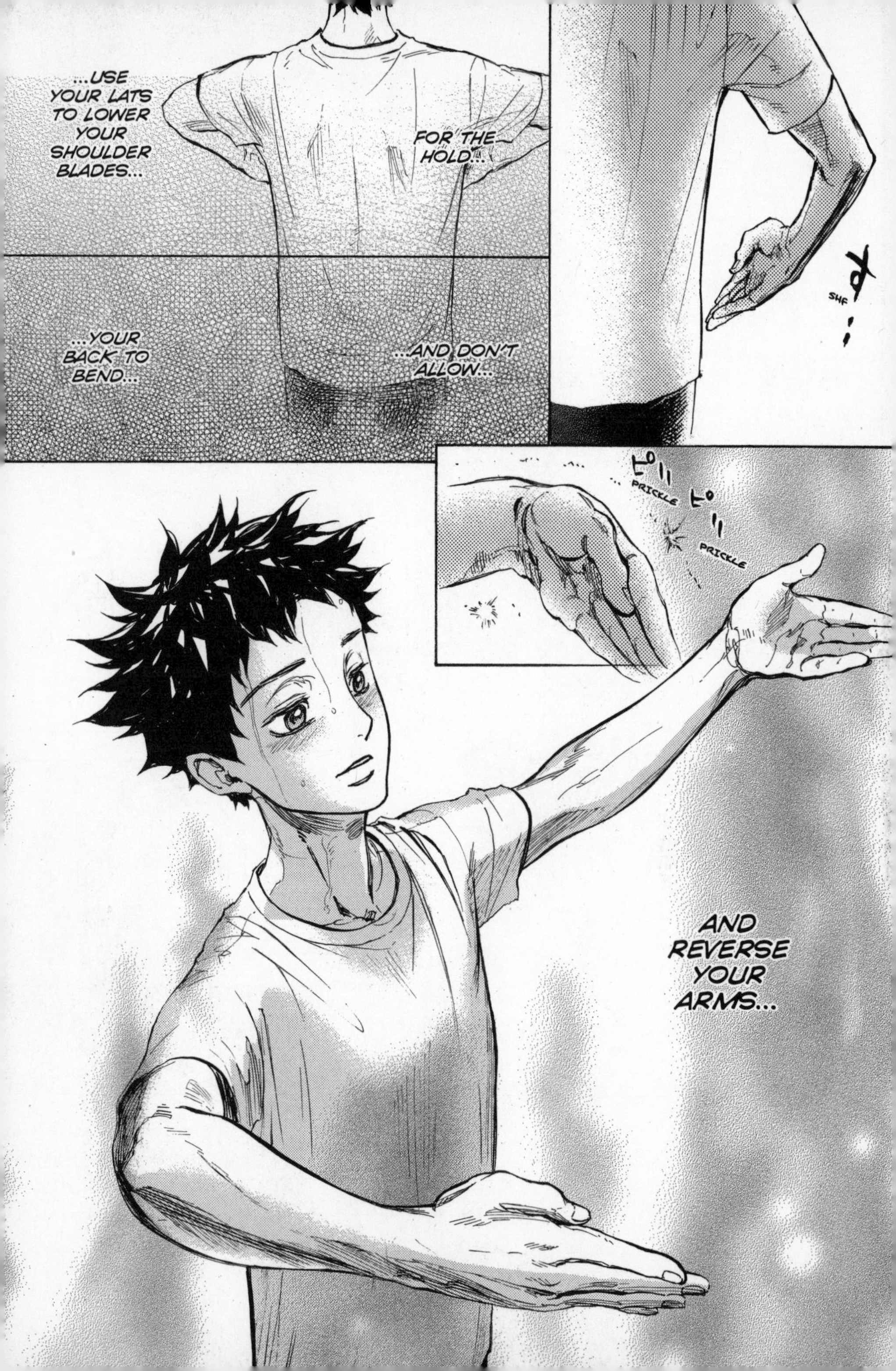

す‥
SHF
FOR THE HOLD...
...USE YOUR LATS TO LOWER YOUR SHOULDER BLADES...
...AND DON'T ALLOW...
...YOUR BACK TO BEND...
ピリ
PRICKLE
ピリ
PRICKLE
AND REVERSE YOUR ARMS...

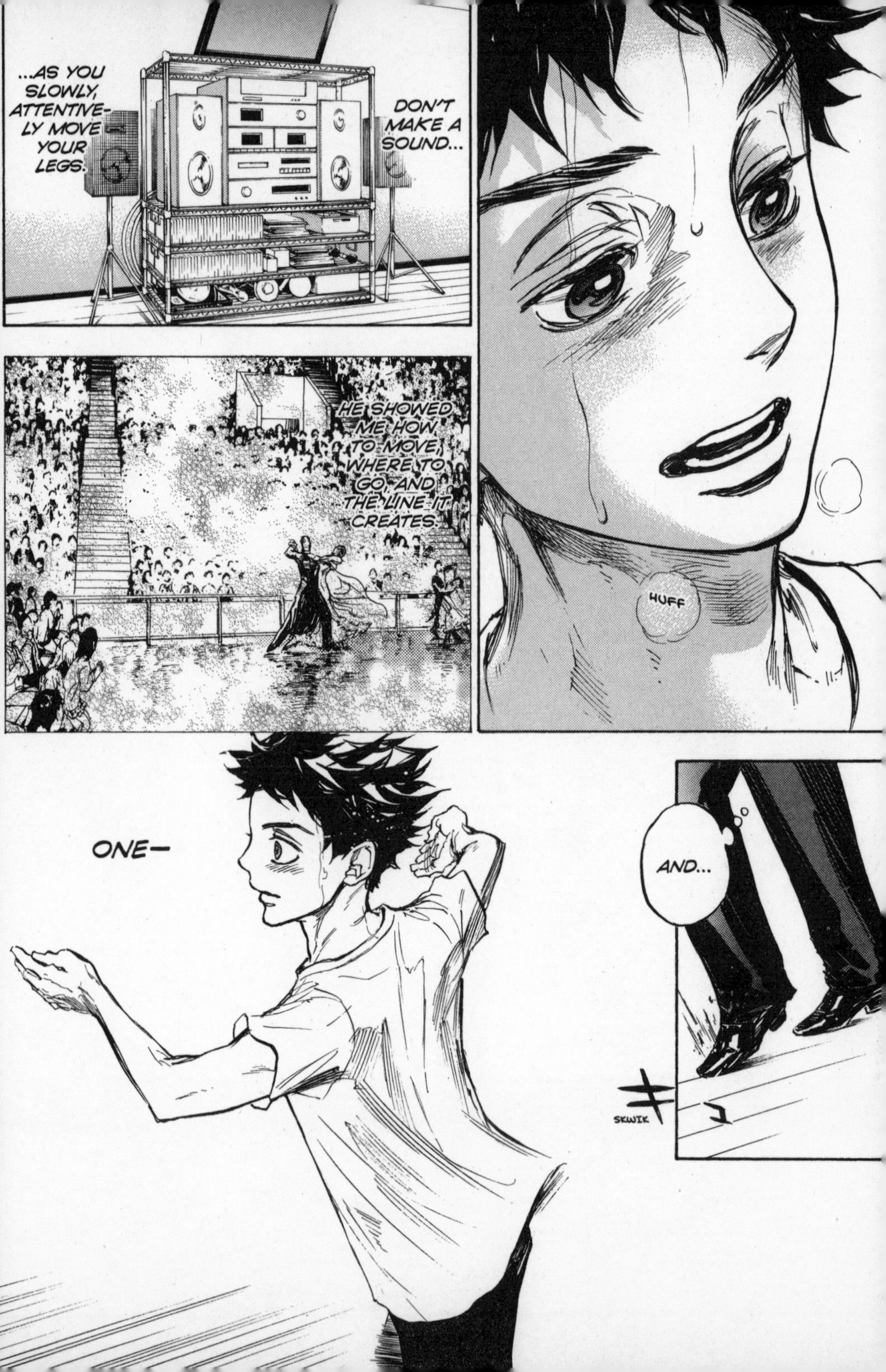
HUFF
DON'T MAKE A SOUND...
...AS YOU SLOWLY, ATTENTIVE-LY MOVE YOUR LEGS.
HE SHOWED ME HOW TO MOVE, WHERE TO GO, AND THE LINE IT CREATES.
AND...
SKWIK
ONE-

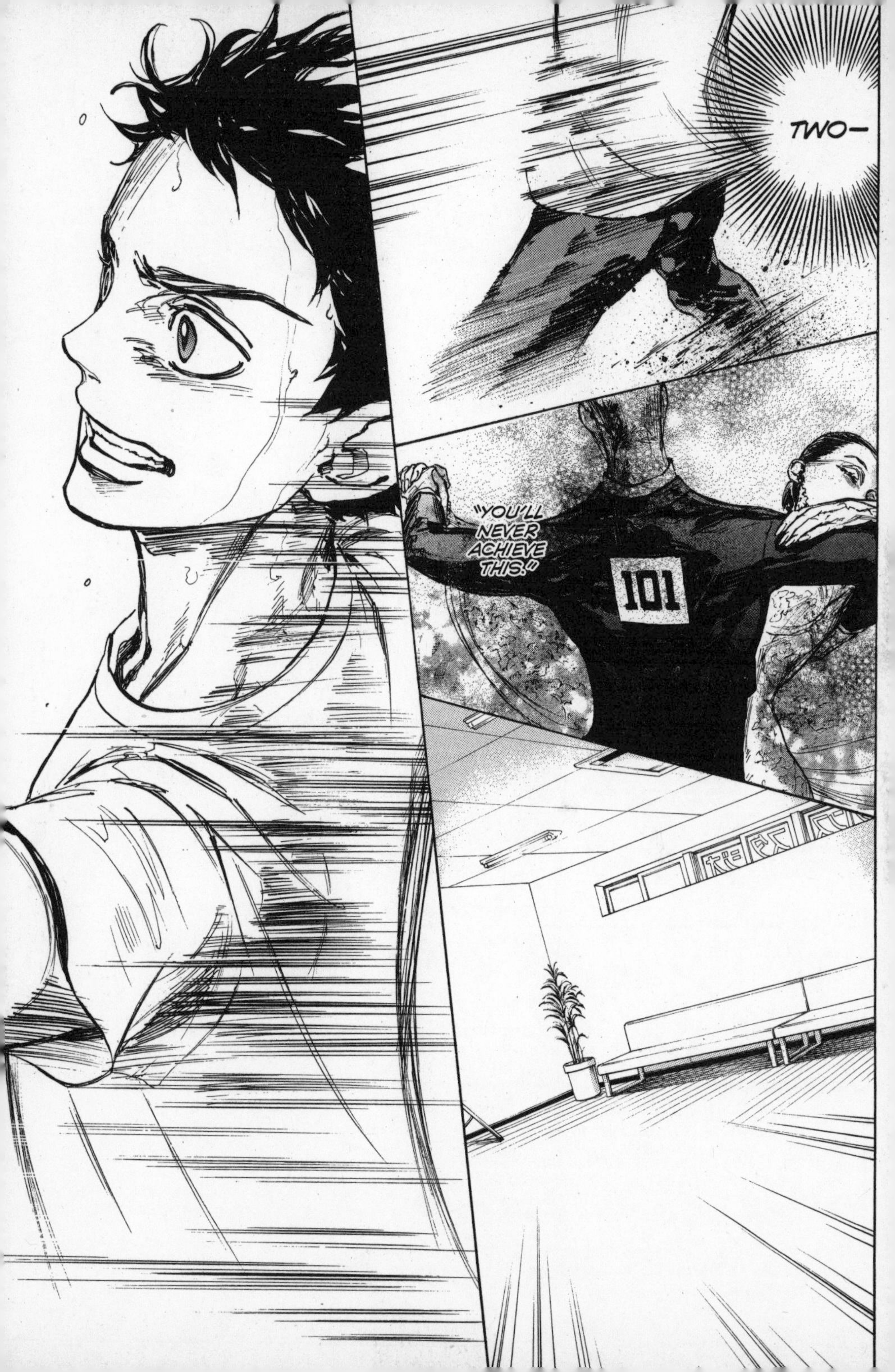
TWO—
"YOU'LL NEVER ACHIEVE THIS."
101

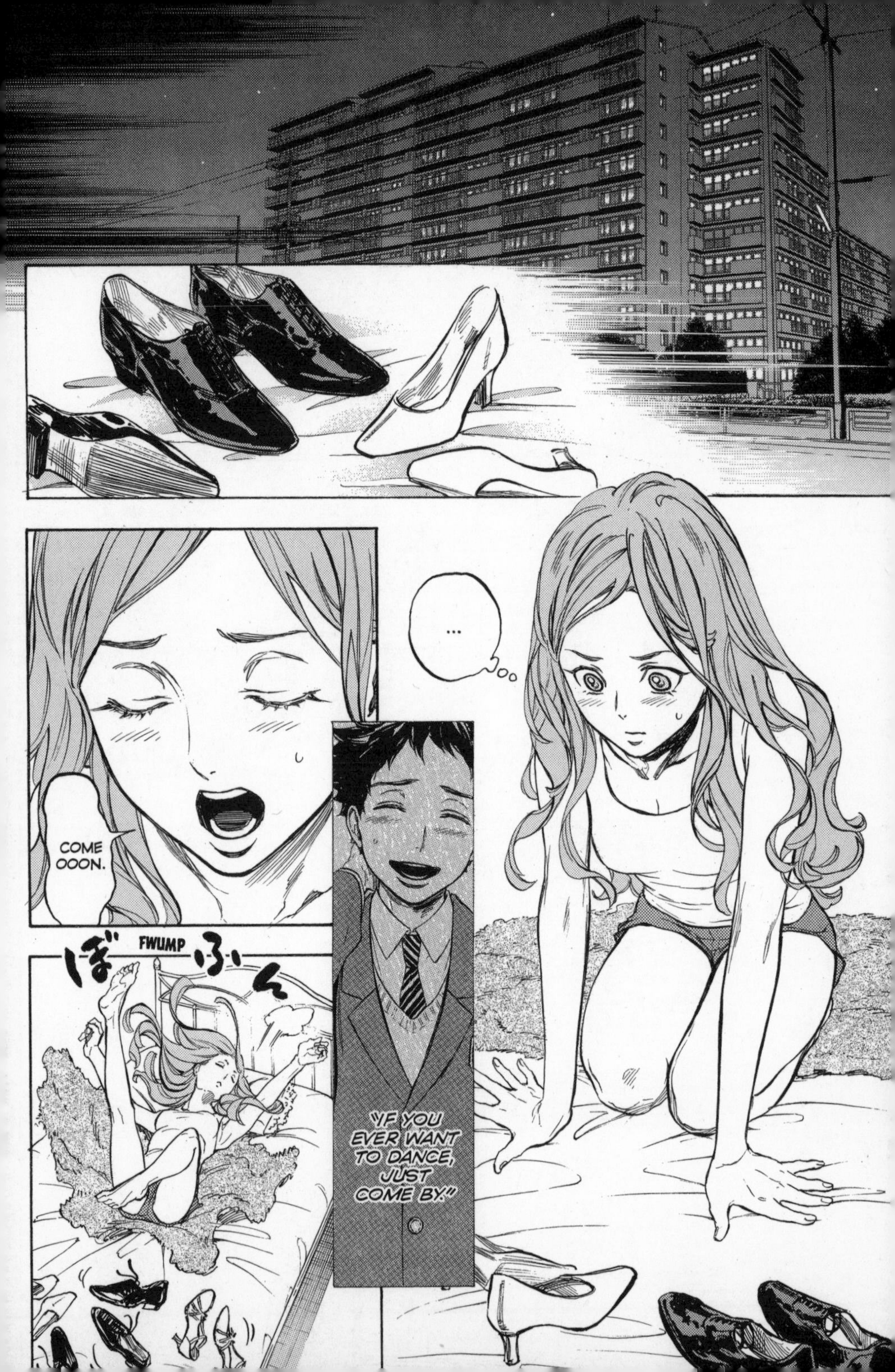
...
"IF YOU EVER WANT TO DANCE, JUST COME BY."
COME OOON.
ぼふん
FWUMP

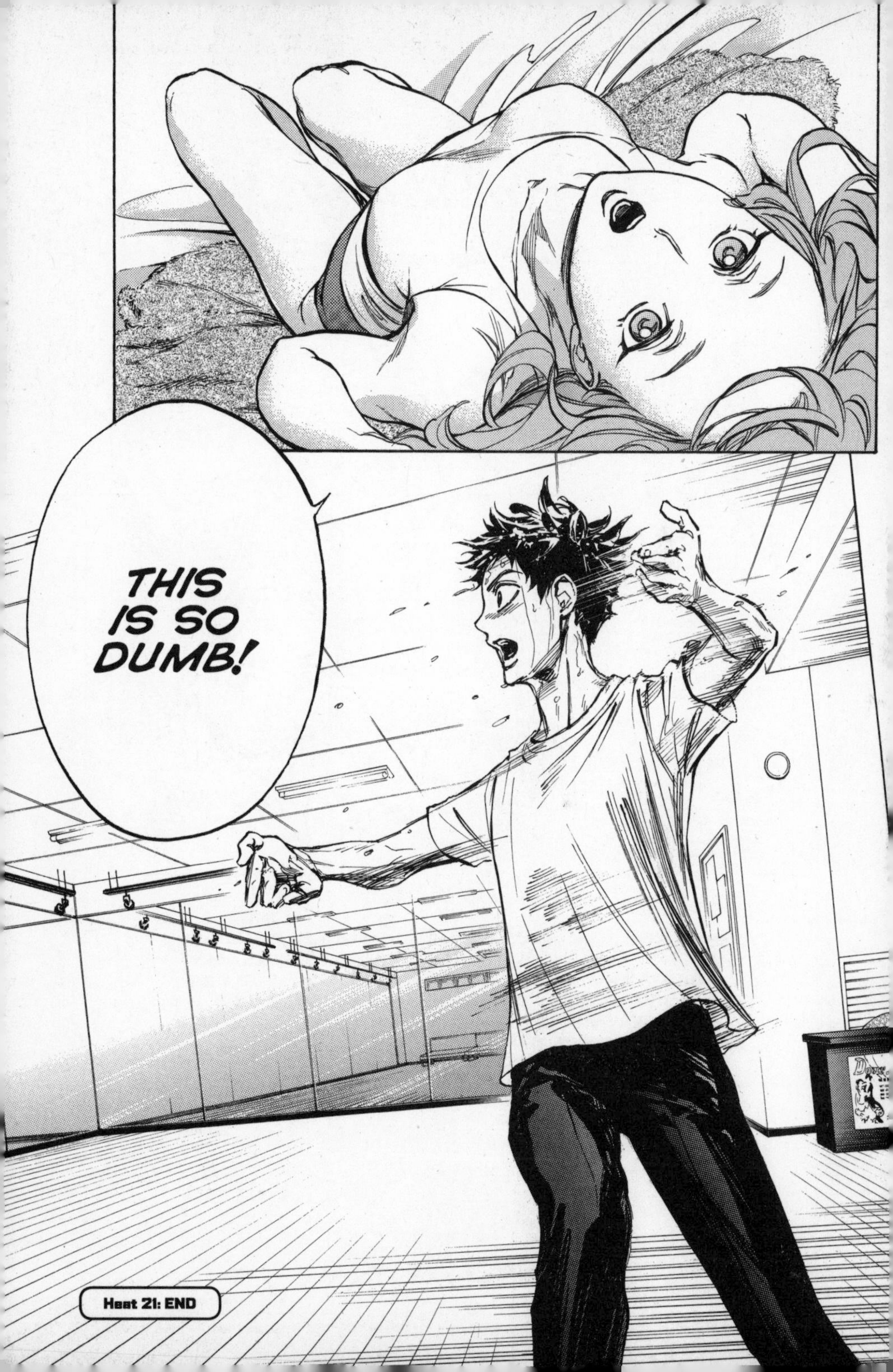
THIS IS SO DUMB!
Heat 21: END

Special thanks!

To all the readers:

THANKS FOR ALL YOUR SUPPORT!
I WAS SO HAPPY SEEING ALL YOUR RESPONSES.
WELCOME TO THE BALLROOM
2013
THANKS FOR ALL YOUR SUPPORT!
WELCOME TO THE BALLROOM
2013
THANKS FOR ALL YOUR SUPPORT!
WELCOME TO THE BALLROOM
2013
THANKS FOR ALL YOUR SUPPORT!
WELCOME TO THE BALLROOM
2013
THANKS FOR ALL YOUR SUPPORT!
WELCOME TO THE BALLROOM
2013
THANKS FOR ALL YOUR SUPPORT!
WELCOME TO THE BALLROOM
2013

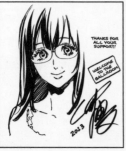

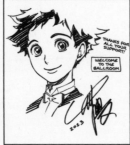

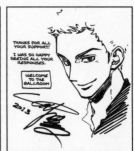

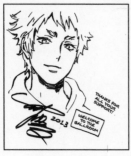

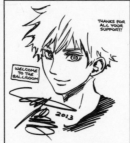

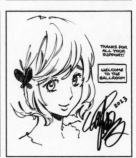

THANK YOU TO EVERYONE WHO ENTERED TO WIN THE GIFT DESIGN AUTOGRAPH CARDS IN THE MAY ISSUE OF MONTHLY SHONEN MAGAZINE, AND FOR ALL YOUR KIND MESSAGES! I WAS HUMBLED BY YOUR GREAT AFFECTION.
WITH HEARTFELT THANKS,

-TOMO TAKEUCHI

The autograph cards were part of a contest in the May issue of Monthly Shonen Magazine. The contest is now closed.

WELCOME TO THE BALLROOM

"YOU HAVE CHII-CHAN, DON'T YOU?"

IN JUST A FEW WORDS, SENGOKU'S PARTNER HONGO THROWS TATARA'S SEARCH FOR A PARTNER INTO *CHAOS!*

AFTER ALL, THAT VERY SAME "CHII-CHAN"—CHINATSU HIYAMA—HAS ALREADY DERIDED BALLROOM DANCE AS BEING TOTALLY LAME. BUT IN ORDER TO JOIN HIS RIVALS ON THE FLOOR OF COMPETITIVE DANCE, TATARA NEEDS A PARTNER. AND SOMEHOW, IT SEEMS LIKE CHINATSU HAS SOME EXPERIENCE WITH DANCE...

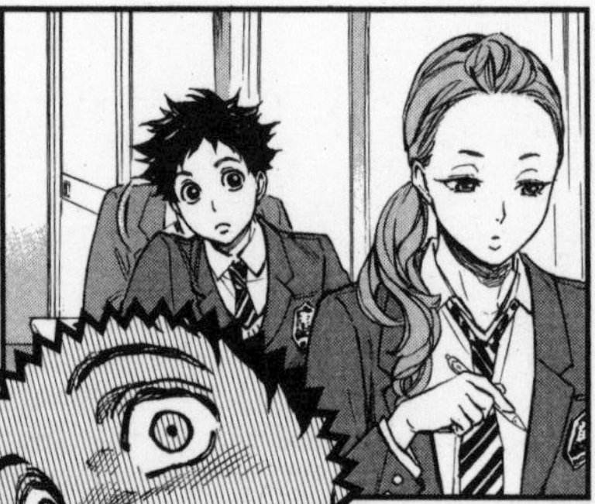

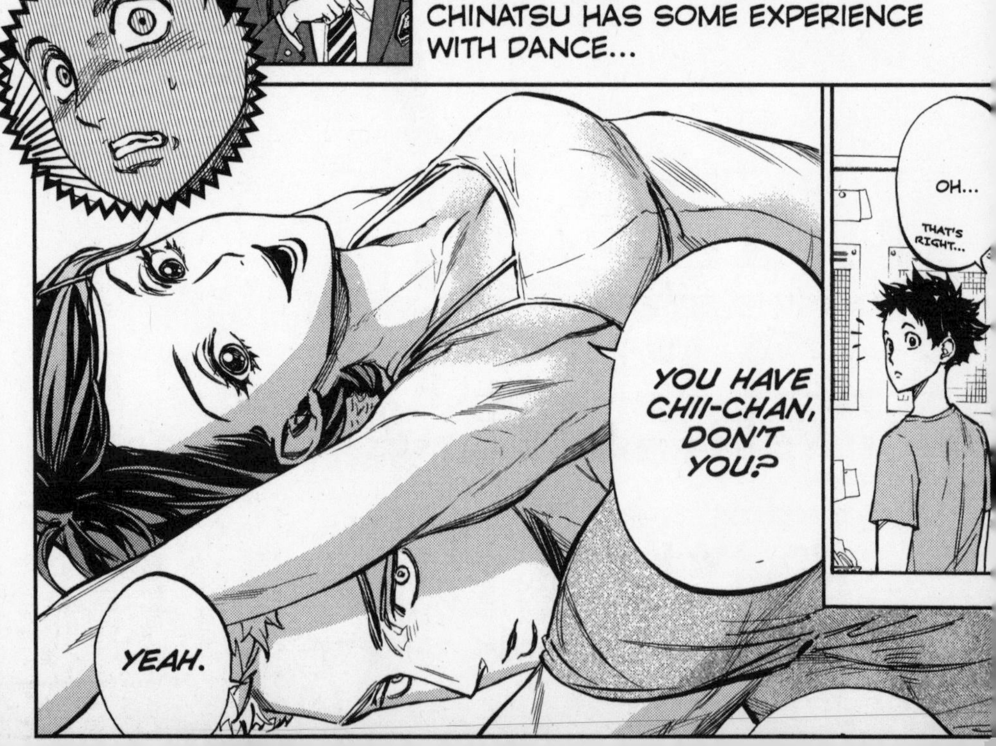
OH...
THAT'S RIGHT...
YOU HAVE CHII-CHAN, DON'T YOU?
YEAH.

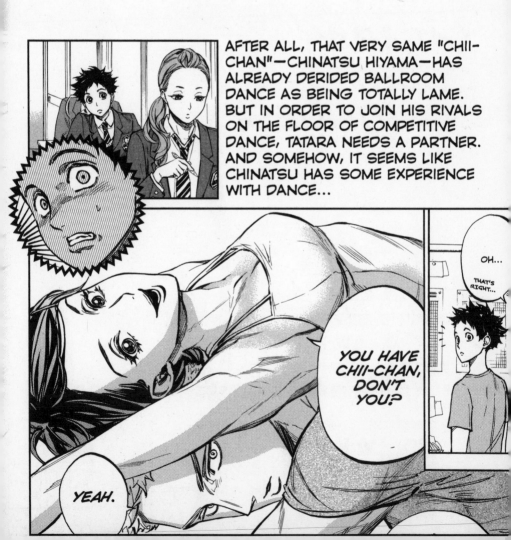